Kit Carson at Thirty

Kit Carson Days

1809-1868

"Adventures in the Path of Empire"

Revised Edition with New Matter

By
Edwin L. Sabin

With Twenty Full-page Drawings by
Howard Simon

Introduction by Marc Simmons

Volume I

University of Nebraska Press
Lincoln and London

Introduction © 1995 by the University of Nebraska Press
Manufactured in the United States of America

☉ The paper in this book meets the minimum requirements of American
National Standard for Information Sciences—Permanence of Paper for Printed
Library Materials, ANSI Z39.48-1984.

First Bison Books printing: 1995
Most recent printing indicated by the last digit below:
10   9   8   7   6   5   4   3   2   1

Library of Congress Cataloging-in-Publication Data
Sabin, Edwin Legrand, 1870–
Kit Carson days, 1809–1868: adventures in the path of empire / by Edwin L.
Sabin; with twenty full-page drawings by Howard Simon; introduction by Marc
Simmons.—Rev. ed. with new matter.
p.   cm.
Originally published: New York: Press of the Pioneers, 1935.
Includes bibliographical references and index.
ISBN 0-8032-9237-6 (v. 1: alk. paper).—ISBN 0-8032-9238-4 (v. 2: alk. paper)
1. Carson, Kit, 1809–1868.   2. Scouts and scouting—West (U.S.)—Biogra-
phy.   3. Soldiers—West (U.S.)—Biography.   I. Title.
F592.C412   1996
978'.02'092—dc20
[B]
95-9473   CIP

Reprinted from the revised 1935 edition by Press of the Pioneers, Inc., New
York.

To

Mary Caroline Sabin

Whose Patient Encouragement is Written
Between the Lines of These Pages

Introduction

Marc Simmons

On the great western frontier, the name of Christopher "Kit" Carson was one to be reckoned with. During his adventuresome life as a fur trapper, guide, mail courier, rancher, Indian agent, and soldier, he ranged much of the country between the Canadian and Mexican borders, participating in more than a few of the major historical episodes that shaped the nation's story of westward expansion. As had happened earlier to Daniel Boone, Carson's popular image by the time of his death in 1868 had accumulated elements of the mythic hero. He was a man, in the nineteenth century, who was admired, even revered, by his fellow Americans.

By the last quarter of the twentieth century, however, the Carson reputation, once so luminous, had fallen on hard times. And it had nothing to do with any new documentary discoveries that suddenly painted him in a reprehensible light. Rather the flip-flop occurred because many scholars and writers adopted the trendy social and political agendas of their day, which dictated that men like Kit must be dethroned and their accomplishments disparaged. Columbus fell victim to the same phenomenon during the quincentenary year, 1992.

Beginning in the 1970s, Carson was transformed from a national hero, noble and self-sacrificing, into an arch-villain and stigmatized as a ruthless racist.[1] That the facts of his life did not square with such a characterization seemed to have little effect. The public remained not so much converted to the revisionist, negative view of Carson, as confused.

Modern readers who wish to examine the evidence and sort the matter out for themselves can do no better than to start with Edwin Legrand Sabin's landmark book, *Kit Carson Days*. When the first edition appeared in 1914, the *New York Times* commended the author for his pains in producing an authentic and valuable volume that could serve equally for reading and reference. Western bibliographer Jack D. Rittenhouse praised it as a pioneer scholarly study upon which all later books have been based. And the late Carson biographer Harvey

L. Carter termed Sabin's product "a monumental work."[2] Those and other accolades still seem well deserved.

Edwin Sabin was born into a middle-class family at Rockford, Illinois, 23 December 1870. Graduating from the University of Iowa in 1892, he launched a career in journalism that lasted until 1900, when he decided to become a free-lance writer of prose and verse. Demands of the marketplace, it seems, pushed him into the writing of boys' books, both fiction and nonfiction, for which there was a large appetite at that time.

Some forty-five titles eventually flowed from Sabin's pen. Increasingly, his interests turned toward figures prominent in American history, especially those associated with the Wild West, like Lewis and Clark, General George Custer, Buffalo Bill, Sam Houston, Zebulon M. Pike, General George Crook, and, of course, Kit Carson. Like other books of the time, Sabin's had a three-fold purpose: to entertain, to impart knowledge of the nation's past, and to provide moral examples for youths to follow.

A growing infatuation with subjects western led Sabin to move with his wife to Denver in 1910 and the following year to California, where he spent the remainder of his life. During his brief residence in Colorado's capital, the author made the acquaintance of an individual who helped focus his interest upon the career of Kit Carson. That was eighty-seven-year-old "Major" Oliver Perry Wiggins, a self-styled former companion of Carson's and a willing teller of tales regarding his own extraordinary exploits on the old frontier. Before his death in 1913, Wiggins spun his yarns in some forty interviews granted to journalists, magazine writers, and historians.

Sabin's excitement at listening to someone who claimed to have traveled with Kit in his early trapping days evidently clouded his judgment, so that he failed to notice the outlandish nature of Wiggins's stories. That experience, nevertheless, prompted him to begin seeking out others yet living who had known the great scout personally, including relatives, friends, and companions of the trail, so that he might record their recollections. In performance of that task, he saved a great deal of information that would otherwise have been lost.[3]

At his new home in San Diego, Sabin completed his first manuscript on Kit, a juvenile book titled *Adventuring With Carson and*

Frémont. Published in 1912, it dealt with the first two government exploring expeditions commanded by Lieutenant John Charles Frémont (1842–44), for which Carson served as a guide. Since Wiggins asserted that he had been a member of both parties and had furnished stirring detail, the author made him a central figure in the book. Therein, Sabin told his youthful readers: "The Oliver Wiggins in this narrative is real. I have talked with him." The statement has the ring of a modest boast.

This book, however, was preliminary to a larger, more serious work for an adult audience that Sabin finished and published in 1914 under the title *Kit Carson Days, 1809–1868.* A second printing followed five years later.[4] It represented the first serious attempt to produce a full and authoritative biography based on archival sources and personal interviews. As such, it stood as a significant improvement over the handful of Carson biographies already in print.

Among those, the earliest and most useful was Dr. DeWitt C. Peters's *The Life and Adventures of Kit Carson, The Nestor of the Rocky Mountains,* initially published in 1858 when Kit was serving as Indian agent at Taos, New Mexico. Kit not only approved its writing (expecting to receive some financial reward), but cooperated by supplying Dr. Peters with a copy of his dictated memoirs.[5] Dime novelists, popular historians, and juvenile writers over the next half-century lifted freely from the Peters biography, essentially presenting little more than inferior rehashes and condensations. But Sabin blessedly took a different track.

Kit Carson Days soon came to be regarded as the standard work on the man who had become one of America's most celebrated frontiersmen. The skilled writing rendered it highly readable, while the fat appendix containing letters, government documents, and other primary material made the book appealing to scholars. No one challenged the author's reliance upon Oliver P. Wiggins as a source of information.

Through the 1920s and into the dark days of the Depression, Sabin's interest in Carson remained high. Using the peerless Bancroft Library at Berkeley, he burrowed deeply and uncovered new nuggets that allowed the filling in of heretofore shadowy parts of his story. By 1935, he had completed an extensive revision and expansion of *Kit*

Carson Days and added a new subtitle, *Adventures in the Path of Empire*.

The manuscript was published that year in two volumes by New York's Press of the Pioneers, bound in green buckram and boxed, in a limited edition of one thousand copies, plus two hundred signed. Today, sets on the rare book market are scarce and expensive. But the work remains in demand as a general reference and as a starting point for all studies on Carson's place in history.

During the interval between publication of the first and second editions of Sabin's book, an important documentary resource became available—the Carson memoirs used by Dr. Peters back in 1858 and afterward lost. In 1926, Blanche Grant, a Taos writer and collector of Carsoniana, lightly edited and printed the memoirs, a publishing event that allowed Kit for the first time to speak for himself.

Strangely, Edwin Sabin in the new, 1935 edition of his biography made limited use of the Carson memoirs, citing Grant's little book infrequently. Perhaps, having already drawn from Peters's standby work that had been based largely on the original Carson document, he saw little that was unfamiliar to him in the Grant publication. Still, his slighting of this key item is puzzling. By contrast, Sabin persisted in using the data collected years earlier from Wiggins.

Owing to the small size of the printing, the reappearance of *Kit Carson Days* provided its author a negligible financial return. In fact, during the 1930s and 1940s an aging Sabin struggled desperately to survive through pursuit of the writer's craft. The kinds of boys' books that had long furnished the mainstay of his income were no longer in vogue, and his attempts to find some other profitable niche in the writing field largely failed. Upon his death at Hemet, California, 24 November 1952, he was listed as a ward of the county.[6]

His Carson book, however, has lived on, gaining new respect with each passing year. As a measure of its durability, the work was even able to withstand the belated exposure of Oliver Perry Wiggins as a complete fraud. In 1952, the year of Sabin's death, mountain man authority LeRoy R. Hafen called Wiggins's stories "questionable."[7] But another fourteen years passed before the full scope of his duplicity was revealed.

Western writers Lorene and Kenny Englert in 1964 published an article proving that the "Major" was an imaginative imposter who had never laid eyes on Kit Carson.[8] Brian W. Dippie's phrase, describing supposed white survivors of Custer's Last Stand as "senile braggarts who told wonderful whoppers," could easily be expanded to include the likes of Oliver P. Wiggins.[9] In the first years of the twentieth century, elderly men who palmed themselves off as colorful frontier paladins were fairly common. Some sought to make money by selling their fabricated narratives, while others, being lonely, merely wished to draw attention to themselves.

Among the self-proclaimed companions of Kit Carson, only Wiggins was taken seriously. Partly it had to do with his stately demeanor and direct manner of speaking, which inspired confidence in listeners. But his acceptance by Edwin Sabin also went a long way in establishing his credibility. For once Sabin started swallowing Wiggins's fabrications, he never looked back. That the Wiggins name failed to appear in any independent western chronicle or receive so much as a bare mention in Kit's memoirs seems not to have troubled him.

Today, of course, "Oliver P. Wiggins," along with the names of fictional trappers he created, such as Ike Chamberlain, Sol Silver, and Bob Dempsey, can be found scattered through histories of the Old West. Using the opening given him by Sabin, Wiggins disseminated his fanciful tales, thereby muddying the waters of history. Modern readers of *Kit Carson Days* simply need to be aware of the situation, so as to steer around Sabin's references to Wiggins and his bogus adventures. Most of the references are brief, and the rest of *Kit Carson Days* is so eminently satisfactory, that skirting them is a tiny inconvenience.

The authentic Kit Carson, as the legitimate record affirms, was a man of honor and courage, a man with strengths and weaknesses, and thus quite human. There is no evidence that he was naturally bloodthirsty, a racist, or an Indian hater, as is routinely charged now by those who have not bothered to examine his career. By and large, Carson was a decent fellow with a strong moral sense, eager to serve his country and his countrymen. Those very qualities attracted Edwin Sabin and led him to write a book from whose pages the real Kit Carson shines.

NOTES

1. For example, historian Andrew Rolle in his biography, *John Charles Frémont, Character as Destiny* (Norman: University of Oklahoma Press, 1991), 63, accuses Carson of being "far more ruthless" than Frémont. In a 1972 dispute which she initiated, anthropologist Shirley Hill Witt of Colorado College publicly called Kit Carson "a terrorist and a genocidal racist." The incident leading to that remark is described in Harvey L. Carter, "The Curious Case of the Slandered Scout, the Aggressive Anthropologist, the Delinquent Dean, and the Acquiescent Army," *Denver Westerners Brand Book,* 28 (Boulder, 1973): 95, 98. The recent literature is rich in slurs cast upon Carson's name.

2. *New York Times,* 17 January 1915. Jack D. Rittenhouse, *The Santa Fe Trail, A Historical Bibliography* (Albuquerque: University of New Mexico Press, 1971), 188. Harvey Lewis Carter, *Dear Old Kit, The Historical Christopher Carson* (Norman: University of Oklahoma Press, 1968), 28.

3. The original notes and correspondence containing the recollections are preserved in the Edwin L. Sabin Papers, Harold B. Lee Library, Brigham Young University, Provo, Utah.

4. Both printings were by A. C. McClurg & Company of Chicago.

5. Reprinted as a Bison Book in 1965 by the University of Nebraska Press, edited by Milo M. Quaife.

6. This and other details of Edwin L. Sabin's life are drawn from the most complete biographical sketch available: Annie Commire, ed., *Yesterday's Authors of Books for Children* (Detroit: Gale Research Company, 1978), 2: 277–79.

7. "Fort Davy Crockett," *Colorado Magazine,* 19 (January 1952): 27.

8. "Oliver Perry Wiggins; Fantastic, Bombastic Frontiersman," *Denver Westerners Roundup,* 20 (February 1964): 3–14. The authors expanded their thesis in a separate monograph issued under the same title (Palmer Lake, Colorado: Filter Press, 1968).

9. "The Custer Mystery," in Ferenc Morton Szasz, ed., *Great Mysteries of the West* (Golden, Colorado: Fulcrum Publishing, 1993), 192.

Author's Statement

Books upon Kit Carson's career may be listed as follows: The Peters *Life and Adventures* (1858 and succeeding editions); Charles Burdette's *Life of Kit Carson* (1869), John S. C. Abbott's *Kit Carson* (1873), Edward S. Ellis's *Life of Kit Carson* (1889), *Life of Kit Carson* in Beadle's Biographical Library Series (of early date), Edwin L. Sabin's *Kit Carson Days* (1914), the brochure *Kit Carson's Own Story of His Life* (1926) edited by Blanche C. Grant, Stanley Vestal's *Kit Carson* (1928), and several juveniles. With the exception of the *Own Story* and the Vestal "The Happy Warrior of the Old West" — as thus sub-titled—the titles mentioned have been out of print.

This present work, KIT CARSON DAYS, was projected to meet the demand for a reissue — with some revision — of the original work of the same title. The result, however, is a work almost entirely rewritten and greatly amended. Much research in the Western field has been done during the twenty years since 1914, and a large amount of information upon Carson, his contemporaries and his times has been made available.

The original edition has of course provided the foundation for this present work. Full advantage has been taken of the data contained in that edition — the excerpts from documents and narratives that are becoming more and more difficult to turn up, and the interviews with and letters from Carson's intimates who have, one and all, since passed from earth.

The form of the original edition has been followed. There is the Appendix, with new matter. The Notes are grouped by themselves. The note numbers in the Text are now placed at the close of paragraphs, as more convenient for the eye. While the Notes are in a measure citations of authorities, they also throw side-lights upon the text and will be found by the general reader to heighten the story interest.

The author is well aware of his indebtedness to a host of co-operates who helped him to compile this new KIT CARSON

Days. It is not practicable to publish the full roll. Mr. W. J. Ghent of Washington went to pains to supply a list of corrections of the old work, and Mr. Allen Lane of California did extensive research and copying in the Bancroft Library, University of California, Berkeley. Mr. Francis T. Cheetham of Taos procured transcripts of original entries in the Taos Parish records. Mr. Charles C. Carson of Colorado, the last of the Carson children, answered many questions as to the family chronology, and times and places. Mrs. Louise A. Puett, daughter of Lindsey Carson, Kit's youngest brother, and her niece, Mrs. E. P. Mathes, both of California, pointed to valuable family material. There are other acknowledgments in the Text and Notes, but they do not cover the obligations due.

Appreciation should, however, be here again expressed, of the courteous and efficient services rendered by the librarians and other staff officials of the Iowa State Library, the California State Library, the Bancroft Library, the New York Public Library, the Hemet (Calif.) Public Library, the Historical Societies and Associations of Missouri, Kansas, Oregon, Idaho, Texas and New Mexico.

Any work featuring Kit Carson should build him into the annals of his times, for he was distinctly a part and parcel of those times. It is necessary to recognize in him other qualities than merely those which clothe him on parade for the worship of the cult of popular derring do. He was no showman in buckskin upon a white horse — he is out of focus in biographies grandiloquent or committedly impressionistic. From the horizoned mass of legendary and factual adventures he emerges most clearly in public documents, homely anecdotes, letters by him, to him, and touching upon him, and the unprejudiced comment of his fellow actors. The real, human Kit Carson is the Kit Carson who has out-lived the spot-light of trappers' yarns and Wild West romance. As such, he is an instance of the survival of the fittest.

Edwin L. Sabin

Hemet, California

Table of Contents

Volume I

List of Illustrations

Volume I

Kit Carson Days

Sabin

Kit Carson Days

Chapter I

The Carson Family

THE Carsons of early Missouri were adventure stock. Of Kit Carson's eight half-brothers and brothers, it is stated by a son of William the eldest: "Every one, without a single exception, went West in search of the Indian and the buffalo; now that the Indian is settled upon the reservations and the buffalo is about extinct, I am at loss to know what this generation can do for a pastime." Therefore, when the boy Kit took to the plains and mountains out of Missouri he not only followed a fashion of the day but he swung true to his heritage. As a son of Lindsey Carson he had to go.

The Carson boys, indeed, set no example. They but contributed their chapters to the family sagas of the day. Of their neighbors, the Cooper boys, an unrecorded number; of the Bent family, four brothers; of the Robidoux family in Missouri, five if not six brothers; of the Sublette family, the five brothers — these and others of close blood kin, from this family board and that, went crusading into the West of the buffalo and the Indian, the beaver and the Don. Home thresholds fronted to the sunset.

The sire of these Missouri Carsons was William Carson, of Scotch-Irish strain, who emigrated from Scotland, or from the north of Ireland, to Pennsylvania, in the first half of the Eighteenth Century. Thence moving southward by that impulse which transfused into the Carolinas and Tennessee so much Scotch-Irish Protestant blood, he eventually laid claim to 692 acres on both sides of Third Creek, in the Loray district of western Iredell County, North Carolina. The Carson grant to this tract, from Lord Granville, is dated December 1, 1761.

The records of this William Carson the First read, in brief, that he was a farmer; that he married Miss Eleanor McDuff

(McDorf?); and that, imprudently drinking from a cold spring on a hot day, before the Revolution, he died, leaving at least five children — Robert, Lindsey (the head of the Missouri Carson branch), Andrew, Eleanor and Sarah. Alexander is mentioned also.

The small covey scattered. The Alexander Carson migrated to Mississippi; Robert Carson, to Kentucky, where he lived out his life; Lindsey and Andrew, to the Hunting Creek settlement in the north of Iredell County. Forthwith, Lindsey, at twenty-two, and Andrew, at twenty, were proved in the fire of the Revolution.

Andrew became a captain under the command of Marion the Swampfox, and while Lord Cornwallis was harrying South Carolina bore dispatches between Marion and Greene. Legends of the battle of Camden, August 16, 1780, accredit him with carrying out in his arms, from the heat of the conflict, the fatally wounded Baron DeKalb, shot down while crossing a creek. A powerfully large man was Andrew Carson, son of the first William. He sleeps in the old family graveyard of the Youngs and Houstons on the banks of Hunting Creek. By marriage with Temperance Young he left sons Washington, Alfred, Robert; and a daughter.

Lindsey Carson's exploits in the Revolution are matters of conjecture, but so sturdy an Indian fighter must have done good service. After the war Lindsey removed to South Carolina, married Miss Bradley and proceeded to raise a brood the flight of which would extend to the Pacific Coast.

This, the first of his two marriages, added to his race William, b. 1786, who effected a union with the Kentucky Boones; Sarah, b. 1788, m. Peyton and lived to an advanced age; Andrew, b. 1790; Moses Bradley, b. 1792; and possibly Sophia, 1794 (?). The mother did not long survive her last child, but died soon after her arrival at the new home in Madison County, Kentucky, where, in 1794, the restless Lindsey resettled.

Here, in Madison County, in 1797, Lindsey took a second

wife, Rebecca Robinson from Greenbrier County, Virginia, and continued the sequence of children. By this connection there were, in all, six more boys and four more girls: one, Elizabeth, m. Robert Cooper of the Missouri (and Kentucky) Coopers; two, Nancy, m. Briggs — a union that reached across the plains to California; three, Robert; four, Hamilton; five, Christopher; six, Hampton; seven, Mathilda, m. Adams; eight, Mary, m. Rubey; nine, Sarshel; ten, Lindsey II. But the last boy, his namesake, the father never saw.

The annals of the Young family, of the Hunting Creek district, North Carolina, assert that Christopher was born not in Kentucky but in Iredell County, while Lindsey and his wife were upon a visit to his brother Andrew. Kit Carson himself always placed his birth in Kentucky. And Iredell County maintains, also, that Carson's full given name was Christopher Houston, in commemoration of that Christopher Houston who was prominent in Iredell County during the Revolution.

Of this brave family of fourteen or fifteen children born to Lindsey Carson by juncture with the Bradley and Robinson clans, the fourteen lived to manhood and womanhood. And that, in itself, is remarkable for the times.

There was one Carson of authentic record in the Far West before the Lindsey Carson cabin had been raised in Missouri. An Alexander Carson (probably of the Mississippi branch, sprung from that Alexander who is listed as a son of the first William) was encountered as a trapper upon the upper Missouri by the Wilson Hunt party of Astorians, in May, 1811. He and his companion, bound down the river, faced about for the still farther West with the Astorians. This Alexander had already been two years in the new fur country. The chances are that he, like other American trappers found by the party, had entered the mountains with the Major Andrew Henry command of the Missouri Fur Company in 1809 bound for the sources of the Missouri.

A Carson is assigned to the fictitious party of Ezekiel Williams upon the upper Arkansas in 1807.

With the advent of the Lindsey Carson family in Missouri, the Carson name began to figure in western affairs. William, the eldest son, returned to Kentucky for his family, and was there held by the Indian disturbances consequent upon the war with England (1812). Here in Missouri Lindsey, the father, and Moses, and by rumor Andrew, served against the Indians and the remainder of the family forted, with other settler families, in one of the local block-houses. Moses soon engaged for the up-river fur trade. In due time, William, Andrew, Robert, Hamilton, Christopher, and Lindsey II, traveled the Santa Fé Trail. By way of the Southwest, Moses went to California. Lindsey II settled in California. By report, Hamilton, of a surety Christopher and Robert, crossed to California. Hamilton was a Pike's Peaker of '59. There are left Sarshel and Hampton. Sarshel was killed in Missouri during the Civil War — the only one, it would seem, of this adventure breed to meet death by violence. The references to Hampton are few.[1]

Chapter II

In Old Missouri — 1811-1826

THE story of Kit Carson days is the story of fur hunt and
Indians; of camp, trading post and fort; of the trapper and
trader followed by the missionary and the explorer, and of
these followed by the immigrant, the soldier and the gold
seeker; of the Santa Fé Trail, the Oregon Trail, the California
Trail; of the acquisition of Texas, a California, a vast New
Mexico and the adjoining Oregon Country, and of a "Great
American Desert" partitioned into fertile states; of the caravan,
the bull train, the prairie schooner, the overland stage, and the
coming of the iron horse; of a wild and unknown country
2,000 miles wide subdued and made known; of the Republic
marching westward across half the continent until all the soil
from the one-time Missouri border to the Pacific, from the Gulf
and the Rio Grande and the mouth of the Colorado to Canada
and Puget Sound, was compacted into one soil under the Flag.

Kit Carson lived to span this era which his activities promoted. He was in at the beginnings; he saw the close. He first
traveled from Kentucky to Santa Fé by ox and mule; before he
died he had traveled from Washington City to the Wyoming
Rockies by rail; another year, and he could have traveled from
coast to coast upon the trail of steam.

The Boones of Kentucky had hailed from the headwaters of
that Yadkin River which, in northwestern North Carolina,
flows southwardly through Iredell County. In 1795 Daniel
Boone, at the age of sixty, had moved westward to the Spanish
Louisiana Province across the Mississippi and had found the
last home, to him, a first Kentucky. Reports from him and his
sons filtered back. Then, without warning, that country was
thrown open to any American. There came the news of the
Lewis and Clark expedition, of the gallant Pike's; so that, as
the initial decade of the young century waxed and waned, the
American pioneer, inspired by the call of a new freedom, again
shouldered axe and rifle and faced onward.

In the spring of 1811, Lindsey Carson, with his wife and nine children, also moved on by ox team and wagon, from Madison County, Kentucky, to the new Boone's Lick district of the even newer American Territory of Louisiana. The youngest child (as yet) was Christopher, born December 24, 1809.

The Carsons and their company of other southerners settled in what is now Howard County, along the Missouri River about 170 miles west of St. Louis. Friends and kin were already here; friends and kin came after. This was the frontier, to be held by the Carsons, the Boones, the Coopers, the Briggses, the Kincaids, by rifle, axe, plough and loom. There soon arose those doughty stockades, Forts Hempstead, Cooper and Kincaid. The name of Linsey (Lindsey) Carson appears upon the roll of old Fort Hempstead, and the annals of old Fort Cooper likewise claim him.

The most practicable trail out of the Missouri borderland was the water trail into the Northwest. Upon the west of the border there lay the indefinite "Indian Country," thus to be designated, with but slight variation, for many a year. And what waited yonder? Wasteland and Indians, by reports. The first promised little of good; the second were near at hand and bad enough, as witness the speedy establishment of Forts Hempstead, Cooper, and Kincaid. The population of the Territory of Louisiana, which comprised that section of the old province north of the Territory of Orleans, the present state of Louisiana, rapidly dwindled, northward from the lower Arkansas and westward from the mouth of the Missouri. St. Louis, with its 1,800 people, was the western metropolis.

St. Louis, dominated by her thriving French citizenship, had been the headquarters of an upper-country fur trade conducted by individuals or at the most by partners. From the very outset it was the French who in the western continent made a business of gathering the pelts of forest, prairie and stream. But now the American nation was definitely fronting upon another West. The national boundary had leaped from the Mississippi to the Shining Mountains. Captain Meriwether Lewis and

Lieutenant William Clark had opened a way to the Pacific itself. And now, at the time when Lindsey Carson from Kentucky unhooked his oxen in Cooper's Bottom of the Boone's Lick district, turned them and the children loose and blazed his homestead site, the Missouri Fur Company of St. Louis was organized with good backing, and the energetic John Jacob Astor of New York was advancing his American Fur Company to the Pacific coast. His trading and supply ship *Tonquin* was en route for the mouth of the Columbia, and the supporting overland party of Wilson Price Hunt had pushed forward up the Missouri River trail from St. Louis.

In this Louisiana Territory, about to be rechristened the Territory of Missouri, Lindsey Carson lived as he had lived in the Carolinas and Kentucky. He led in sundry forays upon the Indians. He and his third son, Moses, were enrolled in the home guards during the War of 1812. In 1814 fingers of his left hand were mangled during an Indian skirmish. In September 1818, before Lindsey, his namesake, had been born, he died by the fall of a limb from a burned tree while he was clearing timber near his cabin. He left a family that had been ever increasing, and a rifle of large bore, with the stock, like his fingers, smashed by an enemy's bullet. His epitaph is written: "A zealous soldier, but in domestic life a man of peace."[2]

Kit, no longer the youngest in the line, was now almost nine years old. Two and one half of these years had been spent under the stockade protection of Fort Hempstead; all had been spent amid the shadows of wilderness perils. He was thoroughly a backwoods and frontier product of local environments where illiteracy was the common lot. The Carsons ran to large frames. Lindsey, the father, was a large man. The son, William, was large. Moses was six feet one and weighed over 200 pounds. Lindsey, the last-born, attained to six feet one inch, was of powerful set-up, could jump twelve feet flat and turn and jump back again. Mary (Mrs. Rubey), who died as late as 1899, was a woman of "noble" appearance. Kit seems to have been the runt in stature, five feet eight or nine, but his endurance supplemented his inches.

By report, his father had designed that he should be a lawyer. Meantime, his widowed mother put him out to learn a trade. When he was fifteen, or early in 1825, she apprenticed him to William and David Workman, the saddlers in near-by Franklin — the chief settlement of the Missouri River border and outfitting point for the land trails into the Northwest and Southwest. The mother married again. There came more children — Kit's half-brother and half-sister by the name of Martin.

William the eldest Carson, very likely Andrew, and possibly Robert, were in the Santa Fé trade. So were several of the Cooper boys. Big Mose Carson was in the up-river fur trade, trapping beaver and fighting Injuns, his whereabouts unknown. Hamilton, Hampton, little Sarshel and baby Lindsey were at home but were free for the out of doors. And Kit, himself, was sweeping the floor and learning to use the awl in the Workman saddlery shop.

During the fourteen years since the Carsons had crossed the Mississippi, government, trader and adventurer had brought the mysterious Farther West nearer to the border. In 1820 Major Stephen Long of the Army, having forged up the Missouri in the first steamboat successfully to breast the upper river, from the site of present Omaha proceeded by horse and mule up along the Platte of the errant voyageur and trapper, to the Rocky Mountains. Then, marching southward, he skirted the eastern base of the foothills, passed the sites of future Denver and Colorado Springs, and returned to Missouri by way of the Arkansas.

The Missouri Fur Company was constantly planting more outposts in that upper river country, and there were half a dozen other companies in the field. General William Henry Ashley of St. Louis, first lieutenant governor of the new state, general of the militia, and Missouri's political leader in state affairs, had entered the fur trade and was making his fortune. In 1822 he had escorted up the river his first party, under that Major Andrew Henry who some twelve years back, while he was in the service of the Missouri Fur Company, had built the first American fur-trade post on the Pacific side of the Stony Mountains, at the Henry Fork of the Snake River in what is now the extreme portion of eastern Idaho.

General Ashley followed his 1822 expedition with others, in command of himself or of his captains. To young Kit Carson, these Ashley expeditions should have been of especial interest, for they numbered upon their rolls Thomas Fitzpatrick, Carson's first employer in the mountains and the announcer of the great South Pass; James Bridger, another of Carson's employers, and the first American to report of the Great Salt Lake; Jedediah S. Smith, whose trail across the desert into California Carson would encounter on his initial trip as a trapper; Jim Beckwourth, the mulatto and Crow chief, a familiar to Carson in both the Northwest and the Southwest; the Sublettes, Milton and William, bold captains and partisans; and others whose names endure in plains and mountain fur-trade history and with whom, in a few more years, Kit Carson, now a boy, mingled as a mountain-man.

Moreover, in the summer of 1823 an expedition of combined soldiers and fur hunters had sought to punish the fierce Arikaras, who were forcibly obstructing the up-river traffic. In the fighting, Mose Carson had served as a trapper lieutenant. There had been no great triumph of arms, but the up-river trail into the Northwest was opened again.

So much, briefly, as regards the Northwest. The Southwest also was being exploited. Objective points in the Northwest were the Three Forks country where sprung the sources of the Missouri, and the Oregon and Columbia region on the other side of the mountains. The Southwest spelled Santa Fé — that enchanted Mexican trading mart of the Spanish Settlements.

Captain Zebulon Montgomery Pike had reported upon it; in 1806 he had found there one James Purcell (or Pursley), a Kentuckian already domiciled and doing well. At present, Santa Fé and the Spanish Settlements were current talk, for trade in that direction promised profitable enterprise equal to that of the fur business of the North.

In June 1813, Ezekiel Williams had returned to Boone's Lick, not far from the Carsons, after experiences on the upper Arkansas, and had brought his word of Santa Fé. The next year he rode back into the West, with Braxton Cooper, of the Fort Cooper and Cooper County family, in his party. The following winter he made another trip, with more Coopers — Joseph and William. Inasmuch as Elizabeth Carson had married William Cooper, these adventurings on the Arkansas River Trail to the western mountains closely touched the Carsons.[3]

The Williams-Cooper parties did not make direct contact with Santa Fé in the Spanish Southwest. Reports of Santa Fé and its territory would be derived from the Pawnees, the Kiowas, the Comanches, the southern Arapahos, and other plains tribes who traded with and fought the Mexicans of the South. The Santa Fé territory was closed territory; the final destination of the foreigner who crossed the alleged boundary of the Arkansas was likely to be the *calabozo* of the interior city of Chihuahua. Here were now languishing Robert Mc-Knight of St. Louis and his companions, who in 1812 had hazarded taking goods to a market not friendly.

In 1821 John McKnight set out from St. Louis for Mexico upon quest of his brother Robert who for nine years had not been heard from, save in enquiries made by Washington. He found Robert confined between the stone walls of the Chihuahua prison. But he found also that rumors were true: Mexico was free from that Spanish rule hostile to Americans. Therefore, he was enabled to bring Robert back with him. The return in the summer of 1822 was chronicled in the *Missouri Intelligencer* of Franklin.[4]

Captain William Becknell of Franklin had advertised in the *Intelligencer* of June 10, 1821, for "seventy men to go westward" on a trading project. He assembled his company at the house of Ezekiel Williams, succeeded in penetrating safely into Santa Fé and in completing his business. The following January he was back in Franklin, enthusiastic over his profits. William Carson appears to have been one of these seventy men.[5]

In the spring of 1822 the Coopers set out. Captain Becknell led another company, with three wagons, and made a new and shorter trail, in defiance of thirst and Indians, across the Cimarron Desert. The Santa Fé trade was fairly started, and the *Missouri Intelligencer* constantly printed items about it.

James Purcell himself, after his nineteen years in those Spanish Settlements, returned to his fellow Kentuckians of the Missouri frontier. James Workman, cousin of the saddler David, in 1825 was back (if romance of the day is to be accepted) with an astounding narrative of fifteen years' sojourn in New Mexico. William Workman, David's brother and saddlery partner, was out on the trail or else about to go.

Therefore, when in 1825 young Kit Carson was put at saddlery service under David Workman in Franklin, it was shutting the cat next to the cream. Northwest and Southwest were on the air with adventurous deeds, the accounts of which focused in Franklin — Franklin, still keenly mindful of that great reception tendered to Major Long and General Atkinson when in 1819 they had stopped off from their steamboat, on their prospective way to the remote Yellowstone. Ashley was reaping fame and furs. And Santa Fé of Nueva Mejico was an assured tangible fact.

Franklin was an eddy formed by two currents. Up the river, for its uttermost sources, by steamboat, keelboat, ahorse and afoot, pressed the men of the fur trade; and down they came bringing their pelts, their squaws, their scars, and their tales of robe and skin, Arikaree, Sioux, Crow and Blackfoot, "b'ar" and "buff'ler" and "ha'r-raisin'." From the outfitting point of Franklin, away into the mystery of the sunsets, there wended the files for Santa Fé — those wagons and pack animals laden tight with merchandise, escorted not only by wide-hatted hairy trader but by broadcloth merchant and health-seeking adventurer. Back to Franklin they came, from the trail to Santa Fé; they came dusty and gay, with their tales of desert rather than of mountain; of Kiowa, Pawnee, Comanche and Arapaho; of storm and thirst and burning sands; of the *cibolero* or Mexican buffalo hunter, and of a unique, romantic city 800 miles by horse and mule across the arid "Indian country" — a city where American energy turned a 40 per cent profit and where American visitors were welcomed by the merry fandango.

As against all this, the saddler's craft seemed dull, indeed, to Kit Carson. In a year he had had enough of it, and the advertisement here copied from the columns of the *Missouri Intelligencer* of October 12th indicates how he left it:

Notice Is Hereby Given To All Persons

That Christopher Carson, a boy about 16 years old, small of his age but thick-set, light hair, ran away from the subscriber, living in Franklin, Howard County, Missouri, to whom he had been bound to learn the saddler's trade, on or about the first of September. He is supposed to have made his way toward the upper part of the state. All persons are notified not to harbor, support or assist said boy under the penalty of the law. One cent reward will be given to any person who will bring back the said boy.   DAVID WORKMAN.

Franklin, Oct. 6, 1826.   16-3

Workman was glad to be quit of his worthless apprentice.

It might well be conjectured that the runaway had set face to the north, on the line of the beaver hunt. This was the readiest trail; there were constant opportunities for a lad to make up-river with trader, trapper or Indian. Anyone who was able of body and was willing to risk his hair was free to join any of a hundred wanderfoot bands, white or red, or both. But Davie Workman's apprentice was won by the lure of the Southwest — of desert and mirage, a foreign land, a foreign people, and profits wrested from great odds. Kit Carson joined a Santa Fé caravan. By the irony of events, David Workman, saddler, at the first chance the next spring, did the same, incited, as may be, by the example of his brother, William.[6]

Kit never again saw that saddlery shop, nor the old homestead cabin on Cooper's Bottom; through upwards of a decade and a half he saw but few of his blood kin. When in the spring of 1842 he returned, man grown, with a half-breed child to the Missouri frontier, he found that the more than fifteen years had, like a landslide, wiped out places and persons.

Chapter III

The Road to Santa Fé — 1826

A LETTER from George H. Carson states: "I often heard my father [William Carson] speak about his brother Kit as a runaway, overtaking him several days after his departure from Franklin on his journey to Santa Fé." Carson family traditions further assert that "Kit followed on a mule his brothers William, Hamilton and Robert and caught them a few miles out of Franklin." A rumor current in Missouri (according to the article, " 'Kit' Carson," by William F. Switzler, in the *Missouri Historical Society Collections,* January, 1900) has it that the brothers faced Kit and his mule about for return home, but that a little way back he let the mule go and joined another outfit. Chroniclers have consigned him to a Bent, St. Vrain & Co. caravan; and George Bent, a son of William Bent the early trader, declares that this "Kit Carson caravan" was in charge of Charles Bent, brother and partner of William Bent. If this is the truth (as seems likely), then all the better for story interest, inasmuch as seventeen years later the ragged runaway, whose fame was now rapidly accumulating, married the sister-in-law of his patron, this same Charles Bent, now governor of New Mexico.

Carson himself never admitted to the runaway escapade. He simply says:

In August, 1826, I had the fortune to hear of a party bound for that country [the Rocky Mountains — that is, New Mexico]. I made application to join this party, and, without any difficulty, I was permitted to join them.[7]

Enthusiastic romancers have made him an official hunter for the caravan, but the early caravans had no appointed "hunters."

As Senator Thomas H. Benton of Missouri had said, speaking before the National Senate in the winter of 1824-25, the journey to Santa Fé was one which with "caravans of men, horses and wagons, traversing with their merchandise the vast plain," savored more of Asia than of America; a journey, as viewed by the *Missouri Intelligencer* of February 12, 1830, requiring "the most steel-formed constitutions and the most energetic natures," as well as "men of high chivalric and somewhat romantic natures."

Out pulled the caravan, one of several dispatched this year from Franklin, for the Santa Fé trade was increasing. The caravan was composed in the main of wagons, with probably a few private lighter vehicles. The year 1826 marked the passing, on the Trail, of pack animals, and the popular employment of wheels for the conveyance of goods. Individuals, however, with pack animals, continued to attach themselves to the wagon trains. And there were the saddle animals and the herd of loose horses and mules — the *caballada*, "cavvy-yard", or "cavvy."

United States territory, as broadened by the purchase of the Louisiana Province from France, extended in the west to the rather indefinite divide of the Rocky Mountains; in the south, to the Red River and at the intangible line of the 100th meridian of longitude (about the line of present Dodge City in southwestern Kansas) only to the Arkansas River. Below the southern limits, all was Mexico and uneasy Texas — which also was of Mexico. Across the summit divide of the Rockies — which were fancifully known as the "Shining Mountains" and the "Stony Mountains" and toward their southern extremity as the "Anahuac" — all was Mexico, in general of vague designation save where specified as California, up to about the northernmost line of present Utah. The western slope of the Northwest and all the Northwest to the Pacific was Oregon, shared jointly by the United States and Great Britain, whose representative was the Hudson's Bay Company.

Kit Carson entered this unplotted West, which he would soon help to map, as stock tender or wrangler (the raw hand's job on the trail) or, since he had been raised on a farm, as a cub teamster.

The course across the plains to Santa Fé lay not as one traveled road but spread into chance-selected trails, for the most part made obscure by the scouring winds and flooding rains.

On the Trail to Santa Fé

As a rule, the country was flat and bare; parties bore on by compass or by landmarks from camping spot to camping spot. Therefore, like other pioneer trails, the trail to Santa Fé was at first merely a loose succession of convenient or necessary stages. Vehicles might take the formation of four abreast, or might stretch out in single file for a mile and more. The column of fours and, later, of twos became imperative in the Indian country for ready defense.

The journey out usually occupied fifty or sixty days; the journey back, when the wagons traveled lighter, could be made in forty days. The distance was about 780 miles, and a well-laden wagon traveled on an average of fifteen miles a day. But in 1826, the time of Kit Carson's first trip, the travel was less systematized, more haphazard and, therefore, less expeditious.

Having ferried the river at Arrow Rock above Franklin, the Kit Carson caravan would strike westward, leaving Missouri through the green prairie of the friendly Osage Indians and, aiming for the Arkansas River, would cross into the Kansas of today. At the height of the trade, in addition to the great heavy, flaring-topped wagons of Conestoga pattern, each drawn by eight mules, there were stylish Dearborn carriages, the conveyances of city merchants and of invalid, for both wealth and health were to be found upon the Santa Fé Trail. Outriders ambled before and upon either flank of the column. Alongside the wagons there trudged booted, whip-popping teamsters or wagoners, changing at times to the near-wheel mules. In the dust of the rear there followed the "cavvy."

As the caravan proceeded into the arid plains of Kansas, discipline would become stricter, for the Pawnees frequently raided here, and just ahead were the grounds of the fierce Kiowas and the equally dangerous Comanches. The horsemen would look to their arms; and at night the wagons would be parked, or joined into a hollow square, the front wheels of one vehicle lapping the rear wheels of another. An opening was left through which the animals might be driven in case of alarm.

The men slept in their blankets around the parked wagons;

the animals were put out to graze, picketed or hobbled, and guards were posted.[8]

Early in the morning, after the rude but hearty breakfast by messes, the captain of the caravan would sign to his lieutenant; the lieutenant would call "Catch up!" To the cry of "Catch up! Catch up!" the teamsters would vie at harnessing their spans and hooking them to the wagons. Presently, from first one crew and then another, would come the bawl "All 's set!" . . . "Stretch out then!"

A noble sight these teams were, forty-odd in number, their immense wagons still unmoved, forming an oval breastwork of wealth, girded by an impatient mass of near 400 mules, harnessed and ready to move again along their solitary way. But the interest of the scene was much increased when at the call of the commander the two lines, team after team, straightened themselves into the trail and rolled majestically away over the undulating plain.[9]

The wagons rumbled, the Dearborns creaked, harness jangled, the horses and mules coughed and snorted, men shouted and sang, and the constant cracking of whip-lashes as the teamsters showed their skill sounded like volleys of gunshots — while anon there tinkled the pendant clapper of the old bell-mare leading the caballada.

The journey had its peculiar fascinations. Indians — to be suspected in every human figure breaking the horizons — and other wild life lessened the monotony of the vast, unbounded reaches. Subject to the season and the presence of Indians, there were dark masses of buffalo; even a solitary old bull was hailed with delight. Bands of antelope swerved hither and thither, "looking at a distance like the shadow of a moving cloud." These, and jack-rabbits, prairie dogs in villages covering acres of ground, badgers and prairie foxes were sighted in great numbers, but to the First Dragoons, upon the Trail in 1829, "buffalo, wolves, rattlesnakes and grasshoppers seemed to fill up the country."

Halts were made at noon for lunch and rest, and at sundown for camp. The men gathered around the mess fires of sage or cottonwood or buffalo chips, to squat with skillet or ramrod spit, or to loll while waiting upon the cooking by others. Such scenes were repeated a quarter of a century later on the Oregon emigrant Trail and the California Trail. Appetite for the most greasy dish was never lacking, says Josiah Gregg in his *Commerce of the Prairies*. The dusk brought sound sleep beside the white-topped wagons under the brightly twinkling stars, while the wolves howled and snarled and the guards occasionally stooped low to limn some suspicious object against the skyline, for the thought of Indians was ever in mind.

There were perils other than Indians. Accidents happened. Rain and hail and sand storms of terrific violence swept the route. Animals stampeded. They and the wagons were struck by lightning. The attack of the elements was appalling; and the caravan, out here upon the havenless pampa, was like a fleet dragging anchors in the midst of an unknown ocean.

The Santa Féans, when on the march through these plains, are in constant expectation of these tornadoes. Accordingly, when the sky at night indicates their approach, they chain the wheels of adjacent wagons strongly together to prevent their being upset — an accident that had often happened when this precaution was not taken.[10]

"The lightning and heavy rumbling of the thunder were frightful," "earth and skies" were so intensely illumined "that the eye could not endure the brightness," "the ground trembled — the horses and mules shook with fear, and attempted to escape."

The soil greedily drank the downpours and was arid again. The Arkansas River, which at times flowed as white and as sweet as milk, was a great blessing. But away from the Arkansas, bewildered by the sameness of the landscape and (as the cross-country traveler Farnham says) by the deep paths made by the buffalo in single file, the caravan might go waterless until men and animals were frantic with thirst.

One of those numerous incidents that have given character to Kit Carson, youth and man, in fact and fiction, occurred when this caravan of the fall of 1826 was about a third along upon the trail, and the Arkansas River, in central present Kansas, was close before. Teamster Andrew Broadus, hastily hauling his gun, muzzle first, out of a wagon, in order to shoot a wolf prowling around the camp, shot himself through the right arm. The bone was shattered but he refused to have the arm amputated, although he was warned of the danger from the wound. By the time the Arkansas was reached the arm had begun to "mortify," as the expression was. Gangrene had set in.

Amputation at once was imperative. Broadus now consented to the ordeal. Peters in his Carson biography says that three members of the caravan, one of them Carson, were appointed to do the job. Carson himself relates, in his *Own Story:* "One of the party stated that he could do it." Accordingly, the flesh was cut with a razor, well above the wound; the bone was sawed through with "an old saw," and the arteries were sealed with a red-hot king bolt. The end of the stump was covered with a plaster of tar from a wagon hub. The operation was a double success, for not only had the arm been removed but the patient recovered. Ere Santa Fé was in sight the stump had healed and Teamster Broadus was active.

Carson undoubtedly assisted in this operation. That he officiated as chief surgeon may be questioned. The whole incident, however, was remarkable enough to be given a permanent place in Santa Fé Trail history. Josiah Gregg[11] chronicles it, although without mention of Kit Carson. He says that the teeth of the handsaw were too coarse for the work and that a set of finer teeth was filed in the back of the blade.

To ford the Arkansas was somewhat risky, on account of the quicksands. Teams were strengthened, and the wagons were snaked through in double time. At the farther shore water was stowed away and food prepared sufficient for a two days' journey. Immediately ahead was a "water scrape," or a dry march across the parched wastes of the Cimarron Desert in southwestern Kansas, between the Arkansas and the sources of the Cimarron River. It was the favorite haunt of the bold-riding Comanches. The Cimarron, below its sources, was only a dry, sandy bed. Herbage was scarce. Mirages lured, gigantic hailstones fell, the surface of the ground was so hard that wagons made no tracks, and the way was easily lost. The Cimarron "water scrape" grew to be the most dreaded stage of the overland trail to Santa Fé. It was at its worst in the fall, for water was then most scant.

But, when that was over — when, having strained through the heavy sandhills that bordered the Arkansas, and crossed the firm, bare plain of the interior, the wagons, with teamsters and all peering nervously ahead out of bloodshot eyes, toiled at last into the valley of the Cimarron and reached the first spring — then there was comparatively clear sailing.

And hereabouts would be met, if not met previously, the first *cibolero,* or Mexican buffalo hunter. As wild as the Comanche, the *cibolero* ranged through the desert like an Arab, clad in trousers and short jacket of goat-skin leather, and flat straw hat. Slung athwart his shoulder he bore bow and quiver, and he had a long lance, suspended beside him in a gaily tasseled case and waving above his head. His pride was his fusil or smooth-bore musket of huge calibre, its muzzle carefully stoppered with a great wooden plug, also tasseled. His stirrup hoods or *tapaderas* swept the ground, and his enormous saddle covered all his pony.

It was considered a good stroke to encounter a *cibolero.* News of the market in Santa Fé might be obtained from him, and also a supply of dried buffalo flesh from his camp where he, his companions and their families were engaged in securing wild meat.

By the landmark of the Rabbit Ear mounds, about where the panhandle of Oklahoma is blunted by New Mexico, the caravan would know that it was upon the straight course. The country grew rougher; mountains were hazily outlined in the northwest. Beyond them there was sequestered the prominent Mexican settlement of Fernandez de Taos. A trail, branching off, led to it and was recommended by the government survey party now in the field. Anybody bound for Taos was at liberty to take that trail, but few did.

The older or the "mountain" division of the Santa Fé Trail did not cross the Cimarron Desert. It followed up the north bank of the Arkansas into what today is southeastern Colorado, turned to the southwest and, approximating the present railroad route over Raton Pass of the Raton Range, passed about forty miles east of Taos and rejoined the Cimarron Desert Trail about 100 miles out of Santa Fé and 100 miles by trail from Taos.

The probabilities are that this fall caravan of 1826 cut across the desert of the Cimarron to avoid the mountain snows and the sooner to reach its destination. When Santa Fé was only some 200 miles on, the caravans dispatched an advance squad of couriers to announce the approach and to prepare the market. By this time the train manifested hard usage. The exceedingly dry atmosphere had shrunk and warped the running gear, the rough road was shaking tires and spokes loose, and at every halt much tinkering had to be done. Strips of green or water-soaked buffalo hide were tightly wound about the parts, as ties, and wedges of hoop-iron were driven into the cracks.

At Turkey River (*Rio de las Gallinas*) the first real token of civilization, or semi-civilization, was encountered: a rude adobe *rancho* at the base of a cliff — prophetic of the future city of Las Vegas. In twenty more miles the first settlement was reached; San Miguel del Vado (St. Michael of the Ford), a forlorn collection of mud huts squatting upon the bank of the rippling Pecos River. Santa Fé was now only fifty miles away. The talk of it waxed more general. Around the mess fires many a tale was told for the benefit of credulous listeners — prankish tales of black-eyed *señoritas,* ready to smile upon the bearded but white-skinned *Americano;* of tasty *frijoles,* crisp *tortillas,* and throat-scalding, belly-tickling *aguardiente* that would make a rabbit bite a rattlesnake; of *baile* and livelier *fandango,* and of the palace with its glass windows and its festoons of Indian ears!

The caravan plodded on. The region was becoming more settled, the greenhorns anxiously looked for the famous city to loom into view. Then, finally, on an early November day, as the first wagons mounted a rocky ridge, a great cheering from the advance was heard. The word went galloping down the column: "Santy Fe! Thar she is!" And when young Carson also gained the crest, he saw in the distance to the northwest, before and below him, a valley dotted with trees yellowed by frost or still green, a valley greenly lined with ditches, cultivated to patches of grain, and blotched with a dun splash of scrambling, flat-roofed, one-story habitations that, according to Gregg, in 1831 resembled brick kilns, and according to Lieutenant Pike, a quarter-century earlier, at a distance reminded the American of a fleet of flatboats moored against a hill.

And this was that mysterious city, the goal of 800 miles!

With Santa Fé a short distance away, caravans usually halted to rub up. Clothing was changed for the best at hand, faces were washed, hair was slicked; teamsters removed the old crackers from their whip-lashes and tied new ones on. All that having been done, the train rumbled and clattered on down the slope, across the plain at the foot of the descent, and in amidst the low hovels. The long-lashed whips cracked, the jaded mules, plucking spirit, tried to gambol, the men swung their hats and cheered. The side lanes and dark doorways erupted other celebrants. Loud and shrill pealed the cries of swarthy men, women and children:

"*Los Americanos!*" . . . "The wagons!" . . . "The caravan is coming in!"

More and more extravagantly then the teamsters flourished their whips, snapping the new crackers and showing off before the black-eyed *señoras* and *señoritas*. The old hands grinned and sputtered their favorite Spanish; the new hands stared. The captain and his aides easily sat their saddles. And young Carson, striving to be the old hand, but in reality as much excited as anybody else, trudged along, as may be, in his dusty boots, or slouched along upon his dusty mule.

"*Muchacho! Un muchacho Americano! Mira!* [Boy! An American boy! See!]" That was he.

The end of this trail down from the outlying mesa — a trail today preserved as a crooked street — was the sun-baked *plaza publica,* or town square, fronted at one corner by the massy one-story, porticoed adobe *fonda,* or public inn, with its thick-walled corral, on another corner by the governor's official quarters, *El Palacio,* and shaded by a few cottonwoods. Halt was made, with the curving line extending out of the plaza and up the trail, while the caravan captain reported to the customs officers ere, wagon after wagon, the goods were broken out for storage and inspection and the teams and emptied wagons corralled.

The arrival of a caravan was a prodigious event for old Santa Fé. It was a visit from another planet. In 1826 very many Mexicans, even of the northern province, had never seen an American, nor had any clear conception of the United States; and for more than twenty years thereafter the Caucasian white skin was a marvel to the natives of the Mexican interior. Lieutenant Frederick Ruxton, that wandering Britisher who in 1846 toured the interior, tells of the embarrassing admiration he drew whenever he bared any portion of his body to take a bath.

This night, and for a succession of nights and days, the officers and men of the caravan were entertained like sailors in a foreign port. Dance and gaming, women, sweet wine and fiery grain liquor were their lot. Paid off with his wage of five dollars in silver a month, accrued from seven or eight weeks of labor, young Kit Carson saw the sights — not omitting the palace with its legendary festoons of dried Indian ears!

Chapter IV

New Mexico and New Mexicans

SANTA FÉ, at the time of Kit Carson's first visit there, was a place of great pretensions but of debatable values. It was the capital of a people, as cited by Senator Benton in his speech before referred to, "among whom all the arts are lost. . . . No books, no newspapers, iron a dollar a pound, cultivating the earth with wooden tools and spinning upon a stick!"[12]

Even in 1826 the town and its environments mustered a population of around 5,000, in which the *rico,* the official, and the *gente principal,* or gentry, were sharply distinguished from the prevailing common classes. They all led a life primitively simple — a life out of step with the world of progress, ruled by ceremony and ignorance, dictated by customs, the military power, and the priesthood. There was not a white, or American, woman in the country, and as yet no potent leaven here of foreigners in permanent residence. As for the term, "white," the Mexican of any class considered himself as white as the Anglo-Saxon, thus setting himself apart from the Indian race. The architecture of the town was severe and ugly although adapted to the land. Buildings, erected of native mud bricks and smeared over with thin mud plaster, were limited to the one story, which was flatly roofed with mud laid upon a thatch of poles. Interiors were lightened by a whitewash of the native *tierra blanca* (white earth) or gypsum. The deep embrasures serving as windows were protected by wooden shutters, iron bars or, here and there, by sheets of laminated gypsum (selenite). Mud front joined with mud front around the central plaza, until at irregular intervals a narrow lane cut through. Nevertheless, amid the pomp and prejudice, dirt and squalor, open vice and doubtful virtue, there was much to interest the visitor from the Missouri frontier.

The blanket-enveloped Mexican, smiling in the foreigner's face, scowling at his back, indolent, graceful, eternally smoking his corn-husk cigarette, and whether *peón, paisano,* what-not, ever a *caballero* or gentleman; the shawled Mexican woman, with her face stained crimson with the oily juice of the alegría plant, a variety of the sesamum similarly used by Egyptian women, or coated with a paste of gypsum to preserve her complexion for the ball; the burros, piled high with enormous loads of corn shucks for fodder, or with wood from the mountains, or with balancing coarsely woven sacks of melons or with slung casks of that white whisky termed "Taos lightning"; market exhibits of melons, baked piñon nuts, peaches from the orchards of the Pueblos and Navajos, native tobacco or *punche,* grapes, bunches of *hoja* or husk for the rolling of cigarettes; the constant gambling, principally at *el monte,* with Mexican cards, by high and low alike, in open booths and gaming-rooms; the religious processions, to which everybody must uncover — in these and other local aspects there was much to see.

As soon as the customs duties had been adjusted the caravans pursued their business of barter and sale. They split into their component units. Detachments might push on for the markets of El Paso del Norte, down the river, and Chihuahua and Sonora farther into Old Mexico.

It usually required three to four weeks to settle caravan business in Santa Fé. The return caravan was loaded with the proceeds of the trading venture, the start back to Missouri was made with the gold dust and the silver bullion, the buffalo robes and furs, the wool, the blankets of the country, the horse and mule stock. Those merchants in the Carson caravan who contemplated return at once to Missouri with wagons would have hastened their departure. The season warned them. Winter threatened desert and plain.

In Santa Fé of this date, and especially in the winter, there could be little employment for an American boy who did not speak the language. Kit Carson, foot-loose and empty of pocket, faced into the north, for Fernandez de Taos. There is no word of his brothers, William, Hamilton, Robert or big Mose, who seems to have appeared in Santa Fé some time in 1826. What impelled Kit to Taos is not stated; but as a trappers' and traders' resort old "Touse" was already infused with American blood, he had heard stories of the place from his brothers and other transients there, and very likely he had made acquaintances who were going there to winter-in.

Taos is about eighty miles north and slightly eastward of Santa Fé. The trail between, like Taos itself, is still without a railroad; but even in Kit Carson's first pilgrimage it was well traveled, plainly marked by wheel and hoof, and by stake and cross topping little heaps of dedicatory stones in sign that here a life had been spilled. As a goal of the earliest caravans, which traveled the mountain route to the Spanish Settlements, and as a port for miscellaneous traffic, Taos was a place second, in New Mexico, only to Santa Fé. Although the actual border was some 150 miles northward, at the Arkansas River, the town was the customs depot of Mexico's northern frontier.

Carson found Taos (familiarly styled "Touse" and Fernandez), an outpost settlement of 500 people, set near the head of fertile Taos Valley (*El Valle de Taos*) with Taos Creek (*El Rito de Taos*) coursing down, clear and cold, between willowed banks, and Taos Peak, sacred to the Pueblo Indians, and now snow-capped and plashed with yellow of the frosted aspens, standing sentinel over the twin *casas grandes* of the Taos Pueblos.

The original appellation of Taos seems to have been Don Fernando or Don Fernandez de Taos. Whether this was in deference to one Fernando, that Vidalpando the early settler whose marriageable daughter, Marie Rose, was carried off by the Comanches and by way of the Pawnees arrived in St. Louis in 1770, there to die as the respected Madame Salé *dit* Lajoie in 1830, aged 107; or in deference to King Ferdinand of Spain — the oldest inhabitants do not agree. The change to San Fernandez was doubtless a tribute to Saint Ferdinand of the Catholic calendar. The grant of town land was issued in 1799. The Taos Indians, occupying their ancient walled pueblo about two miles out of the present town site, hold to the idea that in August, 1556, Roman Catholic sovereignty proclaimed their ownership in the lands for a league around the tower site of their old church; and aver that early in the next century they ceded the site for a settlement *rancho* to a party of discharged Spanish soldiers, as a measure of alliance against the marauding Utes and Apaches. It was in 1760 that the Comanches stormed Taos "Old Town," or *Los Ranchos de Taos,* killed the men and bore away fifty women forted in the Vidalpando house.[13]

Since it was the northernmost New Mexican town contacting the border and was near the southern extremities of those Rockies whose eastern slopes were American territory; and since it was connected by caravans with Santa Fé and Missouri, from the day of the first outland wanderer to these fair parts Taos, through more than a quarter of a century, was a rendezvous for boot and moccasin of the long trails from north and east. Names notable in the fur trade, the goods trade, the adventure trade and the fighting trade registered here; and in its gay hardihood, its co-mingling of whites, reds and breeds, Taos was the Vincennes and Kaskaskia of the old Southwest.

When Kit Carson arrived there in December 1826, he had selected his home port for forty years. During those years he returned to it from all his excursions; and there he is buried — "the hunter home from the hill."

When Lewis H. Garrard (of *Wah-to-yah and the Taos Trail*) saw Taos in 1846 "its walls . . . [were] mica lime washed to a dazzling whiteness." When John H. Fonda was there in the winter of 1823-24 he found dingy one-story structures left to the natural colors of gray adobe. The inhabitants — Spaniards, Mexicans, "Indians, a mixed breed," a few trappers — "were a lazy, dirty, ignorant set." It was a "lively wintering place, and many were the fandangoes, frolics and fights which came off."[14]

At the time of Carson's arrival the principal industries, aside from the barter in trapper goods (furs, robes, blankets, powder and lead, liquor) were the manufacture, from fermented wheat, of the pale "Taos lightning," smuggling and agriculture sufficient to tide the passive *ranchero* over the winter and spring stringencies.

Numerous *acequias* or irrigating ditches divided field from field; there were no fences. The town was a rural, lesser Santa Fé. The mud houses and shops surrounding the central plaza were supplied with mica panes. The houses formed, as today, interior courts or *patios;* living-rooms were provided along the sides with rolls of *serapes* or blankets — divans by day and, when unrolled, beds at night. Sacred relics, rosaries, and images and prints, or *santos,* of the Savior, the Virgin Mary and the patron saint, were the chief ornaments. Bread was baked in outside, beehive mud ovens; *tortillas,* flour and water batter smeared in thin sheets upon a smooth stone, were baked by being propped in front of the fireplace blaze. Fracases of fandango and drinking bout were frequent. The bell of a church, already ancient, called to mass.

It was into this free and primitive life in the little town of San Fernandez de Taos that Kit Carson entered, now, at end of trail, presently to round his seventeenth birthday: a boy strange to country and customs, unable to speak the language, green from the Missouri settlements, very much on his own but self-reliant, quickly observing, and bent upon making his way.

Chapter V

As Fared the Runaway — 1826-1829

As a station upon the fortune seeker's trail, Taos promised not only adventure but enterprise. Young Carson found here society of various sorts. He was thrown with men who became his valuable patrons and long-time friends and fellow citizens.

Taos had its round quota of shaggy trappers, American, French and nondescript, now settled for the winter with or without companions in their lodges. But Don Carlos Beaubien — Charles Hipolyte Trotier, Sieur de Beaubien, born at Three Rivers, Canada — having come out from the St. Louis district of Missouri was already established here and about to marry into one of the prominent Spanish families. In due time he became proprietor of the immense Beaubien and Miranda grant of land and was appointed by General Stephen Watts Kearny one of the first three superior court judges for New Mexico. It was his daughter, Luz, whom Lucien B. Maxwell, Carson's close friend and stanch ally, married — thereby falling heir to the grant upon which he and Carson had gone to ranching together.

Don Carlos, Charles Bent and Ceran St. Vrain, Taosans all, were firmly woven into Carson's life. At this time, 1826, Charles Bent and his younger brother William (who also earned Carson's gratitude for many services) were operating a trading stockade on the upper Arkansas and Charles was much upon the caravan-goods trail between Missouri and New Mexico, with Taos as a stop-over and destined to be his home. He and William were familiar to Taos. Ceran St. Vrain, of the Flemish nobility and of a titled name in the old Province of Louisiana, with Ewing Young and other Taosans, was still out in the Farther Southwest on a fur hunt.

He had left Missouri apparently in May; in August had obtained, at Santa Fé, a trader's passport for self and company, and was known to have headed for the Gila and the Colorado; none of the company had yet reported back in Santa Fé or

Taos in Carson's Day

Taos. Kit Carson, however, came to know Ceran St. Vrain very well, as a member of Bent, St. Vrain & Co., of Bent's Fort and the Indian trade; as a Taosan and a leader in New Mexico in territorial affairs, and as short-time colonel of Carson's own First New Mexico Volunteers.[15]

By reason of the fur-hunt expedition, then, Ewing Young was among the absentees. Kit must have known of Ewing Young, a stalwart of Taos and the Southwest. He had been a member of the Becknell parties from Franklin to Santa Fé in 1821 and 1822 — parties in one of which William Carson is said to have enrolled. Captain Young had been back and forth between Missouri and New Mexico several times on trading and trapping ventures. This summer — 1826 — he, Milton Sublette, Peg-leg Smith the trapper, and others had joined Ceran St. Vrain in the Gila and Colorado River country. To the Spanish people he was Joaquin Jóven, Joon, John, Jon, Yon, and so on.[16]

Don Antonio Robidoux the Frenchman from St. Louis should have been in Taos — where he lived — if he were not at his new trading post among the Utes of the Uncompahgre River over in what is today southwestern Colorado. He and his brother Louis, of Taos and Santa Fé, were Indian traders. Carson saw a great deal of him, in the mountains; and, near the close of twenty years he and Don Antonio marched with the First Dragoons from the Rio Grande to the coast of California, the one as guide, the other as interpreter.

Another American resident of old Taos was Samuel Chambers, Kentuckian who, after his release from Chihuahua with the rest of the Robert McKnight party in 1822, had here settled down, broken in health and fortune.

The boy Kit was taken in for the winter by one Kincaid, an American, of well-known Missouri name, for Fort Kincaid had been a contemporary of Forts Cooper and Hempstead. Variously rendered as Kinkead, Kinkaid, Kincaid and Kincade, the name had advanced from St. Louis to the border settlements, and it is not unlikely that in this Kincaid young

Kit found an acquaintance. He at least found somebody who was acquainted with the Carson and Cooper families.

There was nothing doing in Taos. The caravan-trade season was over; trappers were leaving rather than entering the mountains and no more fur expeditions would be on the move until spring; and there was even less chance of work than in Santa Fé. The distilleries, to be sure, were running in the winter, but they were small businesses and peon labor was cheap. Carson managed to pick up a smattering of colloquial Spanish, and that was about all he did accomplish, aside from profiting, as may be, by the lore of the older Kincaid.

His career through the two years following is somewhat hard to understand when one compares it with his career thereafter and assumes that his brothers were in and out of Taos and Santa Fé. Although he was now at American headquarters in the country, and had been received by Kincaid, he secured no permanent berth with any trapping or trading crew, but merely served, at intervals, as teamster, interpreter, cook — the rôle of the drifter.

One explanation is that in size and means he had nothing to recommend him. He himself told General Rusling, in 1866, that when he first went into the West he "was too small to set a trap." He was of ordinary settler-boy type; he was commonplace in appearance all his life. Few persons, not knowing Kit Carson by reputation, would have picked him out for a valiant. The mountain-men in Taos would have hesitated to burden themselves with a slight and rather dumb greenhorn youth who probably did not look his years.

He was furthermore unwelcome in a trail squad for the reason that he lacked an outfit or the wherewithal for procuring one. A beaver trap cost twelve dollars in St. Louis, and there is no assurance that he had brought a rifle with him. Taos had nobody, in this juncture, who would advance an inexperienced small boy an outfit, or be responsible for him. Kincaid makes unrecorded exit from the scene. His name scarcely breaks the surface of the activities of that period.

Down in Santa Fé again in the spring of 1827 young Carson could find only a job with a caravan bound for Missouri. On the Arkansas, a little more than half way, a Franklin spring caravan for Santa Fé was met. He changed berths and turned back with the caravan to recross the dry stretch of the Cimarron. Luck had favored him.

The chances are that this was the caravan of fifty-two wagons, 105 men, captained by the famed Ezekiel Williams, with which Davie Workman, the saddler, had taken to the long trail. The reunion of ragged runaway apprentice and sarcastic employer who had also abandoned bench and awl should have been interesting.

Stalled in Santa Fé, Kit, scratching for a living and a woolen shirt, forthwith fell into another teamster job, this time with a small train for El Paso del Norte, down the Rio Grande — a trail that well warranted the wage of a dollar a day.

Old El Paso del Norte, which is Ciudad Juarez, in Mexico on the south side of the Rio Grande, opposite El Paso, Texas, was the gateway to the Department of Chihuahua. It was popularly known to traders as "the Pass" — the name being attributed to the ford here (Ruxton), to the course of the river between two high points (Gregg), or to the retreat of refugees from the north, after the Pueblo Indian revolt of 1680 (Gregg). In the boy Carson's time El Paso was chiefly noted for its grape products, "Pass brandy" and "Pass wine."

The caravan trail to El Paso was 320 miles of the trail to Chihuahua, which was still 230 miles onward. It was a trail not without excitement, frequented by bandits and hovered over by the Apaches, for the last 200 miles of its course totally unsettled until the Mesilla Valley at its lower end was reached, and divided into fearsome stages such as the *mal pais* desert of the *Jornada del Muerto* (Day's Journey of the Dead), the dismal *Laguna del Muerto* (Lake of the Dead), a gloomy canyon where the avid Apaches were wont to lurk, and the *Ojo del Muerto* (Spring of the Dead), at the foot of the canyon. The waters of Elephant Butte Dam of modern day have exorcized some of these terrors.

Having been discharged at El Paso, Kit made back over the trail and sought Taos again, there to spend the winter of 1927-28. Kincaid, his first friend in need, is not mentioned. The haven, this second winter, was the quarters of Ewing Young, trader and captain of trappers. Captain Young, bearded Tennesseean, had returned from his trapping trip, of varied fortunes, into the Far Southwest, and was doing a trading-goods business in Taos.

Carson, at eighteen, cooked for his board and lodging; spent what money he had, on the *fandangos* and other frailties which left the winter sojourner in Taos poor by spring; between times listened to the tall tales of Captain Young — a man of might, of few words, the same measure of scruples, but of much daring and of southwestern experiences, which, in the seven years, had carried him beyond the teeming pueblo of the fabulous white-skinned Zuñis and, in defiance of the Spaniard and the Apache, to the rich beaver streams of the unmapped Colorado of the West, the Colorado Grande.

Other men in Taos had been out there, with the captain and with Ceran St. Vrain. Captain Young, ever restless, was planning to repeat; but he did not bid for the services of his cook, the ex-teamster. There were seasoned trappers to be had. In Santa Fé in the spring, Carson once more set his face to the east and to Missouri, in the company of a caravan for the States. And as in the spring before, meeting an incoming caravan on the Arkansas, with it he trailed back to Santa Fé. Thus he was shuttled between poverty and prosperity. His fluency in the spoken Spanish now stood him in a pinch. One Colonel Tramell, trader, needed an interpreter for the onward trip to Chihuahua. Carson hired out for the trip to Chihuahua — a journey of 550 miles, forty days, first south to that El Paso del Norte, thence through the mountains to Chihuahua.

Chihuahua, capital of its department, had the reputation of being a city far superior to Santa Fé. It was practically the *ultima Thule* of the States traders, although venturesome Americans sometimes reached on even to Durango and points west. With its white-washed buildings, their corners faced with stone, its promenade of fashion along the *Alameda,* and its cathedral with façade studded with statues of Christ and the twelve apostles (its doorway arch adorned, on occasion, with Apache scalps), Chihuahua was indeed *ciudad muy grande.*

It was a remotest end of trail for Carson, but Kit Carson was lucky in time and place all his life. Here in Chihuahua he encountered that Robert McKnight whose return to Missouri, in 1822, after nine years' imprisonment in the Chihuahua *calabozo,* had been announced in the *Missouri Intelligencer* of Franklin. John McKnight, who had rescued his brother Robert from durance vile, had long been lying, for the count of the Comanches, amid the sands of the North Canadian country, western present Oklahoma, out from a little trading post that he had attempted. Robert himself was casting dice with Fate again in Chihuahua and vicinity — the first American after Pike to exploit this region. He was in the trader business; and, in line with ways and means, was mining the old copper prospects of the Mimbres (Willows) Apache country, near the sources of the Gila River, 400 miles to the northward, in New Mexico. The workings were called Santa Rita del Cobre — Saint Rita of Copper.

These workings had been in operation before Robert Mc-Knight's and Kit Carson's time there. In 1804 they had furnished employment for 600 peons; a pack road connected with Chihuahua; 100 mules, each laden with 300 pounds of ore or of supplies, traveled back and forth through the dust. McKnight was now intent upon wealth. The gold in the ore paid the expenses of mining, hauling and refining, so that the copper was clear gain. The ore was mined, with pick and shovel only, in great masses of red metal or rich sulphuret, easy to handle. But the country was thoroughly Apache and before McKnight had materialized his golden dream he was delving in a veritable den of rattlesnakes.[17]

Preceding tenants at the mines had founded there a small village of low adobe huts. In the successive occupations of the

premises a fort was erected, triangular in shape, with angle
bastions. The ruins of huts and fort were noted when in 1846
General Stephen W. Kearny's dragoon column to California
camped in the vicinity. Kit Carson was guide for the column,
and narrated of McKnight, his old employer, to Captain Abraham R. Johnston — remarking that at one time the Apaches
ran off eighty of McKnight's pack mules.

While trading and mining together, McKnight had wagons
and pack-trains constantly on the trail between his outpost and
the Chihuahua settlements. He engaged Carson as a teamster.
Carson says in his *Own Story:* "I remained at the mines a few
months driving team. I was not satisfied with this employment, took my discharge and departed for Taos, and arrived
in August 1828."

Possibly so he did, granted that the schedule which took him
to the Arkansas, 400 miles, thence back to Santa Fé, and down
to Chihuahua, 550 miles, and up to the mines, 400 miles, for
"a few months," was one of seven-league boots. Or possibly
the year was 1829.

There is a puzzling reference to young Carson of this period.
The veteran trader, William Waldo, citing a hard battle with
the Comanches in which he and other traders took part under
Charles Bent, in the Cimarron Desert, during the spring of
1829, asserts:

> We had about sixty men. The famous Ewing Young heard of our
> situation, and also that two thousand warriors of various tribes had com-
> bined, and had taken a strong position in a canyon in the mountains,
> which we could not avoid. He first attempted to come to our assistance,
> but was attacked and driven back. Here the boy Kit Carson gained his
> first laurels. Young returned to Taos, and other companies having re-
> turned from their yearly trapping, he increased his force to 95 hunters,
> and, after one engagement, joined us.[18]

Captain Waldo supports this story by linking it with the
escort duty of Major Bennet Riley, who by orders from Washington guarded this caravan of the spring of 1829 to the Arkansas — and, by reason of Indian threats, for a day's march
beyond. The canyon ambuscade also is history.

In any event Carson left the teamster service of Robert Mc-Knight. McKnight in due course settled down in Chihuahua to enjoy, for some half-dozen years, that fortune which he had salvaged from the misfortunes of twenty-five years. Carson, in Taos, whether for a year or a fortnight, in due course heard a call to arms.

"Some time before my [Carson's] arrival" Captain Young had sent a trapping party into the Southwest. The party had fought all one day with the Apaches of the headwaters of the Gila; had been turned back, and here they were in Taos with their story to tell and their losses to recount.

Captain Ewing Young was no man to brook this sort of thing. The trail was to be opened. He at once reorganized for punishment and furs. Carson, on the spot and outfitted at last, at last was admitted to man's estate, for Captain Young enrolled him.

His three years in the country, and his recent hardy experiences at those copper mines in the heart of the Apache range qualified him. Captain Young's observance of him during a winter may have helped his cause. Moreover, at this season, midsummer, Taos would have been pretty well reduced in fighting men.

Carson says in his *Own Story:* "I joined the party which left Taos in August 1829."[19]

Chapter VI

The Trapper's Trail — 1829

BAD as his reputation has been, in the beginning of his intercourse with the invading whites the Apache was not, as a rule, unfriendly or vicious. He soon grew to hate with fierce hatred the Spanish and their descendants the Mexicans, and met deceit and rapine with rapine and deceit.

> You have taken New Mexico, and will soon take California; go, then, and take Chihuahua, Durango and Sonora. We will help you. You fight for land; we care nothing for land; we fight for our rights and for food. The Mexicans are rascals; we hate them and will kill them all.

With such import spoke the Apache chief to General Kearny, in explanation that the newly come Americans who warred with Mexico were approved as allies. But that was only a distinction of the moment. Long before this the Ewing Young, Ceran St. Vrain and kindred companies, rifling the Apache country of furs and game while tempting with the possible booty of arms and of horse or mule flesh, had courted attack. Through trespass without apology, and through other aggressions, it came to be with the Apache as with the tribes by and large in the West: they had to fight, and once settled down to hostility toward everybody who wore a hat they accepted their enforced rôle.

The trappers' solution of the Indian problem was that of the Kentucky settlers and of the army: no offense should be permitted to go unpunished to the utmost. But whereas the settlers and the army were fighting for civilization and the greatest good to the country, the trapper was striving only for private gain.

The list of this vengeful Ewing Young company is still uncalled. The members were Americans, Missouri French, possibly a German or two, no doubt a sprinkling of Mexicans and mixed bloods. Only a few names of the forty odd have been preserved: Ewing Young's because he was leader; Kit Carson's because he had a press agent in Frémont and a Boswell in Sur-

geon Peters; James Higgins's because he shot "big" James
Lawrence — who therefore also received special mention; and
those of François Turcôte, Jean Vaillant, Anastase Curier, who
mutinied.

Captain Ewing Young waived the formality of a trading or
trapping license for his party of this August 1829. Thus Carson
was early initiated into despite for Mexican authority. There
was excuse for the captain's action. When in 1826 he and Milton Sublette and company had followed Ceran St. Vrain into
the Gila country they had operated under a trading license
issued by Governor Narbona of New Mexico. Upon their return to the settlements in the spring of 1827, with their catch
of furs, they found themselves denounced. Governor Narbona
was out, a new governor, Manuel Armijo, was in. Josiah
Gregg, the chronicler, asserts that Armijo, like other governors
of the province, refused to ratify the acts of a predecessor and
accordingly seized the furs as smuggled goods. A license issued
by one administration was voided by the next administration.

In this case, however, Armijo acted not without just cause.
The trading licenses obtained by Ceran St. Vrain, Joaquin Jon,
et al., had been obtained under false pretenses. The trading
expeditions of these small private parties had turned into fur-
hunting and predatory expeditions by large parties of a mem-
bership unlisted. The odor that reached Santa Fé was bad. The
story goes that Captain Young and Milton Sublette stowed
their furs in the house of "a wretch named Don Luis Cabeza
de Vaca," on the outskirts of Santa Fé, until a license that
would make them legal property could be secured from the
new governor. Captain Young worked this plan on his return
from the present trip, by getting a trading license and then
producing the furs as alleged proceeds from trade with the
Indians. The proscribed trapper needed only to pose as the
authorized trader — but for the once, at least, Captain Young
rode to a fall.

The furs brought from the Gila and the Colorado in the
spring of 1827 were seized as contraband. By orders of the gov-

ernor, soldiers forced the Cabeza de Vaca house, killed Don Luis, and under direction of the mayor of Santa Fé the raw pelts — twenty-nine tierces of beaver — were spread to dry. Sublette boldly salvaged two packs bearing his mark, carried them away and hid out among friends while the military searched for him. He managed to reach the frontier with his booty, but Captain Young, growling in his beard, proclaimed that he himself "had been plundered by the Mexican authorities of $18,000 or $20,000 worth fur."[20]

Consequently when he left Taos in August, Captain Young went by no leave of Santa Fé. If he trapped he broke the law anyway, and he was going to trap. That he designed to venture clear into California, this time, is evident. He had fortified himself with two passports that should safeguard his presence, as a foreigner, in settled Mexican territory. The one had been viséd at Washington, March 1828, by the Mexican minister there, but the other was of the current year, 1829, signed by Henry Clay, Secretary of State.[21]

Carson rode for the long trail to the Farthest West, but how far that might be he did not care and probably did not know. It is not likely that Captain Young mentioned his eventual goal to the rank and file. Revenge, the Gila and the Colorado were incentives enough. To blind the authorities he marched his company northward out of Taos, as though for the upper Arkansas and the mountains; but headed into the San Luis Valley of southern present Colorado and there swung about into the Southwest. Santa Fé and its tentacles had been side-stepped. Nobody now would ask for his license. Before him there lay only that wide desert expanse, from the Rio Grande to the California mountains, from the northern frontier of Old Mexico to the Salt Lake, uninhabited by the white race and subject to the will of the lawless.

Although this section of the West was the first to be explored, it was the last to be exploited. The country of the *conquistadores* and the *padres,* distantly heard of by Cabeza de Vaca in 1536, penetrated by Friar Marcos in 1539, by Coronado,

Diaz, Cárdenas, 1540-1542, and thereafter by Fathers Lopez, Rodriguez, Santa María, by Father Baltran and Don Espejo, Oñate, the Jesuit Kino and his companions, seeking souls along the Gila and the lower Colorado; by Garcés, 1768-1776, and by Escalante, it remained as in the beginning. The trails of hoof and sandal made so bravely endured not even in memory; for half a century after 1776 the great, wondrous region between the Rio Grande del Norte and the California missions was unaffected by the outsider. The mission establishments were deserted, the native ceased to worship the meek crosses, the fabulous cities lost their fascination, and the Indian became the *conquistador,* levying upon that civilization which had attempted to levy upon him, and the feeble efforts of which had dwindled to a few shallow indentations along his southern borders. So the Southwest slumbered again.

But the Northwest was awakening. The contrast was an efficient lesson in the difference between New World and Old World government — between American and Spanish supremacy. Since 1803, the date of the opening of Louisiana Province to the Anglo-Saxon, or during but half of that fifty years while the Southwest slept, under impetus from Saxon and Gaul, Americans together, the Northwest had advanced more than had this same Southwest in the almost three centuries from 1539 and Friar Marcos of Nizza. Trappers, American and French, were exploring the secret places of Wyoming, Montana, Idaho, Oregon, Utah, broadening old trails and making new ones, preparing the way for the hosts of civilization. Western New Mexico, Arizona, Nevada, still remained uncharted and neglected.

From 1776 — the year of American Independence, which then signified naught to this vivid, sunny area which long waited to profit by it — for half a century New Spain from the Rio Bravo, the Rio Grande del Norte, to the Colorado lay like an unread book, opened occasionally to the copper mines, to the notes of *Indios bravos* (Comanche, Apache, Navajo) herding their Spanish-Mexican captives into the legendary north, and to the brief mention of reprisal columns from the east and south marching in and out again.

Then, in the spring of 1824, the Pattie party of trappers and traders from Missouri struck into the West — bent first upon the Northwest but soon to turn and to travel to Santa Fé and on to the Gila. Father and son were the Patties — Sylvester and James Ohio, Kentuckians acclimated to Missouri. They divided much of their time between the copper mines where they preceded Robert McKnight and Kit Carson, and the "Heelay" to the West. James followed the Gila down to the Colorado; by narrative, in which fancy rivals fact, ascended the Colorado past the Grand Canyon, pushed northward even to the Yellowstone in present Montana, and circled out by way of the Arkansas and Santa Fé. Heading into the Southwest again he and his father and six others ended their overland trail in jail at San Diego, California, in the spring of 1828.[22]

In 1827 Richard Campbell, an early American trader in New Mexico and later a prosperous *ranchero* near Santa Fé, took a pack train with thirty-five men across the desert, through northern New Mexico and Arizona, to San Diego.[23]

From 1824 onward Captain Young and companion filibusters, joined in time by Ceran St. Vrain and his muster, had been trapping the closed Southwest. Romance does not lack tall tales of other parties of Americans at large in that region, trapping, trading, mining, plundering, working, playing, feasting, suffering, with their presence cited, now and again, in Mexican archives as translated for the Southwest historian.

It is possible that Ewing Young had heard of Richard Campbell's safe trip to California. And while Kit Carson, enlisted under Captain Young, was in no sense of the first American-led party to hazard the Far Southwest, he was of the first trapping party that successfully made traverse from the settlements of the Rio Grande to the Pacific coast and back again.

The Captain Young trail in cut diagonally down through the northwestern corner of present New Mexico. This was the home of the well-formed, light-complexioned, proudly inde-

pendent Navajos: "Lords of New Mexico," but they divided
that sovereignty with the Comanches on the east and the
Apaches on the west. As with the Apaches, in the beginning
they were not openly hostile to the *Americano*. Before their
young men had become old, Kit Carson was their conqueror.

Out of the Navajo country the expedition entered Zuñi land,
the people of which had been reputed to be white. Thus Friar
Marcos of Nizza had defined them in 1539, through having
seen, doubtless, one of their albinos. The belief in a white race
native to the interior of the Southwest persisted for many years.

In Apache land, the Arizona of the future, Captain Young
and all arrived at the head of the Rio Salado, or Salt River.
The Salt River rises near the New Mexican line, and flowing
west through central eastern Arizona empties beyond present-
day Phoenix into the Gila, of which it is the largest tributary.

So far the Ewing Young company had traveled as if in a
hurry and with direct purpose — tracing in part, perhaps, the
course of that first unit which had been turned back. It is
recorded, in evidence, that upon the sources of the Salado one
objective was achieved. Here were encountered the very
Apaches who by their attack had made themselves public
enemies. Whether or not they were the same Apaches, however, was no concern of Captain Young and his riflemen. The
issue at stake was general, not specific. Apaches had bloodied
the trap trail, and blood called for blood. That was trapper
and Indian logic, and Captain Young himself was a determined man, intolerant of denials.

The Apaches were many — covering the hills, Carson says.
This, the White Mountains region of Arizona, with fringes
bordering New Mexico, for more than a generation yet was an
Apache hive. Captain Young had concealed the major portion
of his force amid the camp baggage, and by that he lured the
rascals in. Seeing the booty of packs and mules and munitions
so feebly defended, the Indians trooped down. They were out-
matched in weapons as in guile. Just as they manœuvred, in
numbers, to overflow the camp, the rifles of the ambush opened

a cross-fire upon them. Fifteen or twenty were killed and, pursued by bullets and yells, the survivors joined the rout back into the hills. The wounded who were disabled and the dead yielded up their hair. Whether Kit Carson here took his first scalp is not stated. He had been in the country before — at the copper mines to the south.

Having exacted blood atonement and cleared the trail, the Ewing Young trappers might proceed to the main business of the trip: that of gathering beaver.

The valley of the Salt River was and is of exceeding romantic interest. Ruins of large stone towns, litters of broken pottery, *acequias* or irrigating ditches and reinforced acqueducts twenty-five-feet wide, relate of a vanished civilization. But the trail in, past Zuñi and many a natural phenomenon, and the aspects of the river itself, reduce to Indians and fur, in a narration as colorless as the *parasangas* of the *Anabasis*.

The Rio Salado, christened in 1699 by busy Father Kino, who in one of his pilgrimages surveyed it from a hill top, as formed by the Black and the White Rivers is at first a swift, cold mountain stream, deeply canyoned. Rushing down from the ranges it enters a series of richly alluvial flats and swirls on, with rapid sparkling current, finally to merge with the Gila in southwest central Arizona. Father Kino found the waters of the lower half of its course to be perceptibly brackish, owing to a bed of pure salt; and by that he named it.

Wherever it widened to wooded banks the Salado was a beaver resort. The side streams that fed it were rife with beaver. The Ewing Young company trapped down it, through a virgin territory for the trapper until, having broken free of the canyon in that western divide which looks upon the later-day Roosevelt Reservoir, and finding themselves in more open country they presently turned off, thirty miles short of the Gila, and trapped up the Rio Verde or San Francisco — a tributary coming in from the north.

"A fine, large stream," it has been said of the San Francisco: "in some cases rapid and deep, in others spreading out into wide lagoons. The ascent [was made] by gradual steppes, which, stretching into plains, abounded in timber. The river banks were covered with ruins of stone houses and regular fortification, which . . . appeared to have been the work of civilized man but which had not been occupied for centuries. They were built upon the most fertile tracts of the valley, where were signs of acequias and cultivation."[24]

But of the effect of those walls three feet thick, in places twenty feet high and pierced with small windows or loopholes, upon Kit Carson, Jim Higgins, François Turcôte and all, there is no word. We know only that the pesky Indians had bothered them almost nightly clear to the head of the San Francisco. Animals were killed and traps were stolen. Nevertheless, many beaver were taken and skinned. From the head of the river twenty-two of the men were dispatched back to Taos with the packs of pelts, there to market them and to buy more traps for another hunt. Retaining twenty-one men (among them Kit Carson) and now stocked with the traps of the Taos-bound party, Captain Young prepared for his venture onward to the genial valley of the Sacramento in California.[25]

His choice of Kit Carson as a stand-by is the first definite token of the fact that the trapper pup was making good. During the three years that Carson had been in the Southwest, his career had not indicated any conclusive rise in station. But when Captain Young divided his company he would naturally discard the inefficient and the undesirables for return to Taos under proper leadership, and would keep for the California trip mainly the most skilled and dependable employes.

If he had trapped up the course of the San Francisco, 150 miles, he was now considerably north of present Prescott. Not yet was that northern horizon, dominated by Bill Williams Mountain and the San Franciscos, plumed with the signal smoke of railway trains hurrying travelers of a new generation to the striking point for that Grand Cañon of the Colorado in the still Farther North. Nor had those other trappers, old Joe Walker and Pauline Weaver, with their discoveries roused this

fitfully treacherous Apache land to savage defense of a soil
invaded by the picks of the white treasure seekers. Mindless of
the $500,000,000 in gold, silver and copper under their feet and
eyes, to be tapped a third of a century later, and mindless of
the majestic gorge in that mysterious north beyond the barrier
Colorado Plateau (a region, reported Lieutenant Ives, from his
exploration in 1857-58, doomed by nature to be "forever un-
visited and undisturbed"), Captain Young and his twenty-one
men including Kit Carson, almost twenty, faced again to the
Far West. Roughly speaking, they were halfway from Taos to
the coast; they were cutting loose from pilot streams, and
could only guess at the qualities of the country that lay ahead.

They had been encouraged by friendly begging Indians
(possibly Walapai or Tonto Apaches) with the assurance that
over in the country toward the big water there was much fur;
for through channels of trade in shells and skins and other
commodities passed from tribe to tribe of coast, valley, desert
and mountains the news of peoples and habitats was swapped.
Likely enough, these Indians of the Arizona interior were
merely agreeable when they praised a northern California of
which they knew only by garbled rumors. When they said that
a dry *entrada,* or first march, lay ahead they were within their
limitations, for the Apache exchanged visits with the Mohave
of the Colorado River borders, and Walapai had guided Father
Garcés through.

The Ewing Young party for California camped here near
the head of the San Francisco, or Verde, until provision for the
desert march might be made. Three days of hunting rendered
only three deer, or, by another print, three bear. The flesh of
these was jerked or dry cured in sun and air; the hides were
pouched and filled with water. Then, by saddle and foot, and
driving before them their pack animals, Ewing Young, Kit
Carson who was to be his lieutenant, Jim Higgins, big Jim
Lawrence, the three named Frenchmen and the men unnamed, filed out for the fabled Sacramento Valley in a fabled
Alta California, distant beyond a first lean stretch of 150 miles.

The route westward skirted the Colorado Plateau, which abuts — from the south — upon the Grand Cañon. It spanned a high, bright desert of rocks and gravel — a terrain sundered by canyons and deep washes, and broken by uplifts of colorful tablelands and figured rimrock, and by stark, sharply rising buttes and mountain spurs; with myriad spiny cactus and a harsh vegetation stunted by the parching winds, the long droughts and the chill nights; and with the infrequent rains and the scant snowfalls on the levels quickly evaporated.

If the Ewing Young party had left Taos in August, the season should have been late fall or early winter, for Taos lay 500 miles behind and many and many a devious mile of beaver stream had been trapped. They had been forty men cumbered with pack animals, traveling a rough country that was, moreover, an Indian country, necessitating not only detours but also a conservative pace. The canyoned main streams and their tributaries trapped were not easy of access, and the camps upon the trap lines were not matters of a night. Time had to be allowed for setting and lifting the traps, for skinning the catches and stretching and drying the pelts.

"A country never explored," Kit Carson dictates. But they were not the first through it. Before them there had been Don Juan de Oñate with thirty men in 1604, and Father Francisco Garcés, unsupported save by his faith and his native guides in 1776. Now as a new type of *conquistadores,* whose hope was not any seven cities or heathen souls, but simply fur, through four days they toiled on, pigmies in a vast waste all indifferent to them, in a country absolutely waterless and, to Carson, "burned up"; and drank only at each night's camp from a dole allotted to them out of a hide container. Then, after their rations of dried meat, they shivered in their blankets until dawn.

The mules suffered most. And it was the thirsty mules that in a staggering stampede led them at last to other water, likely a desert tank or sink-hole. Here they all rested for two days. From this camp it was another four days' dry march to the welcome waters of the Colorado and the first fresh meat — a mare heavy with foal, purchased from the Mohave Indians. They camped and restocked here in the Mohave Valley.[26]

The Ewing Young-Kit Carson desert trail of 1829, doubtless counseled by the Indians, may be accepted as having been that of Oñate and Garcés in centuries preceding, and as approximately that adopted, in a succeeding fifty years, by the Atlantic & Pacific link of the Santa Fé system eastward from Needles, and by the still later automobile highway in the section between Kingman and Ashfork. On old maps Young Spring, northeast of Truxton railway station, east of Hackberry, appears to speak of Captain Young, and tourists may weave dreams upon the legend; but Peach Springs is shortly east, and whether the famished trappers drank of living water or of stagnant seepage the records do not say.

The view northward from the highway bridge at Topock, connecting Arizona and California, gives some idea of the valley home of the Mohaves, extending as it did, from above present Mohave City to the Needles and Mohave Cañon at Topock, or about fifty miles by river. Five to fifteen miles wide this valley was, as seen by the mountain-man explorer Jedediah S. Smith in 1826. It has been praised by early travelers wearied of the crisp, falsely bedizened desert amid which it securely nestled; for

. . . to the limit of vision, the tortuous course of the river could be traced through a belt of alluvial land, varying from one or two to six or seven miles in width, and garnished with inviting meadows, with broad groves of willow and mesquite, and promising fields of grain. From either border of this glistening expanse, and contrasting with its emerald hue, rose dark gray terraces, leading, with regular steps, to the bases of lofty mountain chains, whose bold and picturesque outlines are so softened by the distance as to harmonize with the smiling scene below. A pale blue haze, singularly transparent and delicate, lends an exquisite tint both to mountain and valley.[27]

The Mohaves have been a people warlike, able to defend themselves, sturdy, independent, proud, but generally just and friendly to the whites; devoted less to the chase than to the raising of corn, squash, beans and cotton, upon their warm and fertile river bottoms, and to the tattooing of their bronze bodies. The men have been noted for their fine, tall statures; the women, for the favors that they easily granted. When aroused the warriors were fierce fighters and as merciless as other Indians.

First Americans to approach them out of the desert on the east, the Ewing Young-Kit Carson party were not the first Americans to visit them. The very first may be left to tradition; but the James Ohio Pattie trappers would profess to have passed up the Colorado, from the mouth of the Gila, something over three years before; and a little later, or in October 1826, the Jedediah Smith party, breaking a trail from the Salt Lake of Utah southwest to California, had passed down from the mouth of the Virgin in what is now southeastern Nevada. At the Needles of the lower end of the valley they crossed to the west bank by Mohave raft. The Mohaves had been friendly; but when the next year Smith repeated his trip, the same Indians, actuated by the California authorities to keep strangers out, attacked his men ferrying the river and of nineteen killed ten. Smith himself escaped, to reach the California settlements by his trail of the preceding year.

With Thomas Fitzpatrick, Smith's early associate in the mountain fur trade, Kit Carson was to enlist. But in the fall of 1831 Jedediah Smith was dead.

What Captain Ewing Young may have heard, in Taos or upon his expedition with Milton Sublette, of the Smith undertakings, is nowhere stated. What he may have learned from the Mohaves of previous visits from the *Americanos,* is nowhere stated, but it is conceivable that he himself had been in the valley before. In any event, the trail from the Colorado here to the California mountains fronting the coast interior had been demonstrated. And after a peaceful two days of trading with the Mohaves for dried corn and beans Captain Ewing Young and his men all crossed the Colorado of the West, doubtless as Jedediah Smith had first done, by reed raft (for although they were a people ranging on both shores of the river the Mohaves possessed no skin boats) and by swimming their animals.

They marched upon 200 miles of arid, rock-ridged, lava-scarred, dry-lakes plains — the San Bernardino and Mohave Deserts in present San Bernardino County, southeastern California. Kit Carson says that they set a course southwest and in three days came upon the first promise of water — the dry bed of a stream having its source (the Indians must have asserted to this) in the coast range, and flowing northeast until lost in the sands. They followed up the dry bed for two days before striking water; and then followed up the stream for four days.

This stream could have been none other than the Mohave River, which is the only flowing stream with persistent habits in this desert between the bordering western foothills and the Colorado at the ancient home of the Mohaves. The Young-Carson trail and the Jedediah Smith trail before it are the trail today of the railroad and the automobile, flagged as they are by those bottoms of living green, upon the route between El Cajon Pass out of Los Angeles and Needles of the Colorado.

The miracle of the crooked Mohave, with its life-saving desert stations, strongly appealed to the imagination of the desert wayfarer by saddle or foot.

> This is a very singular stream. It may be said to run southeastwardly about two hundred miles, and empty into the Colorado. But on all its length it does not run two miles without entirely disappearing in the sand. So that it presents to the traveler a long line of little rippling lakes, from two to two and a half feet deep, at one time sunken among hard flinty hills or piles of drifting sands, and at others gurgling through narrow vales covered with grass, and fields and forests in which live the deer, the black bear, the elk, the hare and many a singing bird.[28]

Having in nine days made that desert passage which apparently engaged Jedediah Smith for fifteen days, in four days more the Captain Young trappers, having crossed the mountain barrier by way of El Cajon Pass and descended through the western foothills into a country of wide valleys, made sanctuary at the Mission San Gabriel adjacent to El Pueblo de Los Angeles. The date may be reckoned as early in 1830.[29]

Chapter VII

American Trappers in California — 1830

So here was Captain Ewing Young, and here with him were Kit Carson and his fellows, gaunt, burned, bearded or bristly, in tattered patched buckskins, but steady-eyed, unabashed, handling easily their long rifles, and in sooth a little company compact and formidable.

The missions of California still were prosperous, although hampered by interference from the new overlord, the republic of Mexico. Materiality was succeeding spirituality, and the end was near, for secularization loomed upon the horizon and already the priesthood had divided: its power was upon the wane.

However, they yet were fat, these far-flung missions, oozing oil and wine, gathering about them those flocks and herds and lands coveted by the state which had not earned them. San Gabriel Arcángel, old (lacking but two years of being the oldest) and honorable, was mistress over 1,300 Indians, 25,700 neat cattle, 2,200 horses and mules, 14,600 sheep; its vines produced annually 200 barrels of brandy, and twice as much wine; and here were stationed a priest and fifteen Mexican soldiers as guard. The governor of Alta California, in this period 1829-1830, was Colonel José María Echeandía, "a man of scholastic bent and training and of Castilian lisp." California was jealous of trespassers, and particularly of these armed American freebooters whose designs might threaten the security of the province. When Jedediah Smith with his party from the interior appeared at the Mission San Gabriel in 1826 he was summoned to San Diego by Governor Echeandía and forthwith directed to return by the route over which he had entered — instructions which he managed to violate. The Patties, second party of American adventurers overland to the coast of the Southwest, by orders of Governor Echeandía were sent from Lower California up to San Diego and there jailed.

Captain Ewing Young did not tarry long enough at San

Gabriel for action by the governor in San Diego, 140 miles south. There was one day of rest and of trading for meat upon the basis of four butcher knives for one live beef. Then, well aware that he had no license to trap in Mexican territory, avoiding that Pueblo of Los Angeles which was almost to ruin him on his return, he hastened across the little divide of the San Rafael Hills between present Pasadena and Glendale and crowned today with picturesque estates, for the Mission San Fernando Rey de España, some thirty miles to the northwest, as the trail went.

With its 6,500 beef cattle, 550 horses and mules, 3,000 sheep, San Fernando upon its windy plain was of less opulence than San Gabriel. Captain Young tarried but briefly at the vineyards which were San Fernando's pride. He struck for the beaver north.

Of the winter snows upon the crests of the San Bernardino range along whose flank he had descended for San Gabriel, of the snow upon that El Cajon Pass itself, of the snows, ever increasing, upon the Sierra to his right and of the rains in the lower country, as he pressed forward up California's great central valley, there is no comment in the scanty records of the march. By automobile highway through this interior of the state it is 450 miles from Los Angeles to the latitude of San Francisco; it may well have been 300 miles, by trail picked out, day to day, from San Gabriel to the San Joaquin short of San Francisco. But, "we then took a northwest course and passed the mountains to the valley of the Sacramento," Kit Carson narrates, and accomplishes that vague distance in a breath. They had sixty miles of climbing among the ridges north from San Fernando before they made exit into the eastern slopes of the coast range and the lower end of the central valley.

Upon the way north to the San Joaquin, few civilized beings could have been met. The twenty-one missions; the four presidios, San Diego, Santa Barbara, Monterey, and San Francisco; the pueblos, de Los Angeles, Monterey, San José de Guadalupe, all were along the seaboard. Residence by Anglo-

Saxons also was entirely between the mountains and the sea, for aside from the few aliens filtering through with the Smith, Pattie and undeterminate like parties or up from Mexico, the foreign element of Alta California was composed as yet of officers, sailors and supercargoes from the American and English vessels touching at the ports north and south.

Interior California between the ocean-fronting and the desert-fronting divides was a country assigned to the deer, the elk, the antelope, the bear, the wild horse and the wild Indian. And up through this free domain, now green and well-watered with the winter rains, Captain Young pushed at careless speed, scouting along the west foothills and finding the land very pleasant with its abundance of meat and forage. The hunters' paradise should be the trappers' paradise as soon as the prime beaver and otter range farther north were reached.

This was the San Joaquin valley. The Sacramento Valley was an indefinite promised land. At the upper San Joaquin river tributaries beyond lush Tulare Lake there were signs of beaver, but there also were signs of trappers. And presently the Americans overtook their rivals who had been gleaning the beaver pelts. The party was composed of employes of the Hudson's Bay Company of Vancouver, under command of that Peter Skene Ogden for whom Ogden, Utah, is named.

As neither outfit would let the other get ahead, the two must trap together, more or less amicably. To this arrangement the short, dark Ogden probably was nothing loth. Of ranking Canadian birth but said to be from the northern border of New York, he was a jovial and observant man, cloaking his shrewdness with a good-humored courtesy. He had had the best of a poor trapping season, and it was his business, in behalf of the Company, to see that American trespassers fared as leanly as possible in this new field.[30]

The two parties, of which Ogden's muster of sixty French Canadians with a leaven of Scotch clerks was much the larger, trapped the San Joaquin and its tributaries to its delta at Suisun Bay, which is the innermost eastern extension of the Bay of

San Francisco. They crossed to the Sacramento. The Sacramento streams had been well gleaned the previous season by another Hudson's Bay Company detachment under Alexander Mc-Leod. Peter Ogden blithely left the Americans to make the most of what was left and marched on up the Sacramento for the Pit River country and the Vancouver headquarters in the north. Captain Young fell back to the reedy marshes of the Tulares in the south; with the lessening waters and the heat of the summer dry period he advanced to the San Joaquin. Here Kit Carson and all loafed and hunted and repaired equipment, against the time when beaver fur should again be ripe for the traps.

Reports of these camps of armed rough-and-ready strangers had been borne to the Mission San José located some twenty or thirty miles to westward. San José was rich and powerful, possessing 1,800 resident Indians, 13,000 beef cattle, 1,300 horses, 13,000 sheep, and wide lands yielding many fold from the sowings of wheat, barley and corn. Water had been piped from the reservoir to the buildings, gardens and a fountain; and a bell to weigh 1,000 pounds had been ordered for the service of the Faith. But San José was reputed to be a harsh task-master over its flock.

Early in this July there appeared at the trappers' camp the Indian *alcalde,* or overseer, of the mission and company of Joseños or mission Indians out to take a band of runaways who had found refuge in a village of gentiles or unchristianized Indians. The alcalde and company had already summoned the village to surrender the runaways and had been driven off.

By decree of 1826 the Republic of Mexico had freed the California Indians from the obligations imposed upon them as wards of the mission authorities. But spiritual power was slow to yield to temporal power, and the missions clung to their home-rule policy. The padre of San José was determined to capture and punish the mission rebels, who were setting an example all too popular.

Captain Ewing Young willingly engaged to help. Kit Carson and eleven others were detailed to join the posse. The mission force, now brave with these barbarous fighting men and their long rifles, returned to the attack. The *rancheria* put up a good resistance. Only after a day of fighting was the place seized, and burned while from the outskirts the surviving enemy howled their wrath. Threatened, on the morrow, with death for every one of them, the terrified villagers surrendered up their guests.

Captain Don Joaquin might feel secure. He had rendered service. Therefore, taking Carson and three others, on July 11th he boldly presented himself at the mission, showed his passports as token of good faith, announced that he had twenty-two men — one of whom had joined him from the Ogden company — and sought a market for his furs in order to recruit his horse stock. Fortune sided with him. The mission officials were well inclined toward him. Furthermore, at the presidio and port of Monterey, seventy miles southward, there lived the American Don Juan Bautista Cooper, a Mexican citizen of much influence.

Captain John Roger Cooper, who had come from Boston to California in 1823 upon a trading voyage and after settling there had continued in the China trade, was a resident of Monterey and married to Señora Encarnacion Vallejo. He had been re-baptised John the Baptist, and was popularly known throughout California as Don Juan el Manco — John the Cripple — by reason of a deformed hand. Don Juan, a small man, with sandy hair and blue eyes, was a friend at court to Americans in the country.

Don Juan apparently came up to San José. Captain Young may have gone down to Monterey. Through the offices of Don Juan or the mission the furs were disposed of to Don José Asero, captain of a trading vessel in port at Monterey. With the proceeds Captain Young bought horses at the mission.

These naked California Indians had not been so thoroughly terrified, after all. They were thievish rascals. Scarcely had the recruited *manada* been turned out to graze when sixty of the half-broken animals were cleverly stampeded by a night alarm. Fourteen were recovered in the morning — a stroke of fortune again, for the camp had been left almost afoot. The trail of the main herd was plain. Carson and eleven others were ordered to saddle up and bring back those horses. The trail led for a hundred miles, into the Sierra Nevada wilds at the eastern side of the valley. There a halt had been made, for a feast of horse flesh. Men, women and children had gathered at the carnival. The trappers charged the unsuspecting bevy, with their first rifle fire killed eight of the revelers, drove the rest into the brush, and with the beasts, less five or six that had been butchered, and with three captured children, rode back in triumph to Captain Young. The children were turned over to the mission.

The horse-eating California Indians were a race of small resistance power, and subject to many evils. The taste was a mark of indolence and degeneracy. Carson says:

When I first went over into California in 1829, the valleys were full of Indian tribes. Indians were thick everywhere, and I saw a great deal of some large and flourishing tribes. When I went there again in 1853, they had all disappeared, and when I inquired about certain tribes I had seen on the very spot where I then stood, was told by people living there that they had never heard of them.[31]

Captain Young's men were growing restive. This easy California had its appeal. François Turcôte, Jean Valliant and Anastase Curier set out for Monterey, where they announced that they were done with their trapping contract and should go where they pleased — but applied, however, on July 31, for passports back to New Mexico. With this act they wrote their names in history. By order of Captain Young they were returned to the camp, there to be placed under guard. As he states in a farewell letter, October, to his friend Captain Cooper, the Frenchmen in his party had been drawing on account and were bent upon dodging their debts. Moreover, the captain was a man who carried a high head.

Camp in the valley of central California was raised in September. The back trail was taken to San Fernando, for Don Joaquin Jóven was going out. He had planned a venture in mules, but he flaunted Fortune by committing the error of a side trip to Los Angeles. His men likely required this, as a break in training on the eve of another long desert march.

El Pueblo de Nuestra Señora la Reina de los Angeles — the Town of Our Lady the Queen of the Angels — boasted not only a pretentious name but certain more material assets. The population of the pueblo and adjacent ranchos (in all about 1,000) included many representatives of the higher class — *gente de razón* — and a dozen *Anglos* foreigners, chiefly Americans, either citizens or in process of citizenship, several of them married to girls of good family. The houses, to be sure, were little more than hovels of mud, eight feet high, with roofs of reeds and asphaltum, but there was a show of gardens. And entertainment by various devices, not omitting black eyes and shapely ankles and gambling and liquor dens, bid fair to out-rival the charms of old Taos and Santa Fé.

The authorities had been warned of this Don Joaquin Jóven and his trappers from New Mexico. Orders had been issued to Sergeant José Antonio Pico of the military at the presidio San Diego to arrest and hold the interlopers, when found. The alcalde of Los Angeles demanded the captain's trapping license, which was not forthcoming; but to seize these two score barbarians and their bearded leader was more than the alcalde could manage by sheer force.

As to Captain Young, he discovered that his men were getting out of hand. Under the encouragement of compatriots whom they met (there were several of the Pattie trappers resident now in Los Angeles) and of the natives who, encouraged thereto by the alcalde, plied them with liquor, the majority of his men were courting the *calabozo*. Meantime, heaven knew what damage they would commit. And when reinforcements for the alcalde arrived from San Gabriel and from San Diego the captain and his party, drunk or sober, would be in serious plight.

The steady Carson was directed to take three fit men, the
loose horses and the baggage, and go on. The captain would
follow as soon as he could collect the other men. If he did not
appear at the next camp, Carson was to continue to New Mexico and there report that the remainder of the party had been
killed by the Mexicans in California.

Carson started upon the road to San Gabriel. Captain Young
succeeded in making his gather, and followed after. He could
not shake off the enemy. The liquor vendors kept pace and his
staggering, whooping cavalcade defied his orders. Providen-
tially, trapper James Higgins shot "Big Jim" Lawrence from
the saddle and the pestiferous Angelenos fled in dismay.

His [Big Jim's] body was left in the road where he fell upon receiving
the fatal shot. These two men were both Irishmen, and Big Jim was a
burly, overbearing man by nature, and when under the influence of liquor
was intolerable, and Higgins in like condition was uncontrollable. The
men were all suffering from the effects of days of debauchery, and the
major portion of them were intoxicated at the time and could not be
controlled by Young, who, fearing that still more blood might be shed,
as well as apprehensive of trouble with the authorities and people of the
country, did not stop to bury the dead, but continued his march.[32]

Indeed, the effect of the murder upon the escort from the
pueblo was most salutary. As Carson relates in his memoirs
before quoted, the Angelenos did not wait for these men who
so quickly shot one another to turn as quickly upon them.
Captain Young and party joined him before dark. The day
was of the first week in October. Having hovered at safe distance, Sergeant Pico reports the killing on October 7. His command, he states, was too small to detain the Americans.

Well away, Captain Young wrote to Captain Cooper from
his guarded camp beyond San Gabriel:

                                    October 10th 1830
DEAR SIR I received yours of the 8th and am verry sorry that I did not
see you I had like to have Lost all the french that I have with me when
I was in the settle Ment they were all owing me Large Debts and wishing
to not pay them Mutinieed they had Concluded to all remain in this
Country but the Americans were too strong for them and forced them
out much against their wills an Irish Man and an English man in the

rear had a falling out about some very frivilous thing and one shot the other dead of his horse and I could not stop to do any thing with him Left him Lying in the rode where he was kild. It was my Intention to return from Red River [the Colorado] in december and sell what Beaver I had on hand and By Mules but having this dificulty with my Men I cannot have any confidence in them If it was not for some young Americans that is Men of confidence I would not be able to get back to New Mexico therefore I must drop all Idea of the Mule speculation for this year I am going down Red River to the Mouth of the Hela and from there up the Hela to New Mexico every disapointment that A Man could Meet with I have Met with on this trip Since I saw you in St Joseph I have had my horses and Mule stole by the indians I followed them and recovered all my Caviard but five of My Best Mules they kiled to Eat we kild ten or twelve of the Indians next Summer I will return to this country for the purpose of engaging in the Mule trade I want to ascertain how Mules sell in Mexico before I Engage in the speculation I have no idea of taking Mules to the United States from here it would be attended with two Much Risk except there is a peace Made with the Comanses [Comanches] Indians.

Nothing more at present But Remain
yours Respectfully

Mr J B Cooper   E Young

N B I received Mr Hooks Letter but had no opportunity of answering him   E.Y.[33]

Captain Young proceeded to get out of the country. The back trail across the mountains and desert from Mission San Gabriel to the Colorado River again was made in nine days. The men set their traps in the vicinity of the Mohave villages. On the second day a swarm of Indians, estimated at 500 warriors, entered the camp. These might have been in part Chemehueves, who lay claim to the downriver between the Needles and the mouth of Bill Williams Fork, but only the more populous Mohaves, their neighbors on the north, could appoint such a levy of braves. Possibly the Mohaves were mindful of those previous injunctions which had animated them to attack the Jedediah Smith party.

The camp had been left to Carson and a squad while the major portion of the company ran the trap line. The visitors acted suspiciously — there were weapons concealed beneath their unnecessary garments. Promptness and boldness were demanded; Carson had both. With warning word to his camp tenders he then addressed an Indian who spoke the Spanish; ordered him to clear out with all his fellows "inside of ten minutes," for after that any one of them still in the camp would be shot. It was a large order, but the visitors considered the ready rifles, and obeyed.

Where between its lessening successions of canyons the lower Colorado spread into flats of willows and cottonwoods watered by sluggish bayous, it was a prolific beaver stream. The James Pattie party had trapped up from the Gila, four years back, with good success; and three years back (December, 1827) from forty traps set below the mouth of the Gila the Patties had taken thirty-six pelts. The Ewing Young-Kit Carson party should have found the waters and banks replenished, and long undisturbed by trap and pole.

They trapped the west side of the Colorado for the 400 miles to tide-water far below the mouth of the Gila on the east side; crossed when the water grew brackish and the beaver limits had been reached; trapped up the east side to the Gila, 150 miles, and thence up the Gila on a stretch of 300 miles to the mouth of the San Pedro.

The Gila is an ancient and constantly historic trail. The ruins of otherwise unrecorded pueblos lie thickly through its valleys, it was the highway for the padres who sought souls in the *Pimeria Alta* (upper Pima Land) of southwestern Arizona, it was the favorite goal of good Father Kino, where he "administered to the savages the wholesome truths of Christ's redemption"; the Kearny column of '46, overland to California, bore along its course the Stars and Stripes, succeeding the banner of the Cross, and there followed close the feverish emigrants making the old Yuma Trail to the Golden State which was their Cibola.

But when now the Ewing Young party trapped its waters the dusty ruins breathed no romance, the stations of the padres had long been desolate, the teachings of good Father Kino had withered before a blast of savagery, the Kearny column for which Kit Carson himself was to be the guide had not yet stirred to a trumpet call, nor had the toiling emigrant appeared above the eastern horizon. There was only beaver, and beaver was enough.

A typical stream of the desert Southwest where sands and traprock enclose fertile valleys, during the last 400 miles of its course across the state the Gila, at low water, averages 100 feet wide and two or three feet deep; flowing now between banks of green, now between bare borders gray, ruddy, or whitish yellow. Where there was freshened brushy growth, there beaver were.

At the mouth of the San Pedro, which enters from the south, above present Florence, a herd of loose horse stock were grazing. The Apache camp was discovered. The trappers charged in, the Indians fled, the trappers had the herd.

Then, in camp that night, they themselves were aroused by the trampling of hoofs — distant as yet and sounding like welling thunder. Another band of Apaches were approaching, driving before them another herd, as proceeds of a raid into Old Mexico. Lying in wait the trappers delivered a volley, routed the drovers, and on the theory that thieves have no property appropriated the stock.

This herd contained 200 or more horses. "To return the animals to their owners was an impossibility," biographer Peters naïvely chronicles. And since the Captain Young party had accumulated more animals than they could use they cut out the best, killed ten others for emergency rations, and abandoned the rest to the Apaches.

With their claim to the country once more established, they trapped on up the Gila until near its sources across the line of New Mexico of today they were opposite the Santa Rita copper mines. Here they quit the river and marched south the sixty miles to the mines, where Robert McKnight was still holding the fort.

Captain Young took no chances. The bales of pelts were

stored in the mine workings, and while his men continued on to Taos he and Kit Carson applied at Santa Fé for a license to trade with the Indians of the Gila. The bales were packed in from the Santa Rita, whereupon, at the exhibit of 2,000 pounds of beaver so miraculously produced "everyone considered we had made a fine trade in so short a period."[34]

With every man ajingle with silver and hastily primed to the guards the expedition disrupted in Taos. This was April, 1831. Right speedily old "Touse" felt the influx of sudden wealth. But when the money was gone — there was more beaver. Hooray for Californy!

A little may be said of the further adventures of Don Joaquin Jóven, Jon, Joon, John, Yon, and so on: this trader and trapper captain, Ewing Young, cabinet-maker from Knox County, Tennessee, described as a man of heroic stature, alert mind, determined disposition and restless habits. This spring or early summer of 1831 he married Señorita María Josefa Tafoya of Taos, but she did not hold him. In a few months he was off for California again — in October he headed out of Taos, with Moses Carson, Kit's elder half-brother, in his company of thirty, and trapped through to the coast by the Gila route, arriving at Los Angeles in April, 1832. Kit himself had enlisted for the northwest; he never saw the captain again.

David E. Jackson, late a partner of Jedediah Smith and William Sublette in the Rocky Mountain fur trade, but now become Captain Young's associate in the southwest field, had preceded him with letters to Captain John Cooper at Monterey and with five mule-loads of Mexican dollars for the purchase of California mules.

Ill fortune dogged Captain Young. By reason of defective traps his catch of beaver was small; and a number of the mules and horses pointed for New Mexico were drowned in the fording of the Colorado.

He finished out his trapping in California, his company broke up in Los Angeles, he was variously in San Diego, Los Angeles, Monterey. When the Boston school-teacher, Hall J.

Kelley, whose pathetic and at the same time fantastic zeal to colonize Oregon with Americans made him both famous and poor, stopped at Monterey in 1834, northward bound, the captain joined his recruits, for a venture again in horses and mules.

Forewarned by Governor Figueroa of California that Messrs. Young and Kelley were leading a band of horse thieves, Fort Vancouver closed its gates against them. The venture was a loss. On the Willamette the vigorous captain fumed and stormed, farmed and traded; threatened the peace of the Hudson's Bay Company with an improvised whisky still, but yielded to the protests of the missionaries; organized the "Wallamet Cattle Company," in order that the settlers might obtain beef and dairy animals without the restrictions of the Hudson's Bay Company; conducted the appallingly difficult drive of the wild herd from central California over the mountains to Oregon, in the summer and fall of 1837; prospered, shortly, in means and public estimation; built a sawmill — the floods of the winter 1840-1841 carried it away, and on February 15, 1841, he died on his farm near the Willamette. Some say that he died broken in mind and body by his fights with man and nature.

As he died apparently without heirs, his estate, defaulting, "gave the provisional government [1841] of Oregon its first, and, for some time, its only funds." Then, remarkable to relate, in 1854 a stripling, his namesake Joaquin John, just turned twenty-one, appeared with claim to the estate; won, but sold his rights; payment was estopped, and in the final settlement, in 1862, the amount of judgment was slightly over $5,000.

The judgment stood, but there was other judgment subject to question. Young Joaquin had produced, as evidence, an affidavit of identity signed at Taos by Charles Beaubien, C. Carson, Manuel Lefebre — all men of worth; and a copy of his baptismal certificate, by which he had been christened José Joaquin on April 2, 1833, four days after his birth to Señora María Josefa Tafoya — an event that had occurred seventeen months after his father had left his mother and taken off for California, thereabouts to stay. A miracle had happened, seemingly beyond the comprehension of Charles Beaubien, C. Carson, Manuel Lefebre, and the Oregon courts.[35]

The captain had not been on hand to explain. He had been dead, except in memory, for a dozen years; rated as one of the three powers in the Oregon country, "the first being the Hudson's Bay Company, the second, the Methodist Mission"; a man of energy and enterprise, a natural leader, a zealous American, fearless, vindictively courageous, outspoken, of business integrity as he saw it, and of morals adapted to his own interests.

He was the man who, in 1829 opening a trail of his own across the desert to California, set young Carson an example in the mastery of men and circumstances. Carson should have learned much from him; could have had proper pride in having been of that free-foot company which in Taos and Santa Fé spread the word of a new trading world beyond the Colorado.

Chapter VIII

To the Beaver Northwest — 1831

FROM Taos (where, by tradition, he had been popularly called "bub") Carson had gone out with Ewing Young upon the trapper's trail as a promising lad who had yet to learn the tricks of the trade. He had demonstrated that he was a hard worker, but his qualities in a lawless mixed company of freebooters subjected to discipline were yet to be proved. He had come back not only as one of those "young Americans that is men of confidence," who had saved the day for the captain, but (according to his own statements) as Captain Young's lieutenant, upon whose coolheadedness and decision the captain had relied.

The youngest of the Carsons to take to the adventure trail, he had gone the farthest into the west. At twenty-one he had made good, and had his stories to tell. Therefore as man to man he might now meet, in Taos or Santa Fé, his strapping half-brother, veteran Mose, and swap news with him. Might get news of home from his elder brother Andrew, if Andrew were returned from his commission of last year, to St. Louis, for Ceran St. Vrain.

The summer of 1831 would be spent by the majority of the Young trappers in Taos and Santa Fé, for they had plenty of funds or credit and the trapping season was closed. Then, by fall, the money was long scattered, the delights of settlement fracas and fandango had palled, there remained only credit for a new outfit. The beaver trail summoned to the fall hunt.

Carson may have tapered off his celebrations by putting in some time at Bent's Fort trading post, then nearing completion, over on the Arkansas. Adventure tales assign him to the post during its building operations. But: "In the fall of 1830 [1831] I joined the party under Fitzpatrick for the Rocky Mountains on a trapping expedition."[36]

It was to be new country — a much talked of country where white men, Americans, could trap without Mexican interfer-

ence. The pelts there were prime pelts, game was fat for the
pot. But the reasons why Carson did not enlist again with Captain Young are not stated. Service with Thomas Fitzpatrick of
the Rocky Mountain Fur Company may have had greater
appeal. Captain Young, however, already was facing fresh
ventures. The next month, October, he left for California
again, with big Mose in his command. Kit never again saw
him. The two brothers next met fifteen years later, and that
was not in Taos nor the mountains but in California.[37]

Before Kit Carson had fled the saddler's bench in old Franklin for the back of a mule on the Santa Fé Trail, the Northwest
had been well traversed. The impetus given by Lewis and
Clark had gained in momentum; and while the steady exodus
into New Mexico was mainly along beaten lines staked out by
a suspicious Latin government, that to the northwestward was
without law and without restriction, diverging, as it traveled,
where it pleased, free to seek out whatever spots were to its
profit. The trader established his fort, the trapper on his pony
ranged through hill and plain. This was their country: essentially by right of exploration the mountain-man's country; the
commonwealth of him who had succeeded to the *voyageur* and
the *coureur des bois* of the Eastern rivers and lakes.

In the six years (1825-1831) which Kit Carson had spent as
saddler, wrangler, cook, teamster and finally trapper, the
Northwest had advanced rapidly, but its affairs were little
changed on the surface. The Missouri Fur Company in which
Moses Carson had served was defunct; while the great General
Ashley, after having achieved a fortune by those splendid expeditions which he had sent out, and having retired from the
mountains, was about to enter Congress, there to be stout
exponent of the interests of the Far West.

Three of that really brilliant company which enlisted under
him — Jedediah S. Smith, David E. Jackson and William L.
Sublette — bought his fur business from him. Smith has been
noted as the first American by land into California. The name
of Jackson comes down in the famous game resort, Jackson

Hole of northwestern Wyoming. Of William Sublette much might be said: a foremost partisan or captain of trappers, he, the best known among five brothers; a fighter and a trader, and one of the few recorded, besides Ashley, who "amassed a handsome fortune."

The transfer had been made in July, 1826. To the partnership, Smith, Jackson & Sublette, there had succeeded in August, 1830, the Rocky Mountain Fur Company, formed by five other thorough mountain-men, of whom two, at least, Thomas Fitzpatrick and James Bridger, were graduates of the Ashley school. The three others were Milton G. Sublette, brother of William; Jean Baptiste Gervais, unknown to fame because he has lacked a chronicler; and Henry Fraeb (commonly styled "Frapp"), destined to be slain by the Sioux and Cheyennes on Battle Creek near the Little Snake of the southern Wyoming and northern Colorado line.

Thus the Rocky Mountain Fur Company had come into existence, to continue business in the main Rocky Mountains, with the Continental Divide its especial field. Across in the Northwest reigned the Hudson's Bay Company of Great Britain; old, powerful, autocratic, its feet upon the ruins of Astoria. But another fur company was already aiming to wrest from Fitzpatrick, Bridger and partners their legacy. This was the American Fur Company, child of John Jacob Astor of New York whose Astoria had so failed. With a western branch established in St. Louis, during Kit Carson's novitiate of five years in the Southwest, it had waxed stronger, and was now taking decisive steps for advancing from the Missouri River fur trade to the mountain fur trade.

And the fur business was booming. Ashley had given it impetus, Kit Carson entered it in its heyday. Not yet had that Western soil been turned by the plough of a settler; the ground of plain and of valley was suffered to lie despised, while north of the Arkansas and west of Missouri the only incentive for the white man was trade and fur. By keelboat and by caravan the bales from post and rendezvous came pouring into St. Louis;

by keelboat and by caravan went forth the supplies to rendezvous and to post. Not, as in the North before the West was discovered was traffic by water alone; but at the opening of this decade of American supremacy in the trans-Mississippi country the pack train threading lone plain and wooded pass, bearing its cargo, was a recognized institution.

The trading posts were the fur country's principal protection. They were little forts, established in the Indian precincts, and semi-military. They already extended along the Missouri to its headwaters, and well up along the Platte. Beyond the Rockies were the posts of the Hudson's Bay Company, encouraging a flow of furs westward, not eastward. The most aggressive military occupation of the country had been an expedition (boat and horse) up the Missouri to the mouth of the Yellowstone in Montana, by General Atkinson, in 1825, and in 1827 the permanent establishment of Fort Leavenworth, on the Missouri in northeastern Kansas.

The Missouri frontier had advanced 150 miles, from old Franklin to Independence toward the mouth of the Kaw or Kansas River where Kansas City now stands. At Independence landing the goods for the Santa Fé trade were unloaded, and from Independence the long caravans went trailing out into the dusty Southwest as of yore, save that oxen were supplanting mules for teams. Franklin, once "a center of wealth and fashion," gnawed by the river was soon to be abandoned — its graveyard alone remaining as token of the days that were.

The Northwest was still forging ahead of the Southwest, despite the constantly increasing Santa Fé business. To be sure, east of the mountains south of the Platte, in United States territory, during Kit Carson's novitiate Bent's Fort had been founded (1829), about 150 miles north of Taos, upon the "mountain" Santa Fé Trail up the Arkansas. But although from Bent's Fort northward through Colorado to Wyoming there was not a white man's habitation, other than the rude trapper's lodge as movable as the tepee of the Indian, the Salt Lake, the Green River, the Henry Fork of the Snake and the

Snake itself in Idaho, were becoming to St. Louis, base of supplies, as household words. The Rockies were indeed better known to the East than were the Plains.

Two other events of direct bearing upon the trapper and trader West as Carson saw it should be noted. The keel of the steamboat *Yellowstone* had been laid, at Louisville, Kentucky, on commission from the American Fur Company; and this spring, 1831, as the first steamboat to ascend the upper Missouri it had entered the fur trade — thus greatly facilitating the operations of the company which was to crush and swallow the Rocky Mountain Company. For the Southwest, William Wolfskill, with a party of trappers, had broken a new trail from New Mexico to California. It revived, in part, the old Trail of the Padre and won favor as the Old Spanish Trail.

Pointing into the northwest from Santa Fé and Abiquiu of New Mexico, the Old Spanish Trail cut through southwestern Colorado and by a northerly curve crossing central Utah bent for the south, short of the Salt Lake, to follow down the Virgin River, southwestern Nevada, to the Colorado. Thence it swerved off, by way of present Las Vegas, Nevada, to join the desert trail from the Colorado to Cajon Pass of the California Sierra Madre.

The trail through southwestern present Colorado had been pioneered by the Spanish explorer Juan María Rivera, from Santa Fé in 1761; and had been extended into Utah by the padre Francisco Silvestre Velez Escalante, in 1776. The spirit of Father Escalante hovered over it, and names that he dropped — Dolores, Piedra, Las Animas, Ancapagari (Uncompahgre) — endure yet.

William Wolfskill, Kentuckian, Missourian of Boone's Lick in the Carson district, trapper and trader associate of Ewing Young in the Southwest, enthused by news brought to Taos by the returned members of the Young-Carson company and possibly by a letter from the captain himself, California bound — William Wolfscale, known as Wolfskill, backed now by that Henry Hook, Santa Fé trader, whom Captain Young mentions

in his letter to John Cooper, set out from Taos in the fall of
1830 and pushed the Trail of the Padre through to settled California. His route, however, was devious and hard beset, and he
arrived in Los Angeles not until February, 1831.

The trail as finally adopted was a longer, more circuitous
route than the southern routes, but it afforded, through the first
half, stations of grass and water, and throughout it was an
improvement upon Captain Young's trail across the hostile,
barren, arid steppes south of the Colorado. The desert Indians
along it were at first less venomous than the Apaches. As finally
adopted, this Old Spanish Trail, the inception of which proclaimed the glory of God and the Catholic Faith, from a saddle
and pack trail became highway for horse trader and horse
thief. As between the Utah desert country and New Mexico it
was known, later, as the "Durango Trail" for cattle drives and
bandit flights; the Mormons connected with it by a wagon
road from the Salt Lake, and thereafter the western half was
known as the Mormon Wagon Road, and the Mormon Trail
to the Salt Lake. The Mormon settlers for San Bernardino,
California, in the early Fifties, arrived over it, of a time when
the whole trail was marked on the maps "Los Angeles-Santa
Fé Trail." Frémont and Kit Carson, on their marches eastward
across the Mohave Desert in 1844, entered Nevada and Utah
beyond by the Old Spanish Trail, and the San Pedro, Los
Angeles & Salt Lake road approximates the western half of
the trail.

So that today, while travelers by Santa Fé and automobile
between Barstow, east of Cajon Pass, and Needles, view the
aspects of the country seen by Captain Young and Kit Carson,
travelers by the Salt Lake Road and tourists speeding to and
from the Las Vegas gateway to Boulder Dam of the Colorado
may visualize the Mormon Wagon Road and the adventures of
Captain Frémont and Kit Carson upon the earlier trace of New
Mexican traders.

When in September, 1831, Kit Carson, a seasoned hand,
"joined," as he says, the Thomas Fitzpatrick party of trappers

for the northwest Rockies, he allied himself with the most skilled frontiersmen — hunters, trappers, fighters and scouts in one — that the West has produced. The rank and file with whom he trapped into California and back must have numbered men of parts, rovers of mountain experience; but when he engaged with the Rocky Mountain Fur Company he bid for a more inspiring field and atmosphere, where the gay, active *homme du nord — coureur* or *voyageur* — transplanted from Mackinaw, vied with the Illinoisan and the Kentuckian; where the majestic succession of snow-capped mountains invited to manly endeavor; where the air was full of energy, and where the Indian was of type superior to the naked desert Apache and the lethargic, squash-raising Mohave.

Although Carson served only intermittently with the Rocky Mountain Fur Company, and although it existed, under its title, only four years, yet by its stirring history and by the men connected with it early and late it was remarkable. It had rivals, better known; the American Fur Company, whose boast was to be designated simply as "The Company," and the Hudson's Bay Company; but in its search for fur it opened up that bountiful territory now comprising Colorado, Wyoming, Montana, Idaho and Utah; and mustered the majority of the scouts and guides who in after day piloted army detachment and colonist column across plains and passes.

Thomas Fitzpatrick commanded thirty men out of Taos for the north. He had been due with supplies at last summer's rendezvous, he was far behind his schedule, his partners and their camps west of the mountains were still waiting for him. When by marches at speed from the Arkansas up along the foothills he struck the North Platte east of the mountains, fall with its yellowed aspens and first snows in the heights country was well established, the summer and its rendezvous were definitely of the past. In the vicinity of the mouth of the Laramie River in southwestern present Wyoming he was met by his partner Fraeb in search of him.

Rendezvous for the delivery of the supplies and discussion

of business was appointed for the valley of the Powder River, a stretch or two to the north. Word of the reunion place and prospective winter camp was sent over into the west, for the outlying parties there.

Carson says, in his dictated *Story:* "We trapped to the head of the Sweet Water and then on to Green River, and then on to Jackson's Hole . . . and from there on to the head of Salmon River." In what capacity he had "joined" the Fitzpatrick command, whether or not as an independent under agreement to dispose of his furs to the Rocky Mountain Company, is anybody's guess. There is only his word for it that he went into winter camp in the Salmon River country and not in the Valley of the Powder. He left Thomas Fitzpatrick (who with the main party followed, by forced marches, in the early spring) and trapped over to the western slope.

Trapper captain John Gantt and company enter at this stage. Captain Gantt and his partner, Blackwell, had brought a company of seventy men out from St. Louis. In his published *Narrative* of the venture one Zenas Leonard speaks of an encounter by the company this fall, here at the mouth of the Laramie, with Thomas Fitzpatrick. And away over yonder in the Salmon River country of present Idaho, one Warren Angus Ferris, clerk with the American Fur Company, entered in his journal, for the close of October, the news that Fraeb, in search of Fitzpatrick along the Platte, had there met one Captain Ghant [Gantt] leading fifty men for the mountains.

The Gantt and Blackwell company divided into three parties at the mouth of the Laramie; the Gantt command set out to trap up the Sweetwater. Next spring Kit Carson, out of winter camp, looks for and finds this same Gantt, to whom he refers as by previous knowledge.

The Sweetwater link in the early Overland Trail by the South Pass route was already historic. In the spring of 1824 an Ashley party had adopted the route, and the next summer the doughty general himself, surveying it, deemed it practicable for wheels. In 1827 he sent forward over it to the rendezvous at the Salt Lake, a four-pounder cannon drawn by mules.

In 1827 Joshua Pilcher, of the declining Missouri Fur Company, had marched up the Platte and Sweetwater trail, from the Council Bluffs for the Salt Lake Valley, with forty-five men and more than 100 horses, to emulate the celebrated Ashley's successes. And in the spring of 1830 William Sublette, of Smith, Jackson & Sublette, had traveled the route with eighty-one men upon mules, ten wagons of supplies for rendezvous, two Dearborn carriages, some cattle and a milch cow.

Companies and parties recorded and unrecorded had been coming and going, through the half-dozen years, so that the Sweetwater trail was well defined.

"L' Eau Sucrée" the stream is called, in annals dating from the French *engagés* who formed the bulk of the earliest fur-hunt parties — "L' Eau Sucrée," or Sweet Water; a pack-mule laden with sugar having, one time, been capsized in the current. Or, according to Missionary Elijah White, "a company were once passing the stream, and during a drunken carousal, emptied into it a large bag of sugar, thereby, as they said, christening it, and declaring that it should hereafter be called Sweetwater Valley, as long as water ran."[38]

Carson was making his first trip through a region of which he must have heard many trapper yarns. Above the mouth of the Sweetwater, Independence Rock was skirted — an isolated, sudden outcrop into the sagey, desolate plain. Like to Pawnee Rock of the Santa Fé Trail, and to El Moro or Inscription Rock of the Conquistador's trail through Zuñi of Arizona, it served as a bulletin board for all who passed. The names scratched and painted upon it, however, were as yet comparatively few.

It is the first appearance of a strange ridge of granite masses, near a hundred miles long, which stand in the midst of a great plain, in a direction perpendicular to that of the Rocky Mountains. The Sweet Water for nearly half its course, from the South Pass to the Platte, runs near its southern base. Some of the dome-like elevations are about 1500 feet high; apparently no tree or shrub — no beast or bird relieves its stern and lifeless gray; its monumental solemnity. For how many ages, since its upheaval by the primitive fires, has it stood — changeless in summer heats and wintry storms — in untrodden solitude; in awful silence.[39]

The continuous ridge actually commenced about five miles up stream from Independence Rock. The Sweetwater, boiling out from the hill country, issued into the plains through the fissure of Devil's Gate in the lower extremity of the ridge. The trail led around the gorge of Devil's Gate and over the ridge; but by custom wayfarers rode aside, to the brink of the gorge, and looked in. The depth of 400 feet, the bottom width of 400 feet, the length of 1,000 feet, the "deep-toned roar," the "dizzy awe of the downward view," the walls "frowning above the abyss which had sundered them forever," were supposed to impress all beholders.

The Valley of the Sweetwater extended westward for eighty miles above Devil's Gate, with barren slopes and potash flats on either hand, and with the "merry little river" frequently interrupted, in its sparkling course, by cross ledges of granite. The result was a succession of verdant pockets, where were to be found beaver, buffalo, mountain sheep, antelope, deer, grizzly bear and sage chickens. There were short defiles — miniature Devil's Gates; one gained the name Hell Gate, "so called [according to Doctor White] for being the place where eleven whites were once cut off by the Indians."[40]

Twenty-five miles above Devil's Gate the hoary, wild Wind River range far in the northwest was, as the rule, first disclosed, distantly overlooking the trappers' favorite playgrounds of the Valley of the Green. The trail did not follow up the Sweetwater to its sources, but, where the river course turned into the north, it left the stream and proceeded on into the west for the famed Southern Pass — the South Pass, as commonly known, re-discovered and first exploited by Thomas Fitzpatrick himself, in company with Jedediah Smith his captain, in the spring of 1824.

Bleak, wide and open, the Pass, for long a heritage of the Indians, was obscured by reason of a rise so gradual

that but for our geographical knowledge, and the imposing landmarks on our right (the snow-capped peaks of the Wind River Mountains raising their cold, spiral, and barren summits to a great elevation), we should not

Devil's Gate of the Sweetwater Trail

have been conscious that we had ascended to, and were standing upon the summit of the Rocky Mountains — the *backbone,* to use a forceful figure, of the North American Continent.[41]

That the South Pass surmounted the Continental Divide was a fact which did not need to be posted. The Sweetwater had been hastening eastward, for the Platte, the Missouri, and the Gulf of Mexico; from its springs source in the Pass, Pacific Creek went trickling westward, for the Green, the Colorado, and the Gulf of California. Furthermore, every trapper knew that when speckled trout were found in the streams, then the Pacific side of the continent had been reached.

So to trapper, trader and emigrant this down-flowing slope of the smooth swell was Oregon. Having descended to the sandy plain the Kit Carson party struck the headwaters of the Green River, trapped up these to their beginnings, crossed westward into David E. Jackson's covert, Jackson Hole, filed on out through the Tetons and into the Columbia River country and still on northwest to the upper Salmon in northern present Idaho. "Then we came [Carson says] to the camp of a part of our band that we had been hunting, then we went into winter quarters on the head of the Salmon River." Camp was pitched among the friendly Nez Percé Indians.

Carson, aged twenty-two, had now seen the nature of this glorified beaver country of the Northwest; snow-crowned ranges, rushing cold streams, immensely lying valleys flanked by a climbing host of dark pines and firs and spruces, tremendous canyons of red rock and gray rock, chasms and crests alike deemed impassable, patches of bad-lands — in all a wilderness of park and peak, harboring game, the Indian and the pelt hunter.

Chapter IX

The Mountain-Man — His Guise and His Garb

By adopting the profession of trapper Kit Carson entered into one of the two businesses, trapping and trading, a twain closely connected, for which those thousand and more miles of plains and mountain West seemed created. Aside from farming in the state of Missouri, mercantile and trades pursuits in St. Louis and few outlying hamlets like old Franklin, there was naught else west of the Mississippi for an American in his own territory. The deserts and crests and valleys of that vast Indian country, from Missouri to the Stony Mountains, and over and on, represented only fur, fur, fur. This the trapper with his traps, the trader with his trinkets, industriously gleaned for a quarter of a century; after them came the colonist with his ox, the miner with his pick, the husbandman with his plough, the stockman with his alien herds, to reap another and more lasting harvest.

The career of the trapper is romantic, but his record is a very practical one. His service did not end with the beaver; it ended only with the cessation of the Indian wars. The Western trapper was also the Western scout; and Carson, Bridger, Fitzpatrick, Walker, guided into the Western wilds the armies of occupation. Ere the missionaries, a Frémont, the Mormons and the Fortyniners, they were, and their kind. Independent of compass and companionship, they boldly plunged into the broad unknown, there to dwell and to wander month after month. They ante-dated Lewis and Clark, they ante-dated Pike. When the United States acquired Louisiana, the fur hunter with American blood in his veins was within those borders, awaiting the Stars and Stripes.[42]

So swiftly did the trapping business grow after the Ashley successes, that when in 1829 Kit Carson joined the ranks some 600 men were already at work in the mountain regions, for the American market. In the Pacific territory were the Hudson's Bay Company employes, also, of number fully as large.[43]

The American continent was made up of many nationalities; but these men were principally Americans from Missouri, Kentucky and other Southern States, and Frenchmen of Missouri and Canada. These French were good workers and daring adventurers, penetrating far, taking long chances, adapting themselves easily to life among the Indians. They were, indeed, the first trappers and fur-traders; being natural boatmen, they were early dispatched as *voyageurs* and *coureurs des bois* up the Missouri, to explore it and its tributaries. But deft and daring though they were, it was a saying in the mountains that one American was worth, for general service, three Frenchmen. For when the Missourians, including the cool, dead-shot Kentuckians, born woodsmen all, came upon the scene, they and their fellow-countrymen speedily took first rank. The woodsman rather than the boatman was needed upon the plains and in the mountains.

After the Americans and the French there were ranked the Scotch and Irish, Germans, Mexican-Spanish, Portuguese, a very few negroes, and a multitude of "breeds" — mixtures in various degrees of the French and the Indian, French and Mexican, American and Mexican, American and Indian, white and black, what-not; with the darker of two strains demonstrating when the blood was roused.

As upon the frontier, so it was in the wilds beyond, where men of culture were little removed, in manners or speech, from the rude and the ignorant. Some of these men were but visitors. One was Lieutenant George Frederick Ruxton, the young English army officer, to whose veracious chronicles contemporary with old mountain trapper days the files of Western literature are deeply indebted. His last letter to his publisher in 1848, shows how the long trail of the Far West appealed to such spirits:

As you say, human nature can't go on feeding on civilized fixings in this "big village"; and this child has felt like going West for many a month, being half froze for buffler meat and mountain doin's. My route takes me via New York, the Lakes, and St. Louis, to Fort Leavenworth, or Independence on the Indian frontier. Thence packing my "possibles" on a

mule, and mounting a buffalo horse (Panchito, if he is alive), I strike the
Santa Fé trail to the Arkansas, away up that river to the mountains, win-
ter in the Bayou Salade, cross the mountains next spring to Great Salt
Lake and that's far enough to look forward to — always supposing my
hair is not lifted by Comanche or Pawnee on the scalping route of the
Coon Creeks and Pawnee Fork.[44]

Go he did, soon to die by injuries from a fall upon the sharp
picket-pin of an Indian lodge.

Another visitor with keen relish for this mountain life was
Captain Sir William Drummond Stewart — one of those wandering British big game hunters whose double-barreled rifles
have broken the wilderness silence the world over. The American mountain West knew him well; the mountain-man liked
him.

Another was the artist, J. M. Stanley. He was present at
camp-fire and rendezvous in the early Thirties, and his pictures survive to this day. His field was also that of the German
artist Miller (Müller), who accompanied Captain Stewart
from Fort Vancouver.

Aside from these supernumeraries there were the proverbial
black sheep and the "younger son," the ne'er-do-well and the
hater of conventionalities, living the life forced or chosen. Of
such was one Captain Welles, British officer and gentleman,
who had fought at Waterloo and at New Orleans, and now,
when (1846) encountered by Edwin Bryant at old Fort Laramie, sixty years of age, "vigorous and athletic," and "clothed
in the rude buckskin costume of the wilderness." And of such
was William P. Thompson, "a Kentucky hunter in the employ
of a fur company," met, 1845, on the South Platte by Dr. Elijah
White.

He was stopping here by order, to guard goods, and was soon to leave
for Laramy, where he hunted in the savage wilds for the sum of two
hundred and fifty dollars per annum, although an educated, high-minded
young man, of honorable and wealthy parentage.

And of such — the offshoots from a far life — was that
"young Swiss trapper, eight years in the mountains," discov-

ered, 1839, by Thomas Farnham, the traveler, on the "burnt plains of Snake River," west of old Fort Hall.

He learned the silversmith business when in youth; afterward entered a monastery and studied Latin, etc., for the order of Priests; ran away from the monastery, entered the French army, deserted, came to America. Instead of saying his prayers and counting the beads of his rosary, he talked of the stirring scenes of a trapper's life, and recounted the wild adventures of the mountains. Instead of the sublime Te Deum, he sang the martial airs of his native land. Instead of the crosier, he bore the faithful rifle. Instead of the robes of sacred office, he wore the fringed deer skin frock of the children of the wilderness. He was a trapper — a merry mountain trapper.[45]

And akin to such were Lucien Fontenelle, the swart partisan, of blood noble; old Bill Williams, the lone trapper, reputed ex-Methodist circuit-rider; Jedediah Smith, of Bible and rifle; and many another.

As a result of this mingling, at gatherings of the mountain trappers were to be seen "men from almost every country, and almost of every shade of character, from dark sons of Africa to tawney Aborigines, the Creole Canadian, the once polite American, and the adventurous European"; the *engagé,* the greenhorn, the hunter, and "the hardy mountain veteran who has ranged these wilds for more than thirty years. Now as poor as at first."[46]

A curious confusion of language evolved from this confusion of tongues — as might be expected when a French-Canadian acquired at the same time English and Mexican. Lieutenant Ruxton transcribes the lamentations of his trapper friend Laforey, without coffee on the old New Mexican frontier:

Sacré enfant de Garce, voyez-vous dat I vas nevare tan pauvre as dis time; mais before I vas siempre avec plenty café, plenty sucre; mais now, God dam, I not go à Santa Fé, God dam, and mountain-men dey come aqui from autre côté, drink all my café. Sacré enfant de Garce, nevare I vas tan pauvre as dis time, God dam. I not care comer meat, ni frijole, ni corn, mais widout café I no live. I hunt may be two, three day, may be one week, mais I eat notin'; mais sin café, enfant de Garce, I no live, parceque me not sacré Espagnol, mais one Frenchman.[47]

The professed language of the American mountain-man was

equally as unintelligible to the stranger. English, Spanish, French and Indian words served their turn, with many an expression coined for trapper currency. It was a certain rugged, picturesque, straightforward speech — vastly different from the stagy diction of Cooper's Leatherstocking hunters.

"Thar's a gone beaver," shouted Louy, as he discharged his rifle, though without effect, at the diminutive animal [a squirrel], disappearing among the swaying pine branches; "it's many a time this paw's hild a forked stick, with an old nor'west fusil — one of dad's, that's 'under' — when his arm warn't no bigger 'an a beaver tail, to shoot at sich varmin as them. An' when the old shootin' iron 'ud flash in the pan, I 'ud say — Doggone the old thing; you ain't wuth a cuss (I was afraid to swear then); but then, I'ud git as chargin' fâché nor an old buffler an' out 'ud rip dam! Then this old hos 'ud feel kinder like a sick beaver in a trap, or a 'cow' with a G'lena pill in her lights — the dark warn't the place for me then, I tellee; but this coon has 'raised ha'r' so often sence, he keers nothin' now. Mind the time we 'took' Pawnee 'topknots', away to the Platte, Hatch?"

"Wagh! Ef we didn't, an' give an owgh-owgh, 'longside of thar darned screechin', I'm a niggur. This child don't let an Injun count a 'coup' on his cavyard always. They come mighty nigh 'rubbin' me 'out', t'other side of Spanish Peaks — woke up in the mornin' jist afore day, the devils yellin' like mad. I grabs my knife, 'keels' one, an' made for timber, with four of thar cussed arrows in my 'meatbag'. The 'Paches took my beaver — five pack of the prettiest in the mountains — an' two mules, but my traps was hid in the creek. Sez I, hyar's gone coon ef they keep my gun, so I follers thar trail, an' at night, crawls into camp, an' socks my big knife up to Green River, fust dig. I takes t'other Injun by the ha'r an' 'makes meat' of him too. Maybe thar warn't coups counted, an' a big dance on hand, ef I *war* alone. I got old bull-thrower, made 'medicine' over him, an' no darned niggur kin draw bead with him sence."[48]

The Rocky Mountain trappers were of three classes or divisions. The hired trapper was paid yearly wages by the company, was furnished with his outfit, supplies and all, and was under company control absolutely.

The "skin" trapper received no wages, but he was furnished an outfit by a company, and was charged up with the same upon the company books. He likewise was under contract to deliver his furs to the company only.

The free trapper ranked among trappers as the proud *homme du nord* did among the *voyageurs*. He acknowledged no commercial ties; he trapped as he pleased and where he pleased, and disposed of his pelts to whomsoever he pleased. About him, as a character in romance, was a spirit of dash and wild vanity which appeals at once to heart and eye. He loved to be called a "white Injun"; and in his extravagance, as at mountain rendezvous or in border town, no greater compliment could be paid him than to mistake him for an Indian brave.

His hair, suffered to attain to a great length, is carefully combed out, and either left to fall carelessly over his shoulders or plaited neatly and tied up in otter skins, or parti-colored ribands. A hunting-shirt of ruffled calico of bright dyes, or of ornamented leather, falls to his knees; below which, curiously fashioned leggins, ornamented with strings, fringes, and a profusion of hawks' bells, reach to a costly pair of moccasins of the finest Indian fabric, richly embroidered with beads. A blanket of scarlet, or some other bright color, hangs from his shoulders, and is girt around his waist with a red sash, in which he bestows his pistols, knife, and the stem of his Indian pipe: preparations either for peace or war. His gun is lavishly decorated with brass tacks and vermillion, and provided with a fringed cover, occasionally of buckskin, ornamented here and there with a feather.[49]

His horse likewise was adorned, saddle and bridle, "head, mane and tail," with a profusion of fantastic finery, and moreover was "bestreaked and bespotted with vermillion, or with white clay, whichever presents the most glaring contrast to his real color." While the free trapper's squaw rode as proudly, "her horse, selected for his prancing,

and her saddle and baby cradle, are still more elaborately and expensively decorated with pounds of black and white beads, haiqua shells and tin coils, elk teeth and hawk-bells, finger-rings and heavy bracelets, steel top thimbles and cut-glass beads, all glistening in the sunbeams and producing a cheery jingling, as she gallops alongside of her American "hama" (man); their babe lashed in its cradle, and swung to the forehorn of her saddle, while two white parflesh portfolios, beautifully decorated with painted figures, and heavy phylacteries, containing her root-stick, fire steel, sinews, awl, kimp, and other necessaries, are hung to the hind one.[50]

The garb of the mountain-man was eminently practical, and

was apt to be severely plain, because weather-worn. He lived off the country his habitat, and his clothing was supplied by it. Hide and fur was the material, with addition of wool when trader's stock was available. The costume of the Indian was wisely adopted, with such variation as white intelligence or taste, or enforced economies dictated. Shorn of glamor the trapper's equipment and workaday costume might be

one animal upon which is placed one or two epishemores [apishamores: hide saddle-blankets], a riding saddle and bridle, a sack containing six beaver traps, a blanket with an extra pair of moccasins, his powder horn and bullet pouch, with a belt to which is attached a butcher knife, a wooden box containing bait for beaver, a tobacco sack with a pipe and implements for making fire, with sometimes a hatchet fastened to the pommel of his saddle. His personal dress is a flannel or cotton shirt (if he is fortunate enough to obtain one, if not antelope skin answers the purpose of over and undershirt), a pair of leather breeches with blanket or smoked buffalo skin leggins, a coat made of blanket or buffalo robe, a hat or cap of wool, buffalo or otter skin, his hose are pieces of blanket wrapped around his feet, which are covered with a pair of moccasins made of dressed deer, elk or buffalo skins, with his long hair falling loosely over his shoulders, completes his uniform. He then mounts and places his rifle before him on the saddle.[51]

Moccasins, preferably of smoked buckskin, were procured from the Indians by foray or barter, or were made by the trapper himself or his handy squaw. Whereas the legs of the Ohio Valley hunters were sheathed in Indian-style leggins, open at the thigh and tight at the calf, and the same fashion prevailed among the French and the breed bravos in the Northwest, the American mountain-man by and large favored the leather pants of straight cut and easy manufacture — the seam, from thigh to ankle, fringed with thongs, scarlet flannel, or scalp trophies. The outside shirt, the loose coat or hunting shirt, was long and full, extending to the knee, folding across the front and belted at the waist. The fold was a convenient pocket for stowing away small articles. In a way this shirt imitated the *voyageur's* woolen capote or blanket-coat. It was made of smoked buckskin, or on occasion of elk-hide — which was a material inferior, being porous and liable to get soggy. The trapper's hunting shirt, like his trousers, was subject to ornamentation suggested by practice or fancy.

A suit of clothes seldom washed or turned, from the time it is first worn until laid aside. Caps and hats made of beaver and other skins, the skins of buffalo calves, etc. Some of these are fantastically ornamented with tails and horns. These ornaments may be badges of distinction, for aught that I know, but being a stranger in the country I am not able to speak decidedly. You will perhaps recollect to have seen in the "far west" of our own United States the buckskin hunting shirt and leggins gracefully hung with fringes along the arms and sides. But I am sure you have never seen the tasty fashion of fringes carried to perfection. Here they are six or seven inches long, and hung densely on every seam, I believe, both of the hunting shirt and leggins. Indeed, their weight is a great burden.[52]

The fringes supplied thongs or "whangs" for repairing, at spur of the moment, moccasins, saddles, etc. The length was therefore an evolution of the practical as well as of the fanciful. After long use coat and leggins showed many a missing string.

To stain these swaying fringes scarlet was a touch much in vogue. One of Carson's favorite hunting shirts was thus stained. The hunting shirt sometimes was reinforced by a short fringed cape just covering the shoulders.

The pelt of old she-beaver, or of beaver pups, low in value like that of the buffalo calf, was stuff for the wide-brimmed trapper hats. It was preferably sent, by trader caravan, to St. Louis hatters, there to be made up into head-gear, and to be delivered, via caravan, at some rendezvous again. Oliver Wiggins, whose trapper experiences dated back to '38, stated that in the early Forties he and some fellow-trappers consigned a stock of old she-beaver pelts to St. Louis; but that the return caravan conveying the hats was despoiled by the Kiowas on the plains, and that by reason of the ensuing hostilities which cut off traffic between the mountains and the Missouri frontier his whole party went virtually hatless for two years. As a consequence, his eyes and those of others who did not resort to makeshift protection were permanently ruined by sun and snow glare.

Wool hats from St. Louis or Santa Fé were also used in the mountains; and many trappers affected the handkerchief turban, confining the long hair and jutting over the eyes.

Underneath the loose, long hunting shirt, next to the skin, was a regulation shirt (rarely removed) of doe-skin or of wool, slipped on over the head and tied like an open-neck sweater at the throat. For the mountain-man's garb was simplicity itself. "In the mountains," said Joe Meek to Mrs. Victor, "we do not have many garments. Buckskin breeches, a blanket capote, and a beaver skin cap makes up our rig."

Fur cap with ear flaps, or hat with brim tied down, scoop-fashion, by a scarf of cloth or of skin; buffalo robe enveloping body and hips, Indian-wise, and quickly to be thrown aside in case of urgent action; buffalo-hide shoes, fur-side in, reaching well up the leg, grotesque and cumbersome but warm; about the neck a scarf of blanketing or other material available; and upon the hands buffalo-skin mittens, featured the winter costume.

Looped to the hide belt girding the hunting shirt there was the buffalo-hide sheath for the skinning or scalp knife. Hung separately, or else sewed to the side of the sheath was a smaller skin case for the little whetstone by which the knife was kept keen.

An awl, with deer-horn handle, and the point defended by a case of cherry-wood carved by his own hand, hung at the back of the belt, side by side with a worm for cleaning the rifle; and under this was a squat and quaint-looking bullet-mold, the handles guarded by strips of buckskin to save his fingers from burning when running balls, having for its companion a little bottle made from the point of an antelope's horn, scraped transparent, which contained the "medicine" used in baiting traps.[53]

Slung from the belt, or stuck therein, was hatchet tomahawk. From the mountain-man's neck was suspended his pipe-holder, "generally a gage d'amour, and a triumph of squaw workmanship, in shape of a heart, garnished with beads and porcupine-quills." By a hide strap across his left shoulder, under his right arm, convenient to the hand, there depended his horn powder-flask, and the hide pouch containing bullets, flint and steel, and other important accessories. Tucked away in the shirt somewhere was the prized tobacco, in plug or sack; and perchance a razor.

The weapons of the trapper West were those of the hunter East; rifle, pistol and knife. The first-named, the American rifle in its perfection, single shot, flint-lock and muzzle-loader though it was, became famous in Kentucky and demands no encomium. During 100 years, from young Daniel Boone to young Kit Carson, it ruled forest, valley and plain, desert and crest; its spiteful crack sounded across a continent. But in its peregrinations from Kentucky to the Columbia and the Pacific coast it underwent modifications to suit the mountain-man.

As used east of the Mississippi by Kenton, Boone and all, the old Kentucky squirrel rifle was slim stock, long-barreled, and small-bored to fit a ball the size of the proverbial pea. Traveling westward in the browned, nervous hands of the Kentuckian, the Tennesseean, the Georgian, the Carolinan, through Missouri and onward across the muddy boundary river of the fur trade, it readily adapted itself to the newer country.

It still remained heavy, weighing eleven and twelve pounds. A long barrel, forty inches from lock-plate to muzzle, and half an inch, or three-quarters, thick, was retained. The length was deemed necessary for accurate sighting; the thickness, so that the ball could be forced through without deviating the bore a hair's breadth — this, also, contributing to accuracy. But the calibre was enlarged, to deliver a ball that would stop the buffalo, the elk, and the fierce, extraordinarily tenacious Western Indian. The customary ball of the mountain rifle was the half-ounce, thirty-two to the pound, or about half an inch in diameter, which is .50 calibre. The bore varied, of course, on either side of this mark; ranging from sixty to the pound or about a

.38 calibre to twenty-five to the pound, or about a .60 calibre. Subjected as they were to rain, snow and dust, and other vicissitudes of constant camp and travel, not to speak of inefficient cleanings, the mountain-man's rifle demanded reboring once a year. Not always could it be granted this attention, for it had to be sent to St. Louis. Each reboring slightly enlarged the calibre, until the rifle which at the beginning took a forty-to-the-pound ball called for one twenty-five to the pound. The owner cheerfully accepted this progression rather than change to a different piece.[54]

In its pips underneath the barrel there was of course the ramrod. A recess covered by a silver or brass lid, in the right or left side of the stock, was the patch-box. As the Western trapper's rifle, of calibre larger and stock stouter was likely to be heavier than the Kentucky squirrel rifle, a rest for it was sought when time or place permitted. Here the wiping-stick came in handy.

This was a cleaning-rod, supplemental to the ramrod; it was of imported hickory, or was cut from some straight growth native to the trapper's haunts. After about a hundred rounds, at the most, of shooting, the old muzzle-loading rifle ought to be cleaned. The operation of ramming down the patched ball cleaned, after a fashion, each time, until the grooves of the rifling became packed with the powder residue. Then the cleaning-rod, or wiping-stick, must be employed. Camp was the time for this; there was not time during hunt or fight.[55]

On the march the wiping-stick was carried in the bore of the barrel, and projected six or eight inches from the muzzle. It was removed before the shot; but occasionally an excited individual would pull trigger without fore-thought, and the wipingstick would sail out into the air. On the hot trail it was not entrusted to the barrel, but was stowed among the pack equipage. And as before intimated, when whipped from barrel or from pack and planted in the ground with the left fist, while the shooter kneeled and steadied the heavy muzzle upon juncture of stick and fist, it provided an excellent rest for deadly aim.

When the trail and the camp temporarily parted, this wiping-stick was left behind. In such event, a rest when called for was supplied by a pair of other sticks tied and crossed like scissor-blades, or by ramrod and fist. The rest was not necessary but it was convenient in a long and careful shot.

The "dead-center" line shot for the longer barreled, finely balanced Kentucky rifle was a nail head or a charcoal dot or single criss-cross at sixty paces. The plains-and-mountain model should group shots within an inch at 100 yards. It was sighted high to hit a dollar at that distance. The Kentucky front sight, the scant segment of a circle, back up and knife-blade thin, hugging the barrel, was retained; the rear or barrel sight was low, and was merely a bar with a slight notch filed in the middle. The extra or set trigger, straight, and sprung by a feather touch, was universal.

The ascendancy of the mountain-man over the Kentucky hunter gave the St. Louis gun-smith his opportunity, which he speedily embraced. There rose to fame the trade-mark Hawkins. Throughout plains and mountain fur-country the "Hawkins" rifle became sterling, so that to say a horse was a "reg'lar Hawkins hos" expressed the superlative in quality. "Hawkins," in fire-arms, was used as later "Winchester" and "Colt." A first-class rifle cost $40 in St. Louis; a fusil, or smooth-bore like a musket, cost $12 there, but sold at $30 in the Indian trade. Traders had to make their profits. Rifles were not, as a rule, transported for sale; they were too valuable and were personal weapons, not merchandise.[56]

Like the woodsman in the Cooper romances of the Eastern forests, the mountain-man of the West named his favorite and trusted gun. "Old Bull Thrower" was a tickling cognomen. "Old Silver Heels," "Old Greaser," "Knock-him-stiff," "Old Straightener," were acceptable and fond titles. Joe Meek, of Oregon fame, knew his rifle as "Sally," and right glad was he to get her back out of the hands of the Crows. The Western trapper would go to any risk to rescue his piece, not only because his subsistence and very life depended upon it, but also out of sheer love. He was addicted to many wives; a squaw was easily replaced; but for him there was only the one gun — if battered, yet tried and true, the brass-headed tacks in its stock recording the "red niggurs" on whom it had counted "coups." Time and again he had it rebored; and when in a fracas or by a fall it broke at the grasp, he united the two parts with a wrapping of green buffalo-hide.

His execution with it was astounding. Much practice, and the habit of drawing fine with the very fine sight, made him a dangerous off-hand shot. To kill a furious grizzly bear with one solid, round ball driven by old-fashioned black powder was an accepted feat. The fact that the rifle contained but the single load, and that therefore all depended upon the aim, compelled the marksman to do his level best every time.

Yet the reloading, by charger, patch and ball and ramrod, was extraordinarily expeditious. Scout Oliver Wiggins, old trapper of those days, stated that the fire from a small body of mountain-men hard-pressed by the foe was continuous. It was pour powder, ram ball, prime pan, fire; pour powder, ram ball, prime pan, fire, again and again, with only a few seconds intervening. "I tell you, you ought to have heard us," he said. "It was done quicker than you can think." Five times a minute is cited by "Uncle" Bill Hamilton.

"Dupont and Galena [lead]" was the common load, but American powder for the Indian and trapper trade and sold as high as a "plew" [$6] a pint was outbid by the imported "diamond grain," of English make. This to be delivered at $1 the pound, was packed in canisters of fifty-six pounds, or half an English hundredweight. The grains were hard, fine, and glossy black. "By golly," Trapper Wiggins enthused, "with an inch and a half of this rammed down you could kill at not only two hundred, but four hundred yards! It was the grand powder. I never have seen its like since. How it cracked!"[57]

The powder horn's capacity was half a pound to a pound. The pound size was none too large. The Wiggins horn, on exhibit, would contain only half a pound, which, according to the old trapper, on a long march or in a hard "scrimmage" sometimes proved insufficient. It was a black buffalo-horn, for black horns were prized by the mountain-men above white horns, being (by a singular perversion of nature) the more transparent. These horns were not so much carved but were painstakingly scraped and scraped until of the thinness of ising-glass, with every grain of powder visible through their sides. They were stoppered fast at the butt by a wooden plug; and another plug, of deer-horn, protruding for easy extraction, was inserted in the tip. The butt plug was apt to be ringed by brass filagree or by brass screw studs to hold it in place.

From the tip there hung down, some eight inches, by a thong, the metal charger — a small cylinder, with a lip for pouring the powder into the rifle muzzle. It was presumed to hold the proper charge for the rifle. These chargers were usually supplied with the rifle. They hung mouth downward, so that they should not get wet inside. The charger attached to a powder horn picked up on the plains during Indian days had been made from the tip of an antelope spike.

When percussion caps came into general use there came also a handy cap box. This was a flat disk, the thickness of the cap itself, honey-combed with one hundred caps. By a quick jab a cap could be set upon the gun nipple and torn loose. That speeded matters up when one's thumb and fingers were numbed with the cold. The cap box was carried tucked away between hunting shirt and chest, to be kept dry.

The mountain-man's second or reserve barrel was his pistol; in the beginning the long-barreled, large-bored, curved-handle, single-shot and cumbersome flint-lock. The pistol was the trapper's "pup," supplementing the mother arm. When he possessed a pair of "pups" he felt that he could "shine" in any kind of "scrimmage." At first the pistol greatly astonished the Indian, whose alleged comment became historic: "Wagh! White man shoot one time with gun, next time with butcher knife."

Many of the trappers were experts with the Indian weapon

of bow and arrow. This facility saved precious powder and lead, and proved valuable when powder and lead lacked. After a "scrimmage" the wounded Indians were dispatched by their own bows if not by the knife. And in hostile country the bow and arrow proved a silent, economical getter of game. In yet another attribute the native weapon was the superior of the rifle. It was shot by intuitive sense of direction rather than by aim of eye, and in semi-darkness was a weapon unequalled. Many a trapper was spitted, at the camp-fire, by an Indian arrow delivered from outside the circle of light.[58]

The western trappers' knife was of the heavy-bladed and broad-bladed skinning type, very keen at point and edge. For Indian and other Western and Northwestern trade the "Company" knife, the Hudson's Bay knife, that is, was standard. It was imported in great numbers, and sold for a dollar and a half. Upon the blade, close against the hilt, was stamped the sign-mark G. R. — George Rex; token of the English origin. But the American trapper read this otherwise. To him the G. R. stood for "Green River" — that beloved trapping-ground and place of summer rendezvous. The manufacturers of the rivaling American knife therefore bid for the trappers' favor with the brand "Green River" stamped into the blade.[59]

This knife, of six or seven inch blade, single edge, wooden handle, such as may be seen in almost any butcher-shop, was the mountain-man's invariable companion, used for sticking, skinning, scalping, whittling and eating. Weapon and implement in one, it entered largely into his vocabulary. When in a fracas there sounded the hoarse cry "Give 'em Green River, boys!" that was signal for a hand-to-hand conflict, without mercy; a war literally to the hilt. To "go up Green River" was to die by the knife; and "Green River" indicated any action performed to the limit.

The long-handled hatchet was more of a tool than a weapon, employed for knocking beaver on the head (in case that the beaver was found in the trap alive and a short club was not carried), and for cutting fire-wood. It was part of the camp equipage, rather than of the personal. However, at times the trapper would wield it well, in a fight, for it was two pounds of sharp steel.

There should not be omitted the lazo, or lasso, adopted by the mountain-man as by the Indian from the Mexican. This, the lariat and the "rope" of the more modern cow-boy, was handy in many ways. Stories would indicate that in its use the mountain-man was well expert. With it he could catch the wild horse and the half-wild, and with it he noosed some likely squaw just made a widow. As in the case of the bow and arrow, it appealed to the Indian and trapper both, as simple, silent, and startlingly effective.

Mention has been made of the mountain-man's razor. According to one account, when old Hugh Glass was mutilated by a bear, during the 1823 Ashley expedition under Major Andrew Henry, and was abandoned for dead by his companions, his razor was the only article left to him. Oliver Wiggins declared that the trappers of his company, 1838 to 1846, shaved after a fashion only once a year, at most, or for a trip to the settlements. They used their butcher knives. The free trapper brave, however, imitating the Indian, to whom hair upon the face was no mark of merit, shaved or plucked his chin and cheeks clean, permitting himself a moustache alone, or not even that.

Whether free trapper or hired hand, of visage bushy throughout a twelve-month or fastidiously cleared day to day, of skin naturally Saxon light or Creole dark, the mountain-man was *sui generis* — "so long associated with Indians, that his manners much resemble theirs.

The same wild, unsettled, watchful expression of the eyes; that same unnatural gesticulation in conversation, the same unwillingness to use words when a sign, a contortion of the face or body, or movement of the hand will manifest thought; in standing, walking, riding — in all but complexion he was an Indian." [60]

Ahorse or afoot he clung to his rifle. When he was ahorse

carried it held in his right hand, across the saddle-bow, ready for instant service. Rifle slung athwart the back, English fashion, was token of the greenhorn. With rifle across saddle-bow he rode down narrow vale and Taos street. When he moved afoot his rifle was still his close companion.

On going from lodge to lodge to visit his comrades, he takes it with him. On seating himself in a lodge, he lays it beside him, ready to be snatched up; when he goes out, he takes it up as regularly as a citizen would his walking staff. His rifle is his constant friend and protector.[61]

These Western trappers were hard workers, hard players, hard fighters, hard drinkers, extravagant in act as in speech, inured to every excess. They were frank, rough and lawless: frank, for the reason that time and speech were limited, and they despised to use among themselves the wordy deceit of the Indians; rough, because they had to be, to survive their experiences; lawless, because in their haunts there was no law except their own wills. The American trapper was not, like the Hudson's Bay *engagé,* bred to the business, and furthermore he was not under the discipline of the British employe. The rank and

file appeared
to have sought for a place where, as they would say, human nature is not oppressed by the tyranny of religion, and pleasure is not awed by the frown of virtue.[62]

and as Mrs. Victor says, while "a few were brave, independent, and hardy spirits, who delighted in the hardships and wild adventures their calling made necessary . . . all experience goes to prove that a life of perfect liberty is apt to degenerate into a life of license."

Thus it came about that the title "mountain-man" had peculiar significance. One might be a hunter, one might be a trapper, but of hunters and trappers, during the hundred years while the West was becoming the East and a farther West had been opened, there was a long line. "Mountain-man" covered hunter-ship and trapper-ship, and more. For the American it indicated a new race, meeting difficulties of a new degree. As in the frozen north of the British fur regions, there was the greenhorn — the *mangeur de lard* or pork-eater — with his supply of company rations; there was next the winterer, or *hivernan,* who had passed a full season in the wilderness; and after that the veteran, able to go it alone.

"Je suis un homme du nord!" vauntingly proclaimed, on Montreal street and on toilsome portage, the Canadian voyageur-trapper who wore the Nor'west Company button and with dirk and feather ruffled like any game-cock. And now in St. Louis, and up the Missouri and through the length and breadth of the Rockies, there succeeded the equally potent password: "Je suis un homme des montagnes," and, "I am a mountain-man."

Or "mountaineer," of which mountain-man was the variant. General Ashley, leaving the mountains, thus addressed his camp:

Mountaineers and friends! When I first came to the mountains, I came a poor man. You, by your indefatigable exertions, toils, and privations, have procured me an independent fortune. . . . I am now about to leave you, to take up my abode in St. Louis. Whenever any of you return thither, your first duty must be to call at my house, to talk over the scenes of peril we have encountered, and partake of the best cheer my table affords. I now wash my hands of the toils of the Rocky Mountains. Farewell, mountaineers and friends! May God bless you all.[68]

Chapter X

The Mountain-Man — By Mule and By Horse

THE lure of the beaver West took on various appeals. To Robert Campbell, Ashley associate and St. Louis banker, in 1825, the plains and mountains represented health, as they did to John Warner in 1831, and to William Hamilton in 1842, and to Josiah Gregg and many another on the Santa Fé Trail. To Rufus Sage, author of *Wild Scenes in the Rocky Mountains,* the appeal was that of health and the satisfaction of an "innate curiosity, and fondness for things new and strange." To Lieutenant Ruxton it was a like satisfaction, and the out-of-doors free life. To young Oliver Wiggins, to young Kit Carson, it also was that of wanderlust. To Jedediah Smith it was that of profitable observation. To young Jim Bridger, to Zenas Leonard and W. A. Ferris, it was that of livelihood. To General Ashley it was that of business enterprise. To the adventurer the beaver West proffered a field; to the homeless, a home; to the lawless, an asylum.

Thus the voice of this West was subtly adapted to sway almost any heart. Once that voice was heeded, it never was forgotten. After he had entered Congress General Ashley said that his best days were his mountain days, his best friends his trapper friends. Josiah Gregg announced that the lure of the plains remained with him long after he had retired from them. Jim Bridger, decrepit and blind on his Missouri farm, was haunted by the desire for another sight of the great hills and the greetings of some old-time comrade. Jim Baker, his trapping days over, fled from his cabin upon the Denver outskirts and built him another cabin upon his old beaver-ground and battle-ground in northwestern Colorado, there to stay until he died. Lieutenant Ruxton fondly dwelt upon the memory of "my solitary camp in the Bayou Salade," where his only companions were his rifle, his faithful animals and the coyotes, the camp-fire and his pipe. That other Britisher, Captain Stewart, offers his own book "as a sad tho' pleasing memory" of the days that were. Washington Irving who scoured the plains for the buffalo, and the historian Francis Parkman who ate dog in the lodges of the Sioux, wrote thereof with a tinge of regret that those days could be no more. And Kit Carson declared to Surgeon Tilton, who attended him at the last, that "the happiest days of my life were spent in trapping."

Therefore the search for fur was founded upon business and pleasure: profit of purse and profit of body and mind. It not only indulged the hunting instinct and the attribute spirit of conquest which incite any man in any business, but it cultivated that atavism indicated by a bent for personal independence, by rebellion against the dictates of the monotonous and the superficial, even by that fault in the strata of a gentling civilization which appears as an eruptive relish for old clothes and honest dirt.

The price of this liberty afforded by the plains and mountains was constant vigilance lest the liberty be voided. Feasting was threatened by famine, sunshine was countered by storm, warmth was succeeded by bitter cold, ease was punctuated by phenomenal stress, the comfortable camp and the rich beaver trail were thrown into turmoil by the charge of the enemy; there were peace and war, war and peace, with anything possible and with nothing permanent except death.

Taking him by and large, the mountain trapper was intensely practical. Beaver, buffalo and Injuns — fur, meat and ha'r: these were the chief matters occupying his mind. To find the fur and meat he would risk the hair and many a peril besides.

There were company methods of travel until the central camp had been established, whence the trap trails radiated; but the trap trail itself was likely to be a lonely trail. Setting out from the Missouri River border; from old "Touse" or from Bent's Fort in the southwest; from Laramie, Fort Hall, Brown's Hole, in the northwest; from summer rendezvous or winter camp, when the trap season reopened; as headed again for some favorite ground or some new treasure-trove of skins the trapper, when on his own, with a partner, or with a small squad, rode one animal and led another by lariat in hand or by the head-to-tail link — a pack-train mode still in use.

For he had his camp necessities, such as his bedding or robes and blankets, if not a small lodge and his squaw its keeper, to transport; and in a buffalo-hide sack there were his extra clothing and clothing material (such as it was) — moccasins, for a change from wet to dry, 'kerchief or two, perhaps gloves, a dressed deer-skin, squaw "fofarrow" if there were a squaw; and powder, lead, tobacco, bullet mold, articles for trading, various odds and ends that a seasoned traveler in the wilderness will acquire.

This was the "pack-sack," and the contents were the mountain-man's "possibles" — the answer to possible need. In another hide sack were the traps, from six to twenty. This was of course the "trap-sack." These sacks, an inch thick, when cut-up and well boiled or at worst "chawed" dry, provided a measure of provender in emergencies.

Then there was the trapper's iron kettle — his main culinary utensil. It was stowed in one of his sacks, or slung along with the other packs. There might be also a skin sack of tallow, or buffalo fat, pure or mixed with berries or flesh to form pemmican. And after a hunt for meat there were the remnants from the butchering and gorging, in shape of humps and quarters. The trapper's fortunes could be read in the size and the variety of the led-horse load.

When furs had been collected, then to bring them to post or rendezvous he piled them upon pack-animals and transferred his "possibles" and traps to his saddle animal.

All this, to a result that —

The mountaineers in their rude hunting dresses, armed with rifles and roughly mounted, and leading their pack-horses down a hill of the forest, looked like banditti returning with plunder. On the top of some of the packs were perched several half-breed children, perfect little imps, with black eyes glaring from among elf locks. These, I was told, were children of the trappers: pledges of love from their squaw spouses in the wilderness.[64]

The mule and the horse both were favored by the mountain-man: the mule for pack-animal, the horse for saddle-animal. Granted only the choice of mule or horse, many a trapper would take the mule as his companion.

For the uses of the mountain-man the mule had certain advantages — principal among which was its odd but persistent aversion to Indians. When Indians were about, long before their presence was recognized by human being the mule, by up-right ears, by snorts and staring eyes, gave the alarm. Therefore the mule was the trapper's watch-dog.

When he [Killbuck] returned to the fire he sat himself down as before, but this time with his rifle across his lap; and at intervals his keen gray eye glanced piercingly around, particularly towards an old, weather-beaten, and grizzled mule, who, old stager as she was, having filled her belly, stood lazily over her picket pin, with her head bent down and her long ears flapping over her face, her limbs gathered under her, and her back arched to throw off the rain, tottering from side to side as she rested and slept.

"Yep, old gal!" cried Killbuck to the animal, at the same time picking a piece of burnt wood from the fire and throwing it at her, at which the mule gathered herself up and cocked her ears as she recognized her master's voice. "Yep, old gal! and keep your nose open; thar's brown skin about, I'm thinkin'; and maybe you'll get roped by a 'Rapaho afore mornin'." Again the old trapper settled himself before the fire; and soon his head began to nod, as drowsiness stole over him. . . . Sleep, however, sat lightly on the eyes of the wary mountaineer, and a snort from the old mule in an instant stretched his every nerve. Without a movement of his body, his keen eye fixed itself upon the mule, which now stood with head bent round, and eyes and ears pointed in one direction, snuffing the night air and snorting with apparent fear.[65]

This trait in the mule has been noted by other prairie and mountain travelers of overland days.

I must have been sleeping some hours, when I was suddenly awakened by the snorting of my mule. Apprehensive that all was not right, I immediately arose, and taking my pistol, approached the spot where he was fastened.

I found him with eyes fixed, nostrils distended, forefeet firmly braced, and endeavoring, by every means in his power, to break the lariat, which, fortunately, was made of hair, and successfully resisted his efforts.

The first glance convinced me that Indians were near, for a mule will detect an Indian a long distance off by the smell.[66]

In this case the mule had detected a single Indian crawling through the long grass!

Captain Lee Humfreville in his *Twenty Years Among Our Hostile Indians* asserts that the scent of the Indian to which the mule, and the horse also, when unaccustomed, took exception, was the pungent odor of the pipe kinnikinnick or red-willow mixture with which the Indian was permeated. However that may be, whether it was of kinnikinnick, lodge smoke or communism the Indian carried with him a distinct atmosphere. The fact has been potent to authorities other than horses and mules.

Having his mule at hand, the Western trapper might feel assured that no Indian could completely surprise the camp.

The second valuable trait in the mule was its strong attachment for companionship. This attachment was sometimes abnormal, sometimes not; but at all times it was a dominant impulse.

The instincts of the mulish heart form an interesting study to the traveler in the mountains. I would (were the comparison not too ungallant) liken it to a woman's, for it is quite as uncertain in its sympathies, bestowing its affections when least expected, and, when bestowed, quite as constant, as long as the object is not taken away. Sometimes a horse, sometimes an ass, captivates the fancy of a whole drove of mules, but often an animal no wise akin. Lieutenant Beale told me that his whole train of mules once galloped off suddenly, on the plains of the Cimarrone, and ran half a mile, when they halted in apparent satisfaction. The cause of their freak was found to be a buffalo calf which had strayed from the herd. They were frisking around it in the greatest delight, rubbing their noses against it, throwing up their heels, and making themselves ridiculous by abortive attempts to neigh and bray, while the calf, unconscious of its attractive qualities, stood trembling in their midst.[67]

Colonel R. B. Marcy relates of the pathetic affection of a small mule Billy for his own riding mare. Billy would not stay with the other mules, but persisted in traveling and sleeping with the horse.

The sentiment was not, however, reciprocated on her [the mare's] part, and she intimated as much by the reversed position of her ears, and the free exercise of her feet and teeth whenever Billy came within her reach; but these signal marks of displeasure, instead of discouraging, rather seemed to increase his devotion, and whenever at liberty he invariably sought to get near her, and appeared much distressed when not permitted to follow her.[68]

This affection, so lively in the mule and promotive of docility under leadership, is utilized in the pack-trains with their madrina or bell-mare. The scientist Charles Darwin is quoted:

It is nearly impossible to lose an old mule, for, if detained several hours by force, she will, by the power of smell, like a dog, track out her companions, or rather the madrina; for, according to the muleteer, she is the chief object of affection. The feeling, however, is not of an individual nature, for I believe I am right in saying that any animal with a bell will serve as madrina.

The third valuable trait in the mule was the succulency of its flesh in comparison with the flesh of the horse. Either was meat, in extremity, but to the notion of the trapper that of the mule was the better.

As to the endurance of the mule, opinions vary. The mule surpassed the horse in desert work. Of his favorite pair returning with him from Mexico Lieutenant Ruxton says: ". . . the most perfectly enduring animals I ever traveled with. No day was too long, no work too hard, no food too coarse for them." Colonel Emory, with the Army of the West across the southwest desert to California in 1846 records:

Most of the mules belonging to my party have travelled 1800 miles, almost continuously. Two or three times they have all appeared on the eve of death; but a mule's vitality seems to recuperate, when life seems to be almost extinct.

But Colonel Marcy in his report of his winter march from Utah down through Colorado says that the mules gave out first; the horses next; and the oxen "ploughed numbly ahead."

On this other side of the ledger it is claimed also that the mule was more easily stampeded by storm, Indians, or other alarm, than the horse, and was harder to turn.

As a rule, however, the mountain-man's legs were the horse. Mules must be obtained from Santa Fé or California; the horse came more easily as an article of barter or raid. The price value of a horse was whatever circumstances dictated, even up to $50 and $60 in money or trade.

Through several seasons in the mountains "old" Jim Bridger was to be distinguished by his white horse. Carson's favorite horse used in his later years and better bred than common was named Apache. "Old" Bill Williams' storied mount, to which he had the habit of continually talking, is reported by Ruxton as "a crop-eared, raw-boned Nez-perce pony . . . who in dogged temper and iron hardiness, was worthy companion of his self-willed master." According to trapper legend it was a part of Bill Williams until the moment of his death, and was found standing, hunched with cold and starvation, over his body.[69]

The Nez Percé and Flathead stock was considered prime, for these tribes were horse fanciers in a country of abundant grass and pure water. The Comanche stock was as highly prized, for it was likely to be of Spanish blood direct. Bridger's winning race-horse Grohean (gray) was a Comanche animal procured from the Snakes. Charles Bent, with his long black hair streaming in the breeze, charged to the rescue of a caravan upon a horse bearing the split-ear sign of the Comanche.

But regardless of its lineage or raising the trapper's horse at the height of efficiency is seen as

a strong square-built bay; and, although the severities of a prolonged winter, with scanty pasture and long and trying travel, had robbed his bones of fat and flesh, tucked up his flank, and "ewed" his neck; still his clean and well-set legs, oblique shoulder, and withers fine as a deer's, in spite of his gaunt half-starved appearance, bore ample testimony as to what he had been; while his clear cheerful eye, and the hearty appetite with which he fell to work on the coarse grass of the bottom, proved that he had something in him still, and was as game as ever. His tail, gnawed by the mules in days of strait, attracted the observant mountaineers.

"Hard doin's when it comes to that," remarked La Bonte.[70]

The mountain-man's horse was obtained from the half-broken stock of the Indians, and from California. The Snakes, the Nez Percés and the Flatheads were the largest horse-raisers of the northern tribes; and upon them the Crows, the Black-feet, the Sioux and the Cheyennes made heavy demands. The Comanche and the Apache, and in the beginnings the Navajo, derived their horses principally from periodical raids upon the Mexicans. Arapaho and Pawnee on the plains, Ute in the mountains, obtained their horses from both north and south, by lassoing, corralling, or by trade with or theft from their red brethren. And so the field for the trapper was wide. He rarely attempted to catch the wild mustang. That was small, slow work.

Of this native American stock of mountain-man times, writing from the Upper Missouri country the artist Catlin says (1832):

> The horses which the Indians ride in this country are invariably the wild horses, which are found in great numbers on the prairies; and have, unquestionably, strayed from the Mexican borders, into which they were introduced by the Spanish invaders of that country; and now range and subsist themselves, in winter and summer, over the vast plains of prairie that stretch from the Mexican frontiers to Lake Winnipeg on the North, a distance of 3000 miles. These horses are all of small stature, of the pony order; but a very hardy and tough animal, being able to perform for the Indians a continual and essential service.[71]

Not handsome animals, these; but they were the survival of the fittest. Their vari-colored coats would indicate that they did not possess "bottom"; the cow-boy chooses, for his string, the solid colors rather than the mixed of the pinto. But on the contrary the Indian or plains pony, only fourteen hands high, wiry, self-supporting, had tremendous stamina. Though he was never "stabled, washed, rubbed, curried, blanketed, shod, fed nor doctored"; though he may have "not the slightest appearance of blood" —

The amount of work he can do, and the distance he can make in a specified (long) time, put him fairly on a level with the Arabian or any other of animal creation. . . . Treated properly, the pony will wear out two American horses. . . . After endurance, the best quality of the pony is sureness of foot. He will climb a steep rocky hill with the activity and assurance of the mule; he will plunge down an almost precipitous declivity with the ease and indifference of the buffalo. In swamps and quicksands he is only excelled by the elk, and he will go at speed through sand-hills, or ground undermined by gophers, where an American horse would labor to get along faster than a walk, and fall in the first fifty yards of a gallop.[72]

To the Western Indian, horses was the medium of exchange, as wampum was to the Eastern Indian. The most conscientious mountain-man rarely needed to have gone horseless, nor were his animals to be surpassed by any for the work required. It was only the trapper's lawless greed that made him cast covetous eye westward, to the horses of California.

The repute of these, and their worth in the market, caused his mouth to water. Moreover, to steal horses from the Californians was an entertaining and irreproachable act — a prank and a feat in one, attended with small danger save from the journey to and fro. The American trapper early had a supreme contempt for any native of Mexico, rating him as a coward and a braggart.

Horses in California during the Golden Age of the missions were numbered, when numbered at all, not by the thousands, nor by the tens of thousands, only, but by the hundreds of thousands. They roamed at will: once a year, perhaps, to be gathered, after a fashion, in the annual rodeo by the Missions and by the few *ranchos*. In 1849 Thomas J. Farnham estimates the horses still to aggregate some 500,000.

There is no better animal than the Californian cavallo. He presents all colors — from black to white, dappled, mixed and shuffled together in the most beautiful confusion. His head and neck are lightly made — his eyes burn with that kindly yet unquenchable fire so peculiar to his progenitors, the Andalusian Arabian steeds. His chest is broad and full, his loins well knit, and closely laid to the ribs, his limbs clean, slender and sinewy; the embodiment of the matchless wild horse of a green and sunny wilderness.[73]

The gait of the California horse, when ridden by the native, was full gallop. "It is death or banishment for a Californian horse to trot." This gallop

he will keep up, over hill and down mountain-side alike, though a whole day's journey, and generally pressing hard on the rein, the whip or spur being rarely necessary.

Moreover, he was

able to carry his rider sixty and one hundred miles in a day over a rough road, and perform these journeys several days in succession, without other food than could be gathered from the soil on his journey.[74]

Out of greediness, then (for in California were fatness and wenches of easy pillage, strong contrast to the piny slopes and the shy squaws of the great hills), or out of restlessness and bravado (for the mountain-man ever was a wanderer, courting new scenes and new adventures) the doughty bands of the American trapper in romance recklessly dared the thirst and starvation and poisoned arrows and alternate heat and cold of the Great Basin and the Mojave Desert. Like robber barons sallying from the fastnesses of the Rhine they descended upon the peace-loving land of the sun and the vineyard. Shaggy, fearsome and headlong, they sent their reputation before them. The very word: *"Los Americanos! Vienen los Americanos!"* cleared the way; and after a merely nominal resistance upon the part of the missions' uncertain retainers they seized virtually whatsoever they wished — even to dusky half-breed damsels who like the Indian maids themselves did not at all object to the rude-and-rough but ready mountaineer captors. As said Juanita, "the stout wench from Sonora," while she pounded corn in the San Fernando mission court:

"Que vengan — let them come; they are only men, and will not molest us women. Besides, I have seen these white men before — in my own country, and they are fine fellows, very tall, and as white as snow on the sierras. Let them come, say I!"[75]

The discovery by William Wolfskill, Ewing Young and other traders from New Mexico to California in 1830-31 that "in exchange for serapes and blankets large, well-formed, serviceable mules could be obtained," was the foundation for a trade upon these lines between Los Angeles and Santa Fé. Then the notorious excursion of Captain Bonneville's detachment of trappers under the bearded Joe Walker, in 1833, from the Salt Lake across the Great Basin to Monterey, practically opened this trail to California and brought back renewed report of Californian wealth and hospitality. Right speedily the concupiscence of the mountain-man and the frequency of his raids for cattle became so pronounced that the Head of the California Missions made special report thereon to the Governor of that province, declaring that "to oppose these white barbarians it behooves us to make every preparation of defence."

The preparations availed little, as witness:

Pursuing a course W.N.W., on the 27th we met a small party of whites on their return from the mountains, and, yielding to the temptation presented by a luxuriant and well-wooded valley, with a pretty streamlet, the two parties made common camp. Our new acquaintances were taking a large drove of horses, and several domesticated buffalo, with them to the States. Their horses had been mostly obtained from Upper California, the year previous [1840], by a band of mountaineers, under the lead of one Thompson. This band, numbering twenty-two in all, had made a descent upon the Mexican ranchos and captured between two and three thousand head of horses and mules. A corps of some sixty Mexican cavalry pursued and attacked them, but were defeated and pursued in turn, with the loss of several mules and their entire camp equipage; after which the adventurers were permitted to regain their mountain homes, without further molestation; but in passing the cheerless desert, between the Sierra Nevada and Colorado the heat, dust, and thirst were so intolerably oppressive, that full one half of their animals died. The remainder, however, were brought to rendezvous, and variously disposed of, to suit the wants and wishes of their captors.[76]

Juan B. Leandro, reporting to the prefect of San Luis Obispo mission upon the results of a pursuit of marauders who had made off with the mission's animals, says, date May 30, 1840, that he had overtaken the miscreants, 300 miles into the desert; that they had fled his approach, leaving baggage, a few horses tied, and about 1,500 slaughtered. During the pursuit he had seen other bands of thieves with stolen horses aggregating more than 1,000. "The robbers composing the rear-guard were about twenty citizens of the United States."[77]

It takes but little leaven of fiction to conjure up some of these wild forays, retreats, and pursuits; the dash of the dreaded, utterly fearless mountaineers, the stampede of the herds, the tolling of the mission bell, the retreat of the enemy with their spoils, the hasty gathering of the soldiery and the neophytes, the injunctions by the good padre, the valorous pursuit, the dusty, arid desert trail which is marked only by skeletons, the looking back of the hurrying thieves, the looking forward of the would-be rescuers, the rear-guard action, the escape, the return to the mission, and the report; success and horseflesh in the bandits' camp, praise and beef in the mission's court.

The horses and mules found quick sale, in American territory — particularly the mules, the Californian, like the Mexican variety, being highly esteemed in the States, even in Missouri itself, later to be mule center. A favorite market to which the mountain-men brought their stolen stock was Bent's Fort on the Arkansas, where the proprietors, Messrs. Bent and St. Vrain, traded goods for them and thence dispatched them on to Independence and St. Louis.[78]

In time, especially when, while California was still a foreign territory, the beaver hunt began to languish, the Indians offered a market for the stolen stock on a trade basis of furs and robes for horses. And there was the market of the Overlanders to California and Oregon — a persistent market of which, in 'Forty-six and afterward, the retired mountain-man took advantage with the increase of his herd.

Accordingly in 1850 we see the renowned Thomas L. ("Pegleg") Smith, one of the most industrious collectors of horse animals, "in undisputed ownership of hundreds of the most beautiful Spanish horses" and camped with his squaws and Indian herders on the emigrant trail at Bear River in Utah, here doing business upon the basis of a horse for a bottle of whisky or a pound of powder.

In answer to the question as to how he came to have so many horses, he said, "Oh! I went down into the Spanish country and got them." "What did they cost you?" we inquired. "They cost me very dearly," said he. "Three of my squaws lost brothers, and one of them a father, on that trip, and I came near going under myself. I lost several other braves, and you can depend on it that I paid for all the horses I drove away. Them Spaniards followed us and fought us in a way that Spaniards were never before known to do." "How many did you get?" we again queried. "Only about 3,000; the rascals got about half of what we started with away from us, d—n them. I made up my mind to try it over, but then our own people taking the country broke up my plans."[79]

A grievous thorn in the flesh of the California ranchos and missions was this *el Cojo Smit,* the Lame Smith — this burly, red-faced, stump-wearing freebooter "old" Peg-leg; who by one raid in the 'Thirties, with the assistance of Jim Beckwourth, swept the pastures between San Juan Capistrano and the Santa Ana River, twenty-five miles, clean of the best horse stock and thundered out again over Cajon Pass for the desert and the Spanish Trail to New Mexico.

The horse-lifting mountain-man did not always win through to market white or red with even a portion of his hard-earned booty. Descending, with thirty men, upon the California mission herds, trapper Bill Williams drove off fifteen hundred horses. With 200 riders the Californians pursued so closely that on a desert stretch of eighty miles without water Williams lost, by over-driving, two-thirds of his animals. Whereupon he camped at a water-hole and waited for the enemy. After three uneventful days, exasperated by the delay, he retraced the trail and in a night attack he recouped his losses by stealing every animal from the Californian camp! Now with their herd satisfactorily augmented, "the Americans went on their way rejoicing." But they rejoiced too soon. Ere they reached Santa Fé the Apaches in turn attacked their camp, stampeded their whole *caballada,* and left them to find their way on foot as best they might. In the words of Lieutenant Brewerton, who relates the story as in the summer of 1848 it was related to him: "Bill Williams curses the Indians heartily whenever he tells the tale."[80]

As mute witness to the foray, for many years a line of horse and mule skeletons marked the desert trail of the retreating Americans hotly pursued by the California force.

The seat of the mountain-man was the seat of the Indian. The Indian rides with his feet high and his knees well crooked. That other plains rider, the cow-boy, equally as much in the saddle, chooses the opposite position — his feet low, his leg straight from thigh to heel. A similar discrepancy in the science of horsemanship impressed Colonel James Meline, in his tour of the West.

A Mexican or Indian on horseback is readily distinguished at a distance by the ceaseless swinging of his legs. This swing is far from according with our ideas of fine horsemanship. For that matter, there is much really good riding that departs very widely from the rules of the *manège,* or riding-school, and is by no means tolerated at West Point or Saumur. Thus, for instance, it is thought quite the thing to ride with long stirrups — an exquisite rider scarcely touching stirrup with the tip of his long-soled boot. Now, the Cossacks, Bedouins, and Camanches are thought, by judges, to be rather good horsemen, and, at any rate, spend the greater part of their life on horseback. All these people ride with short, and some with very short stirrups. The ratiocination of the matter is plain. They throw the lance, the lasso, or handle the sword, pistol, rifle or bow, seated in the saddle. For such an effort the muscular strength demanded of the arms and upper part of the body cannot be successfully put forth without the leverage, so to speak, of a firm foot pressure. Swing a man in the air by his waistband, and see how far he can send a projectile, and needing the foothold, the Camanche, like a sensible savage, takes it.[81]

But the cow-boy, standing in his long stirrups, also throws the lasso; and the seat of the Californian in the saddle was notoriously "long." As to the practicability of the Indian seat for the mountain-man, we have Kit Carson's own explanation to Colonel Meline:

All the Indians, hunters, and trappers, ride with short stirrups. I am almost bow-legged from it. And they are more important to the Indian than to the white man, as it is only by aid of the stirrup he can shift his position, hanging down on one side, so as to conceal all his body but his leg. . . . On this account, also, they hang the stirrups well forward on the saddle.

According to Oliver Wiggins, who was trained in the Carson company at Taos, the short stirrups, well forward, enabled the rider to pitch free, quickly, when his horse stumbled or was shot from under him.

Of Kit Carson the horseman:

I found, also, that he was a superior shot with his rifle and a remarkable rider, being familiar with many feats of horsemanship learned only among the Indians. Either he or I could with ease pick up a silver dollar from the ground, when going at full speed, mounted on the swiftest pony.[82]

And again of Carson:

He was reputed the most daring and reckless of riders. I had not mounted a horse for months and was still weak and reduced in flesh. But we flew over the rocks, through canyons and across ditches until my blood tingled to the finger-tips. Kit's special delight was to dash down steep hills at full gallop. This new experience made me shudder. But he was far heavier than I and his American horse nearly twice as tall as my little steed. Moreover Indian ponies rarely stumble, so the odds were largely in my favor. Our road was nearly all hills; and after three or four trials I began to enjoy it and to forget the Spanish proverb: "A running horse is an open sepulcher." On foot Carson looks stout and ungraceful. He avers that much riding with the short stirrups of the border has made him bow-legged; but he sits a horse splendidly and rides with rare grace and skill.[83]

This dashing picture of the mountain-man ahorse is subject to place and circumstance. Business-bent on the long trail he employed that ambling gait known variously as the fox-trot, the cow-pony trot, and, when turned into a pace, as the "rack." This latter seems to have been the favorite as it is the easiest and the most rapid. Western narratives of the early day frequently refer to the "trappers' rack."

. . . They encountered a band of a dozen mountaineers, mounted on fine horses, and well armed and equipped, travelling along without the usual accompaniment of a mulada of pack-animals, two or three mules alone being packed with meat and spare ammunition. This band was proceeding at a smart rate, the horses moving with the gait peculiar to American animals, known as "pacing" or "racking", in Indian file — each of the mountaineers with a long heavy rifle resting across the horn of his saddle.[84]

The saddles of the mountain-men were very simple. In the beginning the Indians themselves rode bareback, their bridle a thong looped about the horse's lower jaw; or they affected a skin or hide pad tied on, with or without loops sewed to it for the feet. As intercourse with the Mexicans spread, the use of the saddle, also, spread; and with the arrival of the trappers and traders from Missouri the saddle became quite the thing, although the pad still prevailed for handy service.

The mountain-men themselves did not overlook the advantages of the pads.

I put a pad on my Runner. These pads are made by filling two sacks with antelope hair. The sacks are generally made of buckskin, are seven or eight inches in diameter, and rest on each side of the horse's backbone, being sewed together on top with buckskin. Material is fastened to each side for stirrups and cinch. They would be a curiosity in the East, but are light and elastic, and a horse feels no inconvenience from them and can travel twenty miles farther in a day than under a saddle.[85]

The Indian-made saddle was merely a wooden skeleton, or tree, over which was laid a piece of buffalo-robe, or upon which a sheet of green raw-hide was stretched to stiffen and bind. These trees were manufactured without the slightest regard for the horses' backs, and not infrequently made ghastly sores. Although the side-pieces were somewhat rounded, the seat itself was almost straight between cantle and pommel, which were about eight inches high. The pommel terminated in a round knob (like the horn of today) to which hung a raw-hide loop as a support when the rider threw himself around to shoot under his horse's neck. The cantle was cut away or hollowed in the middle, as a resting-spot for the rider's heel when he was clinging sideways. The stirrup, if any, was of thin wood backed with raw-hide, and was, as before said, hung extremely short.[86]

The mountain-man's saddle, similarly made, would partake rather more of the "States" or the Mexican fashion. In Garrard's *Wah-to-yah and the Taos Trail* the mountain-men Hatcher and Louy rode (January, 1847)

a bare Mexican tree, without pad, cover, or other appendages, save a few long buckskin thongs, tied to the back part of the cantle, and a pair of huge, wooden stirrups, dangling directly under — not forward — the seat.

Garrard himself purchased of the Señorita Lefevre at Taos, for nine dollars, a great Chihuahua saddle, with carved stirrups, flat to accommodate the moccasin.

Oliver Wiggins says that Kit Carson and his men were better fitted than customary with saddles, by reason of Carson's service at saddle-making. And this should bring to mind the fact that in the ranks of the Western trappers, as in the ranks of a Volunteer army, were to be found men of every trade.

The wooden ox-bow stirrup of today, popular on the plains and in the mountains, was the stirrup of the mountain-man. It was somewhat smaller than the cow-boy stirrup or stock stirrup, for the mountain-man wished to be able to wedge his foot in it, and he rode in moccasins. Spurs were not favored. The Indians rarely used them; and the mountain-man was Indian enough to regard them as a superfluity and an incumbrance.[87]

Among the mountain-men there might be seen an occasional Spanish saddle, like that of Garrard's, out of Mexico or California by barter or by methods less exact: cumbrous trees, high of cantle and of horn, hidalgo in their ornamentations, their stirrups "oblong blocks of wood, four or five pounds weight, six inches in diameter one way, and three in the other, with holes in them through which to thrust the feet," as relates Farnham in his California travels. Later, the stirrups, made from bent wood highly carved, had the sweeping hood or tapadera covering the forward portion and protecting the toes.

With such a saddle, the trapper, as pleased as a child, might prance about at rendezvous, for all admiring eyes.

The fur hunter of the Northeast and the far North traveled the waterways. Daniel Boone, Simon Kenton and all were wonted to traverse their vast forest realm afoot. But the hunter, trader and trapper of the mountains and plains West found the Indians already equipped with horse animals and to be upon equal terms he must be similarly outfitted. And the distances to be covered, from the Missouri to the Salt Lake, not only were vast, they were prodigious.

So the *voyageur* and the *homme du nord* to his canoe, the backwoodsman to his legs, and the mountain-man to his horse and mule. Afoot he was badly crippled. Therefore, as in the later battles with the soldiery and with the emigrants, the first thought of the Indians when attacking was to stampede or to steal the mountain-man's saddle and pack animals; and the mountain-man retorted with the same tactics.

Chapter XI

The Mountain-Man — On the Beaver Trail

THE trapping of the beaver has lapsed to a minor art. His fur is no longer a vital factor in the commerce of a nation; no longer are his traits the basis for camp-fire fact and fiction, his circumvention the stake of hard life and ruder death. But there can scarcely be found a more striking evidence of the ordering of this universe, than he.

It seems as though just such a creation as the beaver were needed to toll men into the wilderness and send them hither and thither, opening a thousand trails. The very phase of the beaver's frequenting the streams made this work more thorough, for the streams are the readiest passes of the mountain West. The pursuit of the beaver provided the utmost variety of scenery and adventure: he was to be found upon the plains of the Missouri, the Platte and the Arkansas; upon the deserts of the Colorado, the Gila and the Humboldt; amid the valleys of the Green and the Snake, the Sacramento and the San Joachin; and higher and higher, amid the great mountains, even up to the 10,000 feet elevation. His range was far wider than that of the buffalo, the hunters who sought him outranged the prospector.

The beaver must be ranked, as a communal animal, with the bee. Of a superior grade of intelligence assisted by a very acute instinct, he was the worthy pawn upon the chess-board of fate. It required a like intelligence and instinct to capture him, so that the successful trapper was proud of his calling, the novice was eager to learn.

To this day the work of the beaver is a topic for debate; but whether instinct or conscious reasoning power directed the felling of the trees, the building of the dams, the family relations in the lodges, the mountain-man did not doubt. He *knew;* his mouth was full of anecdotes in substantiation. But—

To give them life and reality, they require all the surroundings of time, place and occasion; there should be the dark night; the wild, whistling wind; the shaking tent with its covering of skins; the roasted venison, bear's meat, or horse-flesh; the rifles standing in the corners; the lamp of bear's grease — in fine, all the similitude of camp life. Then the wild stories of bear fightings, beaver intelligence, Indian deviltry, and hair-breadth escapes, become intensely real.[88]

To the Indian, the beaver was the kin of man, living in the water instead of upon the earth. He was the wisest of animals. To the trapper he was ever a mystery: a creature whose family relations were perfectly codified, even to the extent of a salute's being required, by paw to eye, when a young beaver entered into the company of an old beaver. And when (as was claimed) the experienced beaver would deliberately spring a trap with a stick, or turn a trap upside down, for safety, the admiration of the grisled mountain-man reached the climax.

So, by ennobling the beaver, the mountain-man ennobled his pursuit and vested it with a peculiar fascination. Although his calling was pitiless, it did not have that brutality of the buffalo butcher who succeeded him. The buffalo, stupid, easily confounded, prodigal in his mass, lent naught to the finer feelings. His taking was a mechanical butchery, of little romance and variation, with the main appeal that of flesh.

Then, as a business proposition, the beaver pelts were a staple, the payment was attractive, and the exchange between trapper and trader was prompt. And thus the beaver peopled the unknown with the pioneers best fitted, through inducement of danger, travel, interest and profit, to follow him far.

The outfit of a trapper is generally a rifle, a pound of powder, and four pounds of lead, with a bullet mould, seven traps, an axe, a hatchet, a knife and awl, a camp kettle, two blankets, and, where supplies are plentiful, seven pounds of flour.[89]

This may be taken as the regulation outfit of the company or hired trapper. The awl was a prime necessity in fashioning moccasins and repairing camp and trail equipment generally, and in stretching skins. For the flour the average mountain-man would have substituted pistols. The free trapper "found" himself, and his outfit was governed by convenience and his means.

Oliver Wiggins stated that while a trapper might carry fifteen or twenty traps on his horse or mule, six were about the limit that he could carry while laying his trap line, afoot. J. S. Campion says that a catch of eight beaver was a day's skinning and stretching job.

The traps all were beaver traps — which, as desirable, could be applied to other animals of medium size. The mountain-man, however, made small account of side-issues. He was after beaver, always beaver. There were side-issues, nevertheless, such as mink, otter, martin, and so on. In Coyner's *Lost Trappers* we find the Ezekiel Williams party setting a beaver trap to catch a wolf. In doing likewise a Bonneville detachment under one Montero snagged a prowling Blackfoot Indian, who hobbled off through the snow with the trap still fast to him. And there were other surprises. In *Travels in Mexico,* Lieutenant Ruxton relates of "Rube" Valentine, old trapper, with a bear in his beaver set.

The Newhouse trap, long a standard make, from its beginnings seems to have been the favorite; although St. Louis evidently possessed a negro trap-maker whose goods, like the Hawkins rifle, were considered sterling.

His next visit was to a smith's store, which smith was black by trade and black by nature, for he was a nigger and, moreover, celebrated as being the best maker of beaver traps in St. Louis, and of him he purchased six new traps, paying for the same twenty dollars — procuring, at the same time, an old trap-sack, made of stout buffalo skin, in which to carry them.[90]

A good trap was customarily priced from \$12 to \$16 in St. Louis and at the trading posts. Such a trap had been carefully tempered. There was no economy in buying cheap, experimental traps. According to Wiggins the springs of inferior traps snapped into three and four pieces in the exceedingly cold water. Since spring breakage was always a liability, replacement springs (at \$2 each) were carried among the "possibles." The trap weighed five pounds; with its chain, eight pounds. Weight was necessary for service and in order to anchor the beaver and drown him. The open jaws formed a "set" six inches square.

The progress of a body of mountain-men through the country, while always in fashion alert, sometimes took on the discipline and aspects of a military column. This was particularly the case when the season was opening, and large companies were setting out, later to split into squads. The company would be laden with goods which the Indian coveted, and if from the settlements, would be burdened with greenhorns who must be taught to take care of themselves. And in such a case particularly it would be a miscellany of men as varied in habits as in experience; "the native of France, of Canada, of England, of Hudson Bay, of Connecticut, of Pennsylvania, of New York, of Kentucky, of Illinois, of Missouri, and of the Rocky Mountains, all congregated to act in unison for a specified purpose."[91]

One of the best descriptions of the semi-military progress, through the Indian country, of a trappers' company or brigade, is by the successful leader General Ashley himself, reëmbodied in a report, February, 1829, by Thomas H. Benton, chairman of the Senate Committee on Indian Affairs. The company, with two pack mules and a saddle horse to each man, was divided into messes (as in the Santa Fé Trail caravans), and there were several lieutenants. In fact, the discipline of caravan and of trappers' company were much alike. The camp was laid off, preferably protected by a river or wide stream, in a square, and a breastwork of packs and saddles was erected immediately. The animals were watered and put out to graze under a horse guard; at sunset each man brought in his horse, and picketed him inside the camp. Sentries were stationed. In the morning skirmishers searched the outlying country. Flankers, rear-guard and van-guard were thrown out during the march. "In this way I have marched parties of men the whole way from St. Louis to the vicinity of the Grand Lake, which is situated about one hundred and fifty miles down the waters of the Pacific Ocean, in 78 days."

As for the large party of the times following General Ashley's active supervision:

When the large camp is on the march, it has a leader, generally one of the Booshways [the mountain-man corruption of *Bourgeois,* borrowed from the Hudson's Bay Company title for the factor or resident trader and commander of the fur post], who rides in advance, or at the head of the column. Near him is a led mule, chosen for its qualities of speed and trustworthiness, on which are packed two small trunks that balance each other like panniers, and which contain the company's books, papers, and articles of agreement with the men. Then follow the pack animals, each one bearing three packs — one on each side, and one on top — so nicely adjusted as not to slip in traveling. These are in charge of certain men called camp-keepers, who have each three of these to look after. The trappers and hunters have two horses, or mules, one to ride, and one to pack their traps. If there are women and children, in the train, all are mounted. Where the country is safe, the caravan moves in single file, often stretching out for half or three-quarters of a mile. At the end of the column rides the second man, or "little Booshway", as the men call him, usually a hired officer, whose business it is to look after the order and condition of the whole camp.

The evening camp is pitched at the direction of the "Booshway," who halts at the spot, until the column has gathered around him. The animals are unpacked and their backs examined, and they are turned out under guard to graze, before being picketed for the night. The camp is that of messes, each mess with its own fire and its own cook. Guards for the night are posted. "At times . . . the officer of the guard gives the guard a challenge — 'all's well!' which is answered by 'all's well!' "

In the morning at daylight, or sometimes not till sunrise, according to the safe or dangerous locality, the second man comes forth from his lodge and cries in French, "leve, leve, leve, leve, leve!" fifteen or twenty times, which is the command to rise. In about five minutes more he cries out again in French, "leche lego, leche lego!" or "turn out, turn out"; at which command all come out from the lodges, and the horses are turned loose to feed; but not before a horseman has galloped all round the camp at some distance, and discovered everything to be safe in the neighborhood. Again, when the horses have been sufficiently fed, under the eye of a guard, they are driven up, the packs replaced, the train mounted, and once more it moves off, in the order before mentioned.[92]

The leaders of the organized forces usually went prepared

both to trap and to trade. In their own packs were the catchy and popular articles — "powder, half-ounce balls, flints, beads, paint, blue and scarlet cloths, blankets, calico, and knives," says "Uncle" Bill Hamilton in *My Sixty Years on the Plains*. The trading-goods pack was likely to be a veritable peddler's pack adapted to meet all demands whether by the Indians or by the trappers themselves — for profit was to be had in swapping with covetous trappers at large. "Tea, Sugar, Lead, Powder, Tobacco, Allspice, Pepper, etc.," and Coffee, all at $2 a pound; "coarse cloth" at $10 a yard, "fine cloth" at $20 a yard, are articles of trade mentioned by Zenas Leonard, fur trader and trapper, 1831-1836, in his *Narrative*. "For twenty or thirty loads of powder you can generally get from eight to twelve dollars worth of fur"; and "To get a beaver skin from these Indians [Diggers] worth eight or ten dollars, never cost more than an awl, a fish-hook, a knife, a string of beads, or something equally as trifling."

The Indians' principal medium of trade was buffalo robes, on the plains, beaver, martin and mink in the mountains. The buffalo were killed in enormous numbers; but —

In none of the plains tribes is there the slightest knowledge of traps and trapping. Their invention seems to have stopped short of even the simplest contrivance for catching game, either animals or birds. I have heard of their stealing the traps of a white trapper; but the first time a bungler gets his fingers caught in its jaws, the trap is thrown away as "bad medicine." These seem to be the only aboriginal people in the world who have not some pitfall, spring, or native trap.[93]

There was some knowledge of the snare and the dead-fall among the mountain and desert Indians. The beaver of course could be taken in winter, by spearing them or clubbing them through the ice, at the water-ways and in opened lodges. Of his march down the Humboldt or Mary's River, Nevada, in 1833, Zenas Leonard says:

At this hut we obtained a large robe composed of beaver skins fastened together, in exchange for two awls and one fish hook. This robe was worth from 30 to 40 dollars. We continued travelling down this river, now and then catching a few beaver. But, as we continued to extend our acquaintance with the natives, they began to practice their national failing of stealing. So eager were they to possess themselves of our traps, that we were forced to quit trapping in this vicinity.[94]

The sight of the trappers' effective instruments, and the knowledge of their employment, together with the sudden demand for furs, did start the Indians themselves upon the trap line. But the work was too slow for hunter and warrior spirit, so that —

The Indians of the United States — at least those of Wyoming, Colorado, Idaho and Montana — are very indifferent trappers. The half-breeds, on the contrary, are deadly enemies of the beaver tribe, for they combine the "cuteness of the white man and the dogged perseverance and primitive style of living of their mothers' race."[95]

The free trappers and the solitary trappers collected their furs by trapping until the time arrived to bring them into the rendezvous, or until they had so many that they should send them or carry them to post or town. This might be done by dispatching out a joint pack-train in charge of a few of their number, or by putting the bales in case of a regular caravan, or of a barge down the Missouri or Platte. At the end of the season lone trappers were constantly trailing into Taos or Bent's Fort or Fort Hall or Fort Laramie, with their season's catch.

Oliver Wiggins says that the skins of his company (which was a Kit Carson company) of 1840-1850 were consigned to one of the Robidoux (Robidou) brothers, of St. Joe, who bought them. They were taken in twice a year by a pack-train, or by barge, as happened; unless the Indians were too bad. This Joseph Robidoux whose trading-post of Blacksnake Hills forecasted St. Joseph, Missouri, was proprietor (according to the Wiggins' memory) of a steamboat which operated up and down the Missouri River in the interests of his post, and which often-times met the incoming furs. He had trade connections also with Montreal. Supplies for the Carson trappers of that period were sent out from St. Louis.

A trapping expedition arrived on the hunting grounds is divided into parties of four or five men, which separate for long intervals of time; and as the beaver is mostly in the country of hostile Indians, in and beyond the Rocky Mountains, it is an employment of much hazard, and the parties are under great pains for concealment.[96]

In an organized company, if the physical and Indian conditions of the country admitted, then the out-roaming trappers were expected to converge, at agreed intervals, upon the central camp, to bring in their furs and to report. Thus tab could be kept upon the catches and the fate of the men. But when the country was "bad," and the periodical reporting was not practicable, months or even a year might pass, and the annual rendezvous mark the first reunion. What anxieties were relieved, what fears were substantiated, what tales were told!

To cover the country, then, and because large camps soon exhausted the beaver and the game, the way of the mountain trapper was to divide and to sub-divide until in the height of the season trappers might be working in pairs. This was the smallest customary sub-division. To trap alone was perilous and inconvenient.

By the dictates of common sense and of self-preservation the trapper, at work, ascended the streams in preference to descending them. Doing this, he put himself in a position to meet any Indian sign which would be borne down by the current, and would avoid sending warning of himself, in advance. Furthermore, the beaver cuttings, floating to him, notified him of fur above; while the disturbance that he himself raised, in the water, passed on to ground which he had already covered.

The experienced trapper did not willingly waste his time in seeking the beaver in canyons and in other rapids, or along bare shores, or in the wide, deep rivers. The beaver was to be caught among the smooth, shallowed streams upon whose banks there grew plenty of soft-barked trees such as the willow, the aspen, the cottonwood, and the box-elder. According to Washington Irving:

Practice, says Captain Bonneville, has given such a quickness of eye to the experienced trapper in all that relates to his pursuit, that he can detect the slightest sign of beaver, however wild; and although the lodge may be concealed by close thickets and overhanging willows, he can generally, at a single glance, make an accurate guess at the number of its inmates. He now goes to work to set his trap; planting it upon the shores, in some chosen place, two or three inches below the surface of the water, and secures it by a chain to a pole set deep in the mud. A small twig is then stripped of its bark, and one end is dipped in the "medicine" as the trappers term the peculiar bait which they employ. This end of the stick rises about four inches above the surface of the water, the other end is planted between the jaws of the trap. The beaver, possessing an acute sense of smell, is soon attracted by the odor of the bait. As he raises his nose toward it, his foot is caught in the trap. In his fright he throws a somerset into the deep water. The trap, being fastened to the pole, resists all his efforts to drag it to the shore; the chain by which it is fastened defies his teeth; he struggles for a time, and at length sinks to the bottom and is drowned.

Upon rocky bottoms, where it is not possible to plant the pole, it is thrown into the stream. The beaver, when entrapped, often gets fastened by the chain to sunken logs or floating timber; if he gets to shore, he is entangled in the thickets of brook willows. In such cases, however, it costs the trapper diligent search, and sometimes a bout at swimming, before he finds his game.

As the rule, traps were set in the evening and run in the early morning. Attracted by cuttings or chips floating with the current, or by sign of lodge, pond or canal, the trapper established camp, and having concealed his animals or left them under a camp guard followed up on foot, carrying his traps. When he encountered a fresh beaver slide, a run or path leading out from the water, he sunk a trap at the water's edge. The depth of the set varied. When the trap was set shallow (as it usually was in the runs) it caught the beaver by a fore-foot as he lowered it to climb out. When the bait was planted as a lure, the trap was apt to be set deep, or about ten inches, to catch the beaver by a hind foot as he raised himself to smell.

When traps were set in the beaver channels, at the runs over the dams, or before lodge entrances, they were set ten to fifteen inches, to catch the large beaver, which swam deeper. To bring a beaver pup into camp was to invite ridicule, for pelt of baby beaver and of old she-beaver were practically worthless. But the pelt of the old she-beaver, light in color and coarse in texture, could be employed as material for trappers' hats.

The "medicine" or bait of the trapper had as basis the musky oil which, contained in two small glands in the animal's groin, gives a distinctive scent. It is "a yellow butter-like matter of a very peculiar odour." Some trappers used this alone; others used a recipe of their own,

and it is highly amusing to listen to the high-flown praise the gnarled old "stags" will bestow upon their own peculiar mixture, the receipt of which they treasure as the secret of their craft. A reliable pelt-hunter once told me that the Fur Company trapper, an old veteran, with whom, many years before, he passed his trapper apprenticeship, would not divulge the recipe of the compound he used until his dying day, notwithstanding that they lived and trapped together in the far-off wilderness of the Oregon and Montana forests for six long years. Finally, mortally wounded by an Indian arrow, he revealed, while lying on the ground gasping for breath, the grand secret of his life to his faithful partner.

Assafoetida, oil of aniseed, and other pungent essential oils, are not usually subjects to which hang romantic tales; but this story of life and death proved the contrary.

I was not a little amused when, on returning to civilization from my second trip, several old veteran trappers entrusted me, in whispered confidence, with certain never-to-be-revealed secrets, namely, the names of such drugs for their medicine they could not obtain in the frontier settlements, which they begged me to send them from Chicago or New York. . . . I am not transgressing my trust if I mention that they were of the most varied nature, some of the commonest being oil of aniseed, of amber, of cassia, of cloves, of fennel seed, of tyme, and oil of rhodium.[97]

This "medicine" was carried, jealously guarded, in a small horn bottle, with tight plug. Trapper Osborne Russell speaks of a wooden box for bait. But the tip of an antelope horn was favorite receptacle. In Coyner's *Lost Trappers* a pair of horn vials for two natural secretions are mentioned; the trapper "thrusts a small stick in both of the horns, about an inch deep in the matter," and plants the stick between the jaws of the trap. "A natural propensity prompts the beaver to seek the place whence the scent issues, and he is taken. In this respect the beaver resembles the dog."

If the trap were set near shore, it was placed at the full

length of the chain attached by ring and swivel to the pole driven into the stream bed; for if the caught beaver could drag the trap into a breathing space he would gnaw the imprisoned foot off. The pole itself had to be of dry wood, else the beaver, attacking his tether, would cut the pole in two at the chain and swim away with the trap; but a pole hard-dried made poor gnawing. There was a trick, also, in placing the bait as in placing the trap. If the bait stick were placed high, the beaver was caught by a hind foot as he erected; if low, then by one of his fore feet as he dropped them.[98]

On occasion a piece of wood for a buoy or "float" was hung to the trap, in order that the trap with the beaver in it might be located if towed into deep water. At least two-thirds of the taken beaver had been drowned. Those found still alive were dispatched by a blow upon the head from a club or the hatchet. The "float" entered largely into trapper speech, in expressions such as "That's how your stick floats, is it?" "Danged if I kin read yore float," and, referring to a greenhorn, "I'll gamble on it 'tain't been a month sence he left his mammy's float-sticks."

Mud should be daubed upon the raw top of a freshly cut stake, to weather it; else the beaver would shy clear of the suspicious sign. The trapper who, entering or leaving the water, left a trail, on the shore or bank, that a beaver might cross, splashed water upon it to wash away the human scent. He took care to wash anything that he touched in course of trap setting. The pursuit of the beaver was invested with the ritual and traditions of a guild. There were "musts" and "must-nots"; for to be "up to beaver" one had to avoid putting the beaver "up to trap."

The trap was carried out open, ready to be placed. The trapper must remember

that the farther the place where you leave the bank to enter the river is from where your trap is to be left, the better; for should a beaver get a sniff suggesting human presence on the bank, he will keep to the middle of the stream for a considerable distance, and no "medicine" will allure him to its edge.

When rinsing his bait stick in the water and inserting the shredded end in the medicine bottle he must face the wind, else the odor of him may be blown against the stick.

But if you have inadvertently allowed a single drop of water to trickle off your hand into your medicine bottle, throw it away — you will never catch a beaver with the medicine in it again. On this point I speak not only from my own experience, but on the authority of old white-headed professional trappers who have trapped for a living ever since they were old enough to do so.

Furthermore, never, if that can be avoided, allow a beaver to get free.

How beavers can communicate with each other I, of course, do not know, but that they can, no trapper doubts; certainly if a beaver gets away in any pool from a trap, it is not worth while to waste time by setting any more in it that season.[99]

The trapper while at work was constantly wet by wading and by plunging his arms into the water. In the spring — and throughout all the season in the mountain altitudes — the water was icy cold. By the alternate soaking and drying his limbs and feet grew tender and "rheumaticky." Unless they had been exceptionally well smoked the buckskin moccasins shrank in drying; and when reduced to the one pair the trapper, at ease in his lodge or under his blanket must suddenly bolt for the water and soak his gear again to relieve his badly pinched toes. Buckskin trousers were subject to the same distortion. Therefore:

In the spring, when the camp breaks up, the skins which have been used all winter for lodges are cut up to make moccasins; because from their having been thoroughly smoked by the lodge fires they do not shrink in wetting, like raw skins. . . . For the same reason [the wading], when spring comes, the trapper is forced to cut off the lower half of his buckskin breeches, and piece them down with blanket leggins, which he wears all through the trapping season.[100]

It was the custom to skin the captured beaver on the spot, and take only the pelt, the "medicine" glands and the tail to camp. The trappers' central camp in a busy season was designated by

the hundreds of beaver skins, now drying in the sun. These valuable skins are always stretched in willow hoops, varying from eighteen inches to three feet in diameter, according to the size of the skins, and have a reddish appearance on the flesh side, which is exposed to the sun. Our camps are always dotted with these red circles, in the trapping season, when the weather is fair. There were several hundred skins folded and tied up in packs, laying about their encampment, which bore good evidence to the industry of the trappers.[101]

For at camp the work of "fleshing" or "graining" and curing was done. This "graining" was accomplished best by laying the pelt, inside up, over the official graining block, which was a smoothed stump or a log with rounded, smoothed butt inclined upward, and by scraping the flesh and membranous substance from it. Care had to be used not to scrape into the hair roots. The grained skin was stretched, by thongs along the edges, upon the hoops, and dry-cured in the sunshine. In some case the skins were grained upon the stretchers and the graining blocks were used mainly in the preparation of deerskins. When dry the beaver-skin "is folded into a square sheet, the fur turned inwards, and the bundle, containing about ten to twenty skins, tightly pressed and corded, and is ready for transportation."[102]

In a large camp this work of preparing the skins was assigned to camp-tenders (one-third camp-tenders, two-thirds trappers, was the Bonneville formula); or, in friendly country as among the Utes, the Nez Percés, Snakes, Flatheads, squaws gladly did the work for the flesh of the carcasses or for a pinch of sugar. Unless they were equipped with a squaw or two, isolated trappers and independent trappers had to prepare their pelts with their own hands each day, after the trap line had been run, for delivery at rendezvous, trading post or settlement.

The skins of the fur companies and the traders were branded by a small mark stamped or cut into the inside of the neck. The independent or free trappers did not mark their skins, but each man in the camp kept his catch as a unit. An outside pelt of a bale, or the bale hide wrapper, generally was marked with the trapper's private sign. The bales of Ezekiel Williams of *Lost Trappers* fame were marked E. W. on the outside.

An average skin when cured weighed about a pound and a quarter. Eighty beaver pelts, compactly wrapped and, or, tied with hide thongs, composed the regulation bale for pack trains and weighed about 100 pounds. The best skins were placed in the middle of the bale. The number of skins in a bale varied, however, and fifty-skin bales were not unusual. The finest pelts were the northern pelts, of course; the beaver fur of the southwest country and of valley California was inferior. Cold weather was necessary to make the fur prime, and therefore the spring catch produced the higher quality of fur.

Beaver and otter trapped in April and May are classed A1. I have sold to expert fur buyers furs trapped in June, and these same buyers credited themselves with being able to tell, by the appearance of the fur, in just what month in the year the furs were trapped.[103]

Skins sold to the traders at four, five and six dollars a pound. The best squaw-dressed skins were not only dried, they were softened by rubbing, were smoked in huts of green boughs and rubbed again. Such skins brought $8 and upward, each. The fur market prices were subject to English advices through Montreal and St. Louis.

The Hudson's Bay Company purchased skins by the *plus* or pelt, offering so much regardless of weight. "Plew," the mountain-man's rendering of the French-Canadian *plus* for *pelu*, hair, speedily became the trapper's standard medium of exchange, a unit of value like the dollar and representing six dollars, which was accepted as the value of the average beaver skin. When he said "I'll bet you a plew" or "It's worth four plew" or "It cost me four plew" he was speaking in terms of currency.

The beaver fur was exported in large quantities for the manufacture of hats. So universal was this use at home and abroad that a hat was known as a "castor"; and we read, in old narratives, of somebody "shying his castor into the ring," or "removing his castor."

The "medicine" secretion of the beaver was preserved, along with the fur, as an article of trade, and was styled "castorum" (castoreum). It brought about $3 a pound; was used in medical practice and, later, as a perfume base.

The beaver trapper and the fur trader dealt also in otter, mink and martin, and buffalo robes. The mink and the martin were obtained from the Indians, by trade, or were taken accidentally or incidentally in the traps; but the otter was sought for in course of the pursuit of the beaver. The best market for it was found among the Indians themselves, who invested the skins with "medicine" power. Several of the tribes, such as the Arapahos and Utes, wrapped their braids in otter skin. Eighty otter skins formed a bale, but commanded only about $3 a skin from the traders.

The long tail of the otter made the pelt particularly attractive to the Indian. All the long-bodied fur animals like the martin, otter, mink and weasel were highly esteemed by the Indian. The martin skin, "cased" or removed entire, was valued for quivers. W. H. Hamilton, in *My Sixty Years on the Plains,* states that the martin skin weighs about two ounces and in his time (1842) was worth about $6. "The average pack weighs one hundred and fifty pounds, which, if packed with martin, would mean in value $7,200." The Indians of the Pacific northwest were adepts at taking the martin.[104]

As for the buffalo robe, this was solely an Indian product, for only the squaw would spend the time required to dress down a hide by laborious chipping with a bone flesher. In beaver days a well dressed robe was priced at $5. Ten robes formed a bale weighing eighty pounds.

In changing camp, and upon the march, when the packs grew cumbersome they must be cached or hidden, later to be "lifted" for post or rendezvous. The same disposal was made of the extra supplies, to avoid lugging them about the country. The pack cache (from the French *cacher,* to conceal) was apt to be necessary after the winter camp, in order to lighten the march and the spring hunt.

The manner of digging these holes is upon a high, dry bank, where they sink a round hole like a well, five or six feet, and then dig a chamber under ground, where the merchandise is deposited — after which the well part of it is filled up, and the top covered with the natural sod, and all the overplus earth is carefully scraped up and thrown into the river, or creek, so that nothing is left on the premises to lead to the discovery of the hidden treasure.[105]

The chamber of the cache was lined with dry sticks, grass and blankets. When more convenient, the cache was located under an over-hanging bank or in a natural cave, and the entrance securely closed from sight. By the caving-in of a bank cache the "Frenchman" called Ponto was killed, 1830; whereupon, in the words of Joe Meek, he was "rolled in a blanket and pitched into the river."

The active trapping seasons for beaver were two, the fall and the spring. The fall season may be said to have extended from early September on to the time when the streams were frozen and the valleys were snowed in; the spring season extended from the opening of the streams to the last of May or slightly later. Much depended upon the altitude in which the beaver were hunted, and the climatic conditions encountered. Clerk Ferris records in his *Diary:* "We reached camp in the afternoon [June 3], and ascertained that nothing worthy of recollection, had occurred since I left it. The trappers were all in camp, having ceased to trap, and the spring's hunt was considered over."

On a new trap-line in virgin territory a beaver might be found in every trap; but this did not long continue, and three beaver out of five traps was a gratifying bag. In a few rounds of the traps the majority of the beaver in a colony or stream vicinity had been caught; the remainder had been educated or made "up to trap." When the trapper found his cleverest set sprung (as he alleged) with a stick, or dragged ashore, stake and all and contemptuously covered with mud, he concluded that these beaver were "up to trap" and that he himself was not "up to beaver" in this kind of a bout. Whereupon the squad struck camp and moved on — following up the main stream or else crossing over the next little divide to ascend another tributary. It was the policy to use the main stream as a base line and to trap each side stream to its source.

The depleted territory eventually filled up again from the few beaver left' behind. The beaver produces three or four kittens at a birth. A pair of beaver will multiply industriously, and, says Baillie-Grohman in *Camps in the Rockies,* if unmolested will repopulate a whole mountain stream in a decade.

Faulty as they were in their clean-ups, the mountain-men nevertheless worked destruction. Oliver Wiggins declared that in one season, on the Wisdom River, tributary to the Madison Fork of the Missouri in Montana, he and his company of Kit Carson trappers caught over 2,000 beaver.

Then, with the cowing of the Indian, the trapper, half-breed or white, was free to work unhurried.

I well remember a cluster of small lakes in the Wind River Mountains that presented a woeful picture of desolation. Half-breed trappers had discovered the very secluded dams the previous season, and had made an enormous bag, trapping right from one camp 173 beaver, the inmates of the tarns, which had probably never before been visited by human beings. Traversing the vast and very nearly impenetrable tracts of forest that surrounded the lakelets, I happened to stumble upon unmistakable signs of human travel through the woods. . . . It was the *beau ideal* of a trapper's camp; a small clearing made by their axes was still dotted with skeleton remains of "wickey-ups" bower tents — I might describe them — and strewn about in great number lay birch or willow saplings bent into rings about two feet in diameter, whereupon the beaver skins had been stretched while drying. The half-breed trappers, whom I happened to meet some weeks afterwards, had worked like vandals. Not only was there not a single beaver left, but several of the large dams dividing the lakelets from each other had been ruthlessly torn down by them in their efforts to recover lost traps. . . . Not a sound was to be heard, nor was a solitary living thing visible; and so profound was the death-gloom that hung over the spot, that even the roaring fire that I presently lit, in front of which I stretched myself on my saddle-blankets, failed to chase away the melancholy mood of Nature and man.[106]

Chapter XII

The Mountain-Man — At Camp and Rendezvous

THE beaver-trapper's camp was an affair adapted to the needs of the season and of the outfit. Oliver Wiggins stated that during the active season his Kit Carson company did not take the trouble to erect shelters but slept in their buffalo robes under the spruces, the boughs of which, extending low above the ground, formed (as woodsmen know) dry and fragrant cover. In hostile Indian country a pen or small fort of poles and saplings might be thrown up as a hasty corral for men and beasts.

While the buffalo robe was the popular article of bedding, blankets was much used as being less cumbersome to pack. A great deal of the woolen fabrics brought out to the mountains by the trading caravans was imported. For warmth and durability the British woolen stuffs were far superior to the American and were so recognized by the Indian; and the trapper in American service would go to considerable trouble to procure a Hudson's Bay blanket or blanket-coat or piece of British strouding; would pay, for the blanket, $20.

The Hudson's Bay blanket was a heap better article, twice as good. They charged us over there [east of the mountains] ten dollars a yard for scarlet to make leggins, what we call leggins [wrappings or trouser end-lengths for wading] and here [the Oregon side] we would give them thirty-two shillings. Well, this scarlet would last ten or twelve years, and the other would just go to pieces.[107]

Hamilton in *My Sixty Years on the Plains* states that his party of 1842 used wall-tents as well as hide lodges for shelter. The cabin of the roughest description, of lodge-pine and aspen poles, thatched with grass and boughs, is mentioned in mountain-man narratives of a semi-permanent camp. But the most favored shelter of the mountain-man was the Indian lodge of several buffalo-hides stitched together and erected, upon poles, in a cone shape. It was native to the country, was wind and weather proof, readily taken down and readily set up again, and of a practicability in heating and ventilation which recommended its descendant the Sibley army tent.

The trapper with a wife was particularly partial to the lodge, for putting it up and taking it down was squaw work. The lodges were "sized" by the number of hides used, as five-skin lodges, ten-skin lodges, etc. A ten-skin lodge would measure about fifteen feet in diameter at the bottom and fifteen feet in height at the peak. The ordinary trapper traveling lodge, to accommodate two trappers, or trapper and squaw, was erected of five or six tanned hides, over four or five poles. The Indian lodges were frequently of hides whitened as well as tanned, and either as plain or pictured were habitations with much grace. Captain Howard Stansbury speaks of the lodge of a Sioux chief which was called "The Trader's Lodge." It was formed of "twenty-six buffalo-hides, perfectly new, and white as snow, which being sewed together without a wrinkle, were stretched over twenty-four new poles, and formed a conical tent, of thirty feet diameter upon the ground, and thirty-five feet in height."[108]

When on the march, and camp was to be established, the word was given, and

soon careless groups were loitering on the ground in various positions; others trying to excel one another in shooting; some engaged in mending their clothes or moccasins; here one fondling a favorite horse, there another, galloping, in wild delight, over the prairie; a large band of horses quietly feeding about camp; large kettles supported over fires by "trois-pieds" [three feet], and graced to overflowing with the best of meat; saddles and baggage scattered about; and, to finish the description, fifty uncovered guns leaning against the fort or pen, ready for use, at any moment.[109]

When the stay is to be of some duration, or when the camp is central, the graining block is set up, the stretching frames, four feet square, for the "dubbing" or scraping of deer-skins, are laid out, meat is hung in the trees or upon scaffolds out of reach of prowling beasts; around the fires at night the mountain-men, "whilst cleaning their rifles, making or mending moccasins, or running bullets, spin long tales of their hunting exploits, etc."

Such a camp indeed was home; and as a sanctuary it appealed to Joe Meek, forlorn in the hands of the Crows.

> Soon we came to the top of the hill, which overlooked the Yellowstone, from which I could see the plains below extending as far as the eye could reach, and about three miles off, the camp of my friends. . . . I thought the camp a splendid sight that evening. It made a powerful show to me, who did not expect ever to see it after that day. And it *war* a fine sight anyhow, from the hill whar I stood. About two hundred and fifty men, and women, and children in great numbers, and about a thousand horses and mules. Then the beautiful plain, and the sinking sun; and the herds of buffalo that could not be numbered; and the cedar hills, covered with elk — I never saw so fine a sight as all that looked to me then![110]

So much for the prosperous camp in the mountains when nature and apparently the natives were complacent. And there was the winter season camp. To quote from the *Diary* of Clerk Ferris of the American Fur Company:

> Our camp presented eight leathern lodges, and two constructed of poles covered with cane grass, which grows in dense patches to the height of eight or ten feet, along the river. They were all completely sheltered from the wind by the surrounding trees. Within, the bottoms were covered with reeds, upon which our blankets and robes were spread, leaving a small place in the center for the fire. Our baggage was placed at the bottom of the lodge, on the inside, to exclude the cold from beneath it, and each one of the inmates had his own particular place assigned to him. One who has never lived in a lodge would scarcely think it possible for seven or eight persons to pass a long winter agreeably, in a circular room, ten feet in diameter, having a considerable portion of it occupied by the fire in the center; but could they see us seated around the fire, cross-legged like Turks, upon our beds, each one occupied in cleaning guns, repairing moccasins, smoking, and lolling at ease on our elbows, without interfering with each other, they would exclaim, indeed they are as comfortable as they could wish to be! which is the case in reality. I moved from a lodge into a comfortable log house, but again returned to the lodge, which I found much more pleasant than the other. These convenient and portable dwellings are partially transparent, and when closed at the wings above, which answer the double purpose of windows and chimneys, will admit sufficient light to read the smallest print without

inconvenience. At night a good fire of dry aspen wood which burns clear without smoke, affording a brilliant light, obviates the necessity of using candles. Our little village numbers twenty-two men, nine women and twenty children; and a different language is spoken in every lodge, the women being of different nations, and the children invariably learn their mother's tongue before any other.

In a company somewhat numerous there were always a few jealously guarded books. Joe Meek in the winter of 1830-31 learned to read from a trapper named Green "and soon acquired sufficient knowledge to enjoy an old copy of Shakespeare, which, with a Bible, was carried about with the property of the camp." "Uncle Bill" Hamilton also read Shakespeare, and an Ancient and Modern history, while on the beaver trail. "Byron, Shakespeare and Scott's works, the Bible and Clark's Commentary on it, and other small works on geology, chemistry and philosophy" helped to shorten a winter camp of trapper Osborne Russell and three comrades.[111]

When the camp was pitched among the friendly Indians they added to the conveniences and to the attractions. Meat might be more easily obtained; and there would be horse and foot races, wrestling, and other athletic contests between the two peoples, and target shooting.

Cards were a popular entertainment, with the time-honored game of seven-up or "old sledge" as the leader. "Hand," the Indian game of "pass the button," also was the vogue, particularly in the mixed camps. This consists in one side's guessing in what hand of the other side some object — a small bone, a splinter — is concealed. On occasion the whites and the reds vied in this singularly simple yet intense game, the interest in which was heightened by rhymic singing and beating upon dried reeds or upon the ground; the contestants "working themselves up into such a heat, that the perspiration rolls down their naked shoulders, even in the cold of a winter night." Captain Bonneville had to interfere and order his men out, that they might resume their day's duties after a night's bout at "hand."[112]

The two winter feast-days of Christmas and New Year were observed when it was possible to do so. New Year's Day rarely passed without remark. Even the travel-worn squads of Wilson Price Hunt and Robert Stuart, hastening forth and back upon the Astorian enterprise, 1811-1813, must halt and observe the New Year — the Stuart little company treating themselves, January 1, 1813, to "an old tobacco pouch, still redolent with the potent herb, and smoked it in honor of the day." And in his *Narrative* Zenas Leonard records, of the winter 1831-32:

> On news-years day, notwithstanding our horses were nearly all dead, as being fully satisfied that the few that were yet living must die soon, we concluded to have a feast in our best style; for which purpose we made preparation by sending out four of our best hunters, to get a choice piece of meat for the occasion. These men killed ten buffalo, from which they selected one of the fattest humps they could find and brought in, and after roasting it handsomely before the fire, we all seated ourselves upon the ground, encircling what we there called a splendid repast to dine on. Feasting sumptuously, cracking a few jokes, taking a few rounds with our rifles, and wishing heartily for some liquor, having none at that place, we spent the day.[113]

All in all, with hunters coming and going, with the shout, the song, the ring of hatchet, the curling smokes from the fires, the kettles perpetually on the blaze, the herds of horses, the women and the children, the gay blanketing of Indians and free trappers, the semi-martial, semi-woodsmen atmosphere, a prosperous winter camp in the midst of the wild, snowy hills was an inspiring scene.

Of lesser scale was the camp of three or four trappers, or of the lone trapper; couchant in some sheltered nook secure from the wind, and from the hostile bands of savages who, however, were inclined to keep to their own firesides while the ground was white. Here, in a kind of lethargy, hibernating like the bear, the hardy mountain-men, surrounded by meat and fuel, awaited the spring sun and the spring breezes, and the opening of travel and the beaver streams.

This is the bright side of winter life, but the mountain trapper's life was a constant alternation of the light and the dark.

There were winters of cold such that even the brute vitality of the men, women and animals exposed to it could scarcely endure. The winter of 1832-33 was one, and the winter of 1844-45 was another. Of the latter, Oliver Wiggins, who with a company of other mountain-men spent it in camp at "Eagle's Nest," among some cottonwoods at the mouth of the Cache la Poudre near the foothills of north central Colorado, says that out of his experiences of twenty years as a trapper it was the worst.

Of the winter of 1832-33 Joe Meek relates:

> The frost used to hang from the roofs of our lodges in the morning, on first waking, in skeins two feet long, and our blankets and whiskers were white with it. But we trappers laid still, and called the camp-keepers to make a fire, and in our close lodges it war soon warm enough.
>
> The Indians suffered very much. Fuel war scarce on the Snake River, and but little fire could be afforded — just sufficient for the children and their mothers to get warm by, for the fire war fed only with buffalo fat torn in strips, which blazed up quickly and did not last long. Many a time have I stood off, looking at the fire, but not venturing to approach, when a chief would say, "Are you cold, my friend? Come to the fire"— so kind are these Nez Percés and Flatheads.[114]

The questions before the mountain-man in winter camp were fuel, meat and forage. These questions were settled by the one answer: cottonwood. That sturdy tree, true pioneer, and as much a unit of the Western wilderness as was the buffalo, cheered the camp of caravan, trapper and emigrant and should be adopted as a symbol of the long trail across plains and pass. Wherever the cotton appeared upon the horizon, there was to be expected shelter, wood and water. Moreover, when the cottonwood commenced to bud out, spring had surely come.

The cottonwood fed the trapper's fire, and his stock, and, indirectly, himself. The buffalo frequented, in winter, the cottonwood groves, for the shelter and the browsing upon the bark and twigs. The bark and smaller twigs supplied fodder for the horses and mules also. The boughs were cut by trappers and Indians into sticks and chunks about three feet long, and the bark was scraped off by knives. This bark the horses and mules would munch greedily.

> The moment they saw their owners approaching them with blankets filled with cotton-wood bark, their whole demeanor underwent a change. A universal neighing and capering took place; they would rush forward, smell to the blankets, paw the earth, snort, whinney and prance round with head and tail erect, until the blankets were opened, and the welcome provender spread before them.[115]

Indeed, the animals soon learned to gnaw the pieces, for themselves, as if they were gnawing great ears of corn. The place of a winter camp of whites or Indians was denoted, for some time thereafter, by the bone-white, bone-bare, bone-dry cottonwood stakes scattered about, gleaming like the fragments of skeletons.

The trappers and the Indians recognized two varieties of the cottonwood — the sweet and the bitter. The first was suitable for fodder, the second was unpalatable and poisonous. The Zenas Leonard party under Captain A. K. Stephens, in the fall of 1831, being green to the ways of a country where it was mainly the experts and the fools who thrived, went into winter camp in a bountiful grove of cottonwoods by the Laramie River, and there prepared for winter by hanging up a great quantity of meat. On the first of December they started in to feed the cottonwood bark to their animals.

> But to our utter surprise and discomfiture on presenting it to them they would not eat it, and upon examining it by tasting, we found it to be the bitter cottonwood instead of the sweet cottonwood. Immediately upon finding we were deceived, men were dispatched up and down the valley, in search of Sweet Cottonwood, but returned without success.[116]

So necessary was the cottonwood to the animal life of the West that in time of winter stress the buffalo, wild with famine, would crowd into the groves and thickets, fighting with the domestic brutes for the bark, twigs, and the veriest trash; and the camp had to repel them with shout and shot. When the cottonwood failed the willow was used as emergency rations. When the willow also failed and the lines of winter ever tightened, the men and women must stand idly by and let their weakened horses and mules, unable to paw deep enough to get at any grass, and unable to fight a way out to a grazing ground, perish miserably by cold and hunger.

The winter quarters broke up usually by the first of April. The gaining spring sun and the occasional warm breeze were clearing the snow from the hill-slopes, the tips of pine and spruce were greening, the cottonwood buds were swelling. The final repairs to moccasins, clothing and arms would be hastened, a large batch of bullets would be run, traps would be overhauled, and eager for new scenes, with the men perhaps fat and hearty, the animals gaunt and shaggy, horses' tails gnawed short by the mules, the camp, dispersing in several directions, would gladly set forth upon the beaver-hunt again; gladly, but cautiously, for the Blackfeet and Sioux also had been biding this time when the first fresh grass showed itself.

There now were only three months until the rendezvous — that gay, bustling great summer camp or market, the gathering place for the wild and the free. This feature of mountain life dated from the summer of 1824, when trapping bands of Major Andrew Henry, partner of General Ashley, met at an appointed spot in the open. Heretofore, by the custom of the Missouri Fur Company and the Hudson's Bay Company trappers had been sent out each season from the fur posts, and the fur posts were made the rallying points. But Major Henry instituted an innovation, promptly adopted in 1825 by General Ashley; and the rendezvous in the heart of the fur country proved so flexible, and so satisfactory as to results, that until the decadence of the fur hunt it remained a popular fixture. It drew whites and Indians alike.

The spring fur hunt ceased about the first of June. Then there began a wide movement of trapping parties converging to a common center — to Pierre's Hole, to the Bear River Valley, to the Powder River Valley, or to that rendezvous most famous of all, the Valley of the Green.

At the same time there came on, hastening from St. Louis, Taos, Santa Fé, the pack-trains of partisans and free traders, conveying supplies for the various outfits and goods for the trapper and Indian customers.

As a general thing, by the first week in July the rendezvous was in full force. All along the valley streams were stationed the lodges and brush lean-tos of the influx. Here were the friendly Indians — Nez Percés, Pend d'Oreilles, Flatheads, Utes, Snakes, Arapahos, bringing their furs, robes and skins, eager to swap them for liquor, powder, lead, flints, arms, blankets, and trinkets. Here were the trappers, French, American, what-not, with their own peltries, "lifted" from their caches and piled high upon pack-animals. Squaws and children were working, playing, staring, and clustering at the traders' quarters denoted by piled up bales and boxes or a log "store." The gathering amounted to anywhere from 100 to 1,500 persons.[117]

In the beginning, separate fur companies held rendezvous independently and at separate places. But very soon, or as early as 1830, the one rendezvous answered for all, and the various outfits were encamped either cheek by jowl or else within a radius of a few miles. The trader first upon the ground reaped the harvest, disposing of goods to the whole assemblage; for after the twelve-months of privation the trappers, like the Indians, were illy disposed to resist the alluring sight of those articles among which even the necessities were luxuries.

These succoring companies are always looked for with great anxiety by the people who have been in the mountains any length of time. Many are at times entirely destitute of such articles as would be of great advantage to their comfort — many expect letters or some other manifestations of remembrance from their friends — besides some, who have been strictly temperate (because they could not help it, as the supply of liquor will always be exhausted) look forward with longing anticipations for the supply which is always sent to this country by the owners of these companies; for the purpose of selling it to the men and thus paying their wages.[118]

The rendezvous encampment, in the depths of the Rockies, amid the green underneath the blue and surrounded by the

Rendezvous

snowy ranges, flashed with life and color. It was a bazar of the Far West rivaling any bazar of the Far East.

We reached the camping place. What first struck our eye was several long rows of Indian tents (lodges), extending along the Green River for at least a mile. Indians and whites were mingled here in varied groups. . . . In manners and customs, the trappers have borrowed much from the Indians. Many of them, too, have taken Indian women as wives. Their dress is generally of leather. The hair of the head is usually allowed to grow long. . . . With their hairy bank notes, the beaver skins, they can obtain all the luxuries of the mountains, and live for a few days like lords. . . . The Indians had for the trade chiefly tanned skins, moccasins, thongs of buffalo leather or braided buffalo hair, and fresh or dried buffalo meat. They have no beaver skins. The articles that attracted them most in exchange were powder and lead, knives, tobacco, cinnabar, gaily colored kerchiefs, pocket mirrors and all sorts of ornaments. . . . The peltry bought from the Indians must be carefully beaten and aired, at peril of having objectionable troops billeted upon you.[119]

Here at rendezvous there met and hobnobbed, at one time or another, men of western note either permanent or transient, but men celebrated for deeds and skill where deeds and skill were a daily routine; confabbing, bargaining, buying, selling, swaggering, sporting, eating, drinking, vaunting, while riders galloped headlong hither and thither, robed chief and painted warrior stalked across the sod or posed at their lodge entrance, heralds invited to a feast, squaws screeched, dusky children stared and rollicked, dogs yapped, horses whinneyed, mules brayed, lusty oath and badinage challenged Homeric laughter, and the inevitable fires smoked and crackled under the inevitable pots. On a par with the later cattle round-ups of the plains, the fur round-ups were the welcome to the mountains for the overland missionaries, the greenhorn initiate like Nathaniel Wyeth, and the health-seeker like Dr. Benjamin Harrison II, son of General William Henry Harrison, in 1833.

When the opening reunions had been celebrated, the first tales recited, the preliminary reconnoitering of stranger and new-made friend finished, and the alcohol had circulated, the rendezvous changed in aspects. From inaugural contests in shooting, racing, wrestling, the rank and file turned to sterner business and madcap pranks. At euchre, old sledge, monte and hand, possessions were staked to the last beaver skin, the last animal, the last article of "possibles," and the last squaw. As would be usual wherever men in from the beaver trail, like men in from the range, the long drive, or the diggin's, met off-duty, to uncork at last, "bets were freely made upon everything involving the least doubt — sometimes to the amount of five hundred or a thousand dollars — the stakes consisting of beaver, horses, traps, etc."

Not infrequently the proceeds of months of toil, suffering, deprivation, and danger, were dissipated in a few hours, and the unfortunate gamester left without beaver, horse, trap, or even gun. In such cases they bore their reverses without grumbling, and relinquished all to the winner, as unconcernedly as though these were affairs of every-day occurrence.[120]

The liquor, which was accounted the most valuable asset of the traders, was packed in as refined spirits, in small flat casks which rode easier upon horse or mule. Mixed with water it was the trappers' and the Indians' "whisky" — and a very little, particularly in the case of men who for ten months had been deprived of such stimulant, had a very prompt effect, left a very pronounced thirst for more, and was prolific of bad temper following good.

When inflamed by this fiery beverage, they [the trappers] cut all kinds of mad pranks and gambols, and sometimes burn all their clothes in their drunken bravadoes. A camp, recovering from one of these riotous revels, presents a semi-comic spectacle; black eyes, broken heads, lacklustre visages. Many of the trappers have squandered in one drunken frolic the hard-earned wages of a year; some have run in debt, and must toil on to pay for past pleasure.[121]

The debt account of Johnson Gardner of Gardner's Hole for his rendezvous of 1832 shows an expenditure of $95 out of $346, during ten days, for liquor.

Captain Bonneville bid for trade favors with a decoction of honey and alcohol, half and half — "a happy compound, of strength and sweetness, enough to sooth the most ruffled temper, and unsettle the most solid understanding," which "worked like a charm" by effectually laying out the imbiber.

The Reverend Samuel Parker, 1835, discovered a "day of indulgence" on the march and at rendezvous, when by general agreement the men "drink ardent spirits as much as they please, and conduct themselves as they choose." Clerk Ferris refers to the same custom, in the big winter camp of 1831-1832; at the close of the revel the alcohol casks were bunged again and stowed away.

The price of alcohol in the mountains, at rendezvous or elsewhere, was $1 a gill, or $4 a pint. A blanket was $12; a butcher knife, $2; an axe, $6; powder $4 and $5 a pound or a pint; coffee $5 and $7 a pint; tobacco $2.50 and $3 a plug; sugar $4 and $6 a pint. The prices at the Green River Valley rendezvous of 1838 were: whisky, $3 a pint; powder, $6 a pint; tobacco, $5 a pound; dogs for food, $15 each; *all in trade.*[122]

This last stipulation is to be noted. Cash was a vain commodity in the mountains. The beaver was the standard of value, among the whites, as the horse was, among the reds; and barter by trade was the system in vogue. When it is recalled that beaver averaged say six dollars a skin, that the transportation of goods to the mountains increased their spot-cost, St. Louis, by 400%, and that (according to Nathaniel Wyeth) to recompense him for his trouble, and his perils, the trader counted upon getting a price 600% above this, it may be readily imagined that a trapper's wage account of $250, for instance, was soon wiped out; that the purchasing power of a bale of furs, when applied to munitions and other necessities for a twelve-month future, and luxuries for a short but brimming present, was scandalously cheap — especially when, as Joe Meek claimed, "a thousand dollars a day was not too much for some of the most reckless to spend on their squaws, horses, alcohol, and themselves."

An old trapper, a French-Canadian, assured me that he had received fifteen thousand dollars for beaver during a sojourn of twenty years in the mountains. Every year he resolved in his mind to return to Canada, and, with this object, always converted his fur into cash; but a fortnight at the "rendezvous" always cleaned him out, and, at the end of twenty years, he had not even credit sufficient to buy a pound of powder.[123]

These high lights of the rendezvous are likely to be over emphasized. The rendezvous was founded upon business. It was designed as a clearing house where the fur companies collected their furs and outfitted their hunters for another season. Men of sober mind attended, with full sense of responsibility for the success of the commercial ventures to which they were committed. The partisans and captains of the class of General Ashley, Major Henry, the Sublettes, Fitzpatrick, David E. Jackson, Captain Bonneville, viewed the wassail, took their drams, but kept level head.

The rendezvous was not unreceptive to the missionary; tolerated rebuke, sized up the source, and yielded none of its special privilege in liquor, gaming and women. Here at rendezvous appeared the austere Reverend Samuel Parker, hearty Dr. Marcus Whitman, Missionaries Spalding, Gray, the Lees — all on their way to Oregon. The Sunday sermon of the Reverend Parker to his escort of trappers and Indians out of the rendezvous of 1835 was interrupted by a herd of buffalo which turned his listeners from the Gospel to the chase. Dr. Whitman was well liked; he adapted himself to mountain-man life. Father Pierre Jean DeSmet the Jesuit, arrived in the mountains in 1840, had the respect of all. Kit Carson speaks of him to Colonel Meline:

I admire and venerate that good man. He is the only missionary I ever saw who had the slightest effect upon the trappers. All the Indians, even those who have never seen him, venerate "the long black robe." I remember he came once among the hunters and trappers up in the mountains, and baptized forty-odd children.

The rendezvous, sometimes featured by rival dances and parades by the caparisoned Indians, lasted from ten days to a month, according to the disposition of the trappers and the promptness of the supply caravans. At the close the traders had the furs and the wages; the trappers had little more, except actual necessities and fresh memories, than when they came; the Indians had powder and lead and blankets and some worthless frippery; and —

suddenly the narrow valley of the Green River for ten miles is all alive with horses and mules and human beings. The thousands, perhaps tens of thousands of horses are driven into their several camps and horse pens, lodge poles are taken down, lodges rolled up and packed, beaver bales packed, and pack saddles on the mules, and the long cavalcade for St. Louis impatient to be in motion; the hearty shake of the hand and soul invigorating "God bless you" goes around. The home-bound partner gives the signal by firing his piece, followed instantly by a thousand volleys. The Canadians lead off in that soul-vivifying Canadian boatsong, followed by the Mexican, the English, and the many Indian tongues. As these many natives and languages start off in all directions, the home-bound caravan for the rising sun, the Indian tribes for their distant mountain homes, the mountain trappers moving camp with them, or collecting in small bands, move off to choice trapping fields in the secluded glens of the distant dark mountains, to live over again their life of peril, danger, starvation and feasting, and to come together again with numbers greatly reduced by other sleepless foes. And the romantic valley relapses into its pristine stillness and solitude.[124]

Chapter XIII

The Mountain-Man — Domestic Matters

CONNECTIONS by marriage with the Indians of the country was long a source of strength and protection to the Hudson's Bay Company.

It is their policy, considered by them necessary to conciliate the good will of the tribes. The officers set the example, and have ever encouraged the men to follow it, each taking to be his wife the daughter of a chief, whose grade corresponded with his own. For instance, Governor McLaughlin [McLoughlin] and Mr. James Douglas, holding the highest offices in the company, selected the daughters of the first chiefs of the most important tribes in the country.[125]

But in the mountains the American trapper took a squaw, by custom, not so much out of policy as with the desire to relieve his domestic duties of their drudgery.

The mountains were of course no place for the white woman as so reckoned, and white women, among them, were rarer than the white buffalo. Up to 1836 not a woman's face of American or "white" blood was to be seen in the Rocky Mountains. Then there crossed by the South Pass Mrs. Whitman and Mrs. Spalding, missionary brides.

What the mountain-man needed was not so much sentimental companionship as that physical service which the Indian himself demanded. Returning to his lodge "after days of exhausting exposure and exertions," it was pleasant for him to find there a wife who

removes his stiff-worn clothing; hastens to cook and set before him the best food which she has; offers him a pipe; unpacks the meat which he has brought; and willingly, if her little son has not done it, takes care of the horse.[126]

By training and custom the Indian woman was hardened to harsh labor, and made little of it. Her conquest was accomplished sometimes by a Helen of Troy abduction, but generally by the routine of open purchase, whereupon she moved into her man's lodge. Jim Baker, who as among the last of the mountain-men died, survived by a squaw, in 1898, paid for his first wife, a Snake, a horse; and for his second wife, her sister, a mare and a colt. Thirty beaver skins is quoted again as the price of an able squaw. The women, let it be said, were far more loyal to their ties than were their trapper spouses. This has been so, in fact and fiction, from the beginning of the intercourse between white and red, and is a damning blot upon the American invader's record — contrasting with the faithfulness of the French-Canadian.

I now had to part with my wife and little son, three years of age, which "Spotted Fawn" had brought along to the Fort [Bent's Fort], probably as an inducement for me to remain with her. She had also brought with her from camp a fine bay horse which she knew I valued highly. This horse she left with me; and picking up our child, with a tearful embrace, with a look of sorrow bordering on despair, and one wild, mournful shriek, she was gone from the fort. Her grief at the separation caused the poor woman to lose prematurely her second child, as I have learned since.

A short reunion occurred, in three years, when the white man found his Indian wife waiting for him. But restlessness and opportunity again interrupted, and

I bade them all goodby, parting sadly and reluctantly from the lovely and affectionate "Spotted Fawn," who hung upon my neck and almost refused to let me go. This daughter of "Wolf" was far above the average of Indian women in looks and intelligence, and was nearly white. Her amiable ways, during the years of my pleasant sojourn among her people, had so endeared her to me, that I could not leave on this occasion without promising her that I would return again soon to stay permanently.[127]

But the "permanently" was only white man's word. On the other hand, the trappers had their own woes, as the veteran Killbuck relates in Ruxton's *Life in the Far West:*

For twenty years I packed a squaw along. Not one, but a many. First I had a Blackfoot — the darnedest slut as ever cried for fofarrow. I lodge-poled her on Colter's Creek, and made her quit. My buffler hos, and as good as four packs of beaver, I gave for old Bull-tail's daughter. He was head chief of the Ricaree, and "came" nicely 'round me. Thar warn't enough scarlet cloth, nor beads, nor vermillion in Sublette's packs for her.

The Trapper's Wife

Traps wouldn't buy her all the fofarrow she wanted; and in two years I'd sold her to Cross-Eagle for one of Jake Hawkins' guns — this very one I hold in my hands. Then I tried the Sioux, the Shian, and a Digger from the other side, who made the best moccasin as ever *I* wore. She was the best of all, and was rubbed out by the Yutas in the Bayou Salade. Bad was the best; and after she was gone under I tried no more.

That a sincere attachment, however, broken only by death, might exist between the mountain-man and his squaw we have numerous evidences. The incident of the young Mexican trapper, Loretto, in the Rocky Mountain Fur Company band under Fitzpatrick and Bridger, and his Blackfoot bride, is mountain romance made authentic by Irving. Jim Bridger took his last wife, a Snake woman, to Missouri with him, where his children were in school. Kit Carson married, during his early mountain days, an Arapaho girl of whom he seems to have been truly fond.

At one time during his stay [in the Senator Benton home in Washington, 1847] he was seen to be troubled in mind, and our young friend, Midshipman Beale, being asked to find what had quenched Carson's good spirits, ascertained that he felt it was wrong to be among such ladies when they might not like to associate with him if they knew he had had an Indian wife.[128]

But he added loyally: "She was a good wife to me. I never came in from hunting that she did not have the warm water ready for my feet." Carson was less fortunate in his second venture.

Another mountain-man's wife at once a belle and an appreciated help-meet was the Crow damsel and dame, "Umentucken," the "Mountain Lamb"; first the wife Isabel of Milton Sublette, but upon Sublette's retirement, sick and wounded, quickly transferring her affections, "without even the ceremony of serving a notice on her former lord," to Joe Meek.

She was the most beautiful Indian woman I ever saw, says Meek, and when she was mounted on her dapple gray horse, which cost me three hundred dollars, she made a fine show. She wore a skirt of beautiful blue broadcloth, and a bodice and leggins of scarlet cloth, of the very finest make. Her hair was braided and fell over her shoulders, a scarlet silk handkerchief tied on hood fashion, covered her head; and the finest embroidered moccasins on her feet.[129]

She was a good worker, and a personage of high spirit; Meek jealously guarded her, fought for her, killed for her, and held her safe until, after a year had passed, in a fracas a Bannock arrow pierced her breast.

The Hudson's Bay Company partisan, Peter Skene Ogden, was so devoted to his Indian wife Mary that he bestowed her sweet English name upon the Humboldt River. She, too, was a woman of spirit, for one time dashing alone into the American trappers' camp, she seized her runaway horse and her baby, a strayed pack-horse also, and rode out again followed by the plaudits of the men.

The Indian wife or maiden of romantic fiction is no type figure in beaver-trapper annals. To be sure there was the Indian name more or less symbolical — Deer That Runs, Young Moon, Girl Who Laughs, or one more prosaic — which however less symbolized the bearer than referred to some incident attached to her first days. But in the main the practical minded mountain-man divorced this name from his new domestic establishment; if he did not fully speak the language he may never have interpreted the name, anyway; and he made a convenience of an English name, either on spur of the moment or through some association of ideas. Running Deer, Little Moon, Laughing Girl, "Prairie Flower" of Emerson Bennett's elevated diction, did not "shine" with him even if he were able to lay his tongue to the vernacular. He chose his wife sometimes by approval at first sight, sometimes by advice of other trappers who knew of her, and again by recommendation of the chief or other go-between in her village. As a rule he christened her according to his fancy, with a familiar English designation.

Oliver Wiggins asserted that Alice was a favorite name in the lodges of the mountain-men and that Carson adopted it for his Arapaho girl. Peter Ogden had his Mary, a Flathead or Salish woman; Milton Sublette had Isabel, a Crow; Joe Meek's last Indian wife, a Nez Percé, was Virginia; "Squire" Ebbert's Nez

Percé woman was Fanny; "old" Jim Baker is reported to have dubbed his Snake wives "Monkey" and "Beans."

As has been indicated, the mountain-men's lodge-keepers were widely chosen. The women of various tribes had their reputed good points. The Ute women were the best dressers of deer skin in the mountains. They were industrious if rather stolid wives. The Southern Cheyenne women were experts in quill and bead work and kept a clean lodge. The girls of the northern plains Arapaho were affectionate and merry and were deemed to be superior to the southern plains Arapaho women. Their moccasins and buffalo robes were first grade. The mountain, the northern or eastern Shoshoni woman, a Snake woman, made a thoroughly efficient wife, "up to beaver" in all domestic ways, and very enduring. But a Nez Percé of the Oregon country could not be beat, "no-way." She was neat and obedient and good-natured and capable, and in looks and manners was almost white. The trapper who had a Nez Percé in his lodge was lucky. These Nez Percé damsels

rode their beautiful ponies with perfect *abandon*. They rode "straddle," as all Indian women do, and as their dress permitted. They had buckskin dresses [skirt and tightly fitting waist], fringed at all the seams and beautifully ornamented with bead work. Their jet-black locks hung down in front of each shoulder in heavy braids. Their eyes were large and lustrous and their features were almost classic in the beauty of contour. The Greek model was equalled if not excelled, and the delicate tawny skin, that was susceptible to the keenest emotions, would blush with crimson, or dimple with mirthful smiles. Their dresses, leggings and moccasins were worn with utmost grace of *negligé,* and they seemed entirely unconscious of the charms they possessed. . . . They wore little grass-woven caps, that closely fitted on the smooth combed hair.[130]

The result in the children of these fast-and-loose unions of trapper and buffalo Indian in fur-trade days may be viewed at several facets. Many of the children were left with the mother and her people; others, with an education acquired in a States school or on the frontier, or picked up haphazard in trading post, agency and fort, returned to their mothers' people. Some of the unions developed useful citizens among the descendants, with names respected to this day; but not infrequently the mixture of bloods at first hand fermented in the new vessel, and the half- and quarter-breeds championing the unstable bands of mountains and plains — serving the mother's line rather than the father's — were regarded as vicious elements. Accusations were leveled, for instance, at one or two of the "Bent boys," sons of trader William Bent of Bent's Fort and a Cheyenne woman; and boys who sprang from the marriage of Jim Beckwourth (who himself was a mixture of white and negro blood) and a Crow woman or two (there being one idealized as Pine Leaf, warrior maid, in his biography by Bonner) have been characterized as "regular devils." He had a boy named Kit, after Carson; another called "Panther," remembered by citizens of early Denver.

As said old Jim Baker, when his beard had turned white, although his long flowing cinnamon-red hair had "not a streak of gray in it":

That boy's a half-breed. His mother was a genuine Shoshone Indian. Thar's only one creature worse than a genuine Indian and that's a half-breed. A half-breed has got two devils in him and is meaner than the meanest Indian I ever saw. That boy of mine is a half-breed and he ain't accountable for what he does. It's just the devil in him. Now, I want a squar' deal for my boy.[131]

In connection with this phase, as discussed, of the beaver hunter's domestic habits, it is well to note that by the observation of Francis E. Leupp, formerly United States Commissioner of Indian Affairs —

regarded in its broader aspects, the intermarriage of Indians and Caucasians has nothing to condemn it. There is no barrier of race antagonism to overcome, for the Indian and the white mingle everywhere on a legal and social equality; and the offspring of such a marriage derives from each of the parent races certain traits which work well in combination. With his Indian blood he inherits keenness of observation, stoicism under sufferings, love of freedom, a contempt for the petty things which lay so heavy a burden on our convention-bound civilization; with his white blood the competitive instinct, individual initiative, resourcefulness in the face of novel obstacles, and a constitution hardened to the drafts made upon its strength by the artificialities of modern life.

As to the progeny of mixed marriages, it is impossible to generalize justly. The child of one white and one Indian parent normally inherits the shrewder and more self-seeking traits of his white ancestry. . . . In my own acquaintance, which is large, the good mixed-bloods outnumber the bad. . . . Moreover, it is not their ancestry which makes the vicious specimens what they are; we find the same over-reaching disposition among the better-educated but morally ill-balanced members of all races, whether of pure blood or mixed. It is our common human nature, not Indian nature or white nature, which is to blame.[132]

To the mountain-man the woman in his lodge was an expedient. She represented his nearest approach to domesticity. Upon that other domestic attribute of the white race, the dog, he bestowed small sentiment of companionship. The exactions of a country and people amid which the dog rated as a commodity rather than as a companion were such as to discourage this sentiment. In Coyner's *Lost Trappers,* the Ezekiel Williams party of 1807 took along four dogs, one of them a mastiff and one a greyhound. The former was traded to the Kansas for a horse, "as the party had begun to consider the canine part of the expedition as not only useless, but calculated by their barking to betray them into the hands of the lurking parties of Indians."

The chief took his dog, and Captain Williams his horse, both alike well pleased with their trade. The village generally seemed delighted with the acquisition of an animal so much superior, in every way, to the small, half-starved, half-wolf, roguish-looking breed, which they had in their village.

The mastiff gnawed his tether and rejoined the white march. And after that the canine contingent is mentioned not again, and probably fell by the wayside or landed in the pot.

When in 1839 Thomas Farnham crossed country, from Missouri by the way of the upper Arkansas and Bear River to Oregon, he and his party were supplied with a greyhound for the chase; but half-way they had to eat him. "The noble dog must die!" So they shot him and boiled him. That greyhound is not the best of dog-meat Farnham confirms by adding, remorsefully, "Whether cooked or barking, a dog is still a dog, everywhere!"

Naturally, in traversing the Indian country the trappers would pick up, or acquire as chattels, along with their wives, a following of the Indian dogs. The Zenas Leonard party on their way back from California, in February, 1834, by record consisted of "52 men, 315 horses — and, for provisions, 47 beef, and 30 dogs." The dogs suffered wellnigh humanly from thirst, and Leonard yields to sentiment so far as to declare that "their pitiful lamentations were sufficient to melt the hardest heart."

W. A. Ferris in his diary of Rocky Mountain life speaks of dog followers. One day they were chasing the rabbits — and another day they must be shot, through fear of hydrophobia. Kit Carson, as will be seen later, does speak warmly of the dogs in his camp. But it may be regarded that to the trapper the dog was a nuisance and a peril rather than a pleasure, and that his principal use was to bridge some lean period between fat cow and moccasin soles.

The mountain-man's main dependence for food was the buffalo. He could nevertheless suit his palate to everything available.

"Meat's meat" is a common saying in the mountains, and from the buffalo down to the rattlesnake, including every quadruped that runs, every fowl that flies, and every reptile that creeps, nothing comes amiss to the mountaineer.[133]

Lieutenant Ruxton might have added, to the category, "about every berry and root that grows and every insect that crawls."

"I have," says Joe Meek, "held my hands in an ant-hill until they were covered with the ants, then greedily licked them off. I have taken the soles off my moccasins, crisped them in the fire, and eaten them. In our extremity, the large, black crickets which are found in this country were considered game. We used to take a kettle of hot water, catch the crickets and throw them in, and when they stopped kicking, eat them."[134]

In general efficiency the buffalo headed the list, and from "fat cow" to "pore bull" was welcomed.

> Our knives are quickly hauled from their sheaths — he is rolled upon his brisket — his hide is slit along the spine, and peeled down mid rib; one side of it is cut off and spread upon the sand to receive the meat; the flesh on each side of the spine is pared off; the mouth is opened and the tongue wrenched from his jaws; the ax is laid to his rib; the cavity opens; the heart — the fat — the tender loins — the tepid blood — the intestines, of glorious, savory sausage memory, are torn out — his legs are rifled of their generous marrow bones; all wrapped in the green hide, and loaded on animals, and off to camp.[135]

This custom of propping the dead animal on his stomach, like a boat, with his folded legs as the stays, and butchering him by way of the back instead of the stomach as in the case of domestic cow or sheep or even deer, was mountain-man butchering of approved and practical style.

The plains and mountains habitant was an epicure, and in time of plenty only certain portions of the ton of carcass appealed to him. In particular these were: the *dépouille,* or the strip of fat, sometimes four inches thick, lying along the spine from shoulders to tail; the fleece, or the heavy flesh covering the ribs; the hump and the hump-ribs; the liver, heart, tongue, marrow, tender-loin, and intestines.[136]

The *dépouille* or thick strip of fat was eaten raw, was warmed through or was fried to liquid and drunk. When cold and congealed it was called the trappers' bread, and was thought to be sweet and exceedingly nourishing. The liver was eaten when raw and quivering, and was sprinkled with or sopped in gall, as a sauce. The tongue was fried in the marrow or was boiled until the skin peeled off, leaving the meat tender and juicy. Dried, the tongues were articles of trade and of export, and "hung in clusters from the ceilings of the posts." The marrow ("trappers' butter") was roasted in the bones and the bones were cracked and were licked clean. Or it was turned out, and heated, a pound to a gallon of water, to boiling point; then, mixed with the blood "to the consistency of rice soup," seasoned by a little salt and pepper or gun-powder, it made a fine dish.

"Excellent, most excellent," as says Farnham again. "It was better than our father's foaming ale. For while it loosened our tongues and warmed our hearts towards one another, it had the additional effect of Aaron's oil; it made our faces to shine with grease and gladness."

One must not cut the tender-loin across the grain, but with the grain, in slices, to preserve the juices. The intestines, turned and roughly cleaned (although, as Ruxton remarks, this was not deemed necessary!) taken raw or else wound spirally upon sticks and held to the blaze until broiled, were sucked in like spaghetti. Or, stuffed at intervals with the minced tenderloin, and roasted, as the celebrated *boudins* (sausages) of the trapper, trader and *voyageur* were devoured with smacking zest. Tradition says that nothing in the gustatory line can surpass buffalo *boudins*.

All chronicles of mountaineer and traveler declare that buffalo meat never surfeited, never caused distress. In his *Commerce of the Prairies,* the careful Josiah Gregg declares that "the flesh of the buffalo is, I think, as fine as any meat I ever tasted; the old hunter will not admit that there is anything equal to it. This meat is also very easy of digestion, possessing even aperient qualities. It has often been remarked by travellers that however much buffalo meat one may eat, no inconvenience is ever suffered from it." And Sage narrates, after his initial experience, when, having fried and reduced to a liquid a pan of the dépouille, he drank down six gills of the oily mess: "Strange as it may seem, I did not experience the least unpleasant feeling as the result of my extraordinary potation. The stomach never rebels against buffalo-fat. Persons, subsisting entirely upon the flesh of these animals, prefer an assortment of at least one-third solid dépouille." According to the mountain-men themselves, buffalo fare will "cure despepsy, prevent consumption, amend a broken constitution, put flesh upon the bones of a skeleton, and restore a dead man again to life!" While as for mountain fare generally, it "would make a man shed rain like an otter and stand cold like a polar bear."[137]

The flesh of the beaver was prized by the Indians. It was

occasionally eaten by the trappers but in general was too musky to be relished. The tail, however, was invariably saved along with the pelt and "medicine" for camp. The tail, a foot long, flat and thick and scaly, the trapper boiled in his kettle, or transfixed with a stick and placed before the fire

with the scales on. When the heat of the fire strikes through so as to roast it, large blisters rise on the surface, which are very easily removed. The tail is then perfectly white, and very delicious.[138]

When thoroughly prepared, beaver-tail was of the consistency and appearance of thick gelatin. The liver of the beaver also was eaten; the roasted ham, sliced cold, was likened to pork, and the boiled feet resembled pigs-feet.

The deer and the elk of course were common fare. Mountain sheep was esteemed, and fat dog, an honorary dish among the Sioux and other tribes, was not despised. Panther (the mountain-lion) was rated by many of the trappers, including Kit Carson himself, as being superior to any other meat of hills or of plains, and Ferris writes in high praise of the lynx — which is cat again.

Both horse and mule appeared upon the mountain-man's menu; sometimes by virtue of necessity, sometimes by choice. A. D. Richardson makes Kit Carson say that the flesh of a wild horse

he deemed better than any other meat. A young mule furnished excellent steaks, but meat from an old one was tough, strong-flavored and unpalatable. The most sorrowful meal he ever took was when necessity compelled him to kill and eat a faithful horse which had borne him many hundred miles.[139]

The Ezekiel Williams "Lost Trappers," when almost starved, succeeded in shooting a venerable wild horse, and supped upon him. But although he was "meat," he was, according to their chronicle, so coarse and strong that he was "not fit for a white man to eat." His flesh

would remain in the stomach for a long time, in a state of indigestion, and for several days (eight or ten, they said), "they belched up the old stud as strong as ever."

Fish seems to have figured little in the mountain-man's provender. The dried or the semi-fresh salmon of the Pacific tribes was eaten, at a pinch; and the versatile Joe Meek does relate of a strait wherein trout were caught and eagerly consumed. Fish-hooks were not in the mountain-man's outfit of "possibles," but in the desolate Snake River country one of the Meek party, seeking the reason why his saddle was galling his horse, found in the padding a large brass pin. He held it up with a cry of delight, and

the same thought struck all who saw the pin; it was soon converted into a fish-hook, a line was spun from horse-hair, and in a short time there were trout enough caught to furnish them a hearty and a most delicious repast. "In the morning," says Meek, "we went on our way rejoicing"; each man with the "five fishes" tied to his saddle, if without any "loaves."[140]

Roots and berries were available in great variety — gathered on occasion by the trappers themselves, but usually assigned as squaw work. The sarvice berry, the buffalo berry, the raspberry, gooseberry, huckleberry, whortle-berry, the various currants (black, yellow and red), the prickly pear (boiled and strained), the wild plums, chock-cherries, even rose-buds or berries, were brought into use as variety or as makeshifts. Among roots the camas and the *pomme blanc* were the more common.

In the knowledge of growing things the Indian woman was far ahead of the trapper. This among other assets placed her ahead of any wife imported from the States.

It is surprising what a number of roots, leaves, berries and nuts the squaw will discover. She will go out in the spring with nothing but a fire-hardened stick, and in an hour she will pick a breakfast of green stuff, into which there may enter fifteen or twenty ingredients. Her eye will be arrested by a minute plant that will yield her only a bulbous root as large as a large pea, but which the American would have passed unnoticed.[141]

A tea of the bark of the wild cherry was valued, in the spring, as a blood purifier; and there was another drink termed "bitters."

It is prepared by the following simple process, viz.: with one pint of water mix one-fourth gill of buffalo-gall, and you will then have before you a wholesome and exhilarating drink. To a stomach unaccustomed to its use it may at first create a slightly noisome sensation, like the inceptive effects of an emetic; and, to one strongly billious, it might cause vomiting; but, on the second or third trial, the stomach attains a taste for it, and receives it with no inconsiderable relish.[142]

These "bitters" combined the beneficial effects of a mild "nerve stimulant," a digestive, and an appetizer. They healed the stomach; and Sage is quite confident that if those suffering from the "wasting influences" of "dyspepsy" would drink gall-bitters "and confine themselves exclusively to the use of some one kind of diet (animal food always preferable), thousands who are now pining away by piecemeal, would be restored to perfect soundness, and snatched from the very threshold of a certain grave which yawns to receive them!"

In day of plenty the mountain-man was accustomed to regale himself hugely by devouring prodigious quantities of buffalo and venison as against another day. For upon the deserts, and also among the very hills which might be presumed to have teemed with game; in the times and places "where lizards grow poor, and wolves lean against sand banks to howl," he then faced stark famine. He must resort to the wolf and the coyote; to bleeding the wearied saddle and pack animals and drinking the nauseous fluid, and finally to eating the impoverished flesh; to eking out with the buzzard and the rattle-snake, boiled trap-sack and charred moccasins. Or again, as Zenas Leonard records of desperate want; "after each man had selected two of the best beaver skins to eat as he travelled along, we hung the remainder upon a tree, and started in to try our fortune with the snow shoes." The next morning's breakfast consisted of roast beaver-skin.

The mountain-man was practically carniverous. Kit Carson said to the journalist Richardson: "Our ordinary fare consisted of fresh beaver and buffalo-meat, without any salt, bread or vegetables. Once or twice a year, when supplies arrived from the States, we had flour and coffee for one or two meals, though they cost one dollar a pint." Massalino, the Mexican guide for Captain Gunnison, in the San Luis Valley, Colorado, 1853, stated that he had "lived nine years, on meat alone, at one time, in these mountains, without tasting bread or salt."[143]

Dr. Elijah White, before cited, in 1844 met near Ft. Laramie a French trapper, in the service of the American Fur Company, and then seventeen years a resident of the country. "He had been there so long, that he said he actually dreaded the appearance of a white woman, or anything like refinement."

His story-telling propensity was probably increased by the quantity of tea he drank, of which he declared he had not before tasted in several years, and which acted upon him in much the same manner that stimulous would on another person.

Whatever the cause or the combination of causes, the health of the mountain-men was extraordinary. Says Kit Carson:

During the winter, visiting our traps twice a day, we were often compelled to break the ice, and wade in water up to our waists. Notwithstanding these hardships sickness was absolutely unknown among us. I lived ten years in the mountains, with from one to three hundred trappers, and I cannot remember that a single one of them died from disease.[144]

Other chroniclers of those times make similar assertions. Nevertheless, Clerk Ferris enters in his *Diary:*

A young man by the name of Benjamin Hardiser, who came out last summer [1832] with Bonnyville, but had left him and taken refuge in our camp in the winter, died on the evening of the 8th, of some complaint, the germ of which he had no doubt brought with him from the United States. With the assistance of a man behind him on the same horse, he rode eight miles during the day previous to his decease. We buried him as decently as circumstances would permit the next day, "and left him alone in his glory."

Salt and soap, those two cultures of civilization, with the mountain-man as with the Indian were "extras." At trapper feasts a sprinkling of gun-powder savored a dish if additional savor were desired. Salt itself was procured from various deposits by springs and creeks. Beds of "white stone," probably talc, found here and there, particularly west of the Continental Divide among the valleys of the Salmon, the Snake and the Bear Rivers, provided a substitute for soap. With this material the Indians washed their hair, the trappers (on occasion) their clothing.

Tobacco, solace of the wanderer and the stay-at-home alike, as a prime article of trade and of luxury in the mountains was dear and frequently scarce. The trapper who ran short accommodated himself to circumstances by smoking, pure or as a mixture, the kinnikinnick (killikinick) of the Indian. This was the inner bark of the red willow

which has an aromatic and very pungent flavor. It is prepared for smoking by being scraped in thin curly flakes from the slender saplings, and crisped before the fire, after which it is rubbed between the hands into a form resembling leaf-tobacco, and stored in skin bags for use. It has a highly narcotic effect on those not habituated to its use, and produces a heaviness sometimes approaching stupefaction, altogether different from the soothing effects of tobacco.[145]

The pipe was the least difficult factor in the operation of smoking. There were deposits of soft pipe-stone, white, green, red, prized by the Indians for their medicine pipes; roots and nodules were to be hollowed out; mud might be moulded. And having stuffed his stone, wood or baked-mud bowl with "honey-dew" or "single twist" (a plew a plug) or with the ranker kinnikinnick, the trapper contentedly sucked at the reed stem.

Chapter XIV

The Mountain-Man — The Danger Trail

THE mountain-man on the beaver trail was constantly moving. His camps were of temporary character; he halted a day or so in some likely spot where the signs were good; then he was out and away again. Alone or in company he was closely interested in portents — and if alone, he never was lonely. The sign of other trappers, the tracks of lodge-pole, hoof or foot, the meeting with friend and stranger and enemy, the actions of buffalo, deer and elk, the aspects of streams, near, and of valley and slope, distant, successive expectancy, apprehension, realization — all came in the day's program. For the price of mountain-man existence was vigilance.

The Canadian trappers bore the burden with a song; the Americans, while meeting danger with as much high spirit, presented "a different phase of character."

They seldom smile; the expression of their countenances is watchful, solemn and determined. They ride and walk, like men whose breasts have so long been exposed to the bullet and arrow, that fear finds within them no resting place. . . . No delay, no second thought, no cringing in their stirrups; but erect, firm, and with a strong arm, they seize and overcome every danger "or perish," say they, "as white men should," fighting promptly and bravely.[146]

The stampede of buffalo, the appearance of wild duck swimming hastily against the current of the little stream, the finding of a strayed moccasin — the least unusual token was to be interpreted for good or evil.

It may seem to the reader a trifling matter to note the track of footmen, the report of firearms, the appearance of strange horsemen, and the curling vapor of a far-off fire, but these are far from trivial incidents in a region of country where the most important events are indiced by such signs only. Every man carries here his life in his hand, and it is only by the most watchful precaution, grounded upon and guided by the observation of every unnatural appearance however slight, that he can hope to preserve it. The footmark may indicate the vicinity of a war party hovering to destroy; the report of firearms may betray the dangerous neighborhood of a numerous, well armed and wily enemy; strange horsemen may be but the outriding scouts of a predatory band at hand and in force to attack; the rising smoke may indeed curl up from the camp of friends or an accidental fire, but it more probably signals the gathering forces of an enemy recruiting their scattered bands for the work of plunder and massacre.[147]

The principal danger to the mountain-man was, of course, from attack by Indians. The white invader carried with him his own curse. Lewis and Clark and their men of 1804 met with little opposition from the natives, and, indeed, were furthered by them, until occurred that friction which seems inevitable — a friction arising from the Indians' covetousness and the white man's method of defending his property with death. Numerically the weaker, the whites had to adopt quick, strenuous measures, or lose face; for the Indian, given an inch, will take the ell. The whites and the reds simply could not understand each other. And in the outset the reds could not appreciate what a force, as sure as an avalanche, lay behind the few new-comers. They were as innocent of that power as were the grizzly bears who long had been monarch of the animal kingdom in the West.

The Canadians, by assimilation and by diplomacy, were wonted to placate the Indians; but with the coming of the Americans of the Missouri border matters changed. The Americans were brusque, defiant, fearless, and in a measure contemptuous; inclined to adopt the aggressive whenever circumstances indicated that this was the shortest measure, rather than submit to inconvenience by a stalemate.

Of all the tribes in the fur country, the warrior Sioux and Blackfeet gave the most trouble; the Arikaras were of fierce and treacherous nature; the Crows would extend friendship with one hand and steal the horses with the other; the Utes were offish; the Snakes, Flatheads, Nez Percés, Pend d'Oreilles, were not only friendly but hospitable; the Bannocks were hostile; the Diggers Pai-Utes were assassins.

The annals of the beaver days mention most frequently the

Blackfeet and the Crows. Occupying the heart of the fur country, widely roving, energetic, and powerful in numbers, these
two great tribes were names omnipresent in trapper hearts and
upon trapper lips.

The Blackfeet were the implacable enemy of the whites;
and moreover, inasmuch as their hand was against all the
world save the Arapahos their cousins, wherever they moved
they stirred a ferment. At the climax of their strength, or in
1830, they claimed to a confederacy of 20,000 souls, divided
among four bands: the Blackfeet proper, the Bloods, the Pieg-
ans, and the Gros Ventres of the Prairies. Their territory, northwestern Montana, was regarded as one of the choice beaver
grounds of the whole West. But death was the entrance price
demanded, and this price was paid.[148]

The Blackfoot nation ranged far. By custom they went
a-raiding on foot, yet they were horsemen also, mounting
themselves from their own herds or from the herds of the
enemy. They were a people intensely proud, scornful of aliens
whether white or red, and relentless in their long hates. They
were surrounded by enemies—and they were satisfied to be. On
their west, across the divide were the Flatheads; on their south
were the Crows, on their east were the Sioux and the Cheyennes, and they figured also upon battles with the Snakes, the
Pawnees, the Nez Percés, the Pend d'Oreilles. Nevertheless
they rode almost as they willed, these dark, haughty Bedouins
of the Northwest: they guarded their borders against encroach-
ment, they crossed by the South Pass, by the Wind River Pass,
and many defile less known, to descend upon the herds of the
Snakes and the Flatheads, and through the Home of the Crows
they rode upon visits to the Arapaho of the Colorado plains.

In their rovings, when they saw a trapper head they hit at it.
The Gros Ventres, of Arapaho stock, were the most vengeful
of the bands, and the hardest battles were with these. To the
mountain-man the name "Gros Vent," was the name of the
evil one.[149]

The persistent hostility of the Blackfeet toward the white

hunter had source, it has been asserted, in the blood-shedding by the returning Lewis and Clark company in 1806. That wound was reopened (as suggests Chittenden in *History of the American Fur Trade*) when John Colter, former member of the company but then employed as a trapper, in 1807 aided the Crows in an attack upon the Blackfeet. Thereafter the Blackfeet counted the white men as enemies.

This Colter episode is typical of other episodes all of which put the beaver trapper and fur trader on the spot with one tribe and another. The white man was obliged to share in the blood feuds of the natives. He paid for favors. When he accepted the friendship of the Utes he was in danger of being viewed as their ally by their enemies the Arapahos and other plains tribes. When among the Crows he had to prove his good heart by helping them punish or stand off the Blackfeet and Sioux. As a guest of the Nez Percés or Snakes he joined with them against the Blackfeet, Crows, Sioux. Tribes with which he affiliated not only prized his rifle but valued the trading advantages which they would enjoy through his patronage, and were very willing to limit his privileges among their enemies. The choice forced upon him was frequently to his liking. The Snakes and Nez Percés were fur gatherers and horse raisers as well as buffalo hunters; the Blackfeet were buffalo Indians and horse thieves, and from them, as has been stated, he got only blows and those pelts collected by himself at risk of his scalp.

The long-haired Absaroke or Crows were of character more diplomatic than that of the Blackfeet. Their territory was also a prime trapping ground, being the Big Horn, Tongue, and Powder River country of northern Wyoming, and Montana south of the Yellowstone. The Crows professed to be the white man's friend — and at the same time stole his horses and even the buttons from his coat. They would retain him as an ally against the Blackfeet; they even would temporize with fate by adopting the stranger within their gates — as they adopted Jim Beckwourth the mulatto, Edward Rose, the sinister breed, and others of the fur-hunters and traders: but the beaver-men recognized them as insincere, wily, and the greatest thieves in the mountains. All horses, whether of white camp or red camp, looked alike to the Crows; and in consequence they were constantly being pursued by irate trappers and punished by the bullet. Therefore conflicts with the Crows were successions of spasmodic dashes and rear-guard actions, with the trappers on the offensive; the conflicts with the Blackfeet were a constant give and take.

On the Missouri River trail the Arikaras and the Sioux also were to be avoided, when possible. The Arikaras, stationed in northern South Dakota where the Grand River joins the Missouri, were both fierce and treacherous. Above them were the warlike Sioux — as powerful in the West as the Six Nations had been in the East. But the country of both Sioux and Arikaras (the Arikarees or Rees of the trapper) was as much a buffalo-robe country as a beaver country, and early was subjected to a chain of trading posts.

The popular land trail, the one by the Platte, was infested with the Kiowas, the Arapahos and Cheyennes. The Kiowa, who ranged southward to pester the Santa Fé caravans, have been known as the worst of the essentially plains Indians, and the word "Kiowa!" struck terror to the very soul of trader and settler. The Arapaho, thievish and dissolute, of a dialect difficult for the alien tongue, soon became reconciled to the fur trade; in 1832 Captain John Gantt was permitted to place a trading post on the edge of their territory, at the upper Arkansas. Like the Kiowa they ranged southward from the Platte; but unlike the Kiowa they made victims mainly of the unprotected and defenseless — the lone trapper and the lone greenhorn. The Cheyenne, handsome, dashing, the finest horsemen, barring the Comanche, of the plains, although frequently allied with both Sioux and Arapaho seem to have given the trapper little trouble. In the case of all these plains tribes, the main alleviating factor was the nature of the business intercourse, which was that of buffalo robes, and not of beaver fur. The

Indians who had buffalo robes to sell were more tractable than the Indians from whom the trappers were, in Indian opinion, stealing beaver. Later, when the whites themselves took over the killing of the buffalo and the marketing, first-hand, of the robes, the plains Indians also bitterly resented this intrusion upon their privileges.

West of the mountains the Indians were more friendly. Immediately across the South Pass was the main range of those Shoshoni whose boast was that they never had shed a white man's blood. It must be understood, however, that while to the trappers the Snakes represented the Shoshoni, the unfriendly Bannocks and the cowardly Diggers also were of the Shoshonean family. The Snakes under their great chief Washaki ranged east of the Pass, in the Wind River district, which they debated with the Crows and the Blackfeet; but the Green River and the upper Snake were their territory shared, on occasion, with the Nez Percés. Here, among the Snakes and the Nez Percés, the mountain-man was comparatively at ease.

North of this Snake country was the country of the Nez Percés, the Flatheads and the Pend d'Oreilles, including the celebrated Grande Ronde rendezvous of the Nez Percés. All were friendly, the Nez Percés notably so. They had generously entertained the expedition of Lewis and Clark, and since that time they had never broken faith.

Our history ran its cycle of a hundred years with the record of but one American's blood being shed by a Nez Percé — a case of manslaughter, about the year 1862. Seventy years of friendly intercourse — seventy years in which the Indians patiently endured what they justly considered hardships, for their friendship to the white man.[150]

The mountain-man's favorite program was to hold summer rendezvous or pitch winter camp among the Snakes and the Nez Percés, or to winter even further north, among the Flatheads.

South from the Snake country, in the Uintah region of northeastern Utah, and thence throughout the mountains of western Colorado, were the Utes — dark, square and thick of stature, and for many years, until stung by aggression upon their lands, rather stolid to the white trespasser. In the country of the northern Utes especially the trapper who did not interfere with Ute jealous customs was tolerated. The women, who made good wives, were closely guarded.

North of the Salt Lake there ranged the Bannocks. Trappers upon excursions from the Green River region to the Great Basin southward must be prepared to run the gauntlet of these, a foe not to be despised. In the Great Basin itself there dwelt the Pai-Utes, the Diggers or "Shoshokies" — horseless, small spirited "walkers," but the more to be dreaded because they were assassins using the poisoned arrow. They were in no condition to cope with the well-armed mountain-men, of instant weapons and ruthless methods.

It may be said, then, that west of the Continental Divide the mountain Indians were friendly to the trapper, the desert Indians were unfriendly; and this division corresponded very closely with the boundary line between American and Mexican territory.

Therefore might it be deemed that the territory of Oregon, that vast extent of uneven country watered by the Snake and the Columbia, north of the Mexican boundary line which about coincided with the north line of Utah, and extending from the South Pass to the Pacific, was a trappers' sanctum. Such was far from the case. The Snakes and the Nez Percés in particular were horse-breeders; and hither, to these rich pastures, the Blackfeet, Sioux, Cheyenne, Arapaho, even the far removed Pawnees (horse-thieves almost equal to the Crows) and the Crows themselves, made frequent visits: filing down, over broad South Pass or by crooked passage known to few; raiding and plundering, and with their booty of horses, squaws and scalps retreating to their home sanctuaries.

By such raids the trappers suffered; and taking up arms with the Snakes and the Nez Percés they incurred the displeasure of the more eastern tribes.

There were other Indians. On the upper Missouri the Assiniboines, of Siouan stock — encountered in small hard-riding parties whose village, as like as not, was in the north across the Canadian line. They bore watching. And as neighbors of the Flathead Salish there were the Coeur d'Alênes, a clean and friendly people ranking with the other Columbia country tribes. Their name was popularly supposed to mean Owl Heart, but it rightly meant Awl Heart and in that it was a derisive name applying not to the red man but to the white. For a Skitswish chief had wittily accused a white trader of having a heart the size of the point of an awl and as Awl Heart (Coeur d'Alêne) and as the Awl Heart people he himself and his following were known.

There were Iroquois of the Six Nations of the Atlantic East; employes in the far Northwest of the Hudson's Bay Company — there transplanted by the waterways from Canada; fine canoe-men, trappers, hunters and fighters and roaming, some of them, on their own. There were Delawares from their reservation in the future Kansas; former vassals of the Iroquois, to whom once they had been subjugated; now become great warriors again, great hunters and great travelers enlisted by Frémont, Kit Carson, and other captains. And Shawnees, likewise from the Indian country of a Missouri and Kansas reserve; favorite guides and hunters on the Santa Fé Trail into the Southwest; as restless as the Delawares, penetrating into the beaver Northwest also, but serving more widely in the Southwest; tilting with the Kiowa and the Comanche and outfighting the Apache; as scalp-hunters earning wages in Old Mexico; striking, on horse-stealing raids, into California with free-booter bands of whites and breeds and in the very name *Chaguanosos,* as Spanish rendered, spreading, through missions and ranchos, the dread that once had thrilled Ohio and Kentucky.[151]

In his contacts with the Western Indian tribes the mountain-man acquired a working vocabulary like that of border Spanish and embracing maybe two or three of the important dialects. Residence of some time among a tribe would make him fairly fluent of expression by means of familiarized words and gestures. The Snake dialects of the Shoshonean tongue were of value, for the Snakes ranged on both sides of the divide, and in war and the hunt and horse-trading encountered many tribes. Through captives and captivities languages were exchanged. But the sign language was at the beaver hunter's command. By the use of this he could talk with any Indian met anywhere, and was quite at home in his squaw-shared lodge or in a council: of an extent that, to the amazement of Captain Howard Stansbury in 1850 Jim Bridger, although "unable to speak to either the Sioux or the Cheyenne in their own tongue, or that of any tribe which they could under-stand —

held the whole circle [Sioux and Cheyenne], for more than an hour, per-fectly enchained and evidently most deeply interested in a conversation and narrative, the whole of which was carried on without the utterance of a single word. The simultaneous exclamations of surprise or interest, and the occasional bursts of hearty laughter, showed that the whole party perfectly understood not only the theme, but the minutiae of the panto-mime exhibited before them. I looked on with close attention, but the signs to me were for the most part altogether unintelligible. Upon after inquiry, I found that this language of signs is universally understood by all the tribes.[152]

In his relations with the Indians the mountain-man was incensed chiefly by the loss of his horses and of his traps and contents. The personal risks attached to his calling he accepted more with the attitude of a fatalist. But, as records Zenas Leonard in his *Narrative,*

the Indians, since they have got into the habit of trafficking peltries with the traders, have learnt the value of the beaver, and look upon the trap-pers as poachers, who are filching the riches from their streams, and inter-fering with their market.

Since the beaver hunter had to maintain his mode of travel and of business or quit the mountains, he acted upon the In-dians' principle: "Fight, right or wrong." Since he was of the party fewer in numbers, he aimed to conquer in detail by always striking the harder blow. In the words of old Bill Williams to young Bill Hamilton:

There are five Indians down there who shot at and insulted us. They shall have what they would have given us had they been successful in their attack. Boy, never, if possible, let an Indian escape who has once attacked you.[153]

So these five survivors also were killed.

Trapper-and-Indian battles recorded and unrecorded have wakened the echoes throughout practically every mile of Western country from the Council Bluffs to the mouth of the Snake and from the Three Forks sources of the Missouri to the Gila. There were battles by companies, battles by squads, and battles of the single rifle against odds never quite although almost hopeless.

A small creek at our right, became the scene of a bloody tragedy two months subsequent to our visit. Three trappers, with whom I became acquainted upon my return to the Fort, tempted by the abundance of fur-bearing game common to the vicinity, came here for the purpose of making a summer hunt. While successfully pursuing their occupation, unsuspicious of immediate danger, they were suddenly surrounded early one morning by a war-party of Sioux whose first salute was a discharge of fire-arms, accompanied by a shower of arrows and the sharp thunder of deafening yells.

Two of them fell dead. The remaining one retreated to a hollow tree, close at hand, into which he crawled; and though severely wounded, maintained from it an obstinate resistance till near sun-down — keeping at bay the whole host of savage assailants, and thinning their numbers, one by one, with the deadly discharge of his unerring rifle.

Six warriors lay stiffened in death, and as many more had felt the burning smart of wounds — one of the latter having had his tongue shot out, close to the roots — and still he continued the unequal contest. His triumph would have been complete had not the remorseless crew, as a last resort, set fire to woods and burned him from the shell-like fortress from which they could not drive him. He fell with his companions, mingling his own blood with that of their murderers; and the scalps of the three were treasured as among the horrid trophies of savage victory.

Of these unfortunate men, one, named Wheeler, was a Pennsylvanian; another, named Cross Eagle, was a Swede; and the third, name not remembered, was a native of France. They were men of noble hearts, and much esteemed by all who knew them.[154]

Whether he was in friendly country or not, to the mountain-

man the sight of Indians or of Indian sign was always alarming. Out of experience he soon grew to "know," at a glance,
Indian and Indian sign. Each tribe and each band had their
peculiar method of traveling, their distinctive style of moccasins and of weapons.

Every tribe of Indians make their arrows differently. The Snakes put
but two feathers on their shafts; the Sioux, when they make their own
arrow-points, or buy them, always prefer long, slim points; the Cheyennes,
blunt points, sharp on the edges; the Pawnees, medium points; and the
Crows, Blackfeet, Utes, Omahas, Ottoes, and Winnebagoes, long points.
The Pawnees wrap their arrow-heads with elk sinew, the Crows with
deer, and the Santees [of the Sioux], with sinew taken from the inside of
the shoulder-blade of a buffalo bull.[155]

The arrows of tribe and tribe differed also in the feathers —
the Cheyenne, for example, had a liking for turkey feathers —
and the fashion of feathering; in their length of shaft, in the
so-called "blood grooves" of the shafts, and the paint marks.
An arrow found sticking in the carcass of game or human
being was a message to be read. This knowledge gained by the
fur hunter and trader through contacts with various tribes of
Indians proved of value likewise in the days of the plains and
mountains scouts and guides; enabled Bridger and other
guides to pronounce, from an arrow jutting from the body of
a buffalo bull or of an emigrant, what Indians had been and
might still be in the vicinity. But in due time the smart Indians,
when committing an offense, used the collected arrows of another tribe, so that a killing attributed to the Pawnee might
really have been done by the Sioux!

A war party traveling left no sign of lodge-poles, squaws or
colts. Any roving party of Indians were dangerous. If they
were afoot, they were bent upon war and pillage; were resolved to enrich themselves from an enemy. Whether afoot or
ahorse they were viewed with suspicion. They may have been
disappointed in obtaining scalps and other booty and now
were loth to return to their village without honors. Or they
may have sometime had an encounter with the whites, and
were still unsatisfied in vengeance.

Bear in mind — and this is true of all tribes, notwithstanding the contrary statements by some writers who have had no general knowledge of the character of the Indian, either on the plains or in the mountains — an Indian never for a moment considers himself the aggressor. Sufficient for him is the fact that some member of the village has been lost.[156]

Consequently "old experienced mountain-men leave nothing to chance." If given time, they "forted" behind their packs or bales, behind boulders, logs or trees, or downed animals. When they had cover of any kind a party of trappers were practically invincible. And even when surprised in camp, on the trail, or at his traps, the trapper nevertheless reacted as instantaneously as a wild animal.

"Major Meek" (Joe Meek) arrives in Bridger's camp in the upper Yellowstone country astride a horse with bloody neck.

"News!" exclaimed he. "I have been, me and Dave [Dave Crow], over on to Prior's Fork to set our traps and found old Benj. Johnson's boys [Indians] over there, just walking up and down them 'ar streams with their hands on their hips gathering plums. They gave me a tilt, and turned me a somerset or two, shot my horse, 'Too Shebit,' in the neck and sent us heels over head in a pile together, but we raised a-runnin'. Gabe, do you know where Prior leaves the cut bluffs, goin' up it?" "Yes," said Bridger . . . "Well, sir, we went up there and set yesterday morning . . . and this morning started to our traps. We came up to Dave's traps and in the first there was a four-year-old 'spade,' the next was false licked, went to the next and it had cut a foot and none of the rest disturbed. We then went up to mine to the mouth of the branch. I rode on five or six steps ahead of Dave and just as I got opposite the first trap I heard a rustling in the bushes within above five steps of me. I looked around and pop, pop, pop went the guns, covering me with smoke so close that I could see the blanket wads coming out of the muzzle. Well, sir, I wheeled and a ball hit Too Shebit in the neck and just touched the bone and we pitched heels over head, but Too Shebit raised runnin' and I on his back and the savages jist squattin' and grabbin' at me, but I raised a fog for about half a mile till I overtook Dave."[157]

The Indian's strong aversion to losing his life and his scalp militated against him; he was a poor hand to charge upon a loaded gun. By threatening one Indian and another but firing not a shot, lone trappers surprised in the open were often enabled to beat a safe retreat. With his superior equipment in pistols, good rifle, and full charges of first-grade powder the white man out-ranged the Indian, out-metaled him and as the rule out-shot him. But —

"The Utes," says Carson, "are the best shots in the country, whether Indian or white. I have handled the rifle since I was so high," indicating the size of a small boy, "and shot a good deal" (most men of Carson's skill would have said, "consider myself the best shot in the Rocky Mountains" or "I'll turn my back on no man for rifle-shooting"), "but some of the Utes beat me."[158]

"All Indians dreaded trappers when once brought to bay," "Uncle" Bill Hamilton declares; and "if any reader of this should doubt the fighting quality of the trapper, let him go among any tribe of Indians today, and ask what they think of it. They will invariably answer that it 'costs too much blood to fight trappers.' "

Thought of mercy was a quality infinitesimal. To "rub out," completely and by any means whatsoever, was the ambition of both sides. No warrior prisoners were taken by the trappers; prisoners taken by the Indians were in jeopardy of torture with death following. Upon the battlefield the knife was freely used to dispatch the wounded; white or red searching swiftly, from body to body.[159]

The desire for scalps was the chief impetus toward this. According to Bill Hamilton:

The method of scalping was to run the knife around the head under the hair, cutting through to the skull bone; then taking hold of the scalp-lock and giving it a quick jerk, the scalp would come off and was afterwards dried on a hoop.

The reason that mountaineers scalped Indians was in retaliation and also because Indians dread going to their happy hunting-grounds without their scalps.[160]

To the trapper the scalp of an Indian was moreover an article of trade, a "fancy" scalp from an enemy tribe buying a horse or a squaw.

This custom of scalp-taking, among the mountain-men — and a greenhorn was not considered "broken in" until he had "lifted hair" — effected a callous indifference to human suffering.

In a fight with the Blackfeet an Indian was shot "through the back-bone, thus depriving his legs of all power of motion."

Seeing him fall, Sublet [Sublette] said to me, "Jim, let us go and haul him away, and get his scalp before the Indians draw him in."

We went, and, seizing each a leg, started toward our lines with him; the wounded Indian grasping the grass with both hands, we had to haul with all our strength. . . .

Together, we dragged the Indian to one of our men, also wounded, for him to dispatch. But the poor fellow had not strength sufficient to perforate the Indian's skin with his knife, and we were obliged to perform the job ourselves.[161]

The haste with which the scalp was attacked sometimes proved embarrassing. Men were scalped, and escaped. Scalper and to-be-scalped, the offense and the defense, must engage in a struggle unexpected. The trapper "Doc" Newell, springing from his horse to scalp an Indian who had dropped apparently dead, by the first prick of his knife waked the victim to life again. Blade to blade they fought desperately — the Indian to retain his scalp, the trapper to take it or leave it, he did not care which. For "his fingers were in some way caught by some gun-screws with which the savage had ornamented his coiffure, and would not part company. In this dilemma there was no other alternative but fight. The miserable savage was dragged a rod or two in the struggle, and finally dispatched." Then Newell might loosen his fingers![162]

Other especial foes of the mountain-man were the grizzly bears — the great "white bears" first reported upon by Lewis and Clark. Until made acquainted with the white man's recklessness and the efficacy of his weapons of powder and ball they were absolutely fearless of human intrusion, regarding man as but a species of animal akin to the other wilderness animals which they overawed.

The grizzly was found as far east as South Dakota. He was found in the plains willow and dog-wood thickets along the Platte and the Missouri, as well as back in the hills. His ferocity was early measured, when in 1804 one of the beasts so promptly charged a squad of the Lewis and Clark men that they were forced to leap down a twenty-foot bank, into the river. A sudden encounter with his grayish bulk was always to be feared, and only a fool pursued him into a thicket.

The Grizzly Bear is the most ferocious animal that inhabits these prairies, and are very numerous. They no sooner see you than they will make at you with open mouth. If you stand still, they will come within two or three yards of you, and stand upon their hind feet, and look you in the face; if you have fortitude enough to face them, they will turn and run off; but if you turn they will most assuredly tear you to pieces.[163]

Old Hugh Glass, mountain-man with Ashley, 1823, having come upon a she grizzly in some river-bottoms chaparral was seized before he could set his double triggers and fire, and was torn for the cubs — they being as large as mastiffs. One of the Bonneville men, under Captain Joseph Walker, incautiously following a path into a thicket where a bear was couched with which they all purposed "to have some sport," was set upon and given such a severe wound, tearing the tendrons of his thigh, that he died — and the bear escaped. Trapper Dawson, with the Fowler and Glenn party of 1821-22, was hauled down, when halfway up a tree, by a grizzly; and before guns could be primed afresh and fired his head was in the bear's mouth. When he was carried to camp and examined, it was thought that the fangs had only slit his skin, from ears to the crown of his head — "all of which wounds ware sewed up as well as could be don by men in our Situation." But he insisted that he had heard his skull crack — and in three days he was buried.[164]

Following upon the accident to Hugh Glass, further on Jedediah Smith fairly ran into a grizzly in a brushy bottom in the southern section of the Black Hills, present South Dakota, and was instantly attacked — the animal "taking him by the head first . . . breaking several of his ribs and cutting his head badly."

I asked the Capt what was best   he said one or 2 go for water and if you have a needle and thread git it out and sew up my wounds around my head which was bleeding freely   I got a pair of scissors and cut off his hair and then began my first Job of d[r]essing wounds upon examination I found the bear had taken nearly all his head in his capcious mouth close to his left eye on one side and clos to his right ear on the other side and laid the skull bare to near the crown of the head leaving a white streak whare his teeth passed   one of his ears was torn from his head out to the outer rim   after stitching all the other wounds in the best way I was capabl and according to the captains directions the ear being the last I told him I could do nothing for his Eare. O you must try to stitch up some way or other said he   then I put in my needle stiching it through and through and over and over laying the lacerated parts together as nice as I could with my hands . . . this gave us a lisson on the character of the grissly Baare which we did not forget.[165]

Andrew Sublette, a brother of the more famous mountain-men William and Milton Sublette, while hunting in Southern California in 1854 was so mauled by a grizzly that he died in Los Angeles from his wounds. Having just emptied his gun into an elk Kit Carson was chased into an aspen tree by two grizzlies and there kept for some time — the "worst difficult" of all his mountain experiences, he was accustomed to say.

The trapper, when granted time, placed dependence upon one well-planted ball, but there were instances when fifteen and twenty balls was poured into an animal and at the last he was left in possession of the field. The Ferris *Diary* relates, of such a skirmish: "In his rage he broke down bushes and saplings with such ease, that we concluded that it would be imprudent to meddle with him any more."

This "white bear" and "grissly" of the high plains and the mountains is pictured in extraordinary size up to ten feet by chroniclers who killed him in his haunts, and Kit Carson is emphatic upon his attributes of great bulk. In his conversation with Colonel Meline —

"I have often and again seen grizzlies," said he, "of ten, eleven, and twelve hundred pounds. I distinctly remember killing one in the spring of 1846, that weighed 1200 pounds. Lieutenant Beale told me that he saw one of 1800. Trappers have often told me of numbers rising that weight, and I have no reason to doubt them."

Dr. Peters, in his biography of Carson, says that the grizzly's foot-prints will measure fourteen inches — which would be considered rather out of proportion today; but Dr. Elijah White is authority for a track "twelve inches in length by seven in breadth."[166]

In the contests with wild men, wild beasts and wild nature, serious wounds were received. Hamilton in *My Sixty Years on the Plains* narrates that his party of 1842 carried with them a supply of court-plaster, lint and bandages. But few outfits were so well provided, and the small detachments upon the beaver-streams were prepared for emergencies only by the fact that

in the old days a regular backwoods' science grew up among trappers and voyageurs; they treated gunshot wounds and broken bones, extracted bullets and arrows, or amputated shattered limbs, in a way that would have amazed the faculty, but was singularly successful. The camp-saw and a well sharpened butcher-knife were their surgical instruments; their cauteries, hot irons; and their tourniquets, a handkerchief twisted upon the limb with a stick run through the knot and turned to press upon the artery. Arrows were often drawn through the limb, the feathers having been cut off; and bullets were flirted out of an incision quickly made with a sharp razor. In winter the wounded limb was almost frozen by snow or ice applied before the amputation; in summer there was nothing for it but to suffer it through.[167]

The patient might vent his agony upon a bullet clinched between the teeth — an alleviative which had not gone out of use even as late as the Civil War.

The bone having been shattered at the ankle by a bullet, out in the brush trapper Thomas L. Smith hacked his leg off above the knee with his butcher knife and a key-hole meat-saw; the weather was so cold that the arteries bled very little; while recovering under squaw care in an Indian winter village he whittled a peg; and as "Peg-leg" Smith he rode and stumped hither and thither through plain and desert and mountains for forty years.

Disabled men were transported in the travois or Indian litter — a blanket or buffalo-hide slung between two poles trailing from a horse's rump. Or the poles might be supported by two horses tandem. Zenas Leonard, with a dislocated ankle, declares: "This was the most painful travelling to me, as well as to the others, that I ever experienced — particularly whilst passing over a rough piece of ground." The pole litter was employed by the army also, in Indian-campaign days.

The dressing of wounds was a simple matter. The Indians had good knowledge of healing poultices made from roots, leaves and barks. The softened gum of the pine and the balsam fir was a favorite application by both Indians and whites. But the standard treatment consisted in washing the wound with cold running water (if that were at hand), clapping on a plaster or plug of buffalo wool or beaver fur or wad of tobacco, and bandaging with a strip of hide or blanketing. Nature took its course for good or ill, but the physical system of that western country, like the physical system of the inhabitants, was singularly germ free. Death did occur from gangrene, which poisoned the patient; the more obscure manifestations of blood poisoning from infection were laid to the fever of pain.

The bullet that was lodged too deep for extraction was left in, and the hole was plugged! The head of the arrow that could not be shoved on through until the shaft might be snipped off and withdrawn, and which itself could not be "butchered out" or, by reason of the barbs or the loose wrapping, tugged out, was left in. For better convenience the shaft was hacked away at the surface of the wound; in short time the sinew wrapping of the head yielded (the shaft and head of the war arrow readily parted company) and the remainder of the shaft could be plucked out.

The missionary Dr. Marcus Whitman held a clinic at the rendezvous of 1835 in the Green River Valley, where he

was called upon to perform some very important surgical operations. He extracted an iron arrow, three inches long, from the back of Capt. Bridger which was received in a skirmish, three years before, with the Blackfeet Indians. It was a difficult operation, because the arrow was hooked at the point by striking a large bone, and a cartilaginous substance had grown around it. The Doctor pursued the operation with great self-possession and perseverance; and his patient manifested equal firmness. The Indians looked on meanwhile, with countenances indicating wonder, and in their own peculiar manner expressed great astonishment when it was extracted. The Doctor also extracted another arrow from the shoulder of one of the hunters, which had been there two years and a half.[168]

The hearty food, the active life, and an habitual indifference to fear, endowed the beaver trapper with remarkable endurance and recuperative power. After he had been clawed and bitten and torn from head to foot by the "white bear" and left for dead by his companions, Hugh Glass crawled and crept across country for eighty miles before he was given human help.

In 1860 Mark Ralfe, a young French trapper, was dispatched from Bent's Fort site down the Arkansas with a message to United States troops.

After Ralfe had ridden forty miles, the Kiowas fell upon him, shooting him in three places, and stabbing him in four. Believing him dead, they took his scalp with a dull knife, leaving no hair whatever except a little lock above each ear. After they had gone he recovered consciousness, and with no nourishment except water, walked back to the fort. In a few months he was well again.[169]

John Colter, in 1809, having been granted a head-start by his captors the Blackfeet, ran at top speed for six miles through prickly pear cactus and sage-brush, swam to the middle of a stream and dived underneath the brushwood there. The next day he set forth, naked, famished, dependant upon roots for sustenance, upon a seven days' journey to the Missouri Fur Company's post on the Yellowstone. Jim Beckwourth declares that in one of his foot-races for life he ran ninety-five miles in the day — and he calls upon anybody in Sublette's company of the time to deny the fact. Kit Carson, Joe Meek and four associate trappers, carrying each his blanket and his gun, fleeing the Comanches after a long day's fight behind dead saddle animals, in the hot sun and the reek of powder smoke, ran at a trot all night "and found no water for seventy-five miles."

As Clerk Ferris records, the mountain-man was familiarized, by "hard buffetings," to danger, and had it "impressed upon his mind, as a duty, never to yield to adversity, while a shadow of hope remained; and to scan, even in the most critical moment, the chances of success."

When at last he did succumb, as fate willed; picked off suddenly by arrow or bullet of foe not seen, sinking under wound by man or beast, worn down by privation, or attacked by a rare illness, his shift was short. The wilderness afforded scant measure of mourning or of funeral rites.

When the trapper Marteau, clumsy in his riding, was thrown from the saddle in running buffalo, Carson would send Joe Meek over to see how badly he was hurt.

"What'll I do with him if he is dead?" asked Meek.

"Can't you pack him to camp?"

"Pack h——l," objected Meek. "I should rather pack a load of meat." For, as Meek explained afterward to Mrs. Victor: "We had no time for compassion. Besides, live men war what we wanted; dead ones war of no account."

Accordingly the trapper Ponto, killed by the caving in of a cache, was "rolled in a blanket and tossed into the river." Time lacked. Usually a body was bestowed, more or less hastily, in a grave secret and deep. The Indians would "dig down ten feet to get a white man's scalp," states Hamilton. And so would the wolves. Sometimes a camp-fire was built upon the grave; sometimes logs or boulders were rolled atop the spot. The long beaver trail of the West is dotted with graves so forgotten, so lonely, that we may wonder whether the trump of Gabriel will ever seek them out.

Now in return for the rude life what, beside rude death, was by the mountain-man to be expected? What was the compensation beyond the charm in being free? That excellent young man encountered by Dr. Elijah White received a wage of $250 a year; the skilled mechanic George W. Ebbert hired out to William Sublette "at $150 for six months and $350 a year afterward." Through his nine years in the mountains he averaged eighty skins a year; some years he made $900 for himself — and some years he did not pay expenses. After five years' service as clerk and trapper in the mountains Zenas Leonard returned to Pennsylvania with $1,100; Oliver Wiggins said that the members of his company averaged about $1,000 a year by the sale of their furs — one-third of the aggregate sum went to Kit Carson, and two-thirds were divided among the employes. Joe Meek in his biography claims that as a top trapper he was being paid, at the height of the beaver business, $1,500 a year. But in August, 1839, the traveler Thomas J. Farnham met him in the Bear River Valley.

Meek was evidently very poor. He had scarcely clothing enough to cover his body. And while talking with us the frosty winds which sucked up the valley, made him shiver like an aspen leaf. He reverted to his destitute situation, and complained of the injustice of his former employers; the little remuneration he had received for the toils and dangers he had endured on their account, etc.; a complaint which I had heard from every trapper whom I had met on my journey.[170]

The hired trapper existed by a system almost of peonage: whether his wages were small or large, he was under necessity of making his purchases from the company traders, at exorbitant prices. He was encouraged to stay poor. And as a result, says Zenas Leonard,

scarcely one man in ten, of those employed in this country, ever think of saving a single dollar of their earnings, but spend it as fast as they can see an object to spend it for.

Even as independent trappers selling their catch to the highest bidder, or when by chance or resolution they escaped the wiles of the traders, the mountain-men rarely held fast to their profits. It was not the inability to earn, it was the inability to keep; and by that human nature which attributes one's ill success to other factors than self, Meek and his fellow trappers in blaming the employers were blind to the main chance. Kit Carson saved practically nothing from his own trapping days; Jim Bridger relied upon his trading-post, after his trapping days were over — and he died poor in purse. Oliver Wiggins saved nothing from his beaver days; Joe Meek saved nothing from his beaver days; Jim Baker, having hoarded until he was in possession of $5,000 with which to retire to the States and buy a farm, ere he was beyond Fort Laramie lost every cent of it at monte; and he, too, saved nothing from his beaver days.

It was the destiny of nearly all the mountain-men, free or hired, that they die poor. And as with the beaver trapper, so with the prospector who succeeded to him.

Chapter XV

The Roll Call

IT is the way of the West to receive the new-comer with a certain proper reservation, and to take little on hearsay. When Kit Carson entered the mountains he mingled there with men of service in the Northwest ante-dating his service in the Southwest; men who occupied the scene. Fur trade history had been made in chapters written around the deeds of the Old Guard of the American Fur Company, the Missouri Fur Company, of Ashley, of Smith, Jackson & Sublette, the Rocky Mountain Fur Company, and the free trappers school.

From the view-point of the spring of 1832, when Carson is leaving winter quarters, let us call an honor roll of names then active, about to be active, or already inactive in the mountains.

The popular General William Henry Ashley has retired from the trail; had been elected to Congress, where this past winter he took his seat. Born a Virginian, 1778; by adoption a Missourian, date 1808 if not earlier; slated to be "the most influential man in Missouri, next to Benton," three times married, father of the American beaver trade in the mountains (but with no other child), militia chief, first lieutenant governor of Missouri, powder manufacturer, surveyor, real estate dealer, fur trader, banker, capitalist and politician, out of checkered fortunes he achieved financial success only when he was approaching fifty, but died, at sixty, in 1838. In his rise, a man of slight frame and dyspeptic appearance; in success, owning one of the finest home estates in St. Louis; in death, lying in a neglected grave upon a Missouri farm beside the waters of the river trail that he had stoutly ascended.[171]

As for Major Andrew Henry, fur hunter of 1809, turned lead miner, only to become the Ashley partner in 1822,

> "He is gone on the mountain,
> He is lost to the forest."

A man of "honesty, intelligence and enterprise"; tall and slender, with dark hair and light eyes, and fond of the violin;

first American fur-trade captain to establish himself on the Pacific slope of the northwest Rockies, having turned to Missouri and peaceful pursuits he had submitted to his narrow bed January 10, 1832, in St. Louis his home. His name survives in descendants, and in Henry Lake and Henry Fork of the Snake in the vicinity of his old fort of 1810 — not far from the sanctuary of the Rocky Mountain Fur Company under Fitzpatrick et al., this same winter.

Of Captain Ewing Young enough has been said. David E. Jackson ("Davy" to his friends), of the fur trade and Jackson Hole, as the Young partner on a mule-trading excursion from Santa Fé to California via Tucson and the Yuma crossing of the Colorado has taken perhaps the first negro, his body servant, into California. As the out-come of all his ventures he dies, a poor man, in St. Louis.

Joshua Pilcher: Virginian, hatter by trade, bank director in St. Louis, fur trader of long experience dating to 1819; courtly and indefatigable and noted for his grand tour when, as head of the Missouri Fur Company then in its last days, in 1828-30 with nine men he swung from the Salt Lake Valley country to the British posts of the Columbia, thence around by the line of posts in Canada and down to the Missouri and St. Louis again; in 1832, American Fur Company agent at the Council Bluffs, and active in Company interests, for thereafter he is encountered on the trail to the mountains. In six years he will succeed the jovial, famous General William Clark in the Indian Affairs superintendency at St. Louis; and will die in June, 1847, aged fifty-seven.

Etienne Provot, of the Ashley ranks of 1823, possibly 1822; a leader of Ashley parties; claiming to have preceded Thomas Fitzpatrick over the South Pass, in 1823, and to have preceded James Bridger to the Salt Lake; in 1832 is allied with the American Fur Company, and, according to clerk Ferris, is due at this year's rendezvous with goods from the Company fur post of Fort Union; in 1837 was reported, in the mountains, as "no more," but nevertheless was active yet until, as a respected

French-blood citizen of St. Louis, he died, July 3, 1850. His name, subjected to various spellings, attaches to Provo City, Utah, amid scenes of a fair land that knew him in his beaver days.[172]

Jedediah Strong Smith is only a memory. For nine months his bones have been lying upon Southwest soil. New York State born, a man of high ideals and of steadfast faith in the Christian religion, a combination of the wilderness hunter and the padre explorer, he can ill be spared from an area wherein characters like his are sorely needed. His ambition was to present the world with an atlas and digest of the western country; but he failed of that achievement.[173]

William L. Sublette: "Height six feet two inches; forehead straight and open; eyes blue, light; nose Roman; mouth and chin common; hair light or sandy; complexion fair; face long and expressive; scar on left side of chin." (This description from the passport for that disastrous trading trip upon the Santa Fé Trail, 1831, and cited in Chittenden's *American Fur Trade*.) He is now thirty-three — was born in Kentucky, 1799. An Ashley man of 1823; partner in the firm Smith, Jackson & Sublette which took over the Ashley fur business in 1826; turned trader and fur-trade purveyor in 1830, when with his partners he sold out to the Rocky Mountain Fur Company; in the spring of 1832 is preparing to start from Missouri with his supply caravan for the summer rendezvous; will go into partnership, for the mountain beaver and Indian trade, with Robert Campbell of St. Louis, to operate as Sublette & Campbell, with the depot, in 1837, on Main St., St. Louis. He was a bold, energetic captain of trappers, and trader; a determined and skillful Indian fighter; known to his associate mountain-men as "Billy" and "Captain Billy"; to the Indians as "Cut Face," "Fate," and "Left Hand." He retired, wealthy, from the mountain trade in 1842, aspired vainly to Congress from Missouri, in 1844 married Miss Frances Hereford, a "celebrated but impecunious beauty" of Tuscumbia, Alabama, and installed her upon his farm of 200 acres now within the southwestern limits

Jedediah Strong Smith

of St. Louis; would have been satisfied (1845) with the Super-intendency of Indian Affairs at St. Louis, but his husbandhood and his new plans were soon terminated. He died, in July, 1845, in Pittsburgh while on his way to Washington. For him

it was   "A short life in the saddle, Lord,
                    Not long life by the fire."

His remains rest under a granite shaft in Bellefontaine ceme-tery of St. Louis.

Milton G. Sublette: Younger brother, and associate in the mountains, of William L., and of like aggressive character; said to have enlisted under Ashley and Henry in 1822; slightly less prominent in beaver day annals only because less exploited. A bold adventurer on the Santa Fé Trail and in New Mexico; in 1832 one of the partners operating the Rocky Mountain Fur Company since 1830; this same year seriously stabbed on Bear River by a jealous Rockaway Indian father; by a "fungus" disease of his leg forced to retire, 1835, from his mountain activities and twice to suffer amputation. In December, 1836, while still a young man he died at old Fort William, built by his brother and Robert Campbell and named for his brother, now in 1836 owned, as Fort John, by himself in partnership with Thomas Fitzpatrick and James Bridger and already called Fort Laramie, above the mouth of the Laramie River in Wyoming. Joe Meek succeeded to his Snake wife, the most-beautiful Mountain Lamb.[174]

Robert Campbell: A Scot of County Tyrone, North of Ire-land; at twenty an emigrant in St. Louis; at twenty-one, or in 1825, in the mountains with an Ashley party for his health, and during his ten years' service in the beaver country finding not only health but wealth. In the fur hunt and in St. Louis a close friend and partner of William Sublette; after 1835, one of St. Louis's most prominent financiers, capitalists and business heads; banker, a director in the Missouri Pacific Railroad or-ganization of 1849, owner of the old Southern Hotel, outfitter of and adviser to Government expeditions into the west, a

United States commissioner to the Indians in 1851 and 1869. A man whose word, through over forty years, was good for any amount, "from the Yellowstone to Santa Fé." He died in October, 1879, at the age of seventy-five.

Jean Baptiste Gervais: Missouri, or possibly Kaskaskia (Ill.) Frenchman, but of Canadian stock; a partner in the Rocky Mountain Fur Company — and one who, after he sold out his interests in 1834 for "twenty head of horse beast, thirty beaver traps, and five hundred dollars' worth of merchandise," may have resumed the rôle of free trapper, but is little heard of.

Henry Fraeb: German by blood and accent, partner in the Rocky Mountain Fur Company, associated with Gervais the Frenchman on the beaver trail, favoring with him the streams of northwestern Colorado but reported to have led, with Gervais, a trapping party through the southwest to California in the fall of 1833. At the dissolution of the Rocky Mountain Fur Company in 1834 he sold his interest for "forty head of horse beast, forty beaver traps, eight guns, and one thousand dollars' worth of merchandise," and continued to be a captain of trappers, with Jim Bridger as one of his contacts in the mountains. As "Frapp" he lived, and as "Frapp" and "Trapp" he died — shot while he was forted, with his thirty men, against an attack by 300 Cheyenne and Sioux, at the confluence of Battle Creek and the Little Snake, in northwestern Colorado near the present border-line town of Slater, August 21 and 22, 1841. He was buried on the spot, together with three companions unnamed; and here, after his fifteen years among the vasty plains and hills, the "German Frapp" was left to reap the "fading honors of the dead."

Thomas Fitzpatrick: Carson's first captain for the mountains of the Northwest; Irish born, of the same age as William Sublette, a contemporary of William Sublette, Jedediah Smith, Jim Bridger, commencing with the Ashley company of 1823; fully the equal of William Sublette in activities but serving more meritoriously; beaver trapper, partisan, fur trader, guide and Indian agent; now in 1832 the head of the Rocky Mountain

Fur Company, soon to enter into another short-lived enterprise, that of Fitzpatrick, Sublette (Milton) & Bridger; thereafter, upon the decline of the beaver business and the mountain supplies business, to adapt himself to other issues in the new days in the West. He was selected by Father De Smet as the guide for the Catholic missionary party of 1841 to Oregon and guided the associated emigrant column also; is mentioned, with praise, by the missionary Elijah White as his guide on the way to Oregon in 1842; praised by Frémont as an efficient guide upon the expedition to California, 1843-44; by Colonel Stephen Watts Kearny and Captain Philip St. George Cooke of the dragoons excursion along the Oregon Trail in 1845, by Lieutenant J. W. Abert of the Government exploring expedition out of Bent's Fort into the southeast in 1845; was appointed to the Kearny column for the conquest of New Mexico and California, 1846. Through the recommendation of Senator Benton of Missouri, in the fall of 1846 he received the appointment of Indian agent upon the Upper Platte and the Arkansas, over the Sioux, Cheyenne, Arapaho and "other wandering tribes." With his post at Bent's Fort and elsewhere along the Arkansas he served notably; was "greatly esteemed by the Indians, and among white men since is reputed to have been the best agent these tribes ever had." Married a daughter, by an Arapaho wife, of John Poisal, trader and interpreter known by the Indians as "Old Red Eyes" on account of an inflammation of the lids. To the Indians of mountains and plains Fitzpatrick was "Bad Hand," "Broken Hand," "Three Fingers," because of an injury from a bursting rifle; "White Head" and "White Hair," remindful of a harrowing chase (1832) by Indians, which turned his hair gray. A man of large frame, rather thick-set in later life, still young-looking when employed by Frémont in 1843, with his white hair contrasted with his ruddy complexion, as seen in 1839 by the traveler Wislizenus at Fort Vasquez on the South Platte he then had "a strong spare, bony figure, a face full of expression," and a demeanor revealing "strong passions." He died in 1854, aged forty-five, while in Washington on Indian

business; was given official burial in the Congressional cemetery — but there to lie, by a quirk of fate, in a city unmarked
grave, with his name honored upon no map, and himself to be
　　　"Rolled round in earth's diurnal course
　　　With rocks, and stones, and trees."[175]

Captain Benjamin Louis Eulalie de Bonneville: French born,
reared in New York, educated at West Point; died June 12,
1878, a colonel retired, at Fort Smith, Arkansas; buried in
Bellefontaine cemetery, St. Louis.
　　　"An honest man, close-buttoned to the chin,
　　　Broadcloth without, and a warm heart within."

"Of middle size, well made and well set"; of countenance
"frank, open, and engaging," with a French cast; of "pleasant
black eye," a high forehead, and a bald crown. On leave from
army duty, in the spring of 1832 he is conducting an exploring
and fur-hunting brigade to the South Pass, for the country of
the Green, the Salt Lake, and the Columbia. Rebuffed by
American and British companies alike, he succeeded in fasten-
ing his name to the Great Basin but not to the Salt Lake, in
adventitiously opening communication with California by the
Humboldt River route, sprinkled, as advanced the Star of
Empire, with the blood of wretched Diggers, in over-staying
his leave and exciting army criticism. Too much of the soldier
to make a trader, too easy of reckonings to make a scientist, he
was enough of the performer to inspire an instructive story of
the beaver and Indian West. By this, chiefly, he contributed to
the cause of Western expansion, for his maps, briefly circulated,
soon passed into obscurity. They correctly showed that the Salt
Lake had no outlet.[176]

Captain John Gantt: Carson's second captain in the mountain fur trade; an independent trader who, with his partner
Blackwell, in the spring of 1831 conducted a trapping company
of seventy men out of St. Louis for the mountains, but arrived
at the juncture of the North Platte and the Laramie not until
fall. While Captain Blackwell maintains the supply line Cap-

tain Gantt stays in the field, where, this spring of 1832, Carson
will join or rejoin him and serve with him for a year and a
half. Of Blackwell we know little; of Captain Gantt —
whether by name Gaunt, Gant, Ghant or Grant — we know
more. He was a Virginian appointed to the army from Kentucky in 1817; as captain in the Sixth Infantry of upper Missouri River service was dismissed from the army in May, 1829,
and thus was inducted into his mountain career by bad fortune.
His achievement was that of establishing, on the Arkansas
shortly below present Pueblo, Colorado, the first trading post
by consent of the jealous Arapahos. But owing to various dis-
asters the firm of Gantt ("Baldhead") & Blackwell ("Crane")
failed. Captain Gantt took his knowledge of the country back
to the Missouri, and in the summer of 1835 "Captain Gantt,
Indian trader," was guide for Colonel Henry Dodge's First
Dragoons out of Fort Leavenworth on tour up the Platte and
south to the Arkansas. Following, Captain Gantt was trader,
betimes, among the prairie Indians between the Missouri opposite the mouth of the Platte and the Mississippi (the land of
Iowa) until, in the spring of 1843, as "Captain John Gant, old
army officer and mountain-man," he joined the Great Emigration from the Missouri River frontier for Oregon, to pilot the
column to Fort Hall beyond the mountains; thence he continued on to California; there commanded a company of riflemen "of all Nations" in the Sutter's Fort array for the California internal revolution of 1844; there, in 1845, he contracted
to hunt and punish, with his riflemen force, the horse-thief
Indians; there, in 1846, was discovered by Edwin Bryant (*What
I Saw in California*) as domiciled upon the lower San Joaquin
rancho of the robust Dr. John Marsh (Harvard, 1823). "Captain
Gant, formerly of the U. S. army, in very bad health. . . . He
has crossed the Rocky Mountains eight times, and, in various
trapping excursions, has explored nearly every river between
the settlements in the United States and the Pacific Ocean."
Early in 1849 Captain John Gantt, of many an adventure unrecorded, of ambitions grown old and flesh grown weary,

passed on, short of man's allotted time, in the Napa Valley north of San Pablo Bay inside the Golden Gate.[177]

Nathaniel Jarvis Wyeth: Ice merchant turned Western trader and fur hunter; first enthusiast after John Jacob Astor to attempt to force the lock of the Pacific Northwest commerce with the blade of Yankee enterprise. Cambridge born, Massachusetts educated, business trained, at thirty years of age, having put himself and company through a preliminary "hardening" by a two weeks' camp upon the home river near Boston, in this the spring of 1832 he heads out with his twenty amateur mountaineers to engage in "business" in the Oregon Country beyond the Rockies; in general trading, from which the proceeds were to be shipped by vessels around the Horn; and, again, in the salmon fishery industry, as second string to his fiddle. With his followers daunted by unexpected hardships and sarcastic over his wagon-boat dubbed by Harvard students the Nat-Wyethium, succored upon the trail by William Sublette who then tolerated him as an innocent only later to out-jockey him as a competitor, he was received by the mountains with the fierce battle of Pierre's Hole. He was admired for his gameness, cozened for his ignorance, opposed for his presumption, and the "throat of his prosperity cut with kindness and politeness." The American and British companies would have naught to do with him in business. After a second trip in (this time in behalf of his "Columbia River Fishing and Trading Company") and four years, all told, of struggle, he left his brave Fort Hall as a "stone in the garden" of his smiling countrymen — as a Hudson's Bay Company stepping-stone, by that — and returned to the ice business in Cambridge. Here, with his ambitions shackled, his wanderings o'er, in the close of August, 1856, like the typical New Englander he died on "the spot where he was born."

"Where is it now, the glory and the dream?"[178]

Joseph L. Meek: Beaver trapper, first Oregon sheriff, member of the "provisional" Oregon legislature of 1846, "special envoy" (1848) from the government of Oregon "to the Court

of Washington" and there again meeting Kit Carson, fellow
mountain-man also arrived to distinction; thence returning
with a governor for the officially recognized Territory of Oregon. Joe Meek was born in Virginia in 1810, almost at the time
of the birth of Carson in Kentucky. As another runaway he
entered the mountains in 1829, under William Sublette. Cousin
to one James Polk, Tennessee lawyer and President of the
Republic; himself none the less a dare-devil, a wit, a harum-
scarum, now here, now there upon the fur trail, now prosperous, now poor, with the plantation his school and the mountains his college, he by his narrated adventures and observations
induced one of the most colorful histories of the opening of the
Northwest. In the spring of 1832 he has been camped with the
Rocky Mountain Company men of Fitzpatrick and partners;
Carson's trail and his are due to run together for many a beaver
set and Injun scrimmage ere the change to the Washington
scene.[179]

Andrew S. Drips: Partisan and agent of the American Fur
Company, in the mountain campaigns and on the Upper Missouri; now, this spring of 1832, expected at summer rendezvous
with Lucien Fontenelle and supplies from St. Louis. He was
born in Pennsylvania in 1789, entered the St. Louis fur trade as
early as 1820, died in Kansas City in 1860 — one of the few
mountain-men permitted to reach three score years and ten. In
1842, as the "old mountaineer, Captain Drips" he was recommended to Frémont as the guide for the expedition to the
mountains, and was written to upon the subject, but there fell
to him the agency for the tribes of the Upper Missouri, with his
post at Fort Pierre near the mouth of the Teton or Bad River,
central South Dakota. Thus fate tricked him, for Kit Carson
seized the opportunity for fame which he missed. It was the
turn in the trail. Nevertheless, as duty called, he was the first
Indian agent to fight, with genuine zeal, the introduction of
liquor into the Indian country. While a trader at Bellevue near
the mouth of the Platte in Nebraska and today a suburb of
Omaha he had married an Oto woman, to whom he was faith-

ful husband through many years. The fourth child, a daughter, was born during the battle of Pierre's Hole between the trappers and Gros Vent' Blackfeet at the close of the rendezvous of 1832.[180]

William Henry Vanderburgh: American Fur Company partisan in the mountain hunts whereby the Rocky Mountain Fur Company was steadily harassed. Was an Indianan, by 1823 a fur trader in the Missouri Fur Company, and in that year a captain under Colonel Leavenworth in the attack upon the Arikara Indians. He was ambushed by the Blackfeet, in October, 1832, while he was pressing, reckless of sign, along a side stream of the Jefferson River in the Three Forks country of southwestern Montana. With his horse disabled and himself abandoned by his helplessly stampeded and shattered men, his last words, as he bravely faced the enemy and shot the foremost were: "Boys, don't run." Riddled, he fell; "they uttered a loud and shrill yell of exultation and the noble spirit of a good and brave man had passed away forever. Thus fell William Henry Vanderburgh . . . at the time he perished under thirty years of age. Bold, daring and fearless, yet cautious, deliberate and prudent; uniting the apparent opposite qualities of courage and coolness, a soldier and a scholar, he died universally beloved and regretted by all who knew him" — he, like Jedediah Smith, and the many in trapper rank and file,

> "called upon to face
> Some awful moment to which Heaven has joined
> Great issues, good or bad for human race."[181]

Lucien (B.?) Fontenelle: Third in the trio of American Fur Company partisans in the mountain rivalry; New Orleans Frenchman of aristocratic blood and titled ancestry; a youth born to romance, orphaned by a Louisiana hurricane, made a runaway by an over-strict aunt, exchanging a bank clerkship for the Missouri River frontier, returning to New Orleans, after twenty years, to be identified by and welcomed by an old nurse but to be repudiated by a sister now well married. Again he

became a trader, associated with Andrew Drips at Bellevue post
on the Missouri near the mouth of the Platte and in fur company service leading brigades into the mountains. He was a
swart, foreign-appearing man, of a saturnine temperament and
of excesses which finally brought him to suicide, they say, while
under the influence of liquor, at that Fort John on the Laramie
where, some time previously, his competitor Milton Sublette
had died. Thus did Lucien Fontenelle the apostate seek to be

"No more submitted to the change and chance
  Of the unsteady planets."

Children of his by an Omaha Indian wife have been prominent
figures in the history of Nebraska. A son, Logan Fontenelle,
was head chief of the Omahas in settler days. The house of
another son, Henry, of material and furnishings imported up-
river from St. Louis, in 1841, was long a landmark at Decatur,
and Henry's wife, who had been Emily Papin, of French and
Pawnee strain, passed within the last year or two, aged 109.
Other descendants of Lucien the fur trader carry the family
name, which appears also upon the map of the West.[182]

James Bridger: Major Bridger, "Old Gabe," "Daniel Boone
of the Mountains," "Casapy" or "Blanket Chief"; born in Virginia in 1804, died blind and decrepit on his farm near Santa
Fé (Dallas), Missouri, nor far from Kansas City, in 1881, when
he was almost the last survivor from early beaver days. At
eighteen (1822) an Ashley man; at twenty (1824) the discoverer (on a wager that he would descend Bear River to its
mouth) of the Salt Lake; first exploiter of the wonders of the
Yellowstone National Park — and not believed. Blacksmith,
beaver trapper, captain of trappers, partner in the Rocky Mountain Fur Company, partner next in the short-lived fur firm
Fitzpatrick, Sublette (Milton) & Bridger, partner in the trading firm of Bridger and Vasquez, founder of the Fort Bridger
trading post for emigrants on the Overland Trail to Oregon
and California, and established, 1843, "west of the mountains,"
on Black's Fork of the Green River in southwestern Wyoming,

in the midst of a Mexican grant of almost 4,000 acres. Consulted upon the Salt Lake country by the advancing Brigham Young Mormons, 1847; served as guide for emigrants; was guide for Sir George Gore the Irish sportsman in the Rockies, 1854-55; for the General Albert Sydney Johnston "Utah column" in the Mormon War of 1857-58; for various military and civil expeditions on the plains in the Civil War period, and consulted by General Sheridan as late as 1868; adviser to the survey for the Union Pacific Railroad, building westward in the Sixties; was guide for Captain W. F. Raynolds of the army in the attempted exploration of the Yellowstone Park in 1859-60. He was a man of the spare but powerful type, gray-eyed, brown-haired, of shrewd, quizzical cast of countenance, with his lean square face fringed by a thin beard. Noted for his native wit and his fanciful yarns he also ranked, as mountain-man, plainsman, and guide, above all his contemporaries and was generally looked up to for his knowledge of Indians and topography. He died poor, feeling that he had been defrauded by his Government; but over his body in the Mount Washington cemetery of Kansas City there rises a noble granite monument, the gift of a mindful friend. In this spring of 1832, however, "old" Jim Bridger is about to break winter camp, along with the other trappers in Kit Carson's neighborhood in the Snake and Salmon Rivers territory.[188]

Thomas L. Smith: "Peg-leg" Smith, "Old Peg-leg," among the Mexicans and Californians El Cojo (The Lame) Smit; beaver trapper, Indian-trader, mountain-man, desert freebooter, horse lifter and horse trader, purveyor to emigrants on the trail to California, either the discoverer or the creator of those "three little black hills," 80% virgin gold, known through these almost 100 succeeding years as the Lost Peg-legs and the Peg-leg Mine. Born in Kentucky, 1801; at sixteen a runaway from school and rod; at seventeen a hunter, out of the Boone's Lick district, Missouri, among the Osages, Sacs, Foxes, et al.; at twenty-two, or in 1823 (but more likely, according to the records of the day, in the spring of 1824), a trader with the first wagon caravan, that of Alexander Le Grand, across the plains from the Missouri settlements to Santa Fé, but landing, himself, in Taos; beginning with the fall of 1824, a beaver trapper in west central mountain Colorado (whereby Smith's Fork of the Gunnison), in the Moqui and Apache southwest with Captain Ewing Young, Milton Sublette and others, and elsewhere; in the late fall of 1827 was shot through the leg just above the ankle in a scrimmage with Crow Indians on the sources of the North Platte River, and was forced to amputate his leg; in the spring came out of his buffalo-robe bed among the Utes and donned the peg that he had manufactured. Thereafter he was trapper again, Indian-trader in north and south, fearsome raider upon California horse stock; in 1837, while upon another "trading" expedition, climbed the middle one of three little black hills at the western edge of the Colorado Desert, southeastern California — and in 1849 learned, through an assay in San Francisco, that his keepsake pocket-pieces were fabulously rich nuggets. He headed one or two re-discovery expeditions, but the Lost Peg-legs have remained figments of romance. He was a "stout built man with black eyes and gray hair" and a florid complexion; a "hard drinker, and, when under the influence of liquor, very liable to get into a fight" and to wield his quickly unstrapped wooden leg. In the Fifties and Sixties he was a familiar sojourner in San Bernardino and Los Angeles of Southern California, the mining camps and San Francisco of Northern California. He died, penniless and old and broken, in the San Francisco City and County Hospital, October 14, 1866; is buried in a potter's grave.

Captain Joseph Reddeford Walker: Strapping Tennesseean with the physical and something of the mental characteristics of his fellow townsman Ewing Young; born in Knoxville, 1798; a Missourian of 1818 or 1819; thereafter New Mexico trapper, Spanish captive, Southwest Indian fighter, Missouri sheriff, Southwest trader, mountain-man beaver hunter, captain under Bonneville from the Missouri border into the mountains; breaker of the trail (1833) from the Salt Lake by way of the Humboldt River to the Sierra Nevada range and Monterey of California, and thereby memorializing his name in Walker's Lake, Walker's River and Walker's Pass; guide for emigrants to California by the desert route and for a division of Frémont's company of 1845-46; California rancher and stock-raiser after the American occupation; first among the Arizona prospectors who in the early Sixties opened the Prescott placer region. He was dark and bearded, six feet tall, weight 200 pounds, a thorough frontiersman, mild but resolute, "one of the bravest and most skillful of mountain-men" and especially familiar with the deserts of the Southwest. He died, famous and respected, on a ranch in Ignacio Valley, Contra Costa County, California, October 27, 1876, aged seventy-eight. His request was that upon his stone there be ascribed to him the discovery of the Yosemite Valley.[184]

Michel Sylvestre Cerré: Fur trader, and Walker's associate captain under Bonneville, 1832. St. Louis Frenchman, born 1803, grandson of a pioneer fur-hunter of the Mississippi Valley; "of the middle size, light complexioned," and active, with experience on the early Santa Fé Trail; after the Bonneville expedition, in the American Fur Company; in 1848, representative in the Missouri Assembly; in 1849, clerk of the St. Louis District court; 1858, sheriff of St. Louis County; on January 5, 1860, he passes from earth. The name Cerré still maintains, on an equality with the proud name Chouteau which likewise is a fixture in American fur trade history.

James P. Beckwourth: Jim Beckwourth, Virginia mulatto claiming to Revolutionary ancestry on his father's side but not referring to his mother; "a large, good-humored fellow"; trapper with the Ashley expedition of 1823 and of long, varied career thenceforth, which made him one of the most popular characters in the plains and mountains West of Carson's day. He was a Crow adoption and a Crow chief, alleged army scout in the Florida War of 1836, trader at the old Pueblo post on the Arkansas, where his consort (married in Taos as a successor to his Crow princesses), Madame Beckwourth, was a damsel born

Señorita Louise Sandeville. He was an adventurer on the horse-thief desert trail to California before the Conquest and an actor there in militant proceedings; immigrant trader, occupant, with his "hotel" and trading store, of Beckwourth Valley (1852) and exploiter of Beckwourth's Pass by which in day much later the railroad along the Feather River route crossed the Sierra. The dictated story of his life exceeds the best endeavors of a Ned Buntline but is not without a fair measure of historical values. Returned to the plains and Rockies he was to be seen, with a "Lady Beckwourth," in Denver during the Pike's Peak Rush times of 1859-60. At the end he was again a Crow, only to die by poisoned soup in a Crow lodge of the North Platte country, Wyoming, 1867, aged seventy. Thus his Crow wife, there, retained him in spirit.

Antoine Robidoux: Properly, Robidou; born in St. Louis in 1794, one of several brothers of French family name well established there; is said to have embarked for the mouth of the Yellowstone in 1816 but more likely it was 1819 when the first Government military and exploring expedition ascended the Missouri from St. Louis; a Mexican citizen at Taos in 1822, where after fifteen years he married a Spanish woman; the first fur trader (possibly in connection with his brother Louis) out of Taos, with pioneer trading post, Fort Roubideau, founded 1824-25, among the Utes, near present Delta of southwestern Colorado across the Continental Divide; was longer associated with his Fort Uintah of the same period, at the forks of the Uintah River in northeastern Utah, and destroyed by the Utes in 1844. He traded also with the Navajos and Apaches; was one of New Mexico's earliest American placer miners — setting the fashion by "sinking eight thousand dollars"; was interpreter out of Bent's Fort with the Kearny column, 1846, to California, where his brother Louis, already of two years' residence, was American *juez de paz* of the San Bernardino district; was grievously wounded by a lance thrust at the battle of San Pascual; was granted a pension by Congress in May, 1856; died in St. Joseph, Missouri, founded by his Indian-trader brother,

Joseph, in August, 1860, aged sixty-six. A slender, active Frenchman, of "sprightly disposition and the spirit of adventure," he
was intimately known to Kit Carson. His Roubideau's Pass
across the rampart Sangre de Cristo range, southern Colorado,
between Taos and the San Luis Park and Grand River region
beyond, today Mosca (Musca: Mosquito) Pass, was long a
noted wagon trail.[185]

Moses Harris: "Black" Harris, Major Harris; swart and
shaggy trapper accredited to Kentucky; known first with the
Ashley company of 1823, if not with the initial expedition of
1822; companion of William Sublette, Jedediah Smith, Jim
Beckwourth, Joe Meek, Carson and all; a wit renowned in the
St. Louis and New Orleans press and in the mountains for his
yarn of the "putrified (petrified) peerairie" where even the
songs of the birds had turned to "stun." Following upon his
beaver days in the service of Ashley, the Rocky Mountain Fur
Company, American Fur Company and as free trapper he was
an efficient guide for missionary and emigrant parties to Oregon; in 1836 piloted the Marcus Whitman party as far as the
Green River rendezvous; in 1838 was of the caravan escorting
the missionaries of that spring across the plains; guided the
important emigration to Oregon, leaving the Missouri in the
spring of 1844; remained on the Oregon side of the mountains,
as an Oregon settler and guide, until 1847; and returning that
year to Missouri he died, at Independence, in May, 1849, from
the cholera. Nevertheless he lives on as a mountain-man "as
fearless as an eagle, strong as the elk," as one of the characters
in Ruxton's *Life in the Far West* and Emerson Bennett's
romance, *The Prairie Flower,* and in the epitaph by a contemporary:

> Here lies the bones of old Black Harris
> Who often traveled beyond the far west
> and for the freedom of Equal rights
> He crossed the snowy mountain Hights
> was free and easy kind of soul
> Especially with a Belly full.[186]

William Sherley Williams: "Old Bill" Williams, "Parson"

Williams, "Lone Elk," who is posed in fact and fiction as the most notorious of the beaverday trappers; born probably in North Carolina, reputed to have been a Methodist circuit-rider or itinerant preacher in Missouri if not elsewhere in the West and a proselyting interpreter among the Osage. In his prime (1832) he is described by Albert Pike of Arkansas (*Prose Sketches and Poems,* 1834) as "a man about six feet, one inch in height, gaunt and red-headed, with a hard, weather-beaten face, marked deeply with small-pox. He is all muscle and sinew, and the most indefatigable hunter and trapper in the world." Moreover, was "a shrewd, acute, original man, and far from illiterate." By chroniclers of his trail in his later years is assigned a lank, stooped figure, a pinched leathery visage, Punch chin and nose, small, restless gray eyes, querulous voice, shambling gait, slovenly habits, and a pie-bald, hump-nosed Nez Percé pony familiar, as he himself was, to trappers, traders and Indians from the Three Forks sources of the Missouri to the Gila, and from the lower Missouri to California. An eccentric in speech and manners, an addict of the lone and secret trail and the Indian life, he was the one, of whom, in day of suspicion, Kit Carson is alleged to have said: "In starving times no man who knew him ever walked in front of Bill Williams." He was early upon the plains and in the mountains — in 1848 had been twenty-five years a trapper, according to Frémont; was guide for the Government commissioners who in 1825-26 survived a Santa Fé Trail route from the Missouri to the Arkansas, the Cimarron, and Taos; in 1826 trapped through New Mexico to the Gila with St. Vrain, Ewing Young, et al., and in 1827 lived among the Moquis (Hopi) of north central present Arizona; successively hunted upon the Yellowstone, in northern Texas, and across the Great Basin desert to California with Joseph R. Walker's filibustering party of 1833-34 in the service of Bonneville — evidently revisited California on horse collecting errands, according to the story (before cited) as related to Lieutenant Brewerton; sequestered himself among the Utes and trapped mountain Utah and Colorado, with the Grand River of present

Middle Park, Colorado, as a favorite resort region; learned the Ute tongue, won the Utes' confidence and learned their tribal customs. Was much of a solitary and a mystery; ever a roamer, appearing, as his humor moved him, at camp and rendezvous and trading post, and in Taos and Santa Fé where in bar room and street he dispensed money and goods with reckless open hand. At the last, in the late fall of 1848, he engaged to guide Frémont through the winter fastnesses of the snowy mountains of southern Colorado. The trail failed, the expedition was turned back, and the survivors rallied at Taos in the opening days of February. As soon as it was practicable Williams and Dr. Benjamin Kern of the company went in again to salvage the abandoned baggage. They did not come out, nor were their bodies recovered. The files of the Missouri Historical Society library disclose an obituary:

Bill Williams, well known mountain guide, and Dr. Kearns, were recently murdered by a band of Eutaws. They left Taos in search of scientific instruments and other property lost by Col. Fremont. (Reprint from the *Santa Fé Republican* in *The Brunswicker* (Brunswick, Mo.) of May 21, 1849.)

The petulant jargon of Old Bill Williams lives in Ruxton's *Life in the Far West;* his peculiarities of person and manners are recounted by sundry observers; his name has vanished from Williams Pass, now Sandhill Pass, of southern Colorado's Sangre de Cristo Range, but it endures in Williams River fork of the Grand and Williams River Mountains in Colorado's Middle Park, and in the Bill Williams Fork of the Colorado and Bill Williams Peak and Williams Station, Arizona. He perished, old and discredited, and probably, as he by wont had lived, alone.

> "So long they looked, but never spied
> His welcome step again,
> Nor knew the fearful death he died
> Far down that narrow glen."

Carson was with him, at various times, on the beaver hunt and in camp and trading post; he was of the Carson party that at the decline of the trapping business left the mountains for Bent's Fort.[187]

Richard Owens: Dick Owens, Ohioan and Taosan; Carson's close comrade in many mountain doings in the middle Thirties; his partner in ranching in New Mexico after trapper days; his companion upon the third Frémont expedition (1845-46) and a captain in the Frémont California Battalion following upon the Bear Flag uprising. Owens Lake, in northeastern Southern California — one-time the débouchement of that Owen River which now feeds the Los Angeles water supply from the high Sierra — bears his name, bestowed by Frémont. A man "cool, brave, and of good judgment," whose "dark-hazel eye was the marked feature of his face, large and flat and far-sighted," Frémont remarks in his *Memoirs*. One of Frémont's faithfuls in the controversy with General Kearny over the military and civil rule in California; but of judgment belittled, however, by Lieutenant Colonel Cooke, who refers to "the mutinous conduct of the ignorant Owens." Owens planned to return from New Mexico to California with his States bride, in 1849, and Carson would have joined him out there, to settle, but was unable to remove the family stakes.[188]

Alexander Godey; The third in the trio, Carson, Owens and Godey, who, Frémont comments, would have been Marshals under Napoleon. Godey was a St. Louis Frenchman, Carson's junior by ten years, a very Dumas Musketeer with his gay manners, his flashing black eyes and his long, curling, black silky hair of which he was vain; was a mountain-man of 1837 and a Frémont man with Carson upon the second and third expeditions; was fellow hero with Carson in an Indian pursuit in 1844; was lieutenant in the Frémont Battalion of 1846 and was captured by the Californians in the Kearny affair of San Pascual; served Frémont in the ill-fated fourth expedition, winter of 1848; returned to California in 1849, there to become a rancher and sheep raiser in the Tulare Valley, with headquarters eventually in the neighborhood of Bakersfield of the Tejon district; married María Antonia Coronel, of prominent

Spanish family, but appears not to have been successful with that venture; in 1862 was appointed superintendent of the Tejon Indian reservation, in 1863 was reported as misusing the Owens Valley Indians; was associated with and employed by the great Tejon Ranchos system of General Edward Fitzgerald Beale, Carson's scout partner for the relief of General Kearny's force (1846) and his companion across the southwest desert in 1847; in 1883, at sixty-five, was still an attache of the Beale estate. Died January 19, 1889, aged seventy-one, in the Sisters' Hospital, Los Angeles, and was buried at Bakersfield.[189]

Lucien Benjamin Maxwell: Another of Carson's juniors; in 1832 not yet in the mountains but destined to be Carson's hunting comrade, fellow townsman at Taos, associate under Frémont, ranching partner and generous host. Maxwell was born in old Kaskaskia, Illinois, in 1818 (the same year with Godey); was a son of Hugh H. Maxwell and Odèle Ménard whose family name is featured in early Illinois history; in March, 1842, married, in Taos, Señorita María de la Luz Beaubien, daughter of Don Carlos Beaubien and Paulita Lobata; was hunter with the first Frémont expedition (1842) and served throughout the third; came into the immense Beaubien and Miranda estate of New Mexican land to which his wife was part heir, and operated this, the Maxwell Grant, as sole proprietor, for half a dozen years; was founder of the First National Bank in Santa Fé; after disposing of his ranch and banking business he lost his money in careless expenditures and luckless investments, and died, poor in means, among his children at Fort Sumner, New Mexico, in 1875, aged fifty-seven. A swarthy, burly, open-handed man, of rough-and-ready ways, strong character and warm heart.

Richens Lacy Wootton: Dick Wootton, in later life "Uncle Dick" Wootton, was born in Virginia, of Scotch descent, in 1816 and entered the West in 1836 or 1837, by the medium of a Santa Fé Trail caravan out of Independence; thereafter was fur trader and trapper in the mountains, contacting Carson there and at Bent's Fort and in Taos; was guide for the "Missouri

Column" of Colonel A. W. Doniphan from Santa Fé to Chihuahua, in 1846; was of the Taos party that encountered the in-straggling Frémont men of the fourth expedition, winter of 1848-49, and was one who conducted Frémont himself to Carson's house; was a freighter on the Santa Fé Trail, and one of the first traders at the Cherry Creek diggin's (future Denver) and the first resident merchant, 1859; finally, in 1865, a homesteader in Raton Pass of New Mexico and builder and operator of a toll road there between Colorado and New Mexico; gave way, in 1878, to the Santa Fé railroad, building through his very yard and paralleling his toll road, but lived on, a genial and thrifty rancher, until having retired to a home at the foot of the Pass he there died, in 1893, aged seventy-seven. The original homestead house dominating the old toll road was burned but was restored to serve as a landmark upon the trail, to be saluted by the whistle of the "Uncle Dick," largest freight locomotive in the world.[190]

Pierre Louis Vasquez: "Louee," "Major," and "Colonel" Vasquez, predecessor of Carson in the mountains, having enlisted under General Ashley and Major Henry in 1823 if not in 1822, but at any rate a participant in the battle with the Arikaras in the summer of 1823. Was born in St. Louis in 1798, twelfth and last child of Don Benito Vasquez, captain in the Spanish provincial militia, and Julie Papin Vasquez, said to have been a wife at ten and a mother at eleven. Was an early trapping partner of Jim Bridger in the commands of Jedediah Smith, Thomas Fitzpatrick and others; is erroneously alleged to have accompanied him for the discovery of the Salt Lake in 1824-1825 but may have been of the party that first circumnavigated the lake in 1826; appears to have built a small trading post on the South Platte opposite the mouth of Clear Creek, sometime Vasquez Fork, now within the northern limits of Denver, in the early Thirties, and in the latter Thirties operated, with Andrew Sublette, the post of Fort Vasquez further down the Platte; was the partner of Bridger at Fort Bridger, and there to be seen, as a portly, urbane gentleman with a Spanish-type but American wife, during emigrant days — to be seen, also, traveling the trail, like a grandee, with a relic coach and dusty four, and in Salt Lake City on trading business in connection with the post and with a store maintained in the Mormon capital. Having retired from the mountains and emigrant trade he died, well to do, in September, 1868, aged seventy, and is buried in Mount St. Mary's cemetery, Kansas City. No man was more favorably known in the mountains than Louis Vasquez. Kit Carson saw him at the rendezvous of 1834, on Ham's Fork of the Green. The Vasquez Range of northern Colorado northwest of Denver bear his family name.

Captain Sir William George Drummond Stewart: Seventh Baronet of Grandtully, Scotland, and of family name rendered Stuart as well as Steuart; British big-game hunter and sportsman traveler in western America and as such perhaps the first of the line; a hail-fellow at camp and rendezvous in Carson's time in the mountains, much liked by the mountain-men for his hearty unassuming ways and also for the creature comforts with which he was stocked; a man to be "forever remembered by the mountaineers," declares Carson, "for his liberality to them and for his many good qualities." Between annual trips in which his own outfit joined to that of American or Hudson's Bay Company caravans he wintered in St. Louis, New Orleans and Fort Vancouver. In 1830 had married an American girl of New Orleans. In 1838, at the decline of the beaver hunt and of the rendezvous, he returned to England and to his Scottish heritage; wrote a narrative of his mountain adventures, published in London and apparently pirated in the United States in 1846. He died upon his home estates, 1871, aged seventy-six.

John M. Stanley: Portrayer, in sketch-book and upon canvas, of Far West mountain and desert scenes; present upon the fur trail and at camp and rendezvous in the mid-Thirties; author of *The Trapper's Last Shot,* painted from a sketch made upon the spot during the hard battle, in June, 1838, between trappers and Blackfeet, in which Carson, Joe Meek, Bridger and other mountain-men participated; was artist draughtsman with the

General Kearny column to California in 1846; was a property owner in San Francisco in 1847, having there acquired a lot, corner of Bush and Sansome streets, in Block 2; was delineator with the surveys of Major and Washington Territorial Governor Isaac I. Stevens, 1853-54-55, for the northern route for a Pacific railroad; died in Detroit, 1872.[191]

There are others who would answer "Present": The Lajeunesse brothers, Basil and François, from Kaskaskia and St. Louis to Taos and the mountains — Basil, a Frémont favorite, to die in northern California by a Klamath hatchet's cleaving his skull; the free-trapping brothers Sinclair of Arkansas — encountered by Carson this spring, with William the elder already marked for a Gros Ventre bullet; the Tennesseeans George Nidever and Isaac Graham of the Sinclair company — future heroes of ballad and insurrection in California; the slight and nimble "Squire" George W. Ebbert of Kentucky, now (like Joe Meek, his fellow in the service of the Rocky Mountain Fur Company) three years in the mountains whither he had fled to forget a maid denied him but eventually to seek Oregon, in 1838, with a Nez Percé wife; "Doc" Robert Newell, of Ohio, a recruit of '29 along with Meek and Ebbert in the command of William Sublette out of St. Louis —trapper, Oregon rancher, Indian agent, and speaker of the Assembly; Caleb Wilkins of Ohio, trapping partner of Ebbert and Oregon close friend; trapper Markhead who survived desperate hot-blood affrays in the mountains only to be murdered in cold blood by Mexican captors upon the Taos trail in 1847; Mansfield ("Old Cotton") whose life was saved by Carson's quick aim; LaBonte, made famous by Ruxton and of name perpetuated in Labonte town and LaBonte Creek of Wyoming; young White, a "family pet" from Missouri but of stuff that empowered him to carry Carson out of danger; Samuel Tullock of St. Louis, builder, in this year 1832, of Fort Cass, the American Fur Company post on the Yellowstone; Greenwood, the veteran who incited the Crows to adopt Jim Beckwourth and at eighty in California in 1846, was still able "to shoot an Injun"; Robert Meldrum of St. Louis and the American Fur Company, who with Beckwourth led the Crows into a Blackfeet fortress; the Delawares Tom Hill, Jonas, Manhead — the latter killed by the Blackfeet; Spiebuck the Shawnee; Frazier the Iroquois, killed by the Blackfeet; Alexander, Chevalia, Richards, Montgomery, More, Foy, killed by the Blackfeet, and Baptiste Ménard, crippled for life; "poor Davis," riddled by the Sioux; William (Bill) New, who came out to Bent's Fort with Carson, and was slain by the Apaches, 1850, while fighting with clubbed rifle; trapper Mitchell, adopted by the Comanches; Antoine Godin, breed precipitator of the battle of Pierre's Hole, Carson's partner in a hardy enterprise out of Fort Hall, and at last dead by the vengeance bullet; Edward Rose ("Old Cut-Nose"), the negro breed trapper, guide and Crow interpreter; "Long" Hatcher, Rube Herring, John Smith, the squawman trader of the Bent's Fort trail and later of Denver — these three characterized in Lewis Gerrard's *Wah-to-yah;* and still others —

"... a moving row
Of magic shadow-shapes that come and go."

Chapter XVI

Adventures of Kit Carson — 1832

AFTER the breaking up of those winter quarters of 1831-32 where Carson had entered his twenty-second year, the party of his choice trapped the open stretches of the canyoned, fiercely rushing Snake, crossed back to the Bear, and thence working still eastward they reached the Green. Here they found a party of fifteen other trappers — the free command of William Sinclair of Arkansas and his brother, out of Taos upon the heels of the Fitzpatrick company of last fall. Sinclair said that Captain "Gaunt" and party were trapping in New Park, to the southeastward; thereupon by motive unexplained, whether or not one based upon a previous acquaintanceship, Carson, with three companions, sought for and found Captain John Gantt in the Bull Pen or Colorado's North Park, watered by the sources of the North Platte River.[192]

Accordingly they missed this summer's rendezvous in Pierre's Hole, at the close of which William Sinclair was killed in battle with the forted Gros Ventres ("Take me to my brother," he bade, mortally wounded) and William Sublette was temporarily disabled by a heavy bullet through his shoulder.[193]

The recruited Gantt company trapped through New Park and on across to the Laramie Plains and River of southeastern present Wyoming, thence southward through the wild scenes of central Colorado's front ranges, to the South Platte waters, and in the fall emerged, heavy with fur, upon the upper Arkansas of the foothills regions. Captain Gantt and squad took the Taos trail, to dispose of the catch. The remainder of the company set traps anew, ere the streams froze. The captain returned with supplies. Winter quarters upon the Arkansas were constructed.[194]

In January a horse-stealing party of Indians from the northern country made away, in the night, with nine of the animals that had been turned loose to forage, after a hunting excursion.

In the morning the theft was discovered. Carson and eleven

other men immediately prepared for the chase; mounted and set faces to the trail of hoofs and moccasins. This trended north.

The pursuit along the foothills was made more difficult by reason of the herds of roving buffalo that had trodden out the tracks. The saddle horses were in poor condition, due to short rations of cottonwood bark; the country was rough and snow-bound; and after forty miles of trailing it was thought best, at the approach of dusk, to camp and rest in a patch of timber to be sighted two or three miles before. But some four miles beyond this haven fires sparking into the snowy gloom signaled of the thieves themselves.

The trappers waited only until darkness gathered. Then leaving their mounts tied among the trees of the camp they went stooping and crawling, from covert to covert, through the snow and the cold, until, on a wide circuit, they were posted, unannounced, within 100 yards of the far side of the enemy's camp.

These Indians were fifty Crows. They had built two small forts of logs and brush, as protection against the weather, and thus divided were dancing and singing around their fires, in celebration of their successful horse hunt. The nine stolen animals were picketed just outside the entrance to one of the forts.

The horses were of first importance. When finally the Indians had danced enough and had lain down to sleep, Carson and five comrades, crawling nearer through the snow, with fingers numbed, cut the nine horses' picket ropes. Then they threw balls of snow at the horses to drive them off toward the six trappers in waiting. All was accomplished so deftly that even the Indians' dogs were not disturbed.

The majority of the men now declared in favor of retiring, with the re-captured stock, to the camp upon the Arkansas; for the weather was bitter and the trail was a hunger trail. But the impetuous young Carson and two or three others who had not lost any horses said that the Indians should be punished; the forty-mile pursuit and the cold wait should bring further rewards. This opinion carried; and leaving three men to herd the horses to the saddled animals, the trappers walked boldly upon the camp of the Crows.

Their rapid approach over the creaking snow was heard. A dog barked. The Indians in one of the little fortifications sprang to their feet. To the cracks of the rifles Indians fell; the others ran for the breastworks of the second division, and united with their fellows.

And now in the winter half-light just before the dawn, here in the snowy wilderness, bows twanged, muzzles spat back and forth, with the nine trappers behind trees, the Crows inside their low breastworks. At daybreak the Crows made count of the whites, and charged; at close quarters five dropped; the others dodged back into the fort. But they dared not stay there, to be picked off; with new courage they charged again. Hotly beset, the trappers retired through the sheltering timber to the way camp and their three anxious comrades guarding the stock. The Crows did not press in. Taking the back trail the twelve men, with the recovered animals, thankfully toiled, at evening, into the headquarters camp on the Arkansas.

This is the Carson story as dictated in his own manuscript before cited and as rendered, with a little variation, in the Peters version of his life narrative. A somewhat similar episode is related, of a detachment of Gantt trappers, in March of the preceding year (1832), by Zenas Leonard, and Joe Meek has a rivaling story of the spring of 1831. The prompt reprisal upon red horse-thieves was a common desperate measure — although at no time nor place more boldly performed than in the instance just presented. But there is another and paralleling story of a horse raid by the Crows in the Arkansas country, and retaliation by a Carson party; dated, not in January, 1833, but "in the winter of 1830 or 1831."

By that story, Carson and party were cutting cottonwood timber, five miles below the site of Bent's Fort on the Arkansas, for use in the erection of the post. Indian horse thieves ran the camp herd off, by night; pursuing the next day, on foot, with two mounted Cheyennes, Carson and the eleven men overtook the thieves at twilight, saw the fires sparking amid a thicket, charged in and were met by sixty countering Crows. A volley in time drove the Crows back, the Carson men followed right after, the two Cheyennes meanwhile had rounded up the stock, and the astonished Crows, set afoot themselves, scampered out from the other side of the thicket and kept on going. The Carson party were too exhausted to give chase. The two Cheyennes searched the thicket and found only two scalps; and in the brisk setto not a white man had been injured.[195]

It is necessary to rejoin the Gantt winter camp of 1832-33, seventy miles above the scene of this hasty skirmish.

Captain Gantt decided to make his spring hunt on the North Platte and the Laramie again, in New Park and the plains enclosed by the Laramie Range to the northeast. The fur accumulated since his trip to Taos was "cached" and the march for the north was begun. At the South Platte two men were reported missing, with three of the best horses.

Carson and a companion were dispatched upon the back trail. The two deserters maintained their head start, for the pursuit found the cache at the Arkansas torn open and the beaver "raised"; the 400 pounds of fur and the old camp canoe were gone. Neither the two men nor the bales bearing the Gantt & Blackwell private mark ever were heard of again. The three horses, however, were discovered, having been abandoned in favor of the canoe; and with this satisfaction Carson virtuously hoped that the Indians would get the two men.

Indications are that Carson and partner had been directed to stay here as caretakers of the valuable premises, and to await the arrival of Captain Blackwell, coming from St. Louis, by way of the Arkansas and Bent's Fort, with supplies. They were too late to protect the cache, but nevertheless they stayed on, in the forted camp of the preceding winter; strengthened it against attack, hunted only together, went on night guard turn and turn about, for all the greening country invited the Indian to the plunder trail.

In about a month Blackwell appeared, as if by previous arrangement, with the supplies and with fifteen recruits. And there entered four men from the Gantt camp in the Bayou Salade, come to meet Blackwell and to learn what had happened to Carson and partner, who after all this time had been "given up for lost."

Whereupon the little company, of old men and new men, rode northward for the Bayou Salade, Colorado's South Park basined amid the mountains southwest of present Denver. This Salt Marsh region of the sources of the South Fork of the South Platte, where within three decades historic mining camps had followed upon forgotten trapper camps, and the prospect tunnels in the overlooking hills and the rumblings of the treasure coach outbid the beaver runs in the bottoms and the crack of the eager rifle, was a resort beloved by trappers and Indians. The tasty waters oozing amid the long grasses attracted vast quantities of buffalo; the winters were snowy but were considered mild; and both the Utes of the mountains and the Arapahos of the plains claimed it as a special hunting ground. Trails from north and south, east and west, converged to the Bayou Salade.

Granted that the Gantt winter "fort" was the foundation for the trading post a few miles below the mouth of Fountain Creek at the Arkansas, the trail for the Bayou Salade should have trended up Fountain Creek, among the foothills, and with westward course to the head-waters where, west of Colorado Springs of later day, the Fontaine qui Bouille or Boiling Spring was a sanctuary for visitors of all nations. Here, by established legend, pilgrim Indians of various tribes made offerings to their Manitou or Great Spirit, so that the bed of the clear spring was strewn with beads and amulets. The bubbling tangy water was drunk with gusto by the whites. The place is still Manitou to the dominant race who drink the waters, ascend Pike's Peak by wheel and foot, and view the Garden of the Gods.

Skirting the fantastic red Garden of the Gods a trail from the Boiling Spring climbed the mountain divide and wended on, down and up, for the Bayou Salade.

Whatever was the trail taken by the party, on the fifth day, while the camp was at its early breakfast in the cool grayness among the fragrant sage and pines, the crack of the lookout's rifle and a loud whoop from him spread sudden alarm. As the men sprang to their guns the Indians pelted down for the horses. Fortunately some of these had been hobbled. At the volley the Indians scattered and fled, leaving a dead warrior and taking only one animal.

The camp hastily packed, and made a forced march of fifty miles. The Indian signs ceased; it was hoped that there would be no more trouble. Accordingly the tired trappers went into camp upon the bank of a little stream supposed to be a tributary of the Arkansas.

The barking of a watchful dog aroused them. They could find no reason for his barking; but they brought their horses in closer, and posted an extra guard. Morning broke with the camp and its horses unmolested. It was decided that the dog had barked at prowling varmints.

Kit Carson and three others rode to explore for beaver. Returning at a carefree pace, as they rounded a shoulder of the mountain trail they saw four Indians, armed and painted and mounted for war. By quick agreement they charged at a gallop, only to be welcomed by sixty more reds, the main war party. Without slackening pace or firing a shot they continued headlong on, received at twenty yards the stabs of bullet and arrow, and replying not but reserving the menace of their loaded guns burst the half circle and actually escaped.

The astonished Indians did not push pursuit — which was just as well for the trappers, since one of them had been severely wounded. As to trappers' eyes it was evident that the savages were upon the warpath and lately had been in an affray, the four whites rode hard, and with no little anxiety, for the camp. They found it intact, after an onslaught by this very band. A try had been made for the camp horses; the loose stock had been run off, and four of the men, giving chase, had regained the animals only after an exchange of shots during which an

Indian was killed and a man wounded. Naturally this had not sweetened the temper of the reds, who were vengeance bent. Reckoning that ambush as one of his close calls Carson was moved to say, twenty-five years afterward: "They [the Indians] made a very good attempt, but, thank God! failed."

With one of the wounded men in a rude litter the party resumed the march for the Gantt camp in the Bayou Salade.

Now in mid-spring of 1833 Captain Gantt and presumably Captain Blackwell are in the Bayou Salade, and little had been done except to fight Indians. The course was laid north, into Old Park, or Colorado's Middle Park. But the season was well along, and Old Park had been trapped. The outlook promised little of good, the men grew disheartened. In the dissolution which resulted (the firm of Gant and Blackwell had already been reported through the mountains as insolvent) Carson and two comrades set off for an expedition upon their own account.

They wisely plunged into the timbered regions; and while the Indians were hunting buffalo on the plains and in the parks they trapped unmolested.

Captain Gant, discouraged upon the trap-line, returned to the Arkansas and his trading relations with the Arapahos. Of Captain Blackwell we do not hear again. On the more sequestered streams of central and western Colorado, Carson and his companions finished out the trapping season successfully; and, as free trappers, in the fall took their furs to Taos.

Chapter XVII

The Fight for Fur

WHEN in mid-year, 1833, Kit Carson and two comrades pulled away from the shoaled Gantt and Blackwell ship to seek better fortune, the fur business of the mountains was at the flood.

The Far West was a land crisscrossed by the moccasined foot of the American trapper, for in the past decade the restless beaver hunter from the States had penetrated virtually throughout Northwest and Southwest, between Missouri and the coast. The salient features were accurately mapped in trapper mind — a mind tenacious, like that of Jim Bridger who, in later days, with a piece of charcoal could sketch, off-hand, a range, its passes and valleys, upon a piece of upturned buffalo hide.

It still was a land of romance. Even to the practical mountain-men it held many an *ultima Thule,* strangely peopled like the shores of mythology. For among the trappers there were Gullivers, Hakluyts, Marco Polos, Munchausens. An island in the Salt Lake was for yet some years to be invested by a race of giants, whose enormous cut timbers from time to time washed ashore; in the depths of the desert of the Colorado and of the Great Basin dwelt other giants, armed with clubs; there were canyoned cities, pent from the world, wherein lived white-skinned descendants of the Montezuma. And there were those bubbling springs, geysers, and oddly tinted or ashy tracts, real but made unreal by imaginary attributes, to which the trapper, like the Indian, threw a sop by "making medicine."

It still was a land misunderstood; a land popularly presumed to be forever condemned behind its barrier of the chimeric "Great American Desert" and of the beetling ranges pictured as so snowy and austere. In the words of Senator Benton(1825): "The ridge of the Rocky Mountains may be named without offense as presenting a convenient, natural, and everlasting boundary." And the Robert Greenhow report, fifteen years after, upon Oregon and the Pacific Coast, would declare that this trappers' battleground from the Rockies to the Blue Mountains of Idaho was either a barren waste or else of a climate "sufficient to render any attempts at cultivation entirely fruitless." Its isolation was rendered the more formidable by reason of frigid peaks rising 25,000 feet, as asserted by competent authorities.[196]

But in this debatable region west of the barrier divide there were those favorite summer rendezvous valleys of the Green, the Bear, and the sources of the Snake, and wintering resorts of like nature; there were the Grande Ronde, and Horse Prairie, Brown's Hole, Ogden's Hole, Cache Valley, and many another familiar precinct; all beloved of the mountain-men for their shelter and bounty to meet the human need. There were the recreative delights of the Salt Lake, the Bear Springs, the Soda Springs, of waters hot and cold, of salts and gypsum and iron; on the north the beautiful Flathead Lake and the Pend d' Oreille, on the south of the lovely Utah Lake, with gems of lesser note in between. Here there flowed the varied current of the Green, the friendly stream encountered at the very foot of the South Pass, uniting with the equally varied Grand to form the Colorado; here there coursed the impetuous Snake, canyoned in those stark lava beds to cross which, as said Jim Bridger, "a bird must carry its own provisions"— but a river, nevertheless, to be bridled for the service of man; here there rippled the Bear, flowing into the great lake which, with no outlet, yet never over-spilled; here the Salmon and the Clearwater fed the Snake upon its way to the Columbia; here there sparkled the waters of the Henry Fork, the Sandy, the Godin, Ham's Fork, Black's Fork, the Malade and a hundred other tributaries to the great arterial system; here there were deer, elk, buffalo, sheep, speckled trout, the friendly Indians. As sentinels facing west, the snow-crowned Three Tetons, the trappers' Pilot Buttes, signaled of the prospect.

The crystal of the future already showed two highways branching to the northwest and the southwest beyond the Valley of the Green: the one across desert and mountains for Oregon, the other across desert and mountains for California.

Already, or in 1831, Hall Kelley the Boston schoolmaster had incorporated "The American Society for Encouraging the Settlement of Oregon Territory" and having advanced from New York to Ohio the Church of Latter Day Saints had begun its series of historic moves. Defying the diagnosis of Robert Greenhow and fellow students, in here west of the mountains the utter desolation of the sterile Salt Lake Valley was to blossom and bear and the trap-line streams apparently designed for only fur would neighbor with flock and heard and mine and ranch and Alladin-summoned town.

In his report to Congress upon Oregon, Greenhow the librarian declared that until 1834 there never, at one time, were more than 200 Americans west of the Rockies; yet in 1832 Captain Bonneville had taken in over 100 men, Gantt and Blackwell's seventy of the year before were still to be figured, the Wyeth company joined with William Sublette's supply train, Fitzpatrick is mentioned by Zenas Leonard as leading 112 men, the brigade of the American Fur Company was in the field, the Sinclair little command had wintered on the Green, of the number of detached free trappers there is no count; and there were more than 200 fur hunters, accredited Americans, at the Pierre's Hole rendezvous of that summer.

But whether they were few or many the Americans, crossing the barrier heights by the South Pass and other passes, spread far and wide. Ashley had made known the waters of the Green or Seeds-kee-dee (Prairie-hen) River, and even had tried to descend its canyons by boat — as Major John W. Powell successfully did almost half a century later; had left his name therein for coming explorers to read. He had opened the country of the Bear, east and north of the Salt Lake, the country of Utah Lake and Sevier Lake, southward. With forty-five men and more than 100 horses, Joshua Pilcher had traveled from the Council Bluffs west to the Green; thence with a squad north to Flathead Lake and Fort Colville in present Washington State near the Canadian line, and back by the Athabaska and Red River of Canada to the Missouri and the States. Jedediah S.

Smith had been as far north as the present city of Spokane; he had carried his beaver to the British at Fort Vancouver and his Protestant Bible to the Flatheads, and by his explorations of the country of the Snake and the Columbia, as announced to the War Department, had supplemented the information previously based upon the routes of Lewis and Clark and the Astorians, and to be supplemented again by the notes of Captain Bonneville; he had been as far south as San Diego, had crossed and recrossed the Great Basin, and he, Ewing Young and others had investigated California from end to end. John Colter, Jim Bridger, Joe Meek, Robert Meldrum, and others, had exploited the Yellowstone wonderland.

Trails from New Mexico to California had been opened through the deserts of the southwest. By route north of the Gila Ewing Young had crossed the Colorado at the crossing used by Jedediah Smith on his way south from the Salt Lake, and had struck on through the Mohave Desert to the mission settlements of the latitude of Los Angeles. He had taken the Gila route back and out again. David E. Jackson, by route to the copper mines and thence south of the Gila — a route in part approximated, in after day, by the Butterfield stage line — had crossed the Colorado at the Yuma crossing below the mouth of the Gila and adventuring the Colorado Desert had reached San Diego. William Wolfskill had extended the old Spanish Trail and by route through southwestern Colorado, central Utah and southeastern Nevada to the Mohave Desert region had arrived in Los Angeles. Already a trading business in horses and mules — a business legitimate as well as illegitimate — between the Missouri and California, via Santa Fé or Bent's Fort and the Santa Fé Trail, had set in; the southern route through the valley of the Gila and the more northerly Spanish Trail as amplified by the followers of Wolfskill were beaten to dust by shuffling hoofs. And now in this summer of 1833 the Captain Joseph Walker detachment of the Bonneville expedition is breaking the overland trail from the Salt Lake to California of the north; in so doing punctures the legend of a Rio

Buenaventure, a Rio Timpanagos, and the like, connecting the
Salt Lake basin with the Pacific Ocean.

The Southwest was sufficiently known; the Northwest is
becoming known — the tide of humanity was surely, although
in a manner blindly, forging into the Oregon then present but
of measure yet unreckoned. The debatable ground of the white
race and the red was on-spreading through Wyoming, Colorado, Utah, Idaho, Montana, Oregon and Washington — states
in the embryo and only waiting.

But although the main fur hunts now favored the wide
Oregon country which occupied all of the Northwest beyond
the Shining Mountains, no active American forts or fur posts
existed there — save the rude establishment of the enterprising
Antoine Robidoux, in the Uintah region of northeastern Utah.
Major Andrew Henry's log fort upon the Henry Fork of the
Lewis or Snake was scarcely a memory, and the obscure post
somewhere near the Salt Lake, to which, in 1827, General Ashley's successors had hauled the four-pounder cannon, was no
longer of mention. Only the Hudson's Bay Company posts
west of the longitude of the Blue Mountains of Idaho — that
accepted border line beyond which the Company was presumed
to reign supreme — had persisted as stations of the fur trade
industry.

The fur trade, if prosperous, was waxing complicated also, as
cutthroat methods of an avaricious civilization intruded more
and more. Firmly entrenched upon the western coast, with
headquarters at Fort Vancouver, and dominating that Astoria
which twice had changed hands and now was American by
profitless title, the Hudson's Bay Company, proud, rich, and
powerful, tenaciously gathered to itself the streams of fur heading in north, south and east. Doing a fur business in Oregon
alone of $140,000 annually, with its brigades and its twenty
posts as strictly disciplined as any military force; with its trained
engagés and clerks and bourgeois; with its immense resources
and experience, its employes courteous as man to man but
inflexible as trader to trader — now dining the stranger at a

twenty-foot table lavish with viands and wines, and now refusing him one ounce of supplies to further him upon the onward trail into the fur country—the Hudson's Bay Company by every resource within its means resisted the inroads of the American. When it must outbid, it outbid; when it must undersell, it undersold; when it must deceive, it deceived; when it must play alcohol against blanket, it played; and when it must crush, it crushed.

The whole of this Oregon country was considered, in point of law, contestable ground, and was jointly occupied (again, in point of law) by Americans and British. But the great company, consummate in its machinery, yielded not an inch in the Oregon of today, and the actual common ground was that section before specifically referred to, lying from the Rockies west to the Blue Mountains, the southern portion being technically New Mexico.

The casual American companies, while lending excitement and variety, were only chips in the current. Gantt and Blackwell failed, their company dispersed; Sinclair died the trapper's death, and his little company dispersed; Bonneville swam hither and thither, opened a new trail to California, reported upon the Great Basin, built his useless Fort Nonsense or Bonneville's Folly, which he had vainly named Fort Bonneville, and had to quit; Wyeth, rebuffed by Americans and British alike, was squeezed out of The Rocky Mountain Company, the American Fur Company, the Hudson's Bay Company, grappled until only the two were left.

In the campaign through 1833 and the half dozen years succeeding, until the last regular rendezvous, at Fort Nonsense on the Green above the mouth of Horse Creek, in 1839 — a campaign that decimated the beaver, demoralized the Indian, and killed the goose that laid the golden egg — the Hudson's Bay Company, despite its superb organization, in American transmontane territory was at first under disadvantage; for its organization was met with disorganization under King Alcohol.

Following the splendid example of that British autocracy, the

Northwest Company of Canada, and with true British policy, the Hudson's Bay Company principles were high principles of good business. The company business methods were a striking contrast to those improvident American methods which devastate forests and exterminate fur, fin, and feather.

The Hudson's Bay Company never over-trapped, never overpaid, never connived at offenses in order to receive favors, never temporized with enmity in order to obtain a transient friendship, and never voluntarily debauched business with liquor.

As for over-trapping:

If the annual return from any well-trapped district be less in any year than formerly, they order a less number still to be taken, until the beaver and other fur-bearing animals have time to increase. The income of the Company is thus rendered uniform, and their business perpetual.[197]

As for prices:

A regular tariff was established on the Company's goods, comprising all the articles used in their trade with the Indians; nor was the quality of their goods ever allowed to deteriorate. A price was also fixed upon furs according to their market value, and an Indian knowing this, knew exactly what he could purchase. No bartering was allowed. When skins were offered for sale at the fort they were handed to the clerk through a window like a post-office delivery-window, and their value in the article desired, returned through the same aperture.

As for offenses, no Indian culprit, from murderer to thief, ever was permitted to go unpunished. Even when the company of the American, Jedediah S. Smith, entering upon Hudson's Bay ground in the spring of 1828 was assaulted by the Indians on the Umpqua of Oregon, Chief Factor John McLoughlin at Fort Vancouver instantly ordered out a force to punish the Indians and recover the Americans' goods. Such a policy was maintained by the Company as a measure of self-defense.

As for temporizing with enmity, or for suffering friendship to interfere with business interests, the Hudson's Bay posts would entertain the traveler, but would not supply the alien trader. Factor McLoughlin generously bought the furs of

Jedediah Smith, the castaway, and thereby secured them for his own market; but when Ewing Young entered Oregon, with some hope of pursuing trade with the Indians, he was refused a single article of clothing.

As for liquor, a modicum was furnished, at stated and well separated intervals, to employes as reward of duty. But until the final fight for furs had to be met with American methods, no alcohol went out in trade. And alcohol was not necessary. The Indians knew, as well as did the company, what furs should bring and what goods should cost, and never found their confidence abused.

On the debit side of the ledger, the Hudson's Bay Company existed for its own profit absolutely and only. It was opposed to agriculture as a vocation, for that invited settlers upon the fur grounds, showed the Indian that hunting was not the only livelihood, and narrowed down the company's business. The company discouraged side issues.

It operated in the fur country west of the Rockies and north of present Utah by virtue of that agreement of 1818, extended by provision of 1827, by which citizens of the United States and of Great Britain should have equal rights of trade and settlement in the Oregon Territory. Its fur business was carried on through the offices of strategic trading posts, of which, in 1833, the most easterly in the competitive British-American field was Fort Nez Percé, commonly called Fort Walla Walla, on the Columbia near the mouth of the Snake, in present Washington. The Columbia was the great waterway for brigades descending out of the north and the Canadian northeast with their bales of furs. Brigades by land trapped in California of the south, and companies trapped in the watered Great Basin in the southeast; and detachments, marching eastward and southeastward by the Snake River trail from central Washington encountered the American trappers in that wide no-man's land which, clear to the Wyoming Rockies, was any man's land. The Hudson's Bay Company advanced its posts eastward, up the Snake, into present Idaho, but it never adopted the rendezvous or trading-muster idea of the Americans. It took advantage of those musters, however, by sending agents and convoy parties to them.[198]

Of the two principal American companies, the American Fur Company had possession of the plains. With John Jacob Astor overseeing from New York, and Pierre Chouteau, Jr., directing from St. Louis, with the best organizers and traders in the fur business upon its list of agents, it worked through posts located or in process of location all along the Missouri clear to the Blackfeet country near the river's sources in Montana. Many of these forts, like many of the highly capable agents, were inheritance from former fur businesses which "the Company" had absorbed, thus acquiring, ready to hand, men, territory and munitions. It had installed upon the Missouri the first traffic steamboat, *"The Yellowstone,"* for carrying supplies to the posts and furs to St. Louis. Sternly businesslike, exacting from its employes as much work as possible with as little risk and expenditure to itself as possible, the American Fur Company eventually occupied the whole fur field of the West.

The Rocky Mountain Fur Company's stronghold and headquarters were the mountains, where at the outset it held the advantage in that it knew the country. It had no posts, it worked by means of camps and rendezvous, it was versatile, mobile, and lived afield at a minimum of expense. Of its leaders, Fitzpatrick, Milton Sublette and Bridger had been in the mountains since Ashley's early endeavors of 1823 and 1824. The chances are that Fraeb and Gervais were almost as experienced. Men had been taken over from the Smith, Jackson & Sublette outfit — some of them old Ashley men. The names of Fitzpatrick, Jim Bridger and Milton Sublette should have induced the pick of the mountaineers to join the standard. Robert Campbell and his associate, William Sublette, had the contract to bring in the supplies — which insured competent service.

While the rivalry between the American companies, large and small, and that between American and British outfits was keen, the partisanship did not necessarily extend to all the trapper rank and file — particularly those men who looked to the main chance. There were popular field captains, such as Bridger, who commanded a following without regard to the final destination of the furs. We find, in the Ferris *Diary*, camps of the Rocky Mountain company and the American Fur Company mingling in mutual jollity. Carson, an independent, and other Americans, even trapped in Hudson's Bay Company service.

As has been stated, in the beginning the Hudson's Bay Company forbade the use of alcohol in trading. This was policy as well as principle; but when alcohol was demanded to meet the aggression of the American traders the company changed its policy at large, and bid for patronage with doled out drams.

To be sure, Act of Congress, July 9, 1832, provided that "no ardent spirits shall be hereafter introduced, under any pretense, into the Indian country." The Hudson's Bay Company seized upon opportunity, and waxed generous with the Indian. The American Fur Company, controlling much of the Missouri River territory, was in straits to compete with the British of the northern border and with the small American concerns who could not be closely watched. Until competition was eliminated, whisky had to be fought with whisky.

Indeed, there was no dearth, in 1832 nor for half a century after, of liquor for the Indian trade upon the plains and in the mountains, whither it was transported at first in the flat kegs, on the back of mule and horse, and later in wagons.

In 1841 the caravan of Rufus Sage conveyed, as a portion of its trading assets, twenty-four barrels of alcohol. That kind of thing was profitable rum-running. Each gallon of alcohol was swelled to five gallons by the addition of four gallons of water. A pint of the dilution purchased a buffalo robe of value $5 — or what have you? The original gallon, then, as increased to ten pints, had the purchasing power of $50. And more. There were the devices of measuring out by the gill — with the thumb or finger occupying space in the gill; of raising the bottom of the tin cup with a stratum of paraffin; of befuddling the Indian with a decoction of tobacco and pepper until he could be switched to a keg filled up with plain water — the cheapest dram of all.

So much for the Indian trade as it developed, particularly in the areas of the trading posts. There was liquor aplenty at the rendezvous, but the trappers themselves accounted for most of it when they turned in their pelts or drew upon their wage balances.

Chapter XVIII

Adventures of Kit Carson — 1833-1834

CARSON was back in Taos in October, 1833, with a good catch of fur. By his own account it took him only a short time to dispose of his money, as it had taken to dispose of his beaver, for near the close of the month he was out on the trail again with a "Captain Lee, of the U. S. A., a partner of Bent and St. Vrain" and a few mule packs of goods for the mountain trade.[199]

They struck into the Old Spanish Trail as retraced by William Wolfskill three years before and as now marked by various horse and mule expeditions lawful and unlawful. At the Dolores River in southwestern present Colorado they headed more into the north for the Uintah country of northeastern Utah. In this direction also ran the original Spanish Trail as pioneered by Father Escalante himself. They followed the White River of northwestern Colorado down to the Green, forded the Green and by a march to the northwest reached the trading post of Antoine Roubidoux — located, we are told by other travelers, "at the forks of the Uintah" (Sage), and "on the right bank, in latitude 40°, 27' 45" north, longitude 109°, 56', 42" west" (Frémont), thereby on the Uintah shortly above the Duchesne tributary of the Green.

Here the lively Antoine Robidoux, veteran trader and fond, as Joe Meek alleged, of the Indian game of "hand," had gathered to himself some twenty trappers and traders, their squaws and families, wintering around his log post in their skin lodges. It was scarcely to be expected that Don Antonio, in the trading business himself, would buy trader's goods at trader's prices or share his contracts with Captain Lee. The snow season had set in. Carson and the captain erected their lodge below the post, near the mouth of the Uintah, where there were fuel, and mule shelter and forage, and a friendly Ute village within neighborly distance, and prepared to spend a comfortable winter.

The winter would have passed uneventfully had not a "California Indian" in the Robidoux employ disappeared, one night, with six horses, "some of them being worth two hundred dollars per head." At the request of Robidoux and with the consent of his own employer, the captain (by whom he evidently had been hired as guide and hunter) Carson, with two of the best horses from the trading post and a Ute from the village set out to overhaul the runaway.

He had been cautioned that the fellow was a very shrewd Indian and was one of the best rifle shots at the fort. He and his Ute pursued hard and fast across the winter landscape. The trail was plain. It sped away down along the Green River, through a grim, bare mesa region fringed with rimrock and cut deeply by arroyos. The thief was bound for his home land somewhere in the western Sierras.

Then, on the second day, when the chase had covered 100 miles and the signs were growing fresher, the Ute's mount sickened and failed him. Carson continued alone.

After he had proceeded thirty miles more, he sighted ahead of him the thief and the stolen stock.

The Indian well knew that he was being pursued, and he had seen Kit Carson as quickly as Carson had seen him. Fast and faster they rode, the Indian to reach cover, just before him, where he might make a stand, Carson to catch him ere he did so.

Kit Carson's horse was the swifter, and presently only a hundred and fifty yards separated pursuer and pursued. Both men had down their rifles — but the Californian waited a moment too long. It was his purpose to shoot as he reached the cover, and there, under shelter, to reload in readiness to shoot again, if his first bullet had missed.

Just as he whirled about at the edge of the cover and leveled his rifle, Carson, at speed, loosed a bullet at him. The Indian's gun exploded, but without aim, for he pitched to the ground and instantly died. Kit Carson had shot first. In other words, or Carson's own: "I was under the necessity of killing him."

In due time Carson reached the Uintah camp with the stolen horses.

At the close of the winter a small party of men from the out-side reported that Fitzpatrick and Bridger of the Rocky Moun-tain Fur Company had wintered in the Snake River Valley and were making ready for the spring hunt. Captain Lee and Car-son packed up, in March, and started on to find a market in the Fitzpatrick-Bridger camp.

It was a disagreeable journey of fifteen days, amid the squally, chill weather of early spring, through a country very rough; but at the end of the fortnight they discovered, in camp up on the Snake, the Fitzpatrick-Bridger detachment of the Rocky Mountain Fur Company. Captain Lee traded in his goods for beaver and turned about for Taos. Kit Carson took his dis-charge and engaged to trap with the Rocky Mountain Fur Company again, under his first mountain partisan, Fitzpatrick. But according to his idea there were too many men trapping the territory for the company; and after a lean month he bore away, with three companions, for a less crowded field.

With his select squad he proceeded to trap the heads of the Laramie and upper side streams in the hilly Medicine Bow country sealing the Laramie Plains on the southwest and south, or along the Colorado-Wyoming border; and left the more open regions to the Indians and the strong trapping parties. There was a leavening element of thrifty Scotch blood in Car-son. His age was twenty-four.

Jim Bridger was due to pass this way on his trail to the sum-mer rendezvous in the Valley of the Green. While waiting for him Carson had the adventure to which he was wont to refer as his "worst difficult."

When hunting, afoot, in early evening, about a mile out of the camp he shot an elk on the side of a ridge and was in-stantly charged by two grizzlies in his rear. He had no time to stand on defense; he fled with empty gun for the nearest trees — a line of aspens threading a little draw. By dropping his gun he was just enabled to hoist himself aloft, into a sizable aspen, ere the raking claws could reach him. Here he perched and clung, ten or fifteen feet up, while the two brutes raged below him. It may be true that he thwacked them on the nose with a hasty club. One soon left; the other stayed, bawling and rearing and clawing, and tearing at the small trees, with occasional attempt to uproot the Carson refuge.

The disquieting performance continued until dusk. Then the second bear reluctantly made off. Carson held to his perch until he was convinced that the coast was clear; whereupon he slid down, grabbed his rifle, and reloading as he went, "made for my camp in as great haste as possible." He reached camp after dark, "never having been so scared in my life." The dead elk lay neglected, for wolf meat; and in the morning the hungry camp broke fast on beaver caught during the night.

Bridger — Old Gabe — somewhat testy with an arrow point, now two years old, in his back, eventually appeared with his command in the service of the Rocky Mountain Fur Company. The rendezvous had been appointed for the Green River Valley. Ham's Fork proved to be the spot, owing to the scant grass at the Sandy further upriver.

Now we have followed Carson's *Own Story,* but when we try to check up through contemporary chronicles we are confronted with another confusion of scene and action. Here is Joe Meek, to state that in the spring of 1834 he, with a portion of the Captain Joseph Walker company returning from their junketing trip, 1833, from the Salt Lake across to Monterey of California, on the Bill Williams Fork of the lower Colorado River met with the Rocky Mountain Fur Company detachment of Fraeb and Gervais, in which was Kit Carson.

Two hundred strong, the united parties marched eastward to the Colorado Chiquito — the Flax or the Little Colorado River of central northern Arizona; and here, in true freebooter style, they plundered the Moqui melon patches. For resisting, twenty of the Moquis were shot down; the unripe as well as the ripe fruit was destroyed.

Having thus sown the seeds of hatred and death, and leaving the ruined Moquis to curse the vandal whites, the trappers rode onward across the northwestern corner of New Mexico and struck the headwaters of the Rio Grande del Norte River, in Colorado's San Luis Park. The objective point was South Park.

It would seem that some of the party diverged to Taos, now only eighty miles distant, or to Bent's Fort on the Arkansas; for we find Kit Carson, Joe Meek, William Mitchell and three Delawares, Tom Hill, Jonas, and Manhead (the last-named to be slain in due time by the Blackfeet) on a hunt in southeastern Colorado — "in the country lying between the Arkansas and Cimarron, where numerous small branches of these rivers head together, or within a small extent of country."

On a May morning the six hunters were charged by some two hundred Comanches, those riders of the southern plains equal to their allies, the fierce Kiowas, whose name is a war-whoop. The whites and Delawares barely had time in which to cut the throats of their saddle-mules, and to form a fort of the dead bodies (in trapper style) before the Comanches were upon them, only to recoil before their rifles.

An all-day fight ensued; the trappers strengthened their barri-cade of mule carcasses by digging pits behind. The Comanches charged again, "the medicine-man in advance shouting, ges-ticulating, and making a desperate clatter with a rattle which he carried and shook violently. The yelling, the whooping, the rattling, the force of the charge were appalling." Three of the trappers fired, while the three others reloaded; the Comanche horses shrank from the smell of the mule blood; the warriors could not reach the little fort.

Three medicine-men were killed; and each time the Comanches must retire to choose a new one. During the con-fabs the squaws approached to bear off the slain and to revile the defenders. The red enemy were armed principally with the regulation Comanche long lance attached to a hair rope for re-covery, and with bows and arrows. The siege and the repeated assaults lasted until nightfall, so that without shade and water, pent there under the blazing sun and tortured by dust and heat and powder-reek, the three whites and the three Delawares were desperately put to it.

That the Comanches fought bravely is attested by the record of forty-two killed. Finally, having "lost faith in their medicine," they beat a retreat. When the way seemed to be open the six trappers shouldered blanket and gun and made for the mountains and camp; they maintained a dog-trot all the night, and did not reach water until they had traveled seventy-five miles.

The spring hunt with the main camp was finished off in the Colorado parks; and by trail through that North Park — in whose vicinity Carson, by his own narration, had trapped — we arrive again in the Valley of the Green.

The plains adventure with the Comanches may have happened to Carson sometime, but scarcely in the spring of 1834. For the following order is of record:

Messrs. Pratte, Chouteau & Co. St. Louis. Gentlemen: You will please pay to Mr. Christopher Carson or order the sum of Seventy dollars and have the same charged to Expedition 1834 and oblige yours respectfully, L. Fontenelle. Blackfork of Green River, July 8, 1834.[200]

By this it is indicated that Carson disposed of his furs taken in his spring catch to the American Fur Company, which he hardly would have done had he been trapping with Fraeb and Gervais of the Rocky Mountain Fur Company.

The rendezvous presented troubled waters. Carson's only comment on this rendezvous alleged to be his first, is:

Here was two camps of us. I think that there was two hundred trappers encamped. Then, till our supplies came from St. Louis, we disposed of our beaver to procure supplies. Coffee and sugar were two dollars a pint, powder the same, lead one dollar a bar and common blankets from fifteen to twenty-five dollars apiece.[201]

But at the outset of the gathering the Rocky Mountain Fur Company had executed the following paper:[202]

Whereas a dissolution of partnership having taken place by mutual consent between Thos. Fitzpatrick, Milton G. Sublette, Henry Fraeb, John Baptiste Jerviat and James Bridger, members of the Rocky Mountain Fur Company, all persons having demands against said company are requested to come forward and receive payment, those indebted to said firm are desired to call and make immediate payment as they are anxious to close the business of the concern.

Hams fork June 20th, 1834.

test
    W. L. SUBLETTE for
        BRIDGER & FITZPATRICK.

                          THOS. FITZPATRICK
                          M. G. SUBLETTE
                          HENRY FRAEB

whitness
    J. P. RISLEY for
        FRAEB & GERVAIS.

                          J. B. GERVAIS
                                his
                          JAMES   X   BRIDGER
                                mark

The public are hereby notified that the business will in future be conducted by Thomas Fitzpatrick, Milton G. Sublette, & James Bridger, under the style & firm of Fitzpatrick, Sublette & Bridger.

Hams fork June 20th, 1834.

                          THOS. FITZPATRICK
                          M. G. SUBLETTE

test
                          his
    W. L. SUBLETTE.   JAMES   X   BRIDGER
                                mark

By this the Rocky Mountain Fur Company, of robust lineage, vacated the field. The evil days of bad faith and of concupiscence had disorganized the fur trade. The wassailing and yarning and bartering were rasped by malcontent. Fitzpatrick, the Bad Hand, confirmed the loss of his packs last fall at the hands of the Crows, instigated, he accused, by the American Fur Company. Captain Bonneville had been seducing the rank and file by lavish liquor and by proffers of higher pay. The Cambridge knight-errant Nathaniel Wyeth arrived from St. Louis with a train of supplies and seventy men. He was under contract to deliver the supplies to the Rocky Mountain Fur Company, but the Company members, whether of the old association or of the new, had thrown their business to the more influential William Sublette, already on the spot, and refused to take the Wyeth goods.

At this rendezvous there appeared figures new to the mountains. Among others, two naturalists, Thomas Nuttall and J. K. Townsend, and two missionaries also for Oregon, the Reverends Jason and David Lee, with their assistants, had accompanied Wyeth from the Missouri.

The two naturalists were something, but they were, after all, only guests in a country where others of scientific and inquiring mind had preceded them. The missionaries were something else. They, and not the naturalists nor the dissolution of the Rocky Mountain Fur Company, mark the epoch of the summer of 1834. The beaver hunters were the scouts, the missionaries were the pioneers of the westward march of the American people to the occupancy of the northwest coast. Whereas in the beaver country of the mid-West region the settler followed the miner's pick, in the farther, most remote West the settler followed the Bible of the missionary.

Into this year of 1834 there already was being written one more failure of the American conquest of Oregon by any means, business or social. Even while Carson and his fellow mountain-men were viewing these strangers at rendezvous, in California one Hall J. Kelley, of no name in the mountains, save as brought here in the minds of Wyeth the business man, and the preachers Lee, had proselyted Captain Ewing Young, better known among trappers' lodges, to the colonization of Oregon. By that he had taken an ally from the enemy's ranks, for Captain Young was a fur trader and Kelley blamed the fur trade for his disappointments.

Of this Hall J. Kelley, the Oregon enthusiast, what? He was a New Englander born and bred; a Harvard A.M., Boston school teacher, Sunday-school organizer, text-book writer, surveyor, mathematician, scholar and gentleman. Beginning with 1815, when he was twenty-six years old, roused to his text by the reports of the Lewis and Clark expedition and gathering facts and fancies as a rolling snowball gathers snow, he had been proclaiming of Oregon, ever Oregon. For the purpose of a great 1832 emigration, in 1827 he had issued a fervid circular "To all persons who wish to emigrate to Oregon Territory." He memorialized Congress upon the subject; in 1829 he asked for a grant, to American citizenship, of twenty-five miles in the Columbia district. With the traditional school man's lack of the practical he bid without his host, for under joint occupancy with Great Britain such a grant was beyond the scope of Congress even if Congress heeded his prophetic voice — which it did not. In 1831 he incorporated, in Boston, his "American Society for Encouraging a Settlement of the Oregon Territory," to promote the will of God and the sovereignty of the Nation. He wakened public interest, by the Government he was assured of protection for his colony, but when in the spring of 1834 he at last arrived, by sea and by land via Vera Cruz of Mexico, in California upon his journey to Oregon, he arrived alone and stripped of his settler goods.

He failed to obtain employment, as a surveyor, from Governor Figueroa, suspicious of all foreigners; and his companionship with Captain Young, already in bad favor by reason of certain carelessness with horse brands, was his telling error. This summer, with Young (nothing loath to engage in a trading venture) and eight others, with ninety-eight horses and mules as the nucleus of a stock ranch, he continued on for the land of his dreams. "Nine marauders" convoying fifty-six stolen animals joined him upon the march, and furthered his undoing. Captain Young should have known better, but he was not averse to dispoiling the Latin; he had been educated in that, in New Mexico.

Governor Brigadier-General Don José Figueroa, short in reign, "of Aztec blood, and hence swarthy in color," promptly checkmated the trading operations of these Americans by a dispatched warning to Governor McLoughlin of the Hudson's Bay Company at Vancouver to be on his guard against a party of horse thieves entering from California. The subsequent career, in Oregon, of Ewing Young, innured to rebuffs by Nature and by man, has been related in these pages. Hall Kelley, succored in his needs but, for his associations, refused a seat at the "gentleman's mess" of the McLoughlin table, remained scarce a year. A broken crusader, a pennyless scholar, a ragged surveyor, a proscribed citizen, ill in mind as in body he sailed, in 1835, for home by way of the Sandwich Islands — in his pocket, to help him upon the road, thirty-five dollars from the governor, whose right hand was the hand of Company policy while his left hand was so often the hand of human charity.

Again back in Massachusetts he never again saw Oregon, for both fortune and health deserted him and the little movement that he had headed gathered way without him. When all was over, and Oregon had long been settled, he died, alone and eccentric, in 1874, aged eighty-five.[203]

At the close of the rendezvous of 1834 the brigades, companies and squads trailed out for the east, west, north and south. Carson enlisted with the brigade of Jim Bridger, fifty men, bound for the headwaters of the Missouri in Blackfoot country. Nathaniel Jarvis Wyeth of the new Columbia River Fishing and Trading Company, not yet admitting to defeat in the mountain trade, with the threat (well fulfilled) to "roll into the garden" of Milton Sublette (ill in St. Louis with a "fungus growth" in his leg) and co-operates "a stone which they cannot remove," set forth to build his depot of Fort Hall on the Snake and to clear himself by ventures at the mouth of the Columbia, and in that Oregon to find, in suspicious straits, the Kelley who had first interested him. For the Columbia hastened Captain Bonneville, from his own camp apart on the Bear River, to sweep the country ahead of his fellow struggler Wyeth. And over the Oregon Trail to be, there traveled, in the Wyeth company, from the rendezvous stop-over, the two missionaries Jason and David Lee and their colleagues, bearing their gospel of the white East to the red West.

They also will find in Oregon that Hall J. Kelley whose prophecies they have read. But his ways are not their ways, nor the ways of Wyeth. They will find the indomitable Captain Young, who by his service for the Willamette Land and Cattle Company will encourage American industries. For thus the man of resources wins out over the man of dreams. In due time, but not far distant, being within a year of their arrival, they will find there William A. Slacum, of the Navy, special secret agent investigating American affairs for report to Washington, itself interested. The woes of Kelley the Boston schoolmaster were not vainly suffered.

Chapter XIX

The American Wedge in Oregon

IT may be said that the first invasion of Oregon Territory by the missionaries from the States did not have any conscious purpose of colonizing the Pacific coast. In the spring of 1833, when the *Christian Advocate and Journal and Zion's Herald* of New York repeated the "Macedonian cry" through the Atlantic coast cities, to the Eastern people Oregon was an immense, indefinite fur region beyond the Rocky Mountains, where flowed the rivers encountered by the Lewis and Clark and the Astor expeditions. And while the spasmodic eruptions in Congress, the pronunciamentos of the zealous Hall Kelley, and the business endeavors of Nathaniel J. Wyeth aroused interest from those who were to be the missionary pioneers, nevertheless the initial journey of Jason and David Lee was projected only to plant a Protestant gospel establishment among the Flatheads.

A strange vein of religious fervor was reported to run through the Flatheads and Nez Percés. As records the *Diary* of W. A. Ferris, in 1831:

Their (the Flatheads') ancient superstitions have given place to the more enlightened views of the Christian faith, and they seem to have become deeply and profitably impressed with the great truths of the gospel. They appear to be very devout and orderly, and never eat, drink, or sleep, without giving thanks to God.

Captain Bonneville (1832) found the Nez Percés, Flatheads, Cayuses, observing Sunday and, after a fashion rude but sincere, the ritual and calendar of the Roman church. This custom is explained in a letter of October, 1839, from the Right Reverend Joseph Rosati, Bishop of St. Louis, to the Father General of the Society of Jesus at Rome.

MY RIGHT REVEREND FATHER: Twenty-three years ago [1816] two Indians of the Iroquois mission left their native country, Canada, with twenty-two other warriors and went to settle in a country situated between the Rocky Mountains and the Pacific Sea. That country is inhabited by infidel nations, and especially by those the French call Têtes

Plate [Têtes Plattes, or Flat Heads]. They married there and were incorporated with the Indian nation. As they were well instructed in the
Catholic religion professed by the Iroquois — converted by the ancient
fathers of your society — they have continued to practise it as much as
was in their power, and have taught it to their wives and children. Their
zeal went even further; becoming apostles, they have sown the first seeds
of Catholicity in the midst of the infidel nation among whom they
dwell.[204]

Moreover, throughout the tribes west of the mountains, in
the Oregon Territory of the Northwest, there had been circulating for twenty years the employes of the British fur companies; mainly French-Canadians and good Catholics. The
Indians absorbed much precept and doctrine. And at posts of
the Hudson's Bay Company, in particular at Fort Walla Walla
under Chief Trader Pambrun, pains were taken to impress the
visiting natives with the force of the Roman faith. With Agent
Pambrun this was sincere proselyting — but the fact was not
forgotten that the Christianized Indian was the better Indian
with whom to deal.

The Rosati letter continues:

Eight or nine years ago (about 1830) some of the Flathead nation came
to St. Louis. The object of their journey was to ascertain if the religion
spoken of with so much praise by the Iroquois warriors was in reality
such as represented, and, above all, if the nations that have the white skin
(the name they give Europeans) had adopted it and practised it. Soon
after their arrival at St. Louis they fell sick and earnestly asked — by
signs — to be baptized. Their request was granted, and they received the
holy baptism with great devotion; then holding the crucifix, they covered it with kisses and expired.

The Reverend John W. York, who was a Methodist elder in
St. Louis in 1830, stated to Judge J. Q. Thornton that on September 17, that year, five Indians from the Columbia arrived
in the city seeking religious aid; and that General William
Clark, superintendent of Indian affairs, sent for him and
brethren Alliston and Edmundson for inquiry into the pos-
sibility of the Methodists' replying with missionaries.[205]

The letter, 1839, of Bishop Joseph of St. Louis refers to a

similar delegation but he had previously related in a letter, date of December 31, 1831, to the editor of a Roman Catholic journal in Lyons, France:

Some three months ago four Indians, who live at the other side of the Rocky Mountains, near the Columbia River, arrived in St. Louis. After visiting General Clark who, in his celebrated travels, had seen the nation to which they belong, and had been well received by them, they came to see our church, and appeared to be exceedingly well pleased with it. Unfortunately there was no one who understood their language. Some time afterward two of them fell dangerously ill. I was then absent from St. Louis. Two of our priests visited them, and the poor Indians seemed delighted with their visit. They made signs of the Cross and other signs which appeared to have some relation to baptism. It was truly distressing that they could not be spoken to.[206]

The two Indians died and were buried: the one, Pipe Bard, October 31, 1831; the other, as Paul, on November 10. The two survivors set out for return to their country.[207]

When in after year the artist Catlin read a version of this story as rendered into romance he recalled that the two returning Indians were passengers upon the very steamboat of the American Fur Company by which, in the spring of 1832, he himself was taken to the mouth of the Yellowstone, on his initial trip into the Indian country of the upper Missouri. They are assigned numbers 207 and 208 in his drawings; their Nez Percé names. Hee-oh'ks-te-kin or Rabbit Skin Leggins, and H'co-a-h'co-a-h'cotes-min or No Horns on His Head. The latter died from disease near the mouth of the Yellowstone but the other reached his people.

These two men were part of a delegation that came across the Rocky Mountains to St. Louis, a few years since, to enquire for the truth of a representation which they said some white man had made amongst them, "that our religion was better than theirs, and that they would all be lost if they did not embrace it." Two old and venerable men of this party died in St. Louis, and I travelled two thousand miles, companion with these two young fellows, towards their own country, and became much pleased with their manners and disposition. . . . When I first heard the report of this extraordinary mission across the mountains, I could scarcely believe it; but on conversing with General Clark on a future occasion, I was fully convinced of the fact.[208]

Catlin is accredited with having said to General Clark: "Publish it to the world." But it had already been published. Writing, with date New York, February 18, 1833, to the *Christian Advocate and Journal and Zion's Herald*, G. P. Disoway encloses, for publication, a letter to him from William Walker, sub-agent, interpreter and acting Methodist missionary among his own people, the Wyandot Hurons of Ohio.

"In November last" William Walker had accompanied a committee of the Wyandots sent to inspect the lands "west of the Mississippi River" offered to the tribe by the Government for a permanent home. Said the Walker letter, written January 19, 1833, upon his return to Ohio:

Immediately after we landed in St. Louis, on our way to the West, I proceeded to Gen. Clark's, superintendent of Indian affairs, to present our letters of introduction from the Secretary of War, and to receive the same from him to the different Indian agents in the upper country. While in his office and transacting business with him, he informed me that three chiefs from the Flathead nation were in his house, and were quite sick, and that one (the fourth) had died a few days ago. . . . It appeared that some white man had penetrated into their country, and happened to be a spectator at one of their religious ceremonies, which they scrupulously perform at stated periods. He informed them that their mode of worshipping the Supreme Being was radically wrong, and instead of being acceptable and pleasing, it was displeasing to him; he also informed them that the white people away toward the rising of the sun had been put in possession of the true mode of worshipping the Great Spirit. They had a book containing directions how to conduct themselves in order to enjoy his favor and hold converse with him; and with this guide, no one need go astray; but every one that would follow the directions laid down there could enjoy, in this life, his favor, and after death would be received into the country where the Great Spirit resides, and live forever with Him.

The tale and comments of William Walker and the comments of G. P. Disoway — "Let the Church awake from her slumbers and go forth in her strength to the salvation of these wandering sons of our native forests" — were published in the *Christian Advocate* of March 1, 1833. The effect was instant. With a "Hear! Hear! Who will respond to this call from beyond the Rocky Mountains?" Dr. Wilbur Fisk, now at forty a leading divine and educator, founder and president of Wesleyan College of Middletown, Connecticut, in a stirring editorial summoned Methodism to establish a Flathead mission.

> Let two suitable men, unincumbered with families, possessing the spirit of martyrs, throw themselves into the nation — live with them — learn their language — preach Christ to them — and, as the way is opened, introduce schools, agriculture, and the arts of civilized life. Money shall be forthcoming. I will be bondsman for the church; all we want is men. Who will go? Who? . . . Were I young, healthy, and unincumbered, how joyfully would I go! But this honor is for another. Bright will be his crown, glorious his reward.[209]

Succeeding communications from St. Louis, of dates of April 16 and 17, in the *Advocate* of May 10, stated that General Clark had confirmed the truth of the visit of the Indians, Flatheads and Pierced Noses, who, having been instructed by two Catholic Indians from Montreal, had journeyed 3,000 miles to St. Louis in order to learn further "how the whites approached the Great Spirit." And the fur trader Robert Campbell had replied to inquiries upon the Flatheads, their country, and the means of getting there.

In time the tale had grown until there appeared in print a farewell "Lament" alleged to have been delivered by one of the Indians at the last of several banquets tendered the delegation; taken down on the spot by a young man there present and sent to a friend in the East. The theme was the "White Man's Book of Heaven" which the delegation had been unable to find, and without which the speaker was going back, blind, to his blind people. The oration, as eventually expanded to measured periods and higher flights of imagery and made worthy of a Logan or a Black Hawk or a Chief Joseph, seems to have first appeared in print more than thirty years after its alleged date of delivery.[210]

The fact that there was said to be no one in St. Louis fluent in the Nez Percé or Flathead dialects makes the wonder of the translation all the greater. It has to be propounded that the first delegation were accompanied by an interpreter in the

French or the English, and even at that we have Bishop Joseph's letter which recites of the difficulty of communication. Another wonder is voiced in the contention that the pilgrims had to leave St. Louis without a copy of the "Book of Heaven," which was the Bible.

The legend has persisted that the "Lament" delivered at the banquet was transmitted to the *Christian Advocate* and there published in March, 1833. A query to the Reference Department of the New York Public Library brought the report:

> Our information division has checked through the 1933 file of the "Christian Advocate and Journal and Zion's Herald" and feels reasonably certain that the Indian speech with its reference to "The Book of Heaven" did not appear in it. The many references to the Flathead Indians give some reason for the deputation to General Clark, such as "to inquire of the white man how he ascertains the will of the Great Spirit" (p. 146) and to "inquire for the 'true way to heaven'" (p. 194). It seems reasonable to suppose that if the many writers to the "Christian Advocate" had read a catch phrase such as "to get the white man's Book of Heaven" they would have used it too. It is notable that none of the early writers on the Flathead Indians used the phrase "Book of Heaven" but practically every recent account uses it.
>
> The earliest possible reference to such a phrase we have traced belongs to the year 1850. W. P. Strickland in his "History of the Missions of the Methodist Episcopal Church" (Cincinnati, 1850) says that "a deputation of their principal men was sent on a journey across the Rocky Mountains, to inquire after the 'white man's God' and the wonderful book from heaven" (p. 120).

It is pointed out, however, in support of the Protestant argument in behalf of the speech and its "Book of Heaven" appeal, that a *Christian Advocate* was issued in Pittsburgh also, in 1833.[211]

By the York account, then, the first Indian delegates from the far northwest seeking religious benefits arrived in St. Louis in the fall of 1830; by the letter of Bishop Joseph in 1831 they arrived in the fall of 1831, and by his letter of 1839 they arrived "eight or nine years ago (about 1830)" and were followed, in 1832, by an educated Iroquois and two of his grandchildren; by the letters in the *Christian Advocate* (New York) in 1833 the delegation were seen by William Walker at General Clark's in November, 1832. As described by William Walker they had flattened or receding foreheads and thereby were Flatheads as popularly conceived.

But these men, or two of them, could not have taken the home trail by river, with Artist Catlin, in the spring of 1832; and moreover, his portraits of them do not show the flattened heads. Indeed, the term "Flatheads" implies the very opposite of that notion so generally entertained; for it was originally used in the early northwest, to distinguish the peoples whose head were flat on top from those whose heads were artificially formed to a peak, as among the Chinooks.

Reference to the existing letter-books of General Clark himself, Superintendent of Indian Affairs at St. Louis, indicate that the delegation, whether of Flatheads or Nez Percés or of both, appeared in St. Louis in the fall of 1831. There is a letter of General Clark, dated November 20, 1831, to the Secretary of War, mentioning the influx of Indians from the "North East," and "others from west of the Rocky Mountains visiting me." There is a report, November 22, from the "Ioway Sub Agency," announcing that "Mr. Walter [Walker] and party have called on me, they are all on foot, etc., etc." And a letter of General Clark of December 28 speaks of "the Wyandot Indians & their leaders, who lately explored the Country above."[212]

The idea expressed in 1804 by President Jefferson, that the new Louisiana Purchase would afford an asylum for these doubtful wards the Indians, at last, or in January, 1825, had been presented in proper shape to Congress by President Monroe as one of the final acts of his administration. The result was the establishment of an "Indian Frontier." By treaty of June, 1825, the Osages and the Kaws or Kansas surrendered their vast hunting range in the Southwest, along the Santa Fé Trail. The government hastened to remove here its Indians from the states of the South. The movement of other tribes also was prosecuted — the country so exchanged with them to be "forever secured and guaranteed to them and their heirs or successors," their fate "left to the common God of the white man and the Indian," they themselves, isolated and independent, left "to the progress of events" — an unconscious irony!

In 1835 the boundaries of the "Indian Territory" were defined by the Annual Register of Indian Affairs as "beginning on Red River, east of the Mexican boundary and as far west of Arkansas Territory as the *country is habitable*, thence down Red River eastwardly to Arkansas Territory; thence northwardly along the line of the Arkansas Territory to the State of Missouri; thence up Missouri river to Pimcah [Puncah: i.e., Niobrara] river; thence westwardly *as far as the country is habitable*, and thence southwardly to the beginning."

The italics are the author's. In this Indian Country there dwelt, according to rough estimate, some 100,000 Indians. Beyond the Mississippi the various churches were represented among the Cherokees, Choctaws, Kansas, Pawnees, Creeks, Omahas, Iowas, Delawares, Otoes, Potawatomis, Shawnees, Kickapoos, etc., *as far as the country was habitable*. Truly it was a noble work, in which men and women died, and in which the harvest was great but the laborers were few. Upon the outskirts were the Sioux (approached by way of Fort Snelling, Minnesota), the Comanches, the Blackfeet, the Snakes, the Arapahos — strange, roving, thoroughly wild people, not yet within the fold.

But the delegation of the Columbia River Indians proffered another foothold. Dr. Fisk had called for "two suitable men." He had one such man in mind, and that was the Reverend Jason Lee, a Canadian but an American, once a pupil of his at Wilbraham Academy of Massachusetts, now stationed at Sanstead, Province of Quebec, and employed in missionary work among the Indians of Canada.

The blood of that great New England preacher, the "Apostle of Methodism," Jesse Lee, must have been strong in this other generation. The summons by Dr. Fisk in the *Christian Advocate* had appeared in March; at the Boston session of the

New England Conference in June following, Jason Lee, having resigned his Canadian field, was appointed superintendent of the new Oregon Mission! Tall, stooped, awkward and honest, "of good digestion and a sound mind," he was the choice reflecting Dr. Fisk's excellent judgment.

In August his nephew, the Reverend Daniel Lee, was appointed as his fellow laborer. He, too, "was not an Adonis"; but like his uncle he stood as an example of the plain, orthodox, New England Methodist preacher, and of a youth preördained to the cause of souls.

The *Christian Advocate* had published advice from Robert Campbell, the trader and St. Louis citizen, upon the prospects of the Columbia country, and upon the method of getting there, overland: namely, by escort of fur trader caravan.

And I doubt not but that they would willingly allow a missionary to accompany them; but the privations that a gentleman of that profession would have to encounter would be very great, as the shortest route that he would have by land would not be less than one thousand miles, and when he reached his destination he would have to travel with the Indians, as they have no permanent villages, nor have the traders any houses, but, like the Indians, move in their leather lodges from place to place throughout the season.

Since transportation was the problem, and summer was already well advanced, a voyage around the Horn was discussed. Then in November "notice appeared in the public journals that Captain N. J. Wyeth, of Cambridge, Mass., had recently returned from a tour west of the Rocky Mountains, and that he contemplated returning to Oregon in the following spring."

The way seemed opened. Captain Wyeth was sought in Boston by Jason Lee himself. From Captain Wyeth "valuable information was received respecting the state of the country, the general character and disposition of the Indian tribes inhabiting the Oregon territory; and he likewise manifested a disposition to give every aid in his power to the mission."[213]

Accordingly, when in the last of November, 1833, the Columbia River Fishing and Trading Company ship *May Dacre,* laden with the Wyeth hopes and the company supplies, sailed out of Boston for the port of Vancouver, it bore also the supplies for the prospective missionary station of the Methodist church in Oregon.

And when, on April 28, 1834, the united caravans of Wyeth and Milton Sublette issued from Independence of the Missouri frontier, they convoyed into the West the Reverend Jason Lee, the Reverend Daniel Lee, Lay Missionaries Cyrus Shepard of Lynn, Mass., and Philip L. Edwards of Richmond, Mo.; and assistant Courtney M. Walker of Richmond.

There were two guests of the trail. In 1811 John Bradbury, English naturalist, had ascended the Missouri with the Astorian expedition under Wilson Hunt. Now in 1834 Thomas Nuttall, Englishman, Harvard professor, and botanist, who had been with John Bradbury in 1811, was about to cross the continent. He had as companion J. K. Townsend, ornithologist, whose name is retained in Townsend's Warbler of the Pacific coast.[214]

With seventy men, 250 horses and the missionaries' cattle, the caravan proceeded. Two weeks out Milton Sublette was obliged to turn back for St. Louis and surgical treatment for his leg. William Sublette and his supply train, traveling rapidly, coming from behind gained the lead by night. In June the march crossed South Pass and on the 20th the missionaries pitched their camp amid the rendezvous of whites and reds upon Ham's Fork in the Valley of the Green. Wyeth had to remain two weeks; then, on July 2, with his goods thrown upon his hands by the Rocky Mountain Fur Company and his first disappointment of 1834 encountered, he broke camp and moved on. The presence of the missionaries did not prevent the fur men from celebrating the Fourth as they pleased. Wyeth writes: "I gave the men too much alcohol for peace, and took a pretty hearty spree myself." At the juncture of the Portneuf with the Snake in Idaho he halted the party (126 horses, forty men) in order to build his own fort which should house and distribute his trading goods.

Trader Thomas McKay and his company of Hudson's Bay employes, half of them Indians, were present, and again the missionaries had a chance to study their future charges — even saw them at their devotions, "conducted very seriously, but after a fashion all their own." Jason Lee, who, it is stated, "was a man all liked and respected," and who evidently was making good in trapper opinion, preached to the assembled whites, breeds and natives; then, with his associates, with McKay and with Captain Sir William Stewart the Britisher, he pressed forward down the Snake. Wyeth with his company remained behind to complete the fort, to name it Fort Hall, to hoist over it an American flag of sheeting, red flannel and blue patches, and to salute it "with damaged powder and wet it in villainous alcohol." The day was August 5, 1834. Consigning his post to eleven men, fourteen horses and mules and three cows, in charge of one Evans, he hastened upon the trail of the preceding McKay and the missionaries, for the coast. There he would meet his vessel, *May Dacre* — and another disappointment.

The Lees and their associates had learned much since they had crossed the mountains by South Pass. They might realize how difficult it would be, as Robert Campbell had intimated, to maintain a mission in the Flathead country, so remote, so far from supplies, and so sparsely inhabited. Although they had been well received by the Hudson's Bay employes and the Indians alike, they were faced by a faith already established by teachings and ritual. For in his letter of 1839, referring back to the Protestant endeavors, Bishop Joseph Rosati says, to emphasize the ripeness of the Columbia field:

When these pretended missionaries [the Protestants] presented themselves our good Catholics [the Iroquois instructors] refused to receive them. "These are not the priests we have spoken of to you," they said to the Flatheads; "they are not the priests with long black gowns, who have no wives, who say mass, and who carry a crucifix with them."

But in 1834 six years were to elapse before a Black Robe trod the trail that the Protestant van now trod.

The Lees decided to continue on westward to the lower

Columbia and make that their base. They pressed ahead, through the desolate region along the Snake. At Walla Walla they left their horses and cattle, for later disposal, and embarking upon a wild trip in Hudson's Bay Company log canoes they descended the Columbia to Vancouver of the Hudson's Bay Company. Here they arrived on September 15, to sleep under a roof, after one hundred and fifty nights in trappers' lodges or under the stars.[215]

The landing of the Pilgrim Fathers was scarcely more significant, for the American missions in Oregon meant that the western half, like the eastern half of a continent, was to be settled under a free constitution. From the missionary movement came Whitman, and if we may adapt fancy to fact, Whitman saved Oregon. But even eliminating the patriotic purpose in the ride of Marcus Whitman, a few years of the missionaries of the Protestant Church made the Oregon Territory better known to the eastern people than did all the years of the fur-hunters.

Let us pass to the summer of 1835, and to another rendezvous in the valley of the Green; for inasmuch as the only method of crossing the plains and mountains was that of the spring trading caravans from the Missouri, the annual markets for the next five or six years form paragraphs in the annals of the Protestant missions to Oregon.

At this rendezvous of July and August, 1835, appear the Reverend Samuel Parker, A.M., and Dr. Marcus Whitman, sent forward by the American Board of Commissioners for Foreign Missions to report upon the Oregon field. Parker is from Ithaca, N. Y.; is a native of Massachusetts, a graduate of Williams College and Andover Theological Seminary, has served in both Congregational and Presbyterian charges. Whitman is from Rushville, N. Y.; is a native of New York, a graduate of the Berkshire Medical School of Pittsfield, Mass., is a Presbyterian with Congregationalist tendencies, and a physician more interested in souls than in bodies.[216]

They had left the East in March; had left Liberty, Missouri, May 14, with the American Fur Company caravan, under

Lucien Fontenelle to Fort William (predecessor of Fort Laramie), where Thomas Fitzpatrick had taken the guidance of the march.

These two men, the Reverend Samuel Parker, A.M., and Marcus Whitman, M.D., differed much in character. Mr. Parker, aged fifty-six, was scholarly and serious; Dr. Whitman, thirty-three, was unassuming, lively and adaptable, and quickly attained to fellowship among the mountain-men.

Down the Ohio and up the Missouri to Liberty, Mr. Parker distributed his tracts and held services. He was a studious observer of the land and the people. He and the doctor would not travel on Sunday, at first, and the caravan went on without them—its men offended by the implied rebuke and disgruntled over being burdened with finicky tenderfeet. After a scourge of cholera which they lightened, the doctor and the minister learned that some of the men of the caravan had planned to put them out of the way and thus be rid of their wet-blanket presence.

At the rendezvous, reached August 12, Dr. Whitman extracted arrowheads from the back of two trappers — one being Captain Bridger. By conversation, through an interpreter, with the Flatheads and Nez Percés, Mr. Parker ascertained, to his satisfaction, that "the field was white for the harvest." Dr. Whitman, out of the zeal and energy which characterized him, decided that he ought to return to the East with the caravan, to report in person upon the need of more missionaries, and to bring out a party with the caravan of 1836, thus saving a year of time. Mr. Parker proceeded to the coast with an Indian escort.

He arrived at Vancouver on October 16. Although his stay in Oregon comprised only about eight months (he sailed June 28, 1836, for Connecticut, via the Sandwich Islands) he thoroughly explored the interior of the Columbia basin, the purpose for which he was sent out by the Board. The most notable result of his visit was his book, *Journal of an Exploring Tour Beyond the Rocky Mountains,* which, published with map in

1838, endorsed by Noah Webster, by President H. Humphrey and Professor Edward Hitchcock of Amherst, and written in scholarly manner is the first account, after that by Lewis and Clark, of the upper Platte and the Columbia country — scenery, inhabitants, geology, zoology, climate and customs; and is the very first book devoted largely to Oregon.[217]

While the Reverend Samuel Parker was gathering facts and spreading the Word up the Columbia of Oregon further than the Lees and associates had yet penetrated, Dr. Whitman, aflame with great purpose, was hastening hither and thither through New England, not the least of his encouragements his betrothed, the noble Narcissa Prentiss of Angelica, New York. Dr. Whitman had taken back with him, from the Green River, two Nez Percé boys, that he might present tangible evidence of the work awaiting beyond the mountains. By these, and through his own efforts, he counted upon forming a party for the caravan trip of 1836. In February he and Miss Prentiss were married. He had been appointed a missionary to Oregon by the American Board, and been directed to obtain an associate. He wished an associate for his wife also —

. . . and then light came from an unexpected quarter. In the early spring of 1836 a sleigh, extemporized from a wagon, was crunching through the deep snows of western New York. It contained the Reverend and Mrs. Spalding, who were on their way, under commission of the American Board, to the Osage Indians. The wife had started from a bed of lingering illness, and was then able to walk less than a quarter of a mile.

Dr. Whitman, having heard of the rare courage of this woman, by permission of the board, started in pursuit.

"We want you for Oregon," was the hail with which he overtook them.

"How long will the journey take?"

"The summers of two years."

"What convoy shall we have?"

"The American Fur Company to the Divide."

"What shall we have to live on?"

"Buffalo meat, till we can raise our own grain."

"How shall we journey?"

"On horseback."

"How cross the rivers?"

"Swim them."

Mr. Spalding decided instantly, as for himself. And after prayer, apart, in the tavern at Howard, New York, Mrs. Spalding appeared with beaming face.

"I have made up my mind to go."

"But your health, my dear."

"I like the command just as it stands. 'Go ye into all the world,' and no exceptions for poor health."

"But the perils, in your weak condition — you don't begin to think how great they are."

"The dangers of the way and the weakness of my body are His; duty is mine."[218]

The die was cast. They went — the two women, both tender, each a bride and one an invalid. The maxim on the Sweetwater trail long had been: "No white woman can cross the mountains and live."

The little party numbered five: Missionary Physician Dr. Marcus Whitman, aged thirty-four; Narcissa Prentiss Whitman his bride, aged twenty-eight; Missionary Henry H. Spalding, of Bath, N. Y., who less than three years before had graduated from Western Reserve College, and who was about the same age as Dr. Whitman; Eliza Hart Spalding of Trenton, N. Y., his wife; Assistant Missionary William H. Gray, aged twenty-five, of Utica, who would serve also as agent of farming and mechanics.

From the very beginning the way was made hard for them. At Pittsburgh, Catlin, the artist, told tales of horrors to them, and would dissuade them. At St. Louis the Fur Company declined to convoy them, and yielded only to the insistence of Whitman, who reminded the men how he had succored them in the cholera scourge a year before; how, "from behind the festering spine of a comrade," he had extracted an arrow-head. After the promise of escort, the company's boat passed them at Liberty Landing. A mule kicked Spalding; ague attacked him; a cow, plunging overboard from a ferry, dragged him after; a hurricane leveled his tent, and drenched him again; and before the party, hastening by land after the recreant boat, had reached the Council Bluffs, the company caravan had pulled out and was five days in advance.

Mr. Spalding, sick and discouraged, would have turned back. But his wife, stronger in spirit than in body, declared: "I have started for the Rocky Mountains and I expect to go there!"

With a cavvy of half-broken Missouri mules, fifteen or twenty horses, cattle, two wagons, and mission goods, the three men and the two women, with Whitman as guide, set out to overtake the caravan. Through a series of accidents which delayed the caravan, after a two weeks' chase and after a final desperate spurt (during which Mrs. Spalding fainted) from daylight until two o'clock the next morning the race was won at the Loup Fork of the Platte — the safety limits of the Indian country.

But now that the missionary party had carried their point "nothing could exceed the kindness of the men. The choicest buffalo morsels were always kept for our ladies." The party not only had won the race, but had won the regard of the traders and trappers, who could appreciate pluck. The two women evidently were not going to be a clog, as had been feared. At any rate, willy-nilly, the march must continue; and mustering 200 persons, 600 animals, the caravan proceeded with military discipline up the Platte.

Meat was the sole menu, and fresh meat at that. Once or twice this failed, and the camp went hungry. Mrs. Spalding, with whom the diet seemed to disagree, grew weaker; and at Fort William on the Laramie the captain of the caravan, Fitzpatrick, declared that she had come far enough; she would die for want of bread.

"No," said she; "I started over the mountains in the name of my Savior, and I must go on."

By this time she rode a horse only with difficulty, and preferred the lighter of the two mission wagons. The nineteen wagons of the traders were left, as was customary, at the fort, and the supplies were transferred to mule back; but Dr. Whitman insisted upon taking his light wagon on, for the Columbia. The British big-game hunter Captain Stewart was with the caravan; not to be out-done he took onward a two-mule wagon of his own.

Word had been sent ahead, by an express to the rendezvous, that the "Company" annual caravan was approaching, and that with it were two white women! There was quick excitement in the Valley of the Green.

In short time a squad of the trappers had mounted and were speeding away, on a mad race with rival Nez Percés, to bid the strangers welcome.

Ascending the Sweetwater for the South Pass, the missionaries witnessed this triumphant cavalcade dashing down upon them; carrying in the muzzle of a rifle the white flag of peace, but by whoop and yelp and headlong charge appearing to give it the lie.

On they came, riding faster and faster, yelling louder and louder, and gesticulating more and more madly, until, as they met and passed the caravan, they discharged their guns in one volley over the heads of the company, as a last finishing feu de joie; and suddenly wheeling rode back to the front as wildly as they had come.[219]

Naturally, all eyes were upon the two women, thus initiated into the wild ways of the wildest West. Some of the trappers had not seen a white woman for ten years; the Indians never had seen a white woman. What they, trappers and Indians, saw now, was a slight, dark-haired, pallid, plain-featured young woman in a wagon, gazing back with a studied reserve. This was Mrs. Spalding. They saw, for the other, a large, full, blue-eyed, sparkling-faced, generously featured, brightly haired young woman, in perfect health, upon a horse, returning look for look and smile for smile, as if appreciative of the exhibition. This was Mrs. Whitman.

The gay riders set off for the rendezvous again. The caravan mounted South Pass, where, on this the Fourth of July, Mrs. Spalding again fainted. She was permitted to lie upon the ground and rest.

"Don't put me on that horse again. Leave me and save yourselves. Tell mother I am glad I came."

But from the top the caravan sent back for her. The Southwest has its missionary heroes; the Northwest, its heroines.

Presently the Continental Divide of North America had been spanned; before, the waters flowed west; before, there opened Oregon, where, crushed by horrors and many fatigues, Mrs. Spalding should sleep "under an Oregon clod," and whence, as symbol of martyrdom, there was returned, after thirty-four years, by the hand of Henry Spalding, an old man broken and bereft, only a lock of Mrs. Whitman's hair, of silky texture and reddish-gold color, "indicating the sanguine temperament, with, perhaps, a shade of the nervous."[220]

On the Pacific slope of the Pass the caravan halted, while the little band, at twelve o'clock noon of Independence Day, 1836, six years before Frémont, following in the footsteps of the women, gained the name of the "Path-finder," alighting from their horses and kneeling on the other half of the continent, with the Bible in one hand and the American flag in the other, took possession of it as the home of American mothers, and of the Church of Christ.[221]

Again we are reminded of Plymouth Rock.

Down from the pass the caravan was met now by the charging cavalry of the Nez Percés and Flatheads en masse, arrayed in their brightest and bravest. With this escort the rendezvous was reached. Mrs. Whitman attracted the men, but Mrs. Spalding, ill and slight and reserved, attracted the women. The Indian squaws took her in charge, administered fibrous roots to her which effectively stopped the exhausting bowel trouble caused by the green buffalo meat, and "from that hour she began to mend, and from that hour her future and theirs were one."

Fortunately a Hudson's Bay trading party under John McLeod and Thomas McKay were at the rendezvous; with this party the missionaries traveled westward again. Before arrival at Fort Hall (last American outpost) the light wagon had been reduced to a two-wheeled cart; at Fort Boise (just erected by the British traders as a counter-post to Fort Hall) the cart itself had to be abandoned until it could be brought on by some party unencumbered.

But the indomitable Doctor Whitman had demonstrated his theory. In 1826 Smith, Jackson and Sublette had taken cattle and wagons to the South Pass; in 1832 Captain Bonneville had taken his wagon train over the South Pass to the Green; now in 1836 women, wagon craft and cattle had been taken to the Snake, and on his next trip through a larger outfit would be taken by Whitman to the coast.

The Columbia at Walla Walla was reached September 1, and the good agent Pambrun received Mrs. Spalding in his arms "as if he had been her father." On September 12 the batteaux bearing the travelers rounded the point where stood Fort Vancouver. Flags were waving, songs were resounding, the Hudson's Bay dignitaries Governor John McLoughlin and Factor James Douglass "with stately courtesy" escorted into the fort the first white women over the Oregon Trail. Thus had been performed "an undertaking pronounced impossible by every mountain-man, by George Catlin, and the missionary Lee"; and in Oregon the Protestant church, by importation of the white American family and of American customs, had laid the foundation for the American commonwealth in the Northwest.[222]

Chapter XX

Adventures of Kit Carson — 1834-1835

THE Bridger company with which Carson enlisted for the fall hunt of 1834 trapped the headwaters of the Missouri. "We made a very poor hunt as the Indians were very bad. Five of our men were killed. A trapper could hardly go a mile without being fired upon." Accordingly, having paid well for the privilege of going out lighter than they had come in, the company sought winter quarters again at the forks of the Snake — the juncture of the Snake and the Henry, sixty miles above that new Fort Hall erected last summer by Nathaniel Wyeth.[223]

Ere the camp had broken up for the spring hunt the restless Blackfeet rushed the horse-herd and ran off eighteen animals including Jim Bridger's favorite mount Grohean — a gray of Comanche stock procured from the Snakes. The Blackfeet (likely the Gros Ventres again) had been equipped with snow-shoes, but after a pursuit of fifty miles the posse of trappers, with Carson and Joe Meek in the muster, brought them to bay where the February waist-deep drifts had stalled them and their stolen gather.

The Indians were thirty; the trappers were twelve; the horses were under guard on a bared hillside. The trappers signed for a parley, and at a halfway spot a man from either party met, unarmed, for a talk. The Blackfeet claimed that they had thought to rob the Snakes, not their friends the white men. In a general talk and smoke, with all arms left behind, the Indians agreed to turn over the horses; but when only five, and these the very poorest, were brought in, and the robbers now refused to surrender the thirteen others, there was a mutual rush for weapons.

The battle opened in the snow and among rocks and trees. Carson and trapper Markhead paired off with two of the warriors who, in the rear-guard of the scurrying reds, had posted themselves behind trees. Markhead was having trouble with his gun lock and neglected to watch his Indian. The fellow was taking deadly aim when Carson shifted his muzzle covering his own antagonist and by a quick shot saved Markhead's life. Caught with gun empty he saw that the other Indian, with finger upon trigger, was aiming at his breast. He immediately did a deal of dodging but the ball from the smoothbore grazed his neck and passed through his left shoulder, knocking him flat.

Fortunately the fight was of short duration. The Indians forted amid the rocks and timber and the trappers drew off, to camp for the night about a mile back. The night was extremely cold, no fires could be made lest the enemy be attracted by them, the party were supplied with only saddle blankets for bedding, and Carson suffered severely from his freezing wound.

In the morning the Indians were still in position. Thereupon the party made for the main camp on the Snake. Bridger himself at once led out thirty men, vengeance bent, but the Blackfeet had evacuated their position and had taken the bunch of horses with them.

Remounts were purchased from the Nez Percés and the spring hunt was arranged for the "waters of the Snake and Green Rivers."

On date of May 11, 1835, Trapper Osborne Russell of a Wyeth party out of Fort Hall and then in the vicinity of the upper Snake, northeastern present Idaho, records in his *Journal:*

> Here we met with Mr. Bridger and his party, who informed us that the country around and below was much infested with Blackfeet. They had had several skirmishes with them in which they had lost a number of horses and traps and one young man had been wounded in the shoulder by a ball from a fusee.

It may have been around this time when Carson, trapping, as was his wont, with a party and in a territory of his own choosing, met the adventure which he related to Colonel Meline in 1866.

It was in — let me see — yes, 1835. There were six of us hunters out after buffalo, up in the Snake country. We had made a pretty good hunt, and came into camp at night, intending to start in next morning. Had a good many dogs with us, some of them good dogs. They barked a good deal, and we heard wolves. As I lay by the fire, I saw one or two big wolves sneaking about camp — one of them quite in it. Gordon wanted to fire, but I would not let him, for fear of hitting some of the dogs. I had just a little suspicion that the wolves might be Indians, but when I saw them turn short round, and heard the snap of their teeth, as the dogs came too close to one of 'em, I felt easy then, and made sure it was a wolf. The Indian fooled me that time. Confound the rascal — becoming animated — confound the rascal, you think he hadn't two old buffalo bones in his hand that he cracked together every time he turned to snap at the dogs? Well, by and by we dozed off asleep, and it wasn't long before I was awoke by a crash and blaze. I jumped straight for the mules, and held 'em. If the Indians had been smart, they'd 'a had us all, but they run as soon as they fired. They killed but one of us — poor Davis. He had five bullets in his body, and eight in his buffalo robe. The Indians were a band of Sioux, on the war path after the Snakes, and came on us by accident. They tried to waylay us next morning, but we killed three of 'em, including their chief.[224]

The spot was on the Little Snake, between the mouth of Savery (St. Vrain) Creek and the present town of Slater, at the northwestern Colorado-Wyoming line: in that debatable region "constantly infested by war-parties of the Sioux, and considered among the most dangerous war-grounds in the Rocky Mountains." Hereabouts the veteran Fraeb was killed in 1841. The locality of the Carson adventure is definitely fixed by Frémont in his journal while he was returning from his second expedition, 1843-44. He says: "We passed during the day a place where Carson had been fired on so close that one of his men had five bullets through his body."

The rendezvous of 1835 was held in the Valley of the Green. At this rendezvous there arrived, escorted from Fort William, the first Fort Laramie, by the supplies caravan under Thomas Fitzpatrick, the season's two missionaries Samuel Parker and Dr. Marcus Whitman.

At this rendezvous there occurred Carson's historic duel with the French-Canadian mountain-man called Captain Shunan, or Shuman, or Shunar. In his didactic fashion the Reverend Mr. Parker testifies, upon the pages of his *Exploring Tour:*

A few days after our arrival at the place of rendezvous, and when all the mountain-men had assembled, another day of indulgence was granted to them, in which all restraint was laid aside. These days are the climax of the hunter's happiness. I will relate an occurrence which took place, near evening, as a specimen of mountain life. A hunter, who goes technically by the name of the great bully of the mountains, mounted his horse with a loaded rifle, and challenged any Frenchman, American, Spaniard, or Dutchman, to fight him in single combat. Kit Carson, an American, told him if he wished to die, he would accept the challenge. Shunar defied him. C. mounted his horse, and with a loaded pistol, rushed into close contact, and both almost at the same instant fired. C's. ball entered S's. hand, came out at the wrist, and passed through the arm above the elbow. Shunar's ball passed over the head of Carson; and while he went for another pistol, Shunar begged that his life might be spared.

By Carson's report:

There was in the party of Captain Drips of the American Fur Company a large Frenchman, one of those overbearing kind and very strong. He made a practice of whipping every man that he was displeased with — and that was nearly all. One day, after he had beaten two or three men, he said, that for the Frenchmen he had no trouble to flog and, as for the Americans, he would take a switch and switch them.

I did not like such talk from any man, so I told him that I was the worst American in camp. Many could trash [thrash] him only [they didn't] on account of being afraid and that if he made use of any more such expressions, I would rip his guts out.

He said nothing but started for his rifle, mounted his horse and made his appearance in front of the camp. As soon as I saw him, I mounted my horse and took the first arms I could get hold of, which was a pistol, galloped up to him and demanded if I was the one he intended to shoot. Our horses were touching. He said no, but at the same time drawing his gun so he would have a fair shot at me. I was prepared and allowed him to draw his gun. We both fired at the same time; all present saying that but one report was heard. I shot him through the arm but his ball passed my head, cutting my hair and the powder burning my eye, the muzzle of his gun being near my head when he fired. During our stay in camp we had no more bother with this bully [of a] Frenchman.[225]

In a later day Captain Smith H. Simpson of Taos had it

The Duel With Bully Shunan

from Carson's own lips that the quarrel rooted in a rivalry for
the favors of an Arapaho girl in the camp. The occasion for a
settlement of claims was gladly seized upon. Carson won out,
but had the Shunan horse not reared at the moment of fire the
result might have been different. By all evidence this was the
girl whom Carson married. He was now past twenty-five and
had been in the mountains long enough to see values in a
keeper of his lodge.[226]

When the rendezvous broke up, August 20, Bridger, with
the missionaries, fifty trappers including Carson, and the Flatheads and Nez Percés, headed back north for the Three Tetons, from whose base and the western base of the Wind River
range flowed the waters of the Henry and the Lewis Forks of
the Snake.

The march was begun on August 21; on the 22nd Dr. Whitman turned east, for South Pass and home, to recruit the missionary ranks for the next year. On the 23rd, which was
Sunday, in Jackson's Little Hole the Reverend Mr. Parker's
impromptu church services were interrupted by a buffalo hunt,
the necessity of which he deplored but the tenderloin from
which he enjoyed. On August 25 Jackson's Big Hole was
reached, and Captain Bridger detached a portion of his command to trap the streams.

When I reflected upon the probability that most of these men would
never return to their friends, but would find their graves in the mountains
[records the Reverend Mr. Parker], my heart was pained for them,
and especially at their thoughtlessness about the great things of the eternal
world. I gave each of them a few tracts, for which they appeared grateful,
and said they would be company for them in their lonely hours; and as
they rode away, I could only pray for their safety and salvation.

The trail, ever seeking the beaver, crossed the Teton Pass
and descended into Pierre's Hole, westward, where had been
fought, three years before, the big trapper-Blackfeet battle.
Here Captain Bridger diverged for the northeast and the Three
Forks country of the Blackfeet; Mr. Parker proceeded west,
with his Nez Percés and Flathead escort, for the lower
Columbia.

In the second week of September signs of trappers on ahead of the Bridger march were discovered along a tributary of the Gallatin of the Three Forks. Carson and thirteen or fourteen other men were sent forward to get report, and on the same day galloped into the camp of Captain Joseph Gale and twenty-four men on a hunt out of Wyeth's Fort Hall. It was a reunion, for, as previously narrated by Russell, the Gale command had been met and warned of danger by Bridger and party last spring.

The planet Saturn still governed Nathaniel Wyeth's horoscope. His ship *May Dacre* had been struck by lightning, had come in three months late, at the close of the salmon season. He then had dispatched from Vancouver to Fort Hall, with supplies, his lieutenant, Captain Thing and eight or ten men.

But the Wyeth luck extended to all connected with him. Up among the sources of the Missouri, along the Gallatin Fork the Joseph Gale company had been saddled by never-lightened disaster as by the old Man of the Sea. As Joe Meek remarks: "They had been out a long time. The Blackfeet had used them badly. Their guns were out of order, their ammunition all but exhausted; they were destitute, or nearly so, of traps, blankets, knives, everything. They were what the Indian and the mountain-man called 'very poor.' " Moreover, in the last fracas with the Blackfeet several of the whites had been shot, Richard (Dick) Owens had received almost a death-wound.[227]

Here upon the side stream of the Gallatin the Gale company and the Bridger detachment of Kit Carson and fellows spent a jolly night, spinning yarns and exchanging news of the trail and of the States. In the morning the Bridger party decided to stay and wait for the main company of some fifty whites and twenty Flatheads to come in. A squad of eight started out to set traps on the Gallatin, but had gone only two miles when the foremost pair (said by Joe Meek to have been one Liggit and himself) rode into an ambush of Blackfeet. In short order the Gale camp was roused to arms by the headlong return of the eight Bridger men with eighty Blackfeet whooping at their heels.

Somewhat surprised by their reception at the end of the pursuit trail the Blackfeet halted short and took to the overlooking bluffs. From these they maintained an annoying discharge of slugs from their Nor'west fusils, varied with long-distance arrows. The penned horse-herd suffered. Then adopting more decisive measures they set fire to the long dry grass and the bushes on the windward of the camp.

The camp was located in a pine and aspen copse littered with needles and leaves. The wind blew strongly, the situation ("One circle of fire flame and smoke which united over our heads," as narrates trapper Russell) became desperate. Kit Carson says that the fire died out, as by a miracle, before it had entered the camp. Joe Meek says that the pines caught and that all the defenders were driven into the open, where they used the bodies of dead horses as barricades. Trapper Russell says that by means of a countering back-fire the advancing flames were diverted, and the Indians themselves had to move.

In the tail of the afternoon the Indians withdrew upon a blanket signal from their chief indicating that other enemy were near. The exhausted camp immediately packed up and sought the security of the Bridger main camp — which was found only six miles away and, by reason of the adverse wind, wholly ignorant of the fracas.

Captain Gale's lean command, which but for the opportune reinforcement by the Bridger veterans would surely have been wiped out within a day or two by the Blackfeet, now joined the Bridger brigade for protection. The Wyeth trapping operations in the Rockies were practically at the end.

His contract and that of the other men with the Columbia Fishing and Trading Company having expired, this winter Joseph Gale quit the Wyeth employ and entered the employ of the Hudson's Bay Company; left the mountains in the Joe Meek squad of the exodus of 1840 and settled on the Tualatin Plains of Oregon; and, meeting an emergency, served as the master of the first Oregon-built ship, the schooner *Star of Oregon,* which in September, 1842, with a mountain-man rancher turned sailor again as its captain and green ranchers as crew, sailed from the port of Vancouver for the port of San Francisco.

Badgered by the persistent Blackfeet the united Bridger and Gale parties finished out the fall season of 1835 by trapping westward through the Three Forks country (that of the Gallatin, Madison and Jefferson waters of southwestern Montana) in friendly contact with the Flatheads and Pend d'Oreilles hunting there; breaking southward over the divide at the head of the Jefferson, emerged upon Camas Creek — "the northwest extremity of the great plain of the Snake River." Thence the Gale men traveled down-country to Fort Hall; the Bridger men followed, to go into winter quarters of 1835-36 upon the Blackfoot tributary of the Snake, about fifteen miles above the fort.

Chapter XXI

Adventures of Kit Carson — 1836-1838

To Fort Hall and vicinity there came, this winter, trader Thomas McKay of the Hudson's Bay Company, who had viewed the fort in its beginnings. A breed of Canadian Scotch and Indian blood, handsome and gentlemanly, of "frank, generous disposition" and of leadership qualities as a field captain, he was a man to inspire Carson with confidence.

The mountain fur business among the Americans was badly cut up; where the country was not cursed with hostile Indians it was getting over-trapped; McKay spoke of the Mary's River, to the southwest of the Salt Lake — Peter Skene Ogden's river which in time back had yielded a harvest to Ogden himself, for the Company. "Having heard of Mary's River (now called the Humboldt) and beaver on it was plenty," with Antoine Godin the vengeful breed whose assassination of the Gros Vent' chief had brought on the battle of Pierre's Hole, and four others, Carson joined Thomas McKay for the trap lines of the Mary's in the Great Basin, northern Nevada, separated from the Snake country on the north by a wide divide of bare, bristling ridges, and by plateaus of sage, sand and lava falling away into deep dry canyons.[228]

The Captain Joe Walker company of 1833 had applied the name Barren to the Mary's. Since that year no expedition of record had trapped the stream and McKay evidently expected to do well with his skilled command. But the traps were set in vain; the name Barren had been soundly bestowed.

Down along Mary's River, which, winding and crooked, with its rocky, sterile ridges, its grateful bottoms, its mingling of heat and cold, of springs, alkali ponds, sandy bluffs and grassy camping spots, was destined to be a feature, for 200 miles, of the Overland California Trail already platted by the stars, traveled the McKay and Carson party, clear to the Sinks of the Humboldt. Here, in the midst of a desert desolation characterized by flats of soda and ash, burnt-rock outcrops, stagnation of earth, air, water, and animate life — a region as appalling as the surface of the moon — the Mary's ceased at a swampy lake with no outlet. The water, scummy and green, and specked with wild-fowl, was sucked up by the dry air faster than it could gather to overflow. This is the Sink of the Humboldt.

According to his biographer Charles Burdett, Carson here was sent ahead by McKay, toward the ranges which showed bluish in the west, to be gone a few days and to see if there were not, somewhere, beaver streams. He found a lake of potash, with pumice-stone floating upon it; he found more sinks, and deposits of soda — almost underfoot were the gold and silver which since have made western Nevada famous, but he passed careless glances over their resting-place; he found dried lakes, like saucers, rimmed with low ridges, pulverized mud and ashes for their bottoms; he found many a wonder — but no beaver. And he returned to McKay.

Then upon this country of ruin they turned their backs and partially retracing their outward course they made for the Snake again.

Sage and sand and barrenness encompassed them until as they threaded among the lonely hills they would come upon little valleys which flowing water had made green. When they struck the Snake in southern Idaho the party divided. Partisan McKay turned west down the Snake, making for the Hudson's Bay Company post of Fort Walla Walla, at the Columbia; Carson and the five remaining men set out in the opposite direction, up the Snake for Fort Hall.

The provisions left were poor enough — roots and a little rabbit meat — and the horses left were poor indeed, sad, hard-worked, famished things whom the desert had used cruelly. Fort Hall was still four or five days' march eastward when, reduced to rations of roots, the party adopted the emergency measure of bleeding their animals, carefully closing the veins, and drinking or boiling the blood thus obtained.

The operation could not be repeated on beasts so thin and

weak. The animals themselves, however, might be killed and eaten, bony though they were; but that would put the party afoot. Then, in the midst of the debate, a band of friendly Indians were encountered; from them a comparatively fat horse was obtained; the party feasted at will and thus strengthened were subsisted until they trailed into Fort Hall.

Located "upon the left bank of the Snake River, or Lewis' Fork of the Columbia, in a rich bottom near the delta formed by the confluence of the Portneuf with that stream, in lat. 43° 10' 30" north, long. 112° 20' 54" west," Nathaniel Wyeth's trading station, westernmost of out-posts between the Rockies and the coast yet to fly the Stars and Stripes, reflected much credit upon the Wyeth judgment. It was built of the customary palings or palisades, with a sally-port or double gateway facing the Portneuf across the bottomlands on the south, and with its walls "extending back toward the Snake." The winding Portneuf, with course bent sharply west, entered the Snake about ten miles below the site. After a profitless career of two years the post was transferred, in 1837, by Wyeth to the Hudson's Bay Company. Having now become the British most easterly out-post in this joint territory, as the "stone in the garden" of the American traders it was for nearly twenty years the prize of the Hudson's Bay Company.

The wooden walls were replaced by adobe, which, whitewashed, gleamed afar as a welcome signal to wayfarers forging on across the desert of the Snake. After the hospitable Captain Richard Grant, agent for some fifteen years, retired to settle with his Indian wife and half-breed children at Cantonment Loring, a few miles above, the old post still remained a favorite station for emigrants over the Oregon Trail. It was abandoned by the Company in 1856; in time a new United States military post of Fort Hall, up the Portneuf and dominating the Bannock Indian reservation, continued the name.[229]

The spirit of misfortune was still besetting Fort Hall. By a clever ruse engineered at daybreak two Blackfeet let down the bars of the post corral before the very eyes of the guard and drove out every animal. There could be no pursuit, for now the garrison and the guests alike were afoot. But trader McKay came in, after a month, bringing horses; and now remounted at a price to be paid later the Carson squad rode out with him for the American rendezvous in the Valley of the Green.

The rallying place was Horse Creek, near its juncture with the Green. Again there were the Indians — Snakes, Nez Percés, Flatheads, Pend d'Oreilles, Utes, Bannocks; the mountain-men — hired trappers, skin trappers, free trappers, including the Wyeth former employes who in the main had thrown in with Jim Bridger; and the Hudson's Bay Canadians and breeds — this time in greater number than ever before.

Lucien Fontenelle was due with goods for the American Fur Company camp. On July 2 Thomas Fitzpatrick arrived from St. Louis with supplies for the Fitzpatrick, Sublette & Bridger outfit. With him there arrived Milton Sublette, painfully traveling in a cart by reason of that affected leg which the St. Louis doctors had not cured; and Captain Sir William Stewart the British good-fellow, once more; and, true to the advance report and the confirmation by the returned welcoming committee, the two white women, Mrs. Whitman and Mrs. Spalding, and the other missionaries, Dr. Marcus Whitman, Henry Spalding and William Gray.

July 1 Captain Wyeth had ridden in, on his way back to Boston from the mouth of the Columbia. He was practically done with the fur and fisheries business — his salmon venture had amounted to naught, his Fort Hall trading post did not muster a corporal's guard and was cut off from the Indian trade to the west by the Hudson's Bay new post of Fort Snake or Boise, lower down on the Snake. As for Captain Bonneville, that other trespasser upon the vested rights of the beaver country, he was definitely gone from the mountains by now a year, and with him, the majority of the Gantt and Blackwell trappers.

If there was talk of Texas, where Americans had been fighting for new American territory as important as Oregon, it does not appear upon the surface of rendezvous events. But another empire was in the making, and Carson himself was to play his part in the conquest of the Southwest more largely than in the conquest of the Northwest.

Following upon the rendezvous of 1836 the firm of Fitzpatrick, Sublette & Bridger operated loosely. Rumor merged it with the American Fur Company. Milton Sublette was plainly in a bad way; his active days looked to be over with.

From the rendezvous the missionaries traveled on with the Hudson's Bay Company's brigade of Trader McLeod, for the Columbia. Jim Bridger took out sixty men for the Yellowstone country, and Carson joined the levy. By way of Yellowstone Lake the trapping operations were carried to the Yellowstone Plains, and to Clark's Fork in a region of stream bottoms purpled with the wild plums ripening in the September sun and frequented by careless and greedy grizzly bears.

Here, on Pryor's Fork of the Clark, Joe Meek and Dave Crow were jumped by the Blackfeet while running traps in the plum-thicket bottoms, and Meek, the principal target, barely got off with his horse Too Shebit wounded and eleven balls through his clothes and his blanket coat, extended as he raised an arm.

This was Indian sign with a vengeance. The camp moved down to the Clark, where sixty Blackfeet chased two trappers into the river, forced them to swim their horses across and shot one — poor Howell — so severely that he died in camp.

Out from camp rode the punishment party, of twenty whites, and Nez Percés and Delawares; found the enemy, drove them upon an island in the Yellowstone and fought them from the water and the bank until dusk. In the morning the Blackfeet were gone, but the island foliage and sod were plashed with crimson.

Winter camp was staked beside the Yellowstone, at the mouth of Clark's Fork among pleasant bottom-lands heavily timbered with the sweet cottonwood. Near the close of January, 1837, a Blackfeet alarm was brought in by a hunting party returned with a man wounded and a rifle lost; and when, in the opening week of February, twenty Indians were sighted boldly crossing the open plain for the river, six miles below the camp, a detail including Carson sallied forth in pursuit, and headed them just as they reached the timbered bank. The Indians turned at bay in a nucleus of small old forts built up cone shape of poles now rotted.

The flight was one of give and take, until darkness fell. In the zero temperature the trappers drew off, to wait for morning and another bout. But when, with the dawn, again in the field they hopefully charged the little forts they encountered only silence there. The enemy had gone; the trampled snow inside the pole enclosures was red with blood and strewn with rotted fragments of wood scattered by the rifle balls, and a bloody trail led from the forts to a hole in the ice of the river — the repository of dead warriors.

Wounded had been dragged away upon travois. By the signs of the retreat, and of the several scouting parties that had hovered in the neighborhood, the Blackfeet were in force somewhere in the near territory. Bridger said that now after these drubbings a gather of "five or six hundred" of the enemy from the main village, not far, would come on to wipe out the whole camp.

A sentry was stationed, with the spy-glass, upon a high butte about a mile out and over-looking the plains. The horse stock was kept close in, under guard. Matters were quiet for about two weeks; and then, on Washington's birthday, the "old man" himself again mounted the butte, as was his daily custom, with the glass, to cast an eye around "for squalls." About one o'clock he came down in a hurry. The country ten miles below the camp was alive with Indians.

All hands fell to throwing up a breastworks, six feet high, of poles and brush, to enclose the camp area some 250 feet square. In the stinging cold of this night the double guards posted upon the camp outskirts heard the snapping of frost-bound trees and were amazed by the flashing northern lights which paled the stars and finally deepened to a blanket of blood red over-spreading all the sky above the Indian horde.

However the portent was to be read, the enemy held off. Bridger and six men rode out to reconnoitre. They reported that a "multitude" were assembling three miles below. The breastworks had been strengthened with cut timber a foot and more in diameter, set on end and leaned, close together, against the breastworks on the inside.

It was the third day, February 24, when the enemy came on — a thousand, eleven hundred, fifteen hundred strong, mainly afoot and painted and equipped for war. They came on with shouts and gestures; to camp, half a mile out, to stage a savage war dance, to threaten a charge but only to fire a few shots by advanced scouts (one of which sent Bridger's black cook to the right-about while he was gathering wood and one of which wounded a Spaniard, forestalled in the butte "observatory," in the heel) and, by change of column, with wave of a white blanket from a chief to defile into the north again.

Something about all this — "A wild and fearful scene of barbaric strength and fancy," as his biographer Surgeon Peters puts it — staged in the winter-bound North of frozen plains and river, snapping timber and eerily flaming sky, appealed to Kit Carson's imagination. The purposeful martial host of the dark enemy swelled by band after band trailing in through three days; the energetic stir in the trappers' camp until "we were prepared to receive them"; the full muster of the Indians upon a large island, where they "constructed one hundred and eleven forts"; the confidence in the trappers' camp while it faced a decisive morrow!

They had a war dance. We could hear their songs. We well knew that in the morning they would make the attack. We were prepared. They came, saw the strength and invincibility of our position. They fired a few shots but done no execution and finding that they could not do us any damage by charging our breast works which they declined. They commenced retreating.

We dared them to make the attack. We were only sixty strong, the

Indians fifteen hundred, but there was not one of our band but felt anxious for the fight. Nothing could persuade them to attack us. They departed, went about one mile away. All sat in council. In a short time they arose, one half going in the direction of the Crow Indian country and the other taking the course they had come.[230]

The spring trapping reason passed without great event. The rendezvous of the summer of 1837 was appointed for the Valley of the Green again. The rallying place proved to be on the Green itself, ten or twelve miles below the mouth of Horse Creek — the vicinity of last summer's reunions. During the wait for the supplies from the States to arrive there were games and yarns, and a setto with the Bannocks as a break in idleness.

That started in the Bridger camp, when thirty Bannock warriors galloped in from their own camp of sixty lodges some three miles out, to demand the return of stolen horses recovered from them by a posse of trappers and Nez Percés.

The sharp click of rifle locks punctuated the argument. Bridger himself was holding one of the horses by the bridle, before his own lodge. Bold and unafraid, a Bannock chief jerked the thong from his hand — and on the instant "two rifle balls whistled through his body" [Russell], one of them having been dispatched (as says Joe Meek) by the enraged negro Jim, Bridger's cook. And in the quick flurry a stray arrow pierced the breast of Umentucken, Meek's wife; "the joys and sorrows of the Mountain Lamb were over forevermore."

The Bannocks wheeled in flight. The rifles of the camp cleaned the backs of twelve horses, and now the chase was on. From the island in the Green where the Bannock village had sought refuge while maintaining the fight an old squaw finally advanced, with a pipe in her hand.

"You have killed all our warriors," she called; "do you now want to kill the women? If you wish to smoke with women, I have the pipe."

At rendezvous there appeared, from the Flathead country in the northwest, upon his way from the Columbia to the At-

The Bannocks Sue for Peace

lantic coast, the missionary William H. Gray who had been seen the previous summer westward bound with the Dr. Marcus Whitman party. Mr. Gray, accompanied by two other white men, "Big Ignace," the Iroquois catechist, for St. Louis with three Flatheads (one of whom was an educated young chief, The Hat), and a Nez Percé, was returning East upon mission and personal business. Undeterred by warning that his escort was insufficient he continued his journey, but upon the plains of the lower North Platte was spied by the prowling Sioux.

The whites and the Indians including Ignace fought stoutly on defense, killing fifteen of the Sioux. It is said that in the parley then promoted by a French-Canadian trader among the Sioux Mr. Gray was promised his life and the lives of the two other whites if the five Indians and their "fine horses" were delivered over. That this compromise was understood, much less deliberately effected, who can believe? But the five Indians were killed, the three whites passed through to the frontier; ever after the Flathead tribe accused Mr. Gray of cowardly double-dealing and among the mountain-men he was a byword. The fact that his hat was twice shot through, one of the balls grazing his crown while he was on horseback in the river, shows, however, how dire were his straits. His supporters cite him as a bold, determined man, not readily intimidated; and as one who, only after three hours of fighting during which all his Indians had been killed, upon advice of an interpreter surrendered upon terms guaranteeing safe passage for himself and two white companions.[231]

Thomas Fitzpatrick arrived at rendezvous July 5 with his supply train. Following upon the transaction of business the firm of Fitzpatrick, Sublette & Bridger definitely ceased to be. Milton Sublette was dead. That fungus of the leg had finished him last December, at Fort John on the Laramie. What between the activities of the Blackfeet and the Hudson's Bay Company the fur trade west of the mountains was poor. The Hudson's Bay Company had moved in with Fort Boise, and were pressing closer with Fort Hall, which they practically occupied.

Of the old Rocky Mountain Fur Company field captains only Billy Sublette, Fitzpatrick and Bridger were left on the firing line. But Captain Billy, in partnership with Robert Campbell, was in the general supplies business. Fitzpatrick the Bad Hand now stepped out, as though to contract on his own hook. And old Jim Bridger joined up with the American Fur Company, which had won at last. By its steady westward march of strong trading posts it had elbowed its rival American company into the narrow danger zone flanked by the Hudson's Bay Company's well-covered territory. Henceforth there should be only "the Company" in the American fur trade — as supreme, east of the mountains, as the Hudson's Bay Company, west of the mountains.

A number of the Bridger men went over to Fort Hall, in the service of the Hudson's Bay Company. But Carson and others joined the united brigades of Jim Bridger and Lucien Fontenelle. One hundred and ten strong, the united commands confidently headed for the Blackfeet precincts of the Yellowstone.

Having trapped as they pleased, they pegged winter quarters among the Crows on the Powder River, south of the Yellowstone. Captain Fontenelle went out, with the furs, to Fort John on the Laramie, which the American Fur Company had bought. The winter was cruelly cold — "One of the coldest winters I ever experienced," says Carson — but the buffalo were so plentiful that they had to be kept away from the cottonwood horse-fodder by means of guard fires.

According to the Crows, the Blackfeet had been cowed by smallpox. Villages had left their empty lodges standing and had fled the pursuing pestilence upon a trail of mourning. The spring fur hunt of 1838, under field command of Bridger, therefore was cheerfully pointed for the Three Forks country again. The brigade marched down the Powder, across country to the Little Big Horn, where —

After getting the necessary information from Mr. Bridger concerning the route he intended to take with the camp, we all [the trappers with their traps] started in a gallop in a westerly direction and traveled to the Big Horn and there commenced separating by twos and threes in different directions.[232]

By way of the Yellowstone and its tributary Twenty-five Yard River the Carson party, last week in May, united with the Bridger camp in the valley of the Gallatin. The camp, waxing powerful once more with the inflow of the trapper trains, crossed to the Madison, and following up the valley found, as Carson says, "that the smallpox had not killed all the Blackfeet yet for there was a large village of them in advance of us."

The trail of lodge-poles and horses was three days old. An abandoned death lodge contained nine bodies. Bridger was for turning off and letting well enough alone, but the majority of the men over-ruled him. The village, they said, "did not contain more than three times our number." Therefore on this, the second day, June 3, with the village apparently only one day ahead, camp was established near the trail. In the morning Carson with five men rode ahead of the march to reconnoitre. The village was discovered, about three miles on, beside the river, under a high rocky bench; it was preparing to move, for the horse herd was being driven in.

The Carson squad sped back post-haste to give the word. They went thudding among the ridges enclosing the valley of the Gallatin and alarmed the march, which skirted the edge of a canyon confining a side stream of the Gallatin. The brigade dropped into the canyon and from these headquarters fifteen men ("I, with forty men," says Carson) hastened out to open the battle.

From the edge of the bench above the surprised village the attackers delivered their fire. The Blackfeet warriors, gaining their horses, made for the higher bluffs. The trappers, mounting their own horses stationed below the bench, pursued. Ammunition began to fail, and, as says eye-witness Russell, viewing through a spyglass, "the whites . . . returned toward the camp before about five times their number." Or, in the words of Carson: "We run retreating for our camp. The Indians would often charge among us. We would turn and give fire. They would retreat, then we would continue our course."

The day's mêlée provides incidents. Trapper Doc Newell, dismounting to scalp a downed foe, found his fingers held fast by the scalp-lock ornaments of a suddenly revived Indian and well nigh never got free alive. Joe Meek, unconsciously posing while turned in his saddle in the Gallatin, with bullet pouch empty and the enemy pressing on, was made by J. M. Stanley, the mountain-days artist who was present upon the field, the subject of a canvas "The Trapper's Last Shot." The horse of a Blackfeet woman was killed under her, but amid cheers she seized the tail of her husband's horse and was dragged to safety.

Mansfield, trapper, was pinioned beneath his own fallen horse, which had stumbled upon a point of rocks in the thick of the fray. Six Blackfeet, afoot, dashed for him, to count a coup and take his scalp. At his despairing cry to his fellows: "Tell old Gabe [Bridger] that old Cotton [himself] is gone," Carson, who had noted, sprang from the saddle and stood over him; shot the foremost warrior dead; broke the on-rush, saw only two of the Indian reach cover, but also saw his own mount bolting.

Mansfield's horse was up and away with its rider. Carson shouted, a comrade, White, rode back to the rescue, and two upon one horse they reached the camp.

The enraged Blackfeet came right on. One hundred and fifty of them occupied a high point of ground littered with large rocks, commanding the camp in the canyon, and peppered the camp with long-range shots and derisive yells. Stung by the taunts an old Iroquois, "trained on the shores of Lake Superior," challenged the whites to follow him; stripped to bullet pouch and powder horn, danced his war dance and uttered "the shrill war cry of his nation." Trapper Russell and others "cheered the sound which had been the death warrant of so many whites during the old French war." Then, close after him, they climbed the 300 yards of gradual ascent to the Blackfeet post, "mounted over the piles of granite and attacked them muzzle to muzzle."

Or, as Kit Carson says: "We concluded to charge them, done so."

> It was the prettiest fight I ever saw. The Indians stood for some time. I would often see a white man on one side and an Indian on the other side of a rock, not ten feet apart, each dodging and trying to get the first shot.[233]

The Indians were driven out and down to their horses left in the valley bottoms. They threw their dead into the river, packed their wounded upon horses, and were permitted to go their slow way, "with a mournful cry," toward their village.

The next day the village had moved further up the Gallatin, but had stationed a line of mounted warriors at the previous day's site to attack the pursuit. The old Iroquois and thirty of the whites, with their mouths filled with bullets, charged in from cover by a flank movement and routed the enemy.

The camp on the march now passed by the village unchallenged and this, Carson records, "ended our difficulties with the Blackfeet for the present hunt." Another, smaller village, on Henry Lake, skeletonized by the smallpox sued for peace.

Rendezvous should have been at Horse Creek again, where the trader's quarters were waiting from summer to summer. But the Bridger belated trapping parties, riding in, found tacked upon the door of the log store-house a scrawl from the obliging hand of Black Harris: "Come to Popoazua on Wind River and you will find plenty trade, whisky, and white women."

An express had notified Bridger himself whither to bend his march. With Carson and the other men in his personal company he laid course for the Popoazua (Popo-agie) Fork of the Wind River northeast across the mountains from the

Green — a place chosen by the American Fur Company in hopes of eluding the Hudson's Bay traders.

Here there were Missionary Gray again, returning, with a wife, to Oregon; Missionaries Elkanah Walker and Cushing Eells, also with brides; Missionary A. B. Smith and wife; and a younger missionary unattached, Cornelius Rogers. They had come out with the supplies train of Captain Drips and the Britisher, Captain Sir William Steward.[234]

It was rumored at the rendezvous that "the Company" was done with these gatherings; no more supplies were to be distributed by this method. The mountain festivities appeared to be nearing the end, furs would be delivered at the Company posts, the day of the marts under the blue sky was waning. At the close of the rendezvous of 1838 many of the men left the Fontenelle and Bridger service and struck off for themselves.

A party of thirty including the chronicler Osborne Russell started out up the Wind River; finally joined the main camp of sixty men under Andrew Drips, successor to Fontenelle in the field, and Bridger. But Kit Carson says that he, with seven others, from the rendezvous traveled down to Brown's Hole. Here, in northwestern present Colorado, near the Utah border, an elbow of the Green had formed a deeply sheltered park, some six miles in diameter, among rugged mountains and wild gorges — well adapted, in a later day, for use as a retreat, beyond the law, by cattle rustlers and road bandits. And here the mountain-men William Craig, Philip Thompson and Sinclair (written also St. Clair) were operating the independent trading post of Fort Davy Crockett — "a hollow square of one story log cabins, with roofs and floors of mud."[235]

Carson engaged for a trading trip south into the Navajo country, for horses and mules and merchandise of hair-ropes and the native blankets.

"We traded for thirty mules." From Davy Crockett the animals were sent out to Fort Vasquez trading post on the South Platte about forty miles north of present Denver.

Carson narrates that he spent this winter, 1838-39, as the

hunter for Fort Davy Crockett; and thereafter he was hither and yon on the beaver trail, in the Black Hills of the Laramie Range with Dick Owens, to the head of the Salmon River for the Hudson's Bay Company at Fort Hall, with Bridger again, and on the Grand River of Old Park; was in Brown's Hole, and at Antoine Robidoux' Fort Uintah; up to the fall of 1841. Then he, with Old Bill Williams, Bill New, Mitchell, Fredericks, a Frenchman, all disgusted with profitless trapping, pulled out of the mountains and went down to Bent's Fort on the Arkansas.

As far back as the summer of 1832 the astute Astor, while in London, had noted the advent of the silk hat. In a letter he had recorded the fear that beaver-fur must soon yield to the cocoon, the trap to the loom.

Chapter XXII

The Forking of the Trail

In his own narrative, as taken down from his dictation, Carson appears to say that he left the mountains for the plains and Bent's Fort in the fall of 1840 — which, reckoning from his enlistment in 1831 with Thomas Fitzpatrick, should be 1841. He states that he then contracted as official hunter for Bent's Fort at a dollar a day, and served as hunter until 1842.

The early biographies of Kit Carson, based upon his narration, assign him to Bent's Fort as its chief hunter through eight consecutive years. But he was with Frémont in 1842, and again in 1843-44, and again in 1845-46. Oliver Wiggins, who was in the Carson command from 1838 onward, explains that to supply the fort with a sufficient reserve of meat required in the main two big buffalo hunts a year and that to these the Carson company bent all their energies of the moment. Inasmuch as Carson had quarters at Bent's Fort and at Taos in 1838, his rôle of post hunter may well have embraced four years, of two seasons each, rather than eight years on end.

His hunter contract would not prevent his making excursions into the mountains. Joe Meek claims to have been with him at Fort Davy Crockett in the winter of 1839-40. And he himself says, to Colonel Meline, in speaking of Father De Smet: "I remember he came once among the hunters and trappers up in the mountains, and baptized forty-odd children." Father De Smet's first appearance in the mountains was that of the summer of 1840, at the Green River rendezvous.[236]

The fur rendezvous of 1839 was held near Bonneville's abandoned fort on the Horse Creek tributary of the Green. The rendezvous of 1840 — the sixteenth and last of the annual markets — was held in the same Valley of the Green. From this rendezvous, as from the one of the previous year, disheartened mountain-men scattered to the four winds but not those of the beaver trail.

"Some went to Santa Fé, some to California, others to the

lower Columbia, and a few remained in the mountains trapping, and selling their furs to the Hudson's Bay Company at
Fort Hall."

"Come," said Newell to Meek, "we are done with this life in the
mountains — done with wading in beaver dams, and freezing or starving
alternately — done with Indian trading and Indian fighting. The fur
trade is dead in the Rocky Mountains, and it is no place for us now, if
ever it was. We are young yet, and have life before us. We cannot waste
it here; we cannot or will not return to the States. Let us go down to the
Willamet and take farms."[237]

Supplementing the dictum of John Jacob Astor in 1832, in
1834 *Silliman's Journal* had said, as darkly and more generally:

. . . it appears that the fur trade must henceforth decline. The advanced
state of geographical science shows that no new countries remain to be
explored. In North America, the animals are slowly decreasing from the
persevering efforts and the indiscriminate slaughter practised by hunters,
and by the appropriation to the uses of man of those forests and rivers
which have afforded them food and protection. They recede with the
aborigines, before the tide of civilization; but a diminished supply will
remain in the mountains and the uncultivated tracts of this and other
countries, if the avidity of the hunter can be restrained within proper
limitations.[238]

The exportation of beaver skins from the western plains and
mountains to Europe had risen to 200,000 pelts a year, with no
effort made for conservation — any more than in the slaughter
of the buffalo, later. When the silk hat began to out-rival all
but the very finest beaver hat the market for the poorer pelts
dropped until an ordinary or second-grade skin brought the
trapper only a dollar. Then, when beaver fur was put to other
uses than in hats, the animal had suddenly become scarce; and
although for a squaw-dressed pelt Oliver Wiggins and partners, in the Forties, received eight dollars on delivery at the
Missouri, save in favored localities trapping was a vocation of
small profit.

So rapidly did the beaver business in the mountains decline,
giving way to the buffalo-robe trade of the plains, that in the

summer of 1843 Frémont remarks, of his stop at St. Vrain's Fort on the South Platte close to the Colorado foothills:

> It is singular that, immediately at the foot of the mountains, I could find no one sufficiently acquainted with them to guide us to the plains at their western base; but the race of trappers who formerly lived in their recesses had almost entirely disappeared — dwindled to a few scattered individuals — some one or two of whom are regularly killed in the course of each year by the Indians.[239]

And later in this year, passing along the Snake he learns that very few beaver were left "in this part of the country."

In the combination which produced the decline of the beaver business in the mountains there was another factor: the limitations imposed upon itself by the master surviving American company. The American Fur Company confined its operations to the east of the mountains; the upper Missouri River and the river trails of the plains were its field, and, after 1840, posts and not the rendezvous were its receiving points. When the rendezvous with its caravans, its guests, its reunions, its excesses and brief prosperity went out of the trapper's life a great deal went out; and to the trapper at large the fur business died through over-organization — died not in the free open where bales were tossed upon the affable trader's scales but in the walled court superintended through a wicket by a dole-granting clerk with a pen behind his ear.

There was still the Hudson's Bay Company, firm, but fair and genial; and Captain Bridger the veteran led out a brigade or two. None the less, what with the uncertainties of the future, the constant deflections to the British company and to Oregon, and the scarcity of beaver, the mountains were a land of discontent. The period of transition had arrived; it was a period of unrest — the restlessness of change, the throes of a new birth. The wagons of the emigrants for the Oregon Trail were about to mass upon the Missouri frontier, and in California one Captain Sutter, by the lode-stone of the gold in his mill race, was to draw a citizenship from the very ends of the earth.

The beaver trappers who, through 1839, '40, '41, '42, by

squads and on the lone trail turned their backs, like Joe Meek, Robert Newell, Joseph Gale, Bill Williams, Kit Carson — and, as they thought, forever — upon the trap-line streams, and traveled out with their lean packs, perchance their wives and families, became, one after another, traders, guides, ranchers, Indian agents, prospectors, squaw-men, nondescripts; some sinking, some rising, and not a few unable, the rest of their lives, to adjust themselves to the new conditions of earning that living.

A large proportion of these retired mountain-men were in their prime. Joe Meek was twenty-eight, Jim Bridger was thirty-eight, Robert Newell was not thirty, Joe Walker was forty-two. Kit Carson was verging upon twenty-nine when he purposefully shaped his course for Bent's Fort and Taos of the lower country.

He made exit with a measure of reputation, and the gods of chance were prepared still to favor him; but in no written chronicles coincident with his trapper career does his name appear with any fanfare. As Lewis Garrard comments, 1847, of "the renowned Kit Carson, so celebrated as the companion and guide of Frémont":

Without a desire to detract from Carson's well-earned fame, I can say, in genuine good feeling and full belief, that there are numbers of mountain-men as fearless and as expert as he, though to the reading world little known, whose prowess in scalptaking and beavertrapping is the theme of many campfires, and the highest admiration of younger mountaineers.[240]

That Kit Carson, however, was a name and a figure of pretensions already recognized at Taos and Bent's Fort before the opening of the Forties, may be accepted. The post precincts and the New Mexico of Taos and vicinity saw him as a familiar, in and out. Reports that are not all tradition plunge him into a romance of the latter Thirties — perhaps while he was still of the mountains, perhaps while he was engaged at the fort — with a young French girl, Félicité St. Vrain of St. Louis, relative and protégée of his good patron Ceran St. Vrain, partner in Bent, St. Vrain & Co.

This romance, broken when Félicité was presumably whisked away, back to St. Louis, argues that Carson may have been at Bent's Fort and on the Taos Trail more frequently and of earlier date than his bare statement shows.[241]

Moreover, Captain Samuel Hobbs (*Wild Life in the Far West*) relates that as a captive with the Comanches he met him in the summer of 1837, trading on the plains near Bent's Fort; and speaks of expeditions with him, Peg-leg Smith, John Mc-Intyre, an Irishman O'Neil, the Shawnees Spiebuck and Shawnee Jake, and others, in 1839 as well as in 1840, up the Purgatory, into the New Mexican mountains, to Santa Fé, etc.

Chapter XXIII

Bent's Fort of the Plains

THE Northwest is assured. In the East the Reverend Jason Lee assisted by the two Indian boys is lecturing from Missouri to the Atlantic coast, so that reinforcements of artisans, farmers, money, and "young ladies" may be hastened by land and by sea to that farthest frontier where they "have everything to do, and little to do with." The first territorial petition is in Congress and Oregon's newest legislative champion, Senator Lewis Fields Linn of Missouri, is declaiming the cause of secular occupation. The mountain-men, deprived of rendezvous and supply train are reluctantly wending their way, with their squaws and their children, to the Willamette. At Dubuque, Iowa, inspired by the Welsh civil engineer John Plumbe, a convention has been held, March 31, 1837, to promote a transcontinental railroad.

Down here in the Southwest the great Conestogas still slowly roll (and shall roll for many a year) upon their long way across prairie and desert. Wagons are used exclusively upon the Santa Fé Trail, and oxen have to a large extent supplanted the mules of Kit Carson the boy's day. Old Franklin is of the past. Independence, westward toward the mouth of the Kaw, is the depot point for both the Santa Fé and mountain caravans, but Westport Landing, on the right bank of the Missouri, a few miles above, and its Westport town, adjacent inland, are bidding for business and inviting the future Kansas City. Civilization is ever edging further into the Indian country.

The Indian frontier has been definitely established by Congress; and across it, in present Oklahoma, Kansas and Nebraska, the tribes from east of the Mississippi are located, to dwell forever and naturally, guaranteed against trespass by the whites. The country between the States and the mountains was pronounced to be adapted for Indian purposes only.

Near Independence there have appeared that new sect, the Church of Jesus Christ of Latter Day Saints, in a westward movement of national import yet unread through the atmosphere murky with distrust and ridicule. These strange "Mormons" continue on from Independence to Far West, there to lay, in the summer of 1838, the cornerstone of a Zion Temple. But Missouri declines them; they will be driven forth from Illinois, and thus be led, by hard but sure way, to break the Mormon Trail to the Salt Lake, there to found the Commonwealth of Utah in a State of Deseret that extends its outposts through desolate Nevada and beyond the Sierra of California.

In Texas the decisive battle of San Jacinto (April 21, 1836) has been fought and won to the patriotic chorus:

> For this we are determined, to die or to be free,
> And TEXAS TRIUMPHANT our watch-word shall be.

Of the new republic of Texas, claiming from the Sabine to the Rio Grande, General Sam Houston is president, and Texas is already a potential, if not for some years an actual, part of the Union.

In the northwest, Oregon, and in the southwest, Texas, are ripening for national citizenship. Reaching right and left, Columbia will harvest them with almost the one sweep of the scythe. And straight in the fore, beyond the mountain West, California is being prepared as another segment in the mighty half-circle.

The Bear Flag has not yet been designed, but the Latin unrest is agitated by the ferment of the American adventurer. In 1836 Isaac Graham, the Tennesseean mountain-man of the Captain Sinclair party from Arkansas met by Kit Carson near the Green in the spring of 1832, with sundry fellow conspirators had supported the native Californians' revolt for the cause of home rule headed by youth in the person of Juan Bautista Alvarado, born, himself, at Monterey. On October 6 Alta California, emulating Texas, proclaimed for independence of Mexico until the privilege of native chiefs and home representation should be confirmed.

So set the breeze, faced by Mexico on the Pacific coast as on the Rio Grande. California, loosely swaying, waited only the final coming of a Frémont — received there, as General Taylor was received on the Rio Grande at the same time, without the popular favor, but come empowered to take.

From the originating point of Missouri the lines of interest therefore radiate to Texas, Oregon, California; and in the midst of the fan-shaped field, where the plains roll up to meet the foothills of the Rockies, Kit Carson at Bent's Fort is well within the flutters of the broadly streaming flag.

Old Bent's Fort, Fort Bent, or Fort William, built in the period 1828-1832, was situated upon the north bank of the Arkansas (consequently in American territory) below the present town of La Junta, southeastern Colorado, and about fourteen miles above the mouth of the Purgatory River — that Rio Purgatoire whose name, anglicized, was reduced to the Americanism of "Picketwire." This Rio Las Animas, in full El Rio de las Animas Perdidas en Purgatoire (the River of the Lost Souls in Purgatory) is not to be confounded with another Rio Las Animas, in the southwestern corner of Colorado.

The site was 300 yards back from the river brink on a gravelly "second bank" bared, immediately around the post, of grass and shrubs, but handy to bottom lands productive of coarse forage that might be cut for hay. One hundred and thirty miles west from the fort were the mountains. Thither, up the Arkansas, ran a trappers' and traders' trail for the Fontaine qui Bouille and the South Park and beyond; north from the fort ran a trail to the Bent and St. Vrain posts on the Platte, and to Laramie, 380 miles; southward, over the Raton Mountains ran the trail to Taos, 250 miles, and to Santa Fé; while from the east there came in the mountain division, the oldest route, of the Santa Fé Trail, from Missouri, 530 miles. Thus at the crossroads of the plains wilderness was stationed old Bent's Fort — its dun ramparts a stronghold and a hospice in one.[242]

It stood alone, as the sole eminence overlooking the squatted lodges of the visiting Indians. There were no equal neighbors. The monotonously rolling, almost treeless plains of the buffalo-

range and future cattle-range West surrounded it. In summer
these plains save where threaded by sparsely timbered stream
courses lay brown and parched, blasted by the winds that
swept across in force unbroken for hundreds of miles; and at
the post the sun, reflected from the white-washed inner walls
and the hard clay of the court, fairly blistered all objects
exposed to it. In the winter, with the snow, and the bare
patches, and even the short grass that "scantily concealed the
cold ground"; with the "white chalk cliffs, the leafless trees,
and the chill air . . . the fort mud walls," to Lewis Garrard,
"were abominably cheerless."

But within there were food, shade when needed, warmth
when needed. And always tobacco and conversation. There
were genial days without as within. And from the walls were
to be descried, to the southwest, the entrancing landmarks of
the Spanish Peaks — the Wah-to-yah or Twins of the Indians,
hazy blue or snow-capped, "apparently fifteen miles distant, in
reality one hundred and twenty," with the main range itself
behind them; while farther still, away up beyond the site of
the future Colorado Springs, 170 miles in air-line, there up-
lifted, again "like a cloud on the horizon," the famed "James's
or Pike's Peak."

The fort walls, of large bricks of the native adobe, were
eighteen feet in height, four to six feet thick at the base, taper-
ing off to two feet at the top. They formed a rectangle, running
north and south, 150 feet by 100 feet. At the northwest and the
southeast corners they intersected in the axes of twin towers, or
bastions, thirty feet high and ten feet in diameter, which
swelling out, permitted the defenders to rake the outside of
the walls with gun-fire.[243]

The interior was partitioned into two sections. The larger,
or the eastern section, 100 feet square, was devoted to the trading and living quarters, which occupied a continuous range of
one and two-story, flatroofed clay compartments, backed, Mexican patio style, by the interior of the walls. Here also were
black-smith shop, store-rooms, etc., all enclosing a central court,
and the well.

The walls were extended four feet above the roofs, which, of clay and gravel packed upon poles and brush, formed an excellent moonlight promenade where grizzled trapper and downy clerk alike might sadly reflect that there was not a "white" woman within 500 miles; no, not even at Santa Fé. It constituted also a banquette from which, through loop-holes, powder and ball could be delivered.

The other partition, on the west, was a large corral for the live stock; and beyond the corral, adjoining the wall was the wagon-house, "strongly built, and large enough to shelter 12 or 15 of those large vehicles which are used in conveying the peltries to St. Louis and goods thence to the post. The long drought of summer renders it necessary to protect them from the sun," as says Thomas Farnham.

The main entrance was a thirty-foot gateway in the east wall, looking down stream, or along the Missouri trail, and closed by a pair of immense plank doors faced with sheet-iron studded with bolt-heads. Over the gateway was a sentry box with a mounted telescope, and topped by a cupola belfry for the post bell and flying the Stars and Stripes. In the court a six-pounder brass cannon commanded the entrance gateway; several smaller pieces of ordnance placed here and there commanded the approaches without and the court within. The copings of the lower, corral walls were planted to an abattis of cactus bearing red and white flowers — little symbols of peace nested under the cannon mouth, and appropriate enough when the life of the post inmates were considered. And here and there along the walls there were cages containing native birds — mocking bird, magpie; while the belfry housed a couple of bald-headed eagles. A large press for pressing buffalo robes and furs into bales stood in the center of the court.

Over the headquarters rooms that formed the west end of the court and faced the gateway there was a second-story room, with a billiard table hauled clear from Missouri, and chairs and a table or two, a short but hospitable bar and shelved jugs and decanters and glasses. Among the clerks, traders, trappers

Bent's Fort of the Plains

and travelers were men who could handle a cue; and during the war with Mexico the table was in much favor among the officer transients — as was also the post ice-house which, for them and other guests entitled to special privileges, served to cool pitchers of stirrup-cup more delicate than the raw "Taos lightning."

The motley garrison, as maintained, of sixty to 100 employees, exhibited Americans, English, French of St. Louis and Canada, Germans, Mexicans, Indians, half-breeds, in number augmented by women and children of Mexican and Indian blood. For a period of years the official cook whose products appeared, on state occasions, upon a table with a white cloth and even a revolving caster in the center, was a negress named Charlotte. Her pumpkin pies and her slapjacks were famed from Taos to the Laramie; and moreover she claimed to being "de onlee lady in de dam' Injun country." Her companion, at times, was Rosalie, "half-breed French-and-Indian squaw" and wife of the post carpenter. With her Charlotte shared the honors at the boisterous trapper-trader dances occasionally staged to while away an evening.

Bent's Fort was most advantageously situated for its purposes. Since it was upon the mountain route between the States and Santa Fé it was a candidate for the Mexican trade. Trappers from the mountains traded in their beaver here. A good business was done in horses and mules for the Missouri market. Travelers' needs were supplied with staple merchandise. A heavy trade in buffalo robes was carried on with the Indians.[244]

The southern Cheyennes and Arapahos annually held their winter camp in the Big Timbers, a stretch of huge cottonwoods thirty-two miles below and extending, intermittently, twenty-four miles along the river; in the spring and fall they followed the buffalo back and forth across the Arkansas, with the view of marketing their robes at the post. The Red River Comanches and the mountain Utes likewise engaged in the summer and winter trading. At the height of the robe season there might be 20,000 Indians gathered within easy distance of the post walls.

With its sturdy construction and its military lines the trading post surpassed even Fort Laramie in the north, and was cited by army officers as a model for its kind — as "in reality the only *fort* at the West," according to Colonel Philip St. George Cooke with the Kearny column in 1846. "Rearing its towers over the uncultivated wastes of nature like an old baronial castle that has withstood the wars and desolations of centuries," it welcomed wayfarers like Garrard, Ruxton, Frémont, Francis Parkman, Francis P. Blair, Jr., and mightily stirred the sensibilities of Thomas Farnham, in 1839. He saw, besides the towers as mentioned —

Indian women tripping around its battlements in their glittering moccasins and long deer skin wrappers; their children, with most perfect forms, and the carnation of the Saxon cheek struggling through the shading of the Indian, and chattering now Indian, and now Spanish or English; the grave owners and their clerks and traders, seated in the shade of the piazza smoking the long native pipe, passing it from one to another, drawing the precious smoke into the lungs by short hysterical sucks till filled, and then ejecting it through the nostrils; or it may be, seated around their rude table, spread with coffee or tea, jerked buffalo meat, and bread made of the unbolted wheaten meal from Taos; or, after eating, laid comfortably upon their pallets of straw and Spanish blankets, and dreaming to the sweet notes of a flute; the old trappers withered with exposure to the rending elements, the half-tamed Indian, and half-civilized Mexican servants, seated on the ground around a large tin pan of dry meat, and a tankard of water, their only rations, relating adventures about the shores of Hudson's Bay, on the rivers Columbia and MacKenzie, in the Great Prairie Wilderness, and among the snowy heights of the mountains; and delivering sage opinions about the destination of certain bands of buffalo; of the distance to the Blackfoot country, and whether my wounded man was hurt as badly as Bill the mule was, when the "meal party" was fired upon by the Comanches.

He also drew a fanciful picture of the post in its busy trading season, with the Indians "sliding in and out" through the opened gates till

the whole area is filled six feet deep with their long hanging black locks, and dark watchful flashing eyes; and traders and clerks busy at their work; and the patrols walking the battlements with loaded muskets;

and, at sunset, "the Indians retiring again to their camp outside," there to discuss their goods, "to sing and drink and dance," leaving the fort to the "night sentinel that treads his weary watch away."[245]

The trading goods of the post were powder, lead, paint, brass, knives, blankets, tobacco, cloth, beads, food stuffs such as coffee, sugar, flour, and even abalone shells from California — one shell buying four quality robes. The volume of business transacted was immense. The prize season is said to have been that of 1844; but the heyday of bustle occurred in 1846, when marching overland out of Fort Leavenworth to invade the Mexican Southwest the American soldiery, regulars and volunteers, hailed the sight of the huge new flag "flowing to the breeze, and straining every fibre of an ash pole planted over the centre of a gate."

The brass six-pounder burst in saluting General Kearny; the fort proprietors entertained the officers who visited there; and what with the Kearny column and the following columns, for miles around the grass was cropped close by hungry horses "as if a swarm of locusts had invaded the country," according to Francis Parkman, passing through in August. During the war the post was a commissary base for the army — a forwarding point for supplies for the military needs in New Mexico; and missed no opportunity to furnish remounts and work mules.

Each spring and fall a goods caravan was dispatched and received, in regular course, in trade with St. Louis and the Mexican capital. Smaller expeditions were dispatched, whenever the need, to Santa Fé. The lading of these trains for the Indian and the Southwest trade was as varied as that of a Yankee craft in the palm oil and "black ivory" trade of the Guinea coast.

In September, 1837, the Pawnees attacked a Bent, St. Vrain & Co. train of twelve mule or horse loads of merchandise, in charge of Marcellin St. Vrain (then aged twenty-two), while it was en route to Santa Fé and was "upon one of the forks of the River Arkansas, between Bent's Fort and the Spanish settlements." One man was killed, three wounded, and the company petitioners, Charles Bent, Ceran St. Vrain, William Bent, George Bent, claimed property damages to the amount of $3,271 — citing items as follows:

        1 rifle at $40
       23 robes at $4.50
       38 pairs brogans at $3
        2 Latin missals at $20
        3 fusils at $25
        9 mules and saddles at $75
        3 horses and saddles at $100
       10 lbs. lead balls at 50c
       10 reams paper at $10
       25 lbs. printers' ink, toto $40
        8 pieces moleskin, 428 ½ yds. at $1
       40 pieces domestic, 1,299 ¼ yds. at 50c
        6 pieces calico, 180 yds. at 75c
        1 piece scarlet cloth, 36 yds. at $5
       25 lbs. spring steel at 75c
        8 Spanish bridles at $6 [246]

Inasmuch as the affair occurred south of the Arkansas, in Mexican territory, the damage claim against the United States government was not allowed. The pirate Pawnees were immeasurably the gainers, for the spoils should have been much to their liking. The illuminated devotions (at $20) would please the eye, and the printers' ink provide an abundance of lodge and mourning paint.

When the pilgrimage of the Forty-niners to California set in, old Bent's Fort was a station upon the Arkansas River and Cherry Creek (the future Denver) route. But its hospitality was soon curtailed. This year the Government acquired Fort Laramie as a military post on the Oregon Trail; by tradition commonly accepted Colonel William Bent negotiated for the sale of Bent's Fort for the purpose of a military post in the Indian country of the southern trail. He asked for the property $16,000; $12,000 is said to have been the final offer; and toward

the close of August the colonel, out of patience, summarily
loaded all the goods he could get on his wagons, sixteen in number, set
fire to his premises, and pulled out. A considerable quantity of powder
remained in the fort, and, as the train wound its way down the river, the
ascending flames accompanied by a succession of loud reports told how
effectually the fortress was being converted into a ruin.[247]

The destruction is confirmed in the chronicles of the day.
One Paladay, an employe of the fort, having been sent over,
August 16, toward "Kit Carson's settlement on the Moro,"
southeast of Taos, on return fell in with a government train
bound back to the States. While they were camped "they heard
distinctly a loud report, resembling that of cannon."

They journeyed on — crossed the Arkansas river on the 22nd August,
and came up to the site of the Fort, and saw that the rubbish of the
buildings was all that was left. It had been burnt down by the Indians,
and was still smoking and burning on the 24th, when they left it. They
now were able to account for the report, as the magazine belonging to
Bent had been fired. The guns and traps were consumed, and it is supposed all the goods, books, etc., of Bent's concern, had shared the same
fate. The pack saddles and riding apparatus were not destroyed, as they
were still in the bastions. What had become of Mr. Bent, or anyone connected with the concern, they could not tell; there was no trace of them
or their whereabouts.[248]

On the way down the river, however, the company "saw the
trail of the cattle from the Fort." The rifted buttresses, left
behind, persisted as landmarks for over a quarter of a century.
Rising stark and mute, they presented, to the traveler, "a
strange appearance in these solitudes." Edward Fitzgerald
Beale, late of the United States Navy, hero with Carson in a
famous scouting enterprise and an overland journey, and now
appointed Indian agent for California, on his way to the Coast
in 1853 with his companion Gwinn Harris Heap, "rode all
through the ruins" of a one-time busy establishment which had
already almost become a legend.

It is now roofless; for when the United States refused to purchase it,
the proprietor set it on fire to prevent its becoming a harbor for Indians.
The adobe walls are still standing, and are in many places of great thick-

ness. They are covered with written messages from parties who had already passed here, to their friends in the rear.[249]

Having rendered his old post useless to the Government and the Indians, Colonel Bent himself moved down-river about thirty-five miles into Big Timbers — a place that, three years before, he had agreed with Lieutenant Colonel Emory of the Kearny column was an admirable site for a military post. Here he followed his log cabins trading post with the substantial stone trading post of New Bent's Fort, built in the fall and winter of 1853. This, in 1859, the Government did acquire by lease. Enlarged, it became Fort Wise, Fort Lyon, and Old Fort Lyon as differentiated from the new Fort Lyon, of later date, twenty-five miles up-river or back toward the original Bent's Fort. It was at the new Fort Lyon that Kit Carson died, in 1868; and nearby there died, aged sixty, while still active upon the trail, his long-time patron William Bent.

Chapter XXIV

Bent, St. Vrain and Company

"I Wish I was capable to do Bent and St. Vrain justice for the kindness received at their hands. I can only say that their equals were never in the mountains." Carson pays this tribute to his employers and associates of Bent's Fort, with whom he was more or less connected through much of his career.

Bent's Fort was owned and conducted by the St. Louis trading firm of Bent, St. Vrain & Co., whose trade brand was Quarter Circle B [ )-B]. They established other posts, the principal one being Fort St. Vrain or Fort George, built about 1837 halfway between Bent's and Fort Laramie, on the east bank of the South Platte shortly below the opposing mouth of St. Vrain Creek, and about thirty-eight miles north of Denver. This post, designed for the Arapaho, Northern Cheyenne and Sioux trade, in its last days was the northern terminal of the first pony express route of the plains, which carried mail and packages between St. Vrain, Bent's Fort and Taos and thus served as a link in the communications between northern and southern points; the route also handed down to the emigrant and gold-seeker the Cherokee Trail of the Fifties — pursued first by Cherokees from Georgia for California in 1852 and thereafter popularized by successive other parties seeking gold along the foothills.

The post was a going concern in 1843. Captain Philip St. George Cooke passes the spot in 1845, without mention of a post. In the summer of 1846 Francis Parkman finds only grass-grown ruins there. But it long persisted as a name on the map and as a camping place for travelers; and when in 1859 William N. Byers, pioneer editor in the new Cherry Creek diggin's of the future Denver, brought out his plant of the *Rocky Mountain News,* biding his examination of the newspaper field he stored his precious freight under cover in the old post's walls.[250]

The company had lesser posts in the Canadian River country

of the present Texas Panhandle, for trade with the Kiowas, Comanches and "Prairie" Apaches. By Kiowa tradition, in the winter of 1843-44 K'odal-aka-i or "Wrinkled Neck," a clerk in the employ of "Hook-nose-man" (William Bent), built a log trading-house near the mouth of Mustang Creek of the South Canadian; in the winter of 1845-46 he built one of adobe a little further up the river. This Adobe Fort evidently was the ruins Adobe Walls where, at Thanksgiving time, 1864, Kit Carson engaged in the greatest Indian battle of his life.[251]

Of the members of Bent, St. Vrain & Co., Kit Carson's valued patrons, whose Fort William or Bent's Fort had been preceded by a trading stockade up the Arkansas above present Pueblo, Colorado, the more prominent were William Bent, Charles Bent, and Ceran St. Vrain.

The Bent family themselves were an innovation in the early Western Indian trade, being thoroughly Yankee although of Colonial French and English strain. The grandfather, Captain Silas Bent, commanded the Boston tea party of December 16, 1773; from his son Silas Bent, Jr., first Judge of Common Pleas and Quarter Sessions of the District of St. Louis, there descended the Bents of Bent's Fort. In all, the children numbered seven sons and four daughters.

William Bent, the sixth born, and in the same year with Kit Carson, of medium but wiry figure, dark and pock-marked and with features almost Indian, was resident and in command at Fort William (named for him) but was frequently absent upon trading excursions among the Cheyennes and Arapahos. According to his testimony in 1865 before the Congressional Joint Committee he then had been living thirty-six years around the mouth of the Purgatory — which was to say, at or near Bent's Fort. One of six active brothers, at the time of Carson's accession by the fort he was thirty years old and had still thirty years before him.

An experienced trader, innured to Indian life, in 1835 he took to himself, at Bent's Fort, Owl Woman, a daughter of White Thunder, keeper of the Cheyenne medicine arrows; and in his first widower-hood, in 1847, married her sister, Yellow Woman. Consequently he was a personage of weight among the Southern Cheyennes and their allies. Kit Carson stated in 1865 that he would trust more to Colonel Bent's influence with the plains tribes than to his own.

The Cheyennes called William Bent "Little White Man"; his Kiowa name was "Hook-nose-man." He received his courtesy title of Colonel by reason of his service as guide for the General Kearny column on into New Mexico, in 1846, and as purveyor of supplies to this Army of the West. As an Indian trader he was a marked success, and further showed his business abilities by anticipating the Government at Big Timbers.

In 1859, while operating his post at the Big Timbers, he was agent over the Cheyennes and Arapahos, reporting, however, from St. Louis. He resigned to pursue the more profitable business of government freighting, while also carrying on a trading business with the emigrants pouring through along the Arkansas for the "Pike's Peak gold fields."

He resumed improvements upon a ranch just above the mouth of the Purgatory, whence he had been driven out in 1847 by the Indians. In 1864 he was in the same neighborhood, or on the Arkansas "eighteen miles above Fort Lyon [Wise]." His business on the trail brought him frequently to Missouri, where near Westport the Bent family had a large farm, with the Bent "mansion" upon it — and where his own children, domiciled at times, preferred their buckskins to the linsey-woolsey.

Again a widower, here at Westport he married, in 1867, Adalina Harvey, young daughter of Alexander Harvey (of the upper Missouri fur-trade firm of Harvey, Primeau & Co.) and his Blackfoot wife. This year the colonel removed all his household and chattels to the ranch at the Purgatory. He continued his freighting business. In May, 1869, suddenly taken ill while on his way from Santa Fé to Missouri on another wagon trip, he stopped short on the trail, at the house of his son-in-law, R. M. Moore, of the West Animas ranch lands, adjacent to the

present town of Las Animas, above the Purgatory. He died
there, from pneumonia, May 19; was buried upon the ranch.
He died a year after Kit Carson, a year and a half before Ceran
St. Vrain; thus the three were not long separated.

By his first Cheyenne wife he had four children, Mary, Robert, George and Julia; by his second wife, Yellow Woman, he
had one child, Charles. These all were Bent family names, but
the blood of William Bent the well-born of Colonial lineage
was diverted mainly to Indian veins.[252]

The firm and business of Bent, St. Vrain & Co. engaged three
others of the Bent brothers: Charles, George and Robert. Of
these Charles, a partner, was ten years older than William and
was the eldest in the family; born, not in St. Louis, but in Virginia; rose to be the most distinguished of the four brothers in
the Southwest, for he filled the high post of governorship over
a new American principality and thereby paid with his life.

By William much revered, he was different from him in appearance, being "light complexioned, heavily built, tending to
corpulency." He was early in the Santa Fé trade; was captain
of caravans forth and back, and after the establishment of
Bent's Fort applied himself more to the Mexican part of the
business than to the Indian; maintained domestic quarters in
Taos rather than at the post, although he was sometimes there;
was a leading citizen of Taos, where, in the middle Thirties, he
married Señora María Ignacia Jaramillo, widow of a leading
New Mexican family, elder sister of Kit Carson's wife to be,
and, like all the Jaramillo girls, of a stately beauty — and, when
seen in her widowhood again, in 1847, by Lewis Garrard,
possessed of a "good figure for her age; luxuriant raven hair;
unexceptional teeth, and brilliant dark eyes, the effect of which
was heightened by a clear, brunette complexion."[253]

Singled out by General Kearny in 1846, Charles Bent was
appointed by him civil governor of the newly conquered territory of New Mexico. In the early morning of January 19, 1847,
while he was upon a visit at his Taos home from duties at
Santa Fé, the capital, before the very eyes of his family he was

murdered, between four walls, by up-rising Mexicans and Pueblos, and his bloody gray scalp was "paraded through the streets of Taos."

He was only forty-eight. His hair had bleached in middle life. The Cheyennes around Bent's Fort fondly called him "Gray-haired White-man." He is said to have been the first plainsman to shoe oxen with iron. William Bent forever missed him and his counsel, for they two had been much together upon the trail in the days of their merchant beginnings. Kit Carson, who looked up to him as the senior in the firm and an old, staunch friend, was struck with vengeful horror. And Lieutenant J. W. Abert, who on detached duty from the Kearny column met him in Santa Fé, lamented him as "one in a thousand." Thus, in his prime, beloved and honored, Don Carlos Bent passed from trail and home and state.

Of George Bent, third of the trader brothers and a partner in the firm, less has been written. He was Carson's junior by five years and was two years older than Robert, the fourth brother. He married a Mexican girl, was occasionally in service at the fort — was in command there, during the absence of William, when in July, 1844, Frémont stopped off upon his return from his second expedition — but had residence in Taos, where, in 1843, he was a witness to his friend Kit Carson's marriage. In Taos he received Garrard, in the spring of 1847 while the trial and execution of his brother Charles's murderers were being performed. And the next year he died, from the consumption, at the fort, and was buried in the fort graveyard, beside his younger brother Robert, killed by the Comanches in 1841 at the Pawnee Fork of the Santa Fé Trail. In his will he named Francis P. Blair, Jr., of Missouri, guardian of his two children, and these were thereupon placed in school in St. Louis.[254]

The life of the Bents and the St. Vrains at Fort William was a life well nigh feudal, like the lives of the partisans and factors up the Missouri and in the Columbia country. As chiefs they dressed—

In moccasins thoroughly garnished with beads and porcupine quills; in trowsers of deer skin, with long fringes of the same extending along the outer seam from the ankle to the hip; in the splendid hunting-shirt of the same material, with sleeves fringed on the elbow-seam from the wrist to the shoulder, and ornamented with figures of porcupine quills of various colors, and leathern fringe around the lower edge of the body. And chiefs they were in the authority exercised in their wild and lonely fortress.[255]

But of the St. Vrains themselves, what? Whereas the Bents were of Revolutionary New England ancestry, the St. Vrains, of blood-kin with the house of de Lassus, were of the old French Flanders nobility, representing blood the proudest in Europe. Of this strain was Don Carlos de Hault de Lassus, the last governor of Spanish Upper Louisiana, who in 1804 turned over the province to the French flag, which was immediately succeeded by the Stars and Stripes. In his documents of the proceedings he calls attention to the worthy attributes of his brother, Jacques de St. Vrain, captain of the French navy, *émigré* to Louisiana in 1797, and commander of his Majesty's galliot *Phebé,* in service upon the Mississippi.

The St. Vrains connected with Bent, St. Vrain & Co. were two: Ceran and Marcellin. They were sons of Don Jacques Marcellin Ceran de Hault de Lassus de St. Vrain and Marie Félicité Chauvet Dubreuil his wife, of Spanish Lake, St. Louis County, Missouri. Another son was Felix St. Vrain, agent to the Sacs and Foxes, at Rock Island, and there killed by the Sacs in 1832. There were other sons.

Ceran, born in 1802, and by that senior, in years, to Kit Carson and William Bent, but junior to Charles Bent, was older than Marcellin by a dozen years. He was early a trader in the Southwest and, as has been related, in the summer of 1826 was upon a filibustering fur hunt out of Santa Fé for the Gila and the Colorado. Thence onward he may be considered a resident of New Mexico; first in Taos, where he met, as peers, Don Carlos Beaubien of Three Rivers, Canada, gentility; Captain Ewing Young from Tennessee; Milton Sublette, Don Antonio Robidoux and Don Louis Robidoux, like himself from the St.

Ceran St. Vrain

Louis district; young Kit Carson and other Carsons from the Missouri frontier; the Vigil, the Jaramillo, the Luna clans of conquistador ancestry; David Waldo of the American Waldos, traders and merchants in the Southwest; betimes, Bill Williams, the eccentric trapper; James P. (Jim) Beckwourth, the mulatto breed; Peg-leg Smith, the roisterer; and their fellows in from the mountains and the trap-line; and the Bents his partners. Out of such companionship of trail and camp and settlement the West was made, for the path of Empire, there, was strangely peopled.

As a thick-set, rather portly man, of much grace of manner, and with broad features (swathed, in his trader years, with a black beard) pocked like the features of William Bent, Ceran St. Vrain continued to live at Taos while he was in the firm of Bent, St. Vrain & Co., but was often at the fort. His domestic affairs in Taos were presided over by the Señora St. Vrain, "a darkeyed, languidly handsome woman" (with a sister, "a handsome brunette of some sixteen years,") who greeted the impressionable Garrard in the St. Vrain house in 1847.

Retiring from the Mexican-Indian trade, Ceran St. Vrain, now well-to-do, changed from Taos to the ranch settlement southward on the Mora, where he erected a flouring mill and invested in other enterprises. At the outbreak of the Civil War he briefly functioned as colonel of New Mexico Volunteers, resigned and was succeeded by his lieutenant colonel, Kit Carson; but throughout the war he "threw the influence of his personal character, great popularity, and immense wealth, in the scale of freedom against slavery" — and, incidentally, filled profitable contracts for the subsistence of the troops and reservation Indians in New Mexico. Aged sixty-eight he died, in October, 1870, at Mora, from the apoplexy, and there was buried. He left children by his last wife, Luisa Branch of Taos, and a Spanish grant, the Vigil-St. Vrain Grant, "one hundred miles square, bounded by the Snowy Range, the Rio de las Animas, and the Arkansas" — a little empire which was long a green patch upon the maps, and over the division of which there was some controversy at law.

Now, as to Marcellin St. Vrain, younger than William Bent and Kit Carson, younger than George Bent, a year older than Robert Bent, and therefore a junior among the principals in the Bent, St. Vrain & Co. concern: He was born in October, 1815, tenth child of Jacques de St. Vrain and Marie Félicité Dubreuil, and bore, like his brother Ceran, a family name. Was put at school in the Jesuit college of St. Louis University; following, or in the middle Thirties, he joined his brother in the plains trade; as previously stated, commanded a company train of 1837; with the establishment of Fort George, named for George Bent but soon to be given the courtesy title Fort St. Vrain, he was appointed agent there, and continued his service with the company, not as a partner but as a chief trader. Took a Sioux woman for wife. With the abandonment of Fort St. Vrain save as an occasional depot for a distribution of the company goods he was transferred from his independent command to Bent's Fort and the captaincy, now and again, of its caravans. He was at Bent's in 1846, he was there in 1847; according to Lewis Garrard he was among the most expert of all the post attaches at standing on his head and waving his legs to attract the curious antelope.

About Marcellin, cadet in the St. Vrain line, livelier, slimmer, handsomer than his brother Ceran, and who added to the St. Vrain coat of arms a quartering of the Sioux, there hangs romance. By a chance blow at Bent's Fort, or possibly while he was temporarily again at St. Vrain, in 1848, he killed a young Mexican muleteer. His brother and the Bents advised him to leave the country. He consigned his Indian wife and half-Indian children to his brother Ceran, for maintenance at the Mora, and returned to Missouri, there to stay. At Florissant, St. Louis County, he married, June 26, 1849, Miss Elizabeth Jane Murphy. Having exchanged the free life of the trading post, the caravan and the Mexican southwest for that of the settled prairies, he lived in his latter years upon a farm six miles south of New London, Ralls County, Missouri, and here dying in 1871 was buried in the Salem churchyard, near Center. And here was buried, in 1880, his widow Elizabeth.

Of Marcellin St. Vrain in his retirement we have a description:

> A slightly built man, rather swarthy, with black hair and eyes, about five feet six or seven inches height and weighed only 115 or 125 pounds; and from the time that I can remember him he wore a full beard about six or eight inches long, and black, streaked with gray when he died. Not much of a talker; I know but little of him before 1849, although I heard him speak of Indian fights and buffalo and bear hunting.[256]

The association of Carson, always observant, at Bent's Fort and Taos, with the Bents and the St. Vrains, men of backgrounded breeding and culture, should have somewhat prepared him for another association, that with Frémont.

Chapter XXV

Adventures of Kit Carson — 1838-1842

In the fall of 1838 a Santa Fé caravan of fifty-two wagons commanded by Captain Blunt left Independence, Missouri, for the New Mexican market. It happened that after a short period of truce the Kiowas were again about to break forth — as they had the habit of doing every three years — and the Blunt caravan was warned while on its way by travelers from the west.

The Kiowas were among the fiercest fighters of the Southwest plains. Not even the Comanches and Apaches were so much dreaded, and even the Pawnees did not outrank those painted horsemen with the truly Indian name.

At the Arkansas, in southern Kansas, the much-alarmed train was met by Kit Carson, leading a company of bearded trappers. Right glad was the caravan to see the reinforcement, for many of the teamsters were greenhorns and poorly armed. At the rear, driving the cavvy, there jogged along on a mule a runaway boy of fifteen, who, accoutered with a stained juvenile dragoon suit of blue, and a pistol "as large as the palm of my hand," was out "to hunt Injuns!" This was Oliver P. Wiggins, for twelve years to be Kit Carson's subaltern and close friend.

The Kiowa territory was beyond. After two days' travel, when the danger zone was reached, on the third morning the raw teamsters were amazed to witness the vaunted mountain-men tie their horses to the rear of the wagons, and to pile in, a pair to a wagon, under the canopy-tops. This occasioned grumbling and not a few sneers from the teamsters — utterances treated with silent contempt.

Scarcely had the train got under way, when, from over the sandhills to the north, down poured the whooping Kiowas; riding hard, brandishing lance and bow and shield, flourishing their robes and shouting. But if they thought that they had to deal only with teamsters who foolishly emptied their guns they were much mistaken. Undeterred by the confused parking of the caravan they pelted on — until suddenly from the slightly rolled edges of the wagon tops the long, heavy barrels of the trappers' rifles were poked out and the poised muzzles spat their hot lead. The volley was as deadly as unexpected. Back reeled the remnant of the reds, scurrying and screeching for those sandhills again, and after them raced the trappers, shooting from the saddle. Then the boy Oliver crawled from between the wagon-wheels where he had sought refuge. These warriors of the plains, so different from the tamed Sacs and Foxes with whom he had journeyed from Fort Dearborn, had shamed his small pistol.

Next, the caravan was almost at the forking of the trail, at the crossing into New Mexico. That evening, in the twilight, Ike Chamberlain, Carson lieutenant, approached Oliver, and said:

"Boy, 'stead o' goin' to Santy Fee, how'd you like to travel 'long to Bent's and Touse with us? All right! We take the Bent's trail in the mornin'. There'll be no more Injuns. I'll see Kit again, and if he says for you to come we'll light a fire, after dark where we're campin'. When it flares up, you'll know."

Taos was reached in December. Here Kit Carson, twenty-nine years old, had official headquarters, and operated with a company of forty-five trappers. His assistants were Ike Chamberlain and Sol Silver. Usually half the company were out at a time, under Chamberlain or Silver, after beaver or meat. Chamberlain was a quick-tempered man, a terrific fighter with his fists as well as with his rifle, and Silver had the blackest, bushiest whiskers in all Taos.[257]

Twice a year, in spring and in fall, the whole party went on a great buffalo hunt, to fulfill Carson's contract with Bent's Fort. Obviously no one rifle could stock the larder of this hearty post. Between times there were the beaver, the horse herd, and the Indians.

Carson was the best trapper among all the men, good though they were. The fur trail extended clear to the Wisdom River, north of the Three Forks source of the Missouri. The Blackfeet had quieted, and the Wisdom was found to be virgin ground. At one place a two-foot channel had been dammed and expanded into a shallow pond ten miles wide. From this great collection of lodges forty-three Carson trappers, in 1841, took 3,000 beaver, which Blackfeet squaws dressed for payment in the carcasses and an occasional pinch of sugar. Another time, in Colorado's South Park, by cutting a dam the Carson trappers drained a beaver pond and wading into the muck with clubs, at one attack killed eighty beaver.

The pelts were regularly sent down from the camps, by the Missouri or the Platte trails, to St. Joe — the Blacksnake Hills — where Louis Robidoux the trader handled them. Of the proceeds Carson took ten per cent; the remainder went to the employes — the year's division not infrequently amounting to a thousand dollars apiece for the trappers.[258]

Amid his trading, trapping and hunting out of Taos or Bent's Fort, Carson appears to have served as the Guardian of the Trail. The very existence of Bent's Fort depended upon the communicating trails being kept open. The incident of the Blunt caravan in the fall of 1838 has been told. Another similar incident, of the fall of 1841, is in evidence.

With one sunrise there arrived in Taos an excited group of riders to report that about seventy miles east, on the Santa Fé Trail, a caravan had been held a day and a night by Indians and was in peril of extermination. At the time Carson was suffering from a pistol wound in the right leg; his pistol had fallen and had discharged; the ball passed upward, diagonally, through the calf, and he was in bad shape for six months. But Ike Chamberlain, now aged twenty-six, was on hand, and Carson ordered him to get the men out and take the trail in twenty minutes. A slight delay was necessary (at which Carson, with his characteristic impatience of unreadiness, chafed), to permit some of the men to run bullets. As quickly as possible twenty-five or thirty men took the trail.

Oliver Wiggins, eighteen, and the youngest, accompanied the party, for he had been promoted to man's work, and had just been rewarded by Carson's own new percussion-cap rifle for a recent exploit in which he had summarily turned a Kiowa band and recovered stolen stock.

The rescue horsemen from Taos rode all that day; about two in the morning managed to pass through the cordon, to find the caravan with its oxen almost dead from hunger and thirst. There followed a stratagem similar to that of November, 1838. The Carson men distributed themselves among the wagons, to await the Indian charge. At daybreak, down swooped the reds — to be lured on by a feeble volley of a few muskets and pistols. But when the charge was well inside point-blank range, the whites delivered the first real volley. The charge continued, for to the Indian mind the defenders now had only empty guns.

The galloping warriors were made acquainted with an evolution in fire-arms. The Kit Carson company, according to Wiggins, were maintained in the highest state of efficiency; the revolving pistol had lately been adopted; and springing from cover to the backs of their animals, the trappers met the Indian charge with a counter-charge, shooting right and left *without reloading*. Saddle-pads were emptied, the astonished Indians broke and fled.

These Indians were Kiowas again, with a few Comanches, the two tribes intermingling more or less. More than a score were killed, while the whites lost only one man.

"Ah, what fighters we were, in those days!" sighed old Oliver Wiggins, at eighty-seven, his faded eyes kindling. "Nobody could lick the Carson men! They might kill us, but they couldn't whip us!"[259]

A change had come upon the civilizing weapons of the West. The percussion cap had been invented, cartridges for breech-loading had been experimented with, and the famous Colonel Samuel Colt had brought to comparative perfection his six-shooting pistol. The rifle that young Oliver Wiggins wielded in this affray was the first percussion-cap rifle owned in Taos, and had been bought of the makers, Golcher & Butler of Philadelphia, by Kit Carson in 1840 for $60 gold. According to Wiggins, Carson was alert and his men were alert to secure the most advanced ideas in offensive and defensive weapons; and so his party in the fight of 1841 to rescue the wagon train were armed with the new revolving pistol of Samuel Colt.[260]

Fernandez de Taos was Kit Carson's home port. Whatever of private business he had was in order here. At Taos he centered his horse and mule stock such as his operations required. His herd was pastured out, running loose, in some valley or bottoms to the westward, under the eyes of a wrangler who, like the lad Wiggins, was being proved in faithfulness and mettle. From Taos he dispatched, on occasion, his punitive expeditions. And at Taos he outfitted his company with saddles, as needed — for his short apprenticeship to Davie Workman stood him in good stead.

His domestic establishment was confined to his other station, Bent's Fort. To Bent's Fort he had brought his Arapaho wife; and there he had lost her by death, if not in 1838, then in 1839. By that he had been left with a little daughter, two or three years old. This his first born he named Adaline — a name memorializing his niece Adaline, who was born to his elder half-brother William early in 1810, a few weeks after his own birth near the close of 1809, and was his favorite playmate of childhood in Missouri.

Oliver Wiggins, with memory back to that date 1838, did not have any clear recollection of the Arapaho wife; he recalled well the little girl, and recalled the fact of her mother's being dead; and the remark of Carson that he would be glad to have as Alice's successor "her sister," who, also, "was a good girl." Furthermore, marriage with a sister would naturally occur to him, for that was almost the rule where the first union had been satisfactory, and as has been seen was the custom followed by William Bent and others.

According to the recollection of Wiggins the girl Adaline was a dark, elfish child, playing unrestrained at Bent's Fort and Taos. Carson had friends — William Bent with the beginnings of a half-Indian brood at Bent's, Charles Bent with the beginnings of a Spanish-blood brood at Taos. But with him, himself, away much of the time, the bringing-up of Adaline was a problem. He had to look out for his own; that accorded with his independent nature. Consequently he married again. By accounts more than mere tradition he took for wife, at Bent's Fort, in 1840 or thereabouts, the Cheyenne girl, Making Out Road.

Making Out Road turned out to be a very different kind of "Alice" from Singing Grass. She was a Southern Cheyenne, Waa-nibe had been a Northern Arapaho. She was a belle among the white men of the big fort and among the Indians who gathered there by the thousands; Waa-nibe had been wonted to the customs of her own people alone, where woman was subservient to man. Making Out Road had a temper, and a fondness for the easy life; Singing Grass had had the disposition that fitted her name, and the trail that suited her man suited her. In about a year Carson, no hero to his wife, found himself and all his personal possessions including Adaline thrown out of his lodge. There had been a child which had lived only a month. To Making Out Road the fosterling, an Arapaho, was a poor substitute.[261]

In the spring of 1842 Kit Carson pulled out for Missouri and the settlements. As he says in his *Own Story:*

> In April 1842, the train of wagons of Bent and St. Vrain were going to the states. I concluded to go with them. It had been a long time since I had been among civilized people. I went and saw my friends and acquaintances, then took a trip to St. Louis, remaining there a few days and was tired of remaining in settlements, took a steamer for the Upper Missouri and, as luck would have it, Colonel Fremont, then a Lieutenant, was aboard of the same boat.

With him there went little Adaline, to be placed in school. This was one of the motives of his trip. He might have put her down at Santa Fé, for convent instruction there; that was a custom of Spanish families of Taos and vicinity, for their girls. But like a number of other Americans in the Southwest and

Northwest he preferred, for his child, an up-bringing if not among his own kin, at least among people of his blood.

Jim Bridger consigned his Mary Ann by an Indian wife to the Protestant missions in Oregon; other children to Catholic schooling in Missouri. Joe Meek placed his little Helen Mar with the Oregon missions. George Bent's children in Taos were destined for States' instruction, and to Missouri they went. Many of these fathers living a life beyond the frontiers wished to fit their children for better environments. It was the acknowledgment of a responsibility, the demonstration of an inherent *noblesse oblige* so marked in Carson in his family relations. He took upon himself the education of not only his own children but at least four other dependants.

While considering Adaline, Kit had in mind also young María Josefa Jaramillo of Taos, whom, in February of the next year, 1843, he married. With this union as a prospect his child Adaline, by an Indian wife, was a present problem — particularly as Josefa herself was only fourteen.

Matters should have already been arranged with Josefa and her parents, for by his own narrative Carson returned to Bent's Fort, from his absence with Frémont, in January, and within a month was married to Señorita Josefa. And as a necessary preliminary to the marriage he had already been baptized into the Roman Catholic faith. That ceremony had been performed in the January now past.

The entry in the Record of Baptisms of the Church of Our Lady of Guadalupe of Taos reads, as translated from the Spanish:

In this Church Territory of Taos, on the twenty-eighth day of January, one thousand eight hundred forty-two, I, the Priest in charge, D. Antonio José Martinez, having previously put the necessary religious questions until I was apprised of his being sufficiently instructed in the origins, procedures and aim of Our Holy Religion and the acceptance of it, and as there occurred the sober doubt whether he had been baptized or not, since that was according to the ceremony of the Anabaptists whose errors he condemns, an adult male of thirty-two years of age, I exorcized him, applied the Holy oils, in solemn form baptized *sub conditione* and annointed with the Blessed Ointment, giving him the name Cristobal, the same that he had from his first baptism in the aforesaid Ceremony, but this baptism which I performed was according to the ceremony for adults in conformity with the Roman Ritual: said adult is formerly of the State of misuri of North America; but it is understood that since he passed the age of fourteen years he lives in this town site of Our Lady of Guadalupe of this parish, although pursuing the function of hunter for the region of the North; he says his parents are of legitimate marriage, Linsey Carson and Rebecca Roberson; godfathers were Luis Lee and María de la Cruz Padilla, residents of the same town of Our Lady of Guadalupe, I advised them of their obligation and spiritual relationship and as a act of good faith have signed my name.   ANTO JOSE MARTINEZ[262]

In speaking of his first meeting with Carson, on the steamboat, Frémont says that Carson was then upon his way home from St. Louis after having placed his little daughter in a convent there. Circumstances indicate, however, that Adaline had been left with relatives for her initial schooling, and that her convent days came later — in the period following 1847.

Mrs. L. P. Slaughter of Kansas City, whose mother, Mrs. Leander Amick, was a daughter of Carson's sister Elizabeth (Mrs. Robert Cooper) wrote:

When I was a child, Kit Carson's daughter Adaline, the daughter by his first wife, lived for several years with my parents on a farm between Fayette and Glasgow, in Howard County, this state. There and in a St. Louis convent school she received her education. As my mother refused to accept any money for caring for his daughter, he purchased many presents for her; among them was a mahogany rocking-chair which I still have.

And in another letter:

My sister, if now living [1911], would be 74 years old, and she was about the same age of Adaline Carson, Kit's daughter. Adaline came to our house when she was about 5 years old and stayed with us until she was about 11 years old. I never knew of her attending a school in Fayette but she did attend a country school named Rock Springs school which was about 9 miles from Fayette. When Kit took Adaline away from our home he said he might leave her in St. Louis in school or he might take her with him to California. She was of dark complexion, black hair and dark eyes. Kit visited her several times while she was with us.

It is possible that Adaline was entered, for a term or two, in the old Howard Female Seminary of Fayette. George H. Carson of Fayette, whose recollections have before been drawn upon in these pages, wrote:

> In 1847 my uncle Kit visited all his relatives in Howard County, and the next year, 1848, I think, brought his daughter to Fayette and placed her in school. I know she was in school here in 1849, for I spent most of the summer here and often saw her, myself. My remembrance is, he took her west in the early Fifties.

According to the reckonings, Adaline in the spring of 1842 was five or six years old. Carson's efforts in her behalf were promptly rewarded. His trail opened as he pursued it, for this trip to Missouri resulted in his engagement with Frémont, to further results which warranted his testifying, to Senator Benton, for the Senate committee, in 1848, that he "was under more obligations to Colonel Frémont than to any other man alive."

Just with whom among his brothers and sisters he made reunion while he was again in old Howard County is of only sparse record. After sixteen years' absence from Missouri he found changes in people and land, not wholly unforseen by him. While at Taos and Bent's Fort he had been more or less in touch with news direct from the States, undoubtedly had met several of his brothers, the difficulty had been, to visualize things as they actually were "back home." Nephews and nieces whom he had left as tots and youngsters had grown, and there was a new crop — and likewise a crop of new relatives on the Martin side, by that re-marriage of his mother.[263]

Of old Franklin where he had fiddled away time under Davie Workman the saddler, with eye and ear for the incoming and outbound parties of plains, river and mountains, there was only a vestige, like an abandoned Indian winter or summer camp, with the graveyard as the abiding attestation of a living past. Even the river had changed channel. The new Franklin, down river and safely back from the river, was nothing that he remembered. As for St. Louis — it was too big for him.

Although he saw familiars here, in long hair and leather and blankets — Indians, whites and breeds — and some that he knew; and may have called, as was the custom of the mountain-men and the Indians, upon that dependable stand-by, Robert Campbell, soon his feet hurt, his head buzzed, his stomach revolted and he felt very small.

Carson gladly boarded a steamboat for the river trail to the upper Missouri country. Here among the rough-and-ready deck-hands and passengers he was at home; he spoke their language. His idea appears to have been to return to Taos by way of the Platte route to Fort Laramie, thence south to St. Vrain's and along the foothills to the Arkansas and down to Bent's.

Whether, while in St. Louis, he received a tip, from an acquaintance or from current talk, of an expedition's being organized there for an exploring tour into the mountains, and took a chance of making a profitable contact with it while it was outfitting, is conjecture.

By his own words he voluntarily approached Frémont and offered himself.

Chapter XXVI

On the Trail with Frémont — 1842

HE [Frémont] had been in search of Captain Dripps, an old experienced mountaineer, but failed in getting him. I spoke to Colonel Frémont, informed him that I had been some time in the mountains and thought I could guide him to any point he would wish to go. He replied that he would make inquiries regarding my capabilities of performing that which I promised. He done so. I presume he received reports favorable of me, for he told me I would be employed. I accepted the offer of one hundred dollars per month and prepared myself to accompany him.

This is Carson's relation in his *Own Story*. Viewing the encounter from Frémont's angle, in his *Memoirs:*

On the boat [from St. Louis to the mouth of the Kansas River] I met Kit Carson. He was returning from putting his little daughter in a convent-school at St. Louis. I was pleased with him and his manner of address at this first meeting. He was a man of medium height, broad-shouldered and deep-chested, with a clear steady blue eye and frank speech and address; quiet and unassuming.

I had expected to engage as guide an old mountaineer, Captain Drips, but I was so much pleased with Carson that when he asked to go with me I was glad to take him.

The best of the early biographies of Frémont, that by John Bigelow, states:

Colonel Frémont owed his good fortune in procuring Carson's services to an accidental meeting on board the steamboat above St. Louis, neither having ever heard of the other before, as he was setting out on his first expedition.[264]

Frémont was upon his way to the appointed rendezvous of his party — the Cyprian Chouteau trading post about ten miles in from the mouth of the Kansas, which itself was an estimated 400 miles by water from St. Louis. If, as he declares in his official report for the War Department, he arrived in St. Louis, from the east, on May 22, and broke camp at the trading post on June 10, after "several days" of delay there by reason of outfitting and bad weather, he could have had but a few days for gathering men and material in St. Louis. He records an observation of latitude and longitude made at the Colonel Brant home, his St. Louis quarters, on May 27. He should soon there-after, very likely upon the next day, have taken the boat for the landing at the Kansas River.

Kit Carson himself (and as he says) had not been long in St. Louis, for he had left Bent's Fort in April, the caravan journey to the Missouri settlements would have consumed forty days, and he had visited in Howard County.

Without doubt Senator Benton had written ahead of Fré-mont, to the Chouteaus in St. Louis, requesting them to be getting good men together for the expedition. That would not require great time, but Frémont's time in St. Louis was limited. How many of these men accompanied Frémont up-river on the boat, and how many met him at the trading post, does not appear.

But there were at least two in the company engaged whom Carson knew and by whom he was known. They were Lucien B. Maxwell and Basil Lajeunesse, both of the Santa Fé Trail, Bent's Fort and Taos. Maxwell this year married the Señorita Luz Beaubien of Taos, out of which he trapped and traded; Basil and very likely his brothers including François, future Frémont man, had been *voyageur* trappers and traders by the Platte and Arkansas routes.

Oliver Wiggins asserted that Maxwell accompanied Carson on his trip this spring to Missouri, for a visit among his own kin and friends in his old home, Kaskaskia, in Illinois below St. Louis. That may well be so; he had married Luz in March. It is a matter of guess whether Maxwell already was aware of his choice as hunter for the Frémont column, and whether Carson had received from him a bit of friendly news. They two were allies in love and war in Taos. Indeed, when and where Maxwell received his appointment to the Frémont ex-pedition, whether he and Carson saw each other in Missouri, and what, if anything aside from chance, produced the coinci-dence of a willing-to-do Kit Carson and an about-to-do Fré-mont upon the same boat, in very nick of time when Frémont was lacking a guide, also is a matter of guess. Carson's apparent "luck" stood by him for his engagement for the second expedition, also; as will be seen.

In any event Frémont did not have to cast about very widely for Carson credentials. If he did not find them on the boat itself he found them to his complete satisfaction when he arrived at the Chouteau trading post, where he was housed with Cyprian Chouteau himself, of the American Fur Company.

When in the last of May, 1842, on that steamboat threshing its way up the Missouri from St. Louis, Christopher Carson the mountain-man out of the west met Lieutenant John Charles Frémont, the army engineer out of the east, opportunity joined their hands. Together they entered into fame — they had been enlisted for leading parts in a great drama to be written into the history of the Republic.

Carson was particularly fortunate in that he was the recognized purely American member of Frémont's company. His and Lucien Maxwell's names were the only Anglo-American names featured upon the rôle, but Maxwell was strongly Kaskaskia French in blood and swartly French in appearance. And while Frémont wrote favorably of Maxwell and exploited Basil Lajeunesse and others of his *voyageurs,* the name and blood of Kit Carson had an especial appeal to the American race.

We cannot say that Frémont made Kit Carson, except in public and official favor. Carson performed in character outside of his service with Frémont. He had qualities that would have advanced him along with Jim Bridger and Thomas Fitzpatrick, emigrant and army guides. At the inception of the war with Mexico, had he still been at Bent's Fort and Taos instead of with Frémont he certainly would have been employed as scout or guide in the consequent operations. His office of Indian agent would have fallen to him naturally; he voluntarily, and not through appointment, save locally, entered the Civil War, for which he helped to raise a regiment. But Frémont opened a way to him, encouraged his confidence in his ability to meet larger issues than those to which he had been accustomed, forced his alliterative name Kit Carson (as potent as that of Buffalo Bill) upon the eyes of a public quick to adapt it to the figments of romance, introduced him to powers in State and society from whom he asked nothing, as of record yet disclosed — received nothing not earned; made him only in the sense of making a country conscious of his existing values, and himself conscious that he could demonstrate them under all conditions. Jim Bridger, in Government service, had Carson's opportunities, but he remained the scout; Kit Carson, of the same education, kept pace with his best associates, had that character which realizes the worth of ambitions ever so modest, and developed as the country developed. To be sure he was blessed with favoring environments and connections, there in Taos alone which did not want for social and domestic culture; but he had sought those, they had not sought him.

Both he and Frémont were Southerners. He was of Carolina and Kentucky blood, and was raised in Missouri amid a preponderance of Southerners; Frémont was born in Georgia and raised in South Carolina. Carson was the elder, being now in his thirty-third year, whereas Frémont was twenty-nine. Carson was mature beyond his years, and a father; Frémont was youthfully enthusiastic, and a husband of less than eight months.[265]

The two were opposites. Carson was Scotch-Irish: gray-blue eyed, sandy complexioned (under his tan), light-haired, flat-featured, squat in stature, gritty but ordinarily so lustreless in appearance and manner that few not knowing his name would bestow upon him more than a passing glance. Frémont was of French Creole type: flashing intensely blue eyes, complexion inclining to the olive, thick wavy brown hair, countenance oval and features sharply defined, high-bred and hawk-like, manner distinguished, disposition sensitive, quick, eager and indomitable. Few would forget him.[266]

Frémont was a scholar, of native and acquired attainments;

at this time Carson could not read, nor write more than his own name. His speech, eked out by gestures, was flavored with a jargon of mingled Mexican, Indian and Canadian French terms and frontier English "thar," "fout," "pore," "massa-creed," and so forth. Frémont was fluent in good English and French, and was well founded in their scientific vocabularies; Carson was fluent in colloquial Spanish as well as border English, had picked up *voyageur* phrases as common to the beaver country, had a speaking knowledge of two or three Indian tongues, and was thoroughly founded in the natural aspects of that land which Frémont was to observe scientifically.

Major Andrew Drips, the American Fur Company partisan would have served Frémont well and would have retired probably without distinction. Carson served him better, and gained by that service; as Frémont also gained not only by this contact with a character of rugged honesty but in a new and loyal friendship. While the two men were opposites they were at the same time complements. Frémont the impetuous and obstinate was squared by Carson the cautious and determined; and either could estimate and value the other, for they both were brave, both were of great physical endurance.

It may be that John Charles Frémont was, as has been asserted, intolerant of restrictions, over-ambitious, headstrong, visionary, ill-balanced. "At the time I was with him he was overbearing and conceited," says Oliver Wiggins, in his H. H. Bancroft dictation, referring to the first and second expeditions. "In these days he would have been called a dude." And, in another narration: "We found him a hard man to get along with. He thought he could do anything. We all told him he couldn't run the Platte in that rubber boat and when he upset we were tickled." While Carson himself is put upon record, in his latter days when on occasion he was "quite talkative," as confirming "the accounts we had heard that Frémont, as an explorer, was somewhat of a charlatan," with the additional information that "the worst time the Pathfinder ever had was when on one of his expeditions he disregarded his (Kit's) advice."[267]

Frémont was, however, that kind of man beloved by Westerners: a man who sets out to do his share of the work. He was a man who led into difficulties but he was perfectly willing to lead; he asked no more of his followers than of himself. The friendship between him and Carson, begun in 1842, was maintained, with many mutual expressions of esteem and almost brotherly love, until death took Carson first.

Frémont constantly refers, with generous praise, to Kit Carson's qualities of heart and personality, insures him a welcome as an equal in the Frémont and Benton home, sanctions him as a god-father to one of the children; and Kit Carson declares at the close of his service with Frémont:

> I have heard that he is enormously rich. I wish to God that he may be worth ten times as much more. All that he has or may ever receive, he deserves. I can never forget his treatment of me while in his employ and how cheerfully he suffered with his men when undergoing the severest of hardships. His perseverance and willingness to participate in all that was undertaken, no matter whether the duty was rough or easy, is the main cause of his success.[268]

Now secure of $100 a month for the summer at least, from the Cyprian Chouteau post within the border of eastern Kansas, Carson dispatched two Delaware "runners" to Taos, in order that fifteen of his own company, with trail equipment, should meet him at Fort Laramie.

The expedition left the Chouteau post on Friday, June 10; returned to the mouth of the Kansas, below the post, on October 10. Technically, this expedition, known as "Fremont's First Expedition," was "An Exploration of the Country Lying Between the Missouri River and the Rocky Mountains, on the line of the Kansas and Great Platte Rivers." Theoretically, it was an exploration to acquaint the government with the nature of the "rivers and country between the frontiers of Missouri and the base of the Rocky Mountains; and especially to examine the character, and ascertain the latitude and longitude of the South Pass, the great crossing place to these mountains on the way to Oregon." Officially it was an expedition "ordered by Colonel Abert, chief of the Topographical Bureau, with the sanction of the Secretary of War." But actually, while including the above scope, it was a Benton-Frémont expedition for the political triumph of one, the professional advancement of the other — an expedition, declares Senator Benton, "conceived without its [the government's] knowledge, and executed upon solicited orders, of which the design was unknown."[269]

The bill of Senator Lewis F. Linn, Benton's colleague from Missouri, for Oregon occupation, the bill of 1838, was dead. The Linn bill of the winter of 1842-43 had not yet been announced, and this expedition was a preparatory measure. As Frémont narrates in his *Memoirs,* the design of his exploration was "auxiliary and in aid to the emigration to the Lower Columbia"; his real commission, from the Expansionists headed by Benton and Linn, was to "indicate and describe the line of travel, and the best positions for military posts," as well as to fix the location of the South Pass. As he further admitted, relative to the career which he had also espoused when he married Senator and Mrs. Benton's daughter:

I felt I was being drawn into the current of important political events; the object of this expedition was not merely a survey; beyond that was its bearing on the holding of our territory in the Pacific; and the contingencies it involved were large.[270]

The material contributed by Frémont to the United States indeed proved to be California rather than Oregon. At the very time when, with the unwitting Carson, he disembarked from the water trail for that land trail which bore him forward upon the larger current of life, the American conquest of the Northwest had been potentially accomplished and a new constellation was rising to its place in the flag.

The debate upon the expediency of the American settlement of Oregon, between the expansionists, mainly of the free-soil West, and the anti-expansionists, mainly of the seaboard East and the slave-soil South, was a long debate, extending from the winter of 1820-21 to the summer of 1846. And when at last Government had decided that Oregon, once so remote but now near and looming as an Administration pledge, needs must be had at any cost, the citizenship at large already was in possession: "one of the many events," records Senator Benton, "which shows how little the wisdom of government has to do with great events which fix the fate of countries."

Oregon was made American territory before Kit Carson left the mountains; it was made American territory when in 1834 the American missionaries of the Jason Lee party crossed the South Pass and entered upon the Pacific slope. "For God's sake," Senator George McDuffie of South Carolina dramatically exclaimed, in the debate of 1843, "do not go there." But for God's sake the American of the East had already gone there, and had continued to go there not only for God's sake but for the sake of himself and the national domain.

The trail to Oregon awaited only the white-topped wagon of the emigrant. The secular squad of Thomas J. Farnham, from Peoria, bearing the flag inscribed "Oregon or the Grave" and the following "Quincy" squad of both secular and missionary import, were sporadic gestures. The earnest of the American settlers in Oregon other than the mission workers and the smattering from the beaver trail, the States and California, was yet to be certified.[271]

And then, three weeks before Kit Carson on his buffalo runner equipped with silver-mounted Spanish bridle set out to guide Lieutenant Frémont upon this venture in exploitation rather than exploration; while Congress was dillydallying and the Lord Ashburton-Secretary Webster treaty fixing the northeastern boundary of the United States was being drafted and the report had spread that a spineless President Tyler and an obdurate Daniel Webster were trading the Oregon empire for a Maine cod-fishery, the people had taken matters into their own hands. On May 16, 1842, the American prairie schooner had finally tripped her anchor and had cleared away for Oregon.

At the port of Independence there had assembled, subject to the coming of Dr. Elijah White, newly appointed first sub-

Indian agent for the United States, in Oregon, 112 persons, eighteen wagons, numerous horses, mules, cattle and dogs, hailing from Missouri, Arkansas and Illinois. Dr. White, who in 1836 had gone by ship to Oregon, as missionary physician, by ship returned had been a year in the States, preaching of that promised land beyond the mountains. Oregon was a bandied word in Congress, but this appointment of sub-Indian agent was seized upon as a rift of blue sky in the eddying clouds of debate. The settler migrant who once had left Kentucky for the next frontier hooked up span and yoke again and resumed his westward trek.

The trail for the Pacific coast had been broken by emigrant wheels. Incited by the California tales of one of the Robidoux brothers, probably Louis, possibly Antoine, and by letters from their former fellow citizen Dr. John Marsh, 500 settlers in western Missouri had pledged themselves to a march on California in the spring of 1841. The brew simmered down to the John Bidwell-John Bartleson company of forty-eight men, fifteen women and children, for California, to whom were joined the Oregon-bound party of Father DeSmet — a budget of missionaries, teamsters, hunters and sightseers guided by Thomas Fitzpatrick. Of the Bartleson-Bidwell company, thirty-two men, and Mrs. Benjamin Kelsey and little daughter crossed the Nevada desert to California; twelve others, by late change of mind, at the Bear River had taken the fork-off to the Columbia — several of these, however, only as vagrants, and not to stay.

The van of the definite Oregon settlers, following the skirmishers, marked time for another year.

Not discouraged by the opinion from Captain William Sublette, the experienced mountain-man, that so large a company, of members little acquainted with one another and burdened by women and children, never could get through, the Dr. White command held a meeting in their camp at Elm Grove, twenty miles southwest of Independence, and the first Oregon emigration was organized. It was resolved that every male, over the age of eighteen years, shall be provided with one mule, or horse, or wagon conveyance; shall have one gun, three pounds of powder, twelve pounds of lead, one thousand caps, or suitable flints, fifty pounds of flour, or meal, and thirty pounds of bacon, and a suitable proportion of provisions for women and children; and, if any present be not so provided, he shall be rejected.[272]

Dr. White was required to exhibit, that it should be read, "any document from the War Department, in his possession, showing his oppointment to any office in Oregon territory." He was elected wagon captain; a scientific corps, blacksmith, wagon-maker, master road and bridge builder, and secretary were appointed. Not a member of the company knew the trail beyond the mountains, but James Coates had been as far as Green River, just over the South Pass; so him they chose as pilot of this train fraught with precious lives and hopes.

The meeting adjourned, "to meet again at Fort Vancouver, on the Columbia River, on the first day of October next, the powers of Heaven willing." The emigrant party kept in advance of the government expedition all the way to the South Pass; and when Frémont turned back, to report that the Pass was no canyon but was entirely practicable for travel, the trail of men, women and children, demonstrating the fact, had continued on into the west, for Oregon.

The Santa Fé Trail of 800 miles was for long hereafter the business trail of men. The Oregon Trail of 2,000 miles had now become the domestic trail of families, whereon was lived the daily life of the home in transit, and each night's camp was the townsite of an hour.

At this date, 1842, the Platte River and South Pass route to the western slope was not news. General Ashley and other fur hunters of prominence had vouched for it, there was Captain Bonneville of the Army to testify of it, returned missionaries had borne witness to it, trader caravans and missionary parties of both men and women had traveled it, and the Reverend Samuel Parker's minutely written narrative of his trip through from the Missouri had appeared. The country be-

All the Way to Oregon

tween the South Platte and the Arkansas, and that along the mountains of the western border, also comprised in Frémont's orders, had been reported upon by Major Stephen Long's expedition of 1820 and Colonel Henry Dodge's march with his dragoons in 1835.

In view of the growing pains of the American people: the popular enthusiasm for an independent American Texas still claimed by a jealous Mexico, the swelling insistence upon that Oregon still claimed for British occupancy, the quickening impulse to extend the Monroe Doctrine to coveted California should England seek ownership there — in view of this unrest, the tense relations with Mexico over Texas and unpaid damage claims of American citizens, the debateful relations with England in the Columbia country, the question of the balance of power upon the continent involving all the great Southwest and the great Northwest clear to the Pacific coast, the War Department, with eye and ear to the rumblings from the far horizons, made preparations by securing an up-to-date and detailed topographical report upon that mid-region which constituted the western frontier. That the report might encourage the passage of settlers into the region, and thus open it and improve the trails; and the passage through it, and thus further warrant military protection by the establishment of handy posts looking westward, was a matter for tacit approval by the Government.

The acquisition of the Southwest and California came about through act of war. The acquisition of the Northwest more happily came about through measures of peace. The Frémont official report upon the frontier between the settlements and the Oregon country was adequate from every angle, makes good reading today, and when printed, the next spring, just in time for another and greater emigration to the Columbia, was widely read. With its fascinating high-lights of adventure and romance, cleverly inserted throughout, it was the first popular travel report made authentic by dry-as-dust-Washington.[273]

The real Frémont report, however, was contained in the

address of Senator Linn, introducing the official report to the Senate and moving that it be printed for Congressional and public distribution.

In executing his instructions, Mr. Frémont proceeded up the Kansas River far enough to ascertain its character, and then crossed over to the Great Platte, and pursued that river to its source in the mountains, where the Sweet Water (a head branch of the Platte) issued from the neighborhood of the South Pass. He reached the Pass on the 8th of August, and describes it as a wide and low depression of the mountains, where the ascent is as easy as that of the hill on which this Capitol stands, and where a plainly beaten wagon road leads to the Oregon through the valley of Lewis's River, a fork of the Columbia. He went through the Pass, and saw the headwaters of the Colorado, of the Gulf of California; and, leaving the valleys to indulge a laudable curiosity, and to make some useful observations, and attended by four of his men, he climbed the loftiest peak of the Rocky Mountains, until then untrodden by any known human being; and, on the 15th of August, looked down upon ice and snow some thousand feet below, and traced in the distance the valleys of the rivers which, taking their rise in the same elevated ridge, flow in opposite directions to the Pacific Ocean and to the Mississippi. From that ultimate point he returned by the valley of the Great Platte, following the stream in its whole course, and solving all questions in relation to its navigability, and the character of the country through which it flows.

*   *   *   *   *   *   *

Eight carts, drawn by two mules each, accompanied the expedition; a fact which attests the facility of traveling in this vast region. Herds of buffaloes furnished subsistence to the men; a short, nutritious grass, sustained the horses and mules. Two boys (one of twelve years of age, the other of eighteen), besides the enlisted men, accompanied the expedition, and took their share of its hardships; which proves that boys, as well as men, are able to traverse the country to the Rocky Mountains.[274]

As far as the *Congressional Globe* (the back-country circulating library of that day) carried, these words were carried. Senator Linn interpolated the Frémont report somewhat, as in his declaration of "a plainly beaten wagon road" westward leading from the Pass. But in this, in the reference to the Platte and Sweetwater trail, the easy crossing of the divide, the practicability of wheeled vehicles, the plentiful subsistence for men and animals, the presence of two boys in the company, the governing motivations of the enterprise were read. And although the Linn expansionist bill calling for military posts along the Oregon Trail to the Rockies and one at the mouth of the Columbia, and the promise of 640 acres to every adult American settler in Oregon, was lost in the House, the cause of "on to Oregon" had been advanced.

As for the navigability of the Platte — Frémont's rubber canoe had been wrecked in the upper rapids, and lower down his bull-boat, drawing four inches, had immediately grounded.

When the personnel of the Frémont command is considered, interest attaches especially to the leader; to Carson the guide, Lucien Maxwell the hunter, Basil Lajeunesse who became a Frémont favorite rivaling Carson, bristly-headed and tow-headed Charles Preuss, the plucky German topographer, and the lads Henry Brant, aged nineteen, son of Senator Benton's niece Sarah Benton Brant (Mrs. J. B. Brant) of St. Louis, and Randolph Benton, aged twelve, son of Senator Benton himself. That the two youths were left at Fort Laramie on account of Indians threatening the trail onward was not mentioned by Senator Linn.

From the Cyprian Chouteau trading post where the expedition organized, Carson had sent word of his plans to his company at Taos. Oliver Wiggins relates:

> The order from Kit direct was the cause of rejoicing among our crowd, and we started in time to reach the fort ahead of the government party.
>
> We hurried away late in June with laden pack horses, and pushed east and north along the Indian trail, up through Pueblo, then a Mexican village of adobe buildings, up through the old trail fourteen miles east of the present city of Colorado Springs, crossing Cherry Creek at Denver, where at that time there was not even a cabin or permanent tent, and joining the party at the fort. We trappers were not engaged as a part of the Fremont company, but the territory through which we were to travel was wild and the Indians were plentiful, and Kit, with his usual foresight, preferred to have his men within call in case of trouble. It was a continuous hunting trip for us, with plenty of big game along the route. We lived much like Indians as we traveled, and I can not say that we were not much like them except for racial differences.

Fremont went 110 miles west of Laramie to Sweetwater River, then up the Sweetwater. Leaving that stream we journeyed through unbroken mountains and forests to Atlantic and Pacific Springs, on the West Slope. About thirty miles west of the Springs Kit left Fremont, rejoined us, and we returned with our pelts to Taos, where we spent the winter. Fremont had learned many things heretofore unknown to the government, and when we parted company it was with the understanding that Carson was to act as guide for a second expedition the next year.[275]

Having marched up the valley of the Kansas River for a short distance by the Santa Fé Trail, a little beyond present Topeka, Kansas, the Frémont company crossed the river from the south to the north side, using the ford and following the road of the fork-off, here, for the Platte and the mountains and Oregon. Signs of the emigrant company three weeks in the lead were plain.

In ferrying equipment across the river the rubber boat with its air compartments (a species of craft which later excited the ridicule of the Carson veterans) was capsized. The precious stock of coffee was lost and Carson and Maxwell were made ill from their scramblings in the water.

The course led northwest through Kansas, into Nebraska, and to the Platte near present Grand Island. At the forks of the Platte the company was divided. The main party under Clément Lambert as chief and Carson as assistant proceeded by the Oregon Trail route up the North Platte, for Fort Laramie; Frémont himself, with four others including Lucien Maxwell and Basil Lajeunesse, traveling light, proceeded up the South Platte on an exploring tour to Fort St. Vrain and thence, by march northward across country, to the rendezvous at Fort Laramie. The presence of Maxwell insured a welcome at Fort St. Vrain, for he "had spent the last two or three years between this post and the village of Taos."

Previous to the division of the company Frémont had had occasion to observe Carson in action, and Carson had had opportunity to read the character of this, to him, new manner of man. A states-bred man but a man who showed trail experience; something of the dandy but nothing of the popinjay; a captain in command but prompt to fall to with the best of them; a captain and a comrade in one — a leader with the enthusiasm of a greenhorn but without the greenhorn's blatant ignorance.

For when Frémont, the young lieutenant serving history, once had plunged into the great prairie between the Kansas and the Platte he was in his element of knight errant. The atmosphere of the wide open, like that of the lofty peaks beyond it, so vast, so mysterious and immutable, infused his blood with the wine of life; as did the deeds fostered by the inhabitants.

He enjoyed the spectacle of Carson when, responding to an alarm, "without a saddle, and scouring bareheaded over the prairies, Kit was one of the finest pictures of a horseman I have ever seen." He enjoyed the camp and trail alarms — "in an instant, every man's weapon was in his hands, the horses were driven in, hobbled and picketed, and horsemen were galloping at full speed in the direction of the newcomers, screaming and yelling in the wildest excitement." The buffalo hunt was contagion to him. "My horse was a trained hunter, famous in the West under the name of Proveau, and, with his eyes flashing, and the foam flying from his mouth, sprang on after the cow like a tiger." Young, himself, with the spirit of romance, on the first stormy night he assigned young Brant and Benton to guard duty out there in the dark with Kit Carson the Indianfighter as their companion.

Maxwell would relate to Carson of Frémont at the Arapaho and Cheyenne village on the march to St. Vrain's; how there Frémont, as by his own confession:

remarked near some of the lodges a kind of tripod frame, formed of three slender poles of birch, scraped very clean, to which were affixed the shield and spear, with some other weapons. All were scrupulously clean, the spear head was burnished bright, and the shield white and stainless. It reminded me of the days of feudal chivalry; and when, as I rode by, I yielded to the passing impulse and touched one of the spotless shields with the muzzle of my gun, I almost expected a grim warrior to start from the lodge and resent my challenge.

All this sort of thing was tenderfoot "fofarrow" (fanfaron,

the French would put it), of course, and would not shine among mountain-men; but Carson, who was to appreciate the spirit of Scott's "Lady of the Lake," should have appreciated the spirit of this also.

Frémont and his squad were entertained at Fort St. Vrain by nimble Marcellin St. Vrain, the Bent-St. Vrain agent in charge there. At the Fort Laramie rendezvous with the Lambert-Carson detachment they were met by alarm indeed. The detachment had camped on the North Platte trail with Jim Bridger, who was convoying a party of traders out to Missouri. Bridger and his party warned that the Sioux, Gros Ventres and Cheyennes were on the warpath in revenge for the casualties suffered in the battle of last August, over on the Little Snake, with Captain Fraeb and his trappers — the battle in which Fraeb himself had been killed; the Sweetwater route, beyond Laramie, to the South Pass, was bad medicine.

This news, coming from an old campaigner like Bridger, spread consternation among the French of the in-going company — burdened as they were with two boys. Carson openly agreed with Bridger, whose opinion he respected, upon the gravity of the situation. Now at the Fort Laramie camp he made his will — undoubtedly to provide for the future of little Adaline; which apparent lack of confidence in his leader and the French employes impressed Frémont to the effect that "among the circumstances which were constantly occurring to increase their [the men's] alarm, this was the most unfortunate; and I found that a number of my party had become so much intimidated, that they had requested to be discharged at this place."

On the other hand, Mr. Fitzpatrick, "whose name and high reputation are familiar to all who interest themselves in the history of this country," had set out from Fort Laramie with the emigrant company, to take them safely through clear to Fort Hall.

It is noticeable that throughout the remainder of Frémont's story of this first expedition the name of Carson figures only formally, with "Mr." Carson substituted for the fond "Kit," and that Thomas Fitzpatrick was chosen as guide for the second expedition.

Anyway, in the midst of alarms Frémont wavered not an inch. Against the advice of the resident traders at Laramie and at Fort Platte, below, and probably of Carson (whose advice, however, does not appear to have been asked after he had made the gesture of the will), having left the two boys and one man who took his discharge, he set on for the Pass. Carson served to guide through several by-ways of the trail — ostensibly for the purpose of finding better forage.

As happened, the trip in and back to the post incurred no direct opposition from the Indians, save in words; few Indians were sighted; the chief actual peril was that when, during the return, in the Red Narrows of the Platte the rubber boat was wrecked and it crew barely escaped drowning.

At the western foot of the South Pass, Frémont faced to the north, with intent to follow the western slope of the mountain divide and turning the upper end of the range skirt the eastern slope back again, by crossing the heads of the Yellowstone. But he remembered his limiting instructions and considered also the travel-worn state of his company. Therefore, aiming for the highest peak in sight, having traversed a wildly romantic region of verdure, parks, lakes, tumbling waters, precipitous canyons and ridges, ice, flowers, and beaver sign — a region that astonished even "our guides" and was unknown, therefore, to the "wandering trappers," he sent Carson and the majority of the other men back to the camp where the reserve mule stock was pastured — and after a night's sound sleep proceeded, with Topographer Preuss, Basil Lajeunesse, Clément Lambert, and two other Frenchmen, to climb the peak.

At the summit each man, after Frémont, stood in turn upon the platform crest of this, adjudged to be the highest peak in the Rocky Mountains — a lofty solitude never before invaded by human foot. To a ramrod stuck into a fissure of the rocks Frémont slung his trail flag bearing an eagle upon a peace pipe in the field of stars, that it might briefly wave where flag had never waved before. A bee, resting for a moment on a knee of one of the men, he pressed between the leaves of a specimen book. And having overlooked the jumbled world below and made notes, he and Topographer Preuss with their squad descended from Frémont's Peak of the Wind River Range of the Wyoming Rockies; rejoined Carson and Maxwell and the others at the mule camp beside Frémont's Lake.

Accordingly Kit Carson was not to carry to Taos and the pretty ears of Josefa a story of his having climbed, with Lieutenant Frémont of the Army, the highest mountain of all the Rockies; and Lucien Maxwell himself had lost out.[276]

By Carson's own narrative:

> Fremont accomplished all that was desired of him and then we returned. Arrived Fort Laramie, sometime in September.
> During the expedition I performed the duties of guide and hunter. I, at Laramie, quit the employ of Fremont, he continuing his march for the States, taking nearly the same route as that by which he had come.
> I went to Bent's Fort in January 1843, departed for Taos. In February of same year got married to Senorita Josepha Jaramilla [Jaramillo], a daughter of Don Francisco Jaramilla [Jaramillo].

The whereabouts of the Carson retainers from Taos, during the debate at Fort Laramie and the trip out and in again, is not of official records. According to Wiggins, the party hovered about the line of march, living merrily, albeit with an eye out for Indians, while ready for an emergency summons from Kit. Of the Indian "war parties" they made light. "Only hunting parties," Wiggins asserts. The reports of the army man's rubber-boat contraption greatly amused them. Thus they put in time with profit while waiting for the prime pelts season to open. The present season was still summer.

There were contacts, however, with the Frémont camps. Bearded Sol Silver maintained, in his reminiscences, that he and Kit and Lucien Maxwell sweat and swore for three hours in essaying the squaw job of setting up a Sioux lodge obtained by Frémont from the Indians at Laramie. As narrated by Frémont, the squaw of a young Indian enlisted at the fort finally had to tackle the problem. Through her it was mastered.[277]

Carson united with his own band just in time to go on the trap line. He had his government vouchers, cashable at Laramie or any other trading post, but he could not be too well heeled for his venture with Josefa. Beaver pelts were money. The chances are that he seized opportunity to pillage those recently visited recesses of the Wind River Range where the fresh beaver sign had been so plentiful. When the lakes and streams there were closed by winter and with his party he was liable to be snowed in he traveled by easy stages to Laramie, possibly, or to St. Vrain, trapping the last of the open waters as he went. The packs could not be too heavy.

And in January he went on from Bent's Fort over to Taos and Josefa.

A page from the Marriage Records of the parish reads, in translation:

In this Church Territory of Taos, on the sixth day of February one thousand eight hundred forty-three, I the Priest in charge, D. Antonio José Martinez, having completed certain matrimonial investigations at the desire of Christopher Carson, single, legitimate son of Linsey Carson and of Rebecca Roverzon, formerly of Misuri of the North America, and resident of the town of Our Lady of Guadalupe, with María Josefa Jaramillo, single, legitimate daughter of Francisco Jaramillo and of María Polonia Vigil, she formerly of the village of Santa Cruz de la Cañada and resident of the same town of Our Lady of Guadalupe, and the banns being published in this parish of my charge three feast days *inter Missarum Solemnia* which were the 29th of last January and 2nd and 5th of the present month, and there having resulted no objection whatsoever either annulling or impeding I have married them and administered the holy sacrament *in facie Ecclæ*. Sponsors were George Bente and Maria de la Cruz Padilla, Witnesses present Juan Manuel Lucero and José María Valdez, all residents of the town of Our Lady of Guadalupe, with the others who were present, and as an act of good faith I have signed my name.   ANTO JOSE MARTINEZ[278]

By thus abandoning the domestic lodge and Indian connections and definitely tying up with white-blood culture, Kit Carson made a long step that put him ahead of many of his trail-fellows. He was well supported in his new marriage. Padre Martinez, officiating, was a power in northern New Mexico. A man of learning and active intelligence, he took part in secular affairs independently of his priestly privileges. In 1835 he had printed and issued, at Taos, the first newspaper of the province of New Mexico — *El Crepusculo* (The Dawn), of brief but lusty existence. Through his press he issued textbooks and tracts for the education of novitiates studying under him. The bloody insurrection of 1847, to oust the Americans from the province, is charged to him; but in 1849 he with Ceran St. Vrain and Antoine Leroux, the noted guide, were delegates to the organization convention at Santa Fé and in 1851 he was the president of the first assembly of the newly accredited Territory of New Mexico. His zeal in politics and his defiance of the authority of the diocese caused him to be read out of the Church, ere the close of the Fifties, and he persisted in his schisms to his death in 1867. Kit Carson, in time, was to be ranged against him.

The Jaramillos were highly connected — an elder sister of Carson's bride was the wife of Charles Bent. The Vigil family was constantly growing in influence, and was of the few book-educated Mexicans of the northern district. The head of the family, Donaciano Vigil, of Taos, had been military secretary to Governor Armijo, was now captain of the militia at Taos, and as secretary of the provisional territory would succeed, as second civil governor, the first governor, Charles Bent.

Of the witnesses there were George Bent, and José María Valdez of prominent Spanish family and destined to be colonel of New Mexican Volunteers in a companion regiment to Carson's, in the Civil War.

Señora Carson, born in March, 1828, was just rounding out her fourteenth year, and therefore was some nineteen years younger than her husband. Slim and willowy as a girl, as a woman she was slender and unusually tall, topping Carson by almost a head: "rather dark, very dark hair, large big bright eyes, very well built, graceful in every way, quite handsome, very good wife and the best of mothers," wrote her niece, Mrs. Scheurich of Taos.

"A style of beauty," observed Lewis Garrard, seeing her in Taos in April, 1847, four years after the wedding, "of the haughty, heart-breaking kind, such as would lead a man, with the glance of the eye, to risk his life for one smile. I could not but desire her acquaintance."

The Carson men declared fiesta to signalize the eventful homecoming of their chief. By the Stanley Vestal account:

Silver told my father that when Kit got back to Taos there was a great celebration, and that he (Sol) got drunk and fell off his horse, and was laid up for three days as a result of this spree. This was in January, 1843.[279]

The first child of Kit and Josefa was long in arriving, and was of short stay. It was Charles (christened for Charles Bent), born May 1, 1850, only to be taken away in the next May. But after this the household increased with gratifying regularity. There came William, 1853, named for William Bent and Carson's eldest half-brother, both; Teresina, or Teresa, 1855, of same name as that of fourteen-year-old Teresina Bent whom Carson was helping to support since the murder of her father; Christopher, Kit Jr., 1858; Charles again, 1861; Rebecca, 1864, named for Carson's mother; Stella, 1866; Josefita, little Josephine, 1868, named for her mother.

These seven children were left orphaned when in 1868 Carson died only a month after the death of Josefa his wife. A happy union of twenty-five years had been but briefly discontinued.

Chapter XXVII

Carson Makes a $300 Turn

IN the early summer of 1841, six armed companies, 270 men, Texans and recruits from the States, together with fifty traders, officials and so on, set out from Austin, the capital of the Republic of Texas, with the purpose of extending the Lone Star flag to the Rio Grande — the alleged western boundary. They believed that the New Mexicans of that part of Mexico were ripe for the change of rule. This was the famous "Santa Fé Expedition" chronicled in two volumes by Journalist George W. Kendall of the New Orleans *Picayune,* volunteer and correspondent with the column.[280]

The dispersal, capture, execution or incarceration of the armed invaders by the forces of Governor Armijo excited reprisals made in the name of Texas but committed by American free-booters as well as Texans. In April, 1843, fifteen professed Texans under one Captain John McDaniel seized the Santa Fé Trail outfit of young Don Antonio José Chavez, from Santa Fé for Independence and reduced, by reason of severe spring weather, to five servants, five mules, and one wagon conveying a quantity of bullion and a few furs. Here at the Little Arkansas, 100 miles within American territory, the Chavez outfit was plundered and Don Antonio (whose very family in New Mexico had befriended the captive Texans of 1841) was murdered in cold blood.[281]

At this time Kit Carson, having finished off his honey-moon after a fashion, was about starting from Bent's Fort as hunter with a Bent, St. Vrain & Co. goods caravan for Missouri. Josefa would do well left to the ministrations of her relatives in Taos, but it behooved him to be earning wages again, for he was a husband with a station to maintain among people of quality. The quips and grins of his Taos *compañeros* and the comfort of the domestic pipe smoked in the sunshine beside his threshold alike had staled. The foot-loose Dick Owens, now of Taos, a kindred spirit, had engaged for the same caravan to the States.

Moreover it was another spring. Maxwell was in Missouri — whether word from him to Taos broke out the news that Lieutenant Frémont had been scheduled for a second exploring trip, whether the news was carried through the channel of Bent's Fort as a budget of Ceran St. Vrain's or the Bents', Charles Bent being Carson's brother-in-law; whether the project had been spoken of (as Oliver Wiggins declares it had) at the close of the first expedition; and, indeed, whether Kit Carson was at all informed upon this second venture, is a question open to discussion.

There is no official statement that Frémont had figured upon the services again, so soon, of Carson for whom Josefa had been waiting. But the caravan from Bent's should arrive at the Missouri about the time when, conceivably, another expedition was mustering there; or, encouraged by reports met along the way, a man could spurt ahead or across country. That the glamor of Frémont and $100 a month invested Kit Carson is supported by the fact that he was quick to throw in with his "accidentally" refound commander.

During this spring Colonel Jacob Snively, assumed to hold a Texas commission, was raising a regiment of 800 men to prey upon Mexico's Santa Fé Trail commerce until Mexico should cry quits with the Texas Republic. One Colonel Warfield, displaying a commission from President Sam Houston himself, had been assisting by levies made in the far north of the trading posts along the South Platte east of the foothills — at Fort Lancaster, ten miles above Fort St. Vrain, had enlisted, in February, the misdirected zeal and presence of Rufus B. Sage, still pursuing his *Wild Scenes* theme.

The muster was known to Governor Armijo in Santa Fé. There should have been rumors of it in Taos and at Bent's Fort and along the Trail. The proposed business had ugly angles to it, for while it struck at Mexican commerce it hit American commerce also; the two were inseparable, especially since American goods in American wagons were traveling with Mexican trains. Moreover, Texas had ambitions to treat for this Santa Fé and Chihuahua trade. And furthermore, once let the Tejano and Mejicano nations war along the Trail, then scalps and plunder would summon the gleeful Comanches, Apaches, Kiowas, Cheyennes, Arapahos, Spanish or Southern Utes, and what not?

When in May the Bent-St. Vrain caravan toiled into Walnut Creek, 250 miles from Bent's Fort, here were encamped the dragoons detachment of Captain Philip St. George Cooke, on regulation escort duty, as far as the crossing of the Arkansas, with the first spring caravan for Santa Fé — bearing the trading proceeds from the last fall caravan for the States as well as consignments to the Mexican market. "The train of Armijo and several traders . . . a great number of wagons and in the party there was about one hundred men — Mexicans and Americans," Carson says. But as of record, sixty wagons, of which twelve or fifteen were American owned, and "seventy-five thousand weight of merchandise."

Captain Cooke was even-minded so far as a dragoon could be when anchored to the desert trail by a ball-and-chain appendage in guise of stolid ox teams and timorous freighters, but he reported that his caravan convoy was in a flutter. At the Little Arkansas, three marches to rear, a Mexican trading outfit had been robbed, burned, destroyed — the cold and bloody body of its owner, Don Antonio Chavez of Santa Fé, had been found cast into a ravine. Pirates' work! The crossing of the Arkansas was only 150 miles before, a large band of desperadoes from Texas were reported in waiting there upon the Mexican side of the border, he would assure the caravan of safety while it was upon American soil but the caravan had stayed the order of its going until the road to Santa Fé itself should have been opened by Governor Armijo.

A courier was needed, to inform Armijo of the straits of his caravan and bring back the guaranty that a strong Mexican escort should march to the border without delay; else, as Captain Cooke feared, he and his squadron of yellow-legs would be rationed on poor water and worse whisky for the rest of the summer while the wagon train balked at the crossing.

Carson rode on to the camp of the wagon train. He was his

own recommendation. "Hello, Kit! *Cómo 'stá,* Don Keet? We're in a scrape, Kit — we hear there's a thousand *bandoleros Tejanos* waiting to murder every one of us, 't other side the river; the same as murdered Chavez. *Sí, los mismos, señor — los malditos Tejanos, demonios sin lastima!"* Said a booted teamster, undertone, with jerk of head: "You know these *pelados* won't fight, but we who *kin* fight won't stand by an' see 'em butchered, so we likely all will lose our ha'r." Said the grave Mexican wagon-master, with a beck: "Could you take word of us to Santa Fé and Don Manuel the governor? *Por amor de Dios, señor!"*

Carson phlegmatically reckoned he could.

"We will pay you $300 gold."

Carson reckoned he would, if his train captain would let him off.

Carson luck! Frémont (if there were a Frémont) could wait. Three hundred dollars in pocket — full three months' wages at one stroke, a surprise for Josefa, a coup notched in the score of law and order: all by the mere ride of a few hundred miles! Not that he was fond of favoring Armijo who was in no great favor on either side of the border, nor that he, and a heap more, Americans and natives both, in Taos, would be sorry were all New Mexico taken over by Americans under any white man's flag; but these fellows weren't real Texans in the main — they'd been hired from everywhere, and these attacks upon wagon trains were like to turn into an Injun warfare that respected the rights of nobody.

This episode of Carson and the wagon train is here touched up with fancy. He himself says only, in his dictated *Own Story:*

> I was spoken to in regard of carrying the letter to Armijo in Santa Fé. They offered $300.00 for the performance of the duty. I agreed to carry it. I left the train and started for Taos.

With his $300, and the dispatch to Governor Armijo, and Dick Owens as company, he rode back to Bent's, 250 miles — thus side-stepping the Texans and the Cimarron trail. From Bent's it was some 250 miles over to Taos by the Taos Trail.

William Bent said that a big band of Utes were somewhere off yonder, primed for trouble; if they did not strike the kind they wanted, in shape of plains Injuns, they were liable to take whatever offered. Their hearts were bad. He lent Carson his best racer as a led-horse. Dick Owens stayed at the fort. A man with an extra mount is better off with only himself to tend to.

Carson found the fresh Indian sign, scouted the Ute camp, hid out and circuited it in the night. Reached Taos, turned over his dispatch for the *alcalde* to forward to Santa Fé by open road, and had four days with Josefa.

But Taos was in a fever. A party of the Texans had surprised a camp of Mexican soldiery holding the Santa Fé Trail at Mora village in the southeast — had killed, dispersed and plundered, and left the town terrified; but the soldiers had rallied, pursued, and by another surprise had set the Texans afoot. Captain Ventura Lobato had marched from Taos with militia and Pueblo Indians to scout the Texans at the Arkansas while Armijo and an army were advancing — he had been driven back with loss and there was mourning and wrath in Taos. The Pueblos who had hated the governor and had not wished to fight the Texans their brothers in hate had been put in the van. Now they were wailing their dead and were threatening the lives of all the Mexicans and Americans in Taos.

And Armijo with his army of 600 had retreated to Santa Fé.

This shedding of New Mexican blood white and red in the cause of Texas lost that cause in New Mexico. One might say that here began a feud which extended to the Civil War — which strongly influenced New Mexico for the Union by enthusing its native people, under Kit Carson and others, to face the Texas Confederates bent upon invading from the south.

Kit Carson in Taos received the Armijo dispatch for the wagon train; started back with it and with a Mexican companion by the Bent's Fort trail again, and when half way sighted and was sighted by the Utes.

The Mexican said: "You have a good horse. Mount him and

run. They can't catch you. I will stay. I don't think they will
hurt me, but they will kill you." Sol Silver, in his transmitted
reminiscences before cited, claims this act of cavalier for himself; Carson's official biography speaks of a Mexican boy, his
original dictation speaks of "this man." He was moved to follow the advice but changed his mind. "No; if either of us goes
under we'll both go under but we 'll take a couple of scalps
with us." The episode calls for no heroics; a white man could
scarcely do otherwise.

The Utes came on rapidly. An old chief in advance, grin-
ning, made the feint of shaking Carson's hand but at the same
time clutched his rifle. They two "tussled" for that, until with
a blow Carson wrested it free. The chief's young men arrived
en masse; Carson and his Mexican sat knee to knee, facing in
oposite directions, with guns cocked, while for thirty minutes
the jostling, jabbering, menacefully gesturing Indians tried to
take them at disadvantage. As Carson relates in his life story:

Some would ride about us examining their guns, open their pans, knock
the priming of their rifles and many other manouvers endeavoring to
frighten us or to induce us to change our positions, that they might fire
and kill us before we could return the fire. We watched them closely,
determined that the first that would raise his gun should be shot.

The reds gave up and made off. The two express riders lost
no time in taking to the trail again. At Bent's Fort that trail
ended, for Armijo's dispatch of instructions to the caravan was
a dead letter document. The Cimarron trail to Santa Fé was
open. The train had crossed the river border and was upon its
further way. Captain Cooke and his dragoons had found a part
of the Texans on the United States side, had arrested the whole
outfit, less than 200, taken their arms and sent them to the
right-about. No thanks to Governor Armijo, however.

Carson luck again! For behold:

A few days before my arrival at the Fort Frémont had passed. He had
gone about seventy-five miles. I wished to see him and started for his
camp. My object was not to seek employment. I only thought that I

would ride to his camp, have a talk and then return. But, when Fremont saw me again and requested me to join him, I could not refuse and again entered his employ as guide and hunter.

Apparently by this, another happy accident like that of the meeting upon the steamboat out of St. Louis the year before, Kit Carson joined the adventuring John Charles Frémont at El Pueblo settlement of white and breed hunters at the mouth of Fountain Creek seventy-five miles up the Arkansas from Bent's Fort. But Frémont had not come to the settlement from the east; he had come down from the South Platte in the north — he had passed Bent's Fort only as he "passed" it when he was traveling out by a route from the Missouri taking him 150 miles north of the fort.

From Fort St. Vrain, some forty miles north of present Denver, on July 6 he had started Lucien Maxwell to Taos for mules and had followed in order to meet him, returning, at the Fountain Creek pueblo on the Arkansas. Maxwell, Taos bound, made the pueblo July 9; Frémont reached it at noon, July 14 — and "had here the satisfaction to meet our good buffalo hunter of 1842, Christopher Carson, whose services I considered myself fortunate to secure again."

According to the Peters biography of Kit Carson, Carson was at least five days in returning from Taos to Bent's Fort; he may have been seven. He stopped at the fort, then rode the seventy-five miles up the Arkansas to find Frémont; is reported by Frémont between noon of July 14 and the morning of July 16. The coincidence of time and place is remarkable. Lucien Maxwell had passed through the pueblo on July 9, on his way to Taos. He might easily have taken word to Bent's Fort of Frémont's presence in the country — if he went by way of the fort — in time for Carson to get the information. Or somebody from the pueblo may have notified the fort. Five days, apparently, intervened between the day Maxwell, riding from Frémont, reached the pueblo, and Carson, seeking Frémont, found him there. The round distance of 150 miles could have been readily covered within that period.

Maxwell however need not have gone by way of Bent's Fort. He would strike the mountain branch of the Santa Fé Trail at present Trinidad south of El Pueblo (present Pueblo city), and by that cut out the Bent's Fort leg.

Further discussion of Kit Carson's extraordinary prevision is provoked by the Oliver Wiggins statement that the Carson men under Ike Chamberlain joined the Frémont party on July 4, at Fort St. Vrain — which was the day Frémont reached the post.

Chamberlain, the lieutenant under Carson, started for the fort in time to reach there July 4, and that very day something happened that resulted in a serious breach between the Carson and Fremont parties. St. Vrain's people, assisted by the Fremont men, were having a celebration. It had been a long time between Fourth of July celebrations with us fellows out on the plains, and we wanted to get in on a little of the fun. I was out with the horses some distance from the fort, and a sergeant of the Fremont company was in charge. I insisted upon going to the fort, and Pat White, the sergeant, refused permission . . . Pat thought he was physically capable of making me submit to his orders, but when I went into the fort I asked them to send a wagon out after the sergeant, while I enjoyed the fun.[282]

Maxwell had ridden on from the pueblo, with two men, for Taos, all unaware that the Spanish Utes were between him and his goal and that in Taos the Pueblos, roused by the sacrifice of their warriors in the battle with the Texans, had proclaimed for vengeance upon the "foreigner" residents and had compelled his own father-in-law, Don Carlos Beaubien, to flee (as Frémont heard) to Santa Fé. Whether Carson brought the Taos news to the pueblo is not stated.

In any event he knew conditions. He found the pueblo and Frémont alarmed lest Maxwell should be waylaid by the Utes — the same Utes who had tried out him, himself. And there were the reports of the Taos uprising. But he evidently was on fire to enlist again with Frémont — maybe he had engaged so to do, maybe he was making opportunity. Regardless of Maxwell's problem (but Maxwell was now either definitely dead or definitely alive) and of the troubles in Taos where he had left his wife of six months, he became a Frémont man pledged to a long journey — how long, no one might say.

Frémont was convinced that owing to the disturbances he could get no mules or other trail munitions from Taos — and especially from Beaubien, whom Maxwell was to solicit. Therefore Carson was sent back to Bent's Fort with a requisition upon it. From Bent's he was to cross country northward and rejoin Frémont at St. Vrain's. At Bent's he may have left word for Josefa to be notified not to expect him home for some time — granted that she had not already bade him a resigned *"A Dios."* The $300 in gold would keep her from want, and she had relatives and friends to keep her in spirits. Her husband Kit was gone from her a year. During that time she heard from him only once; he was at Fort Hall and setting onward for the Columbia.[283]

Carson maintained his remarkable celerity. Despatched "immediately," he left the pueblo for Bent's again, presumably on the 15th, and had been two days at Fort St. Vrain, forty miles north of Denver, when Frémont arrived there, July 23. That bespoke a willing spirit. To quote Theodore Talbot, writing in his journal at Fort St. Vrain:

Fri. July 21st. Fitz and Gilpin went up to Lupton's, returning with Christopher Carson, Mr. Fremont's guide last year, who he had again engaged in capacity of Hunter. He brought nine mules for Mr. Fremont, bought at Bent & St. Vrain's Fort on the Arkansas R.[284]

Chapter XXVIII

On the Trail with Frémont — 1843-1844

FREMONT's second expedition again was one, Senator Benton alleged, in which the administration at Washington was entitled only to the credit of compliance, not to any credit of origination. It was authorized by the War Department to pursue on the west side of the Rockies, in British-American joint territory, the same objects that had been pursued on the east side, in American territory, by the first expedition; or, technically, "to connect the reconnoisance of 1842 with the surveys of Commander Wilkes on the coast of the Pacific Ocean, so as to give a connected survey of the interior of our continent." It is know, officially, as the "Exploring Expedition to Oregon and North California, in the years 1843-44." Practically, it exceeded its province rather more than even enterprising Frémont could have forseen. It not only embraced the Mexican territory of Utah, western Nevada, and California, colored with romance the Salt Lake and the contrasting features of the Great Basin, but achieved a dramatic climax by its passage across the snow mountains into the spring land of California where all nature smiled and life apparently was so easy.

Oregon received the due of Oregon, but California was made news. In its reported aspects it was as much news to the general public, and to Washington also, as the Great American Desert of the Indian Country between the Missouri and the mountains was in its aspects of fertility as reported by the first expedition. And it was further away — therefore the more inviting.

"His first expedition barely finished, Mr. Frémont sought and obtained orders for a second one," Senator Benton informed his public. The Oregon machine worked smoothly, but how early in the game this second expedition was contemplated is not of definite record. Frémont says only, in his *Memoirs* of more than forty years later, when speaking of Senator Linn's endorsement of the report of the first expedition: "In the meantime the second expedition had been planned."

The second expedition left the Kaw, or Kansas (Westport) Landing, the foundation of Kansas City, May 29, 1843, and returned there July 31, 1844. Frémont broke camp before-time, hastened by cryptic orders from Mrs. Frémont, who had opened a dispatch from his corps commander directing him to return to Washington and explain why he was taking a twelve-pounder cannon upon a strictly scientific survey into territory not yet within the limits of the United States. The howitzer had been supplied, in addition to patent small-arms, as a weapon of defense against hostile Indians, by Colonel Stephen Watts Kearny, commanding the Third Military Division, from the Government arsenal at St. Louis.

Colonel J. J. Abert, chief of the Topographical Corps, may rightly have feared that a field-piece in the train of Lieutenant Frémont might impose unwarranted military power upon a party committed to civil functions. Mrs. Frémont (and her father the senator) were convinced that the lieutenant was being recalled in favor of some West Pointer slated for the glory of leadership. West Point jealousy was an abiding obsession with Senator Benton. He cherished a feud with the Military Academy and its graduates — held himself to be the equal of any Regular Army professional and would have promoted himself over either General Scott or General Taylor in field command in the war with Mexico.[285]

Lieutenant Frémont got away with his howitzer, only to abandon it during the winter ascent of the Sierra Nevada. It lay crippled and mute there among the foothill piñon ridges southeast of Lake Tahoe of the Nevada-California border for half a dozen years — a prodigy to the Diggers and the jackrabbits.

By his adding this cannon without authority from the War Department Lieutenant Frémont made Colonel Kearny subject to reprimand. By inciting the lieutenant to start before he was prepared to start, and to put himself out of reach of his superiors, without his knowing the reason therefor, his mentors did him an unkind turn. Senator Benton asserts that Frémont knew nothing of the howitzer query until his return from the expedition. Nevertheless he must have known that he was being encouraged to disregard new orders.

The cannon episode did not bend the course of history. Historically it was of small importance. Frémont took the piece, but he would have fared as well, or better, without it. That it saved his party in the one really threatened Indian attack is debatable. The party were prepared for battle, with their animals herded in; had Carson and other men of experience, and were equipped with the Hall breech-loading rifled carbines — flint-locks, to be sure, but using a ready ball-and-powder paper cartridge.

Writers have said that by his flight from orders Frémont probably averted "early disaster" from the expedition. The disaster, however, if any, would have been that to his own ambitions and to the supporting plans of his political backers. The expedition was his only by favor, as a government employe. Had he been actually relieved, another officer would have carried out the government orders — as other officers did in subsequent explorations. As to disaster, again, the expedition as conducted by him was not, in practical results, history making. The tide of westward emigration had definitely set in. He opened no trail for that. His voluntary or privately directed excursions had little bearing upon the National future save that they incidentally (and mistakenly) brought the Salt Lake into the Mormon horizon. His trespass upon California soil did not produce the conquest, which was fore-ordained; and while it freshened the public interest in California, that interest was already a potential factor in the shaping of destined events.

The alleged disaster was shelved only to incubate a greater real disaster — one to himself after all. When he undertook insubordination upon his own responsibility, his previous record was in evidence against him if it were needed for the purpose.

In formally applying to Colonel Kearny for the howitzer issue along with other munitions "required May 8," Frémont stated that the hostile nature of the Indians upon the projected route required that the party "be furnished with every means of defence which may conduce to its safety." He must have had a conversation with Colonel Kearny, for the colonel, in ordering the issue to be made, by Captain William C. Bell, commanding at the St. Louis Arsenal, referred to the fact that Lieutenant Frémont was to leave tomorrow, "and therefore has not the time to hear from Washington, in reply to an application for arms and ammunition." Kearny, a friend of Senator Benton and of the Brant family in St. Louis with whom the Bentons and Frémont were intimate, and therefore disposed to favor Frémont, assumed the whole responsibility for the issuance of the requisition. Frémont obtained the howitzer, "1 carriage complete with harness, 500 pounds of artillery ammunition, 200 tubes filled."

As may be seen in the documents upon exhibit in the *Appendix* to this work the business was not lightly dismissed at Washington. It even came up before the Senate. Frémont had gone far beyond reach, but he had been reprimanded for the high-pressure methods that he had employed in obtaining the howitzer, and Colonel Kearny and Captain Bell had been reprimanded for issuing the howitzer. The small arms obtained — 4 pistols with 2 pairs holsters, 33 carbines, with 5 kegs rifle powder — were also short- order measures, but were allowable.

In their waywardness John C. Frémont and George A. Custer were much alike. In their idolatry of their captains who could do no wrong Jessie Benton Frémont and Elizabeth Bacon Custer were one person. But Frémont defying the authority of General Kearny, his superior, in conquested California, and General Custer taking to himself the prospective round-up of the Sioux and Cheyennes on the Little Big Horn — there they are.

The effect of the headstrong Frémont upon Kit Carson was tempered by Carson's habitual repression and self discipline.

It is not to be said that Carson and the others in the second
expedition knew that the howitzer was contraband, but there
must have been discussions regarding that sudden march beyond the settled frontier, following the receipt by Frémont of
the courier dispatch from St. Louis. They all were the kind of
men to admire independent action. When time came, Carson
himself was minded to flout the orders of Frémont's superior
officer by deserting in the night.

Lieutenant Frémont had started with a shortage of animals.
By this also he courted disaster while avoiding other disaster.
His force was larger than that of 1842, listing as it did thirty-
nine men — the majority of the employes being, as before, Missouri and Canadian French, but the full roll including names
such as Patrick White, two Campbells, Henry Lee, and so on.
Lucien Maxwell, about to return to Taos from Missouri, joined
the party at the Kaw Landing camp. He found there comrades
from the first expedition. But Thomas Fitzpatrick and not Kit
Carson was the guide at hand. There were several supernumeraries, bound across continent; among them a young
man, Frémont's peer in brilliancy and of greater military en-
dowments but with his future yet in shadow. This was William Gilpin, twenty years of age, one-time page to Andrew
Jackson, at twelve a cadet (for less than a year) at West Point,
when fourteen a second lieutenant of dragoons in the Semi-
nole War, 1836; unsuccessful applicant, 1838, for assignment
to lead a government exploring party to the Columbia; editor
of the Missouri *Argus,* St. Louis — a Benton paper, secretary
of the Missouri General Assembly and friend in the Benton
family; soon now to be major and lieutenant colonel of Missouri Volunteers in the war with Mexico, 1846, and as sole
supporter of Abraham Lincoln in Jackson County, Missouri,
1860, appointed first governor of Colorado Territory, 1861,
there to serve in holding the West in the Union. Of William
Gilpin, not second to even the Old Roman as a champion of
National manifest destiny, much is still to be written. Neither
Senator Benton in his manifestos nor Frémont in his *Report*

and *Memoirs* give him his character as an attaché of the expedition.[286]

"The camp equipage and provisions were transported in twelve carts, drawn each by two mules; and a light covered wagon, mounted on good springs, had been provided for the safer carriage of the instruments." Emboldened by the gusto with which Frémont's explorations were being hailed, and summoned to the march by the energetic Dr. Marcus Whitman, this spring there had gathered upon the Missouri border the largest muster, to date, of emigrants for Oregon. At Elm Grove station on the trail the Frémont company found the camp of J. B. Chiles and others, including women and children, with not Oregon but Alta California as their goal.

The Chiles wagons were freighted "with goods, furniture, and farming utensils, containing among other things an entire set of machinery for a mill which Mr. Childs [Chiles] designed erecting on the waters of the Sacramento River." When in March of the next year the Frémont company straggled down to the Sacramento, the emigrant company had been long arrived and Chiles was settled upon a farm.

Fitzpatrick and Carson were not the guides, this year, for Frémont upon the Overland Trail. The guide was the dust from the wheels of the groaning wagons, the smoke and the ashes of the wayside camps, and the scars in the rocks and sage.

At Fort St. Vrain, reached in the first week of July, Frémont found no replacement of animals. He had bargained without his hostage. He left Fitzpatrick and the baggage here while Lucien Maxwell posted south to get mules at Taos and he followed after to meet Maxwell, returning, at the pueblo on the Arkansas.

Here Kit Carson appeared. Here was encountered another stalemate: Maxwell might not be able to produce the mules. Carson confidently rode back to Bent's Fort to solicit the aid of the Bents. Delaying not for word from Maxwell, Frémont left instructions for him to come on (if he came at all) to Fort St. Vrain, within time limit of ten days; and with detour to inspect the Boiling Springs of Colorado's Manitou he himself, with his detachment, put into St. Vrain again on the seventh day. "My good and reliable friend, Kit Carson," already was there, "with ten good mules, with the necessary pack saddles." Fitzpatrick was directed to take the main baggage and the major portion of the company, and by way of Fort Laramie proceed to rendezvous at Fort Hall. With him there went a recruit of much value: Alexander Godey, known as a good hunter, and admitted to be "in courage and professional skill a formidable rival to Carson." On the next expedition Richard Owens would complete the trio of experts in the Frémont service.

There is no further mention of Maxwell; he had not appeared by the morning of July 26 — Frémont had waited two days, he says, in order to rest his animals, and in the afternoon of July 26 he pulled lodge stakes for Oregon.

His party of thirteen employes were picked for dependability and comradeship. Topographer Preuss, Basil Lajeunesse and his brother François, and Kit Carson were among them. The howitzer which had trundled with him to the Arkansas trundled with him and his thirteen onward into the mountains. Throughout the journey to the point of its abandonment it did not fire a hostile shot, but it paid for itself in lending morale.

Frémont had planned to cut northwest through the mountains, from Fort St. Vrain, and strike the Green River west of the South Pass; thence extend his first survey, which had terminated there, to the Columbia at a point where the Commodore Wilkes survey of the Oregon coast had confined itself. He hoped to find, on the way to the Green and the Oregon Trail, passes for wheeled vehicles which would provide a new road across the divide, adapted for emigrants through the central plains.

Nobody at St. Vrain's knew of such passes. Even Kit Carson and Thomas Fitzpatrick and Alex Godey apparently were dumb on the subject. Or if they did deliver opinions, Frémont reserved his own judgment for his own experience. That was

proper, since he was the final authority and was committed to
make his reports from first-hand data; but nevertheless Carson — and for that matter Marcellin St. Vrain with his constantly out-going and in-coming trappers and Indians — should
have had a good idea of the character of this mountain region
of central north Colorado, abutting on the famed New Park
or Bull Pen on the west and the Laramie Plains on the north.

On the way in Carson hunted assiduously, and with fair
success. His dozen retainers from Taos, commanded by Ike
Chamberlain, hunted on their own hook, according to Oliver
Wiggins, and had a royal good time. The instruments carriage
and the howitzer met with difficulties in the wildly rough
country, but the cannon, hastily swung into battery, broke an
Indian charge and thus early won respect. Frémont was enabled to cite that his party, unsupported, might not have withstood this sudden charge by greedy Arapahos and Cheyennes
returning from defeat by the Snakes.

In later day the Overland Stage from Denver to Salt Lake,
by way of Fort Collins, the Medicine Bow mountains, and
Bridger's Pass, approximated the route that Frémont sought to
open, but he was forced into the north short of his goal, and
emerged upon the Sweetwater east of the South Pass.

At the Sweetwater he now found a "broad, smooth highway,
where the numerous heavy wagons of the emigrants had entirely beaten and crushed the artemesia [sage]." The welcomed
trail, comparatively smooth to the battered hoofs of the animals, was followed over the South Pass and down, and to the
valley of the Bear River. Fitzpatrick would be waiting at Fort
Hall, and the Columbia waited far beyond; the summer was
waning and Frémont had told his wife that he would be home
in eight months: but the mysterious Great Salt Lake beckoned
in the hazed southwest.

"Its islands had never been visited; and none were to be
found who had entirely made the circuit of its shores. . . . It
was generally supposed that it had no visible outlet; but among
the trappers, including those in my own camp, were many

who believed that somewhere on its surface was a terrible whirlpool, through which its waters found their way to the ocean by some subterranean communication." This, from the official report by Frémont; and since the romance of that fabled inland sea had colored "our desultory conversations around the fires at night," and scientific observations of the locality were lacking, he seized the opportunity to relieve his excited mind and set doubts at rest.

It was not that the existence of the lake needed to be established. Carson would tell him that Jim Bridger had viewed it and tasted it eighteen years back — that trappers in a bull boat had paddled in a circuit of its waters and that Joe Walker had marched part way around it. But as Frémont comments in his excuses for making the side trip, the previous white men at the lake had been seeking beaver, and were "caring very little for geography."

The side trip was not made through any sudden impulse of Frémont's. In the *Frémont MSS* in the Bancroft Library of the University of California Mrs. Frémont characterizes Colonel J. J. Abert, chief of the Topographical Corps, as "a placid, indolent man," thereby a person of small imagination. It would seem that no revised map of the western interior beyond the Utah mountains was examined for the information of either Abert or Frémont — it is certain that the Bonneville map of the basin country and the still better Albert Gallatin map to which Jedediah S. Smith contributed, were not examined by anybody interested in the projected expedition, else Frémont would not have chased the mirage of that waterway flowing from the Salt Lake region into the Pacific Ocean. The values of this legendary desert salt lake sequestered off the line of overland travel should have appealed to Colonel Abert in the line of scientific phenomena, but were not of the spirit of those orders for a practical continuance of the reconnoissance of 1842 "so as to give a connected survey of the interior of our continent."[287]

This "interior of our continent," however, was a broad expanse to the more imaginative Senator Benton, Senator Linn, and Lieutenant Frémont their agent. Nothing in the practicable territory of Mexican or British and American tenancy, there west of the Rocky Mountains, was without interest. And that Frémont was given wide latitude in his private instructions is evidenced by the fact that he again was equipped with a rubber boat. A boat would be necessary for an exploration of the great lake, and should come in handy were a river route from the Great Basin to the Pacific Ocean developed.

With the keen enthusiasm of a Balboa (as he says), from a butte above the débouchment of Weber's Fork Frémont gazed, in the morning of September 6, upon the glistening waters of the sluggishly rolling lake. Carson was there beside him. He had been detached from the march in order to obtain provisions at Fort Hall, but had returned in time to miss nothing. It is doubtful if he had ever before seen the lake — "the Inland Sea, stretching in still and solitary grandeur far beyond the limit of our vision." There should have been a studious, calculating gleam in his usually mild blue eyes as he squinted at the shore-line and those distant islands rearing darkly above the immutable surface.

The islands, perhaps rocky and bare, perhaps delightfully wooded and possessed by strange fur and feather, perhaps the secure citadels of an unknown, gigantic lake tribe whose immense cut timbers (by trapper legend) occasionally drifted ashore, were to be investigated.

Considerable manoeuvering was required before the embarkment for the first voyage. Camp was pitched beside the Weber Fork, a log corral for the animals and a small fort for the camp keepers were erected. The rubber boat was unpacked, reinforced with patches and seam cement — and pronounced to be a "possible" although inferior to the boat wrecked in the Platte rapids. But there had been no time to inspect it before that hurried take-off from the out-fitting camp.

On September 8 the boat was launched for the voyage down the Weber to the lake. This night in camp shortly back from the lake the men's dreams were bad medicine — the day dawned with evil in the air. Carson himself was no less superstitious than his mountain contemporaries, whether white or red. By report he would not (if he could avoid it) start an enterprise on Friday, and when he had failed to score with a fair shot at standing game he would not try again. The "medicine" was against him.

On the morning of September 9, 1843, the rubber boat was dragged through the deep ooze and floated into soundings. With its captain and crew — John C. Frémont the army man, Kit Carson the mountain-man, Preuss the German draughtsman, Basil Lajeunesse and Baptiste Bernier the voyageur trappers — it cleared away for the nearest island. Another Columbus caravel, it. Even the steady Carson, out of his element here, betrayed nervousness. As Frémont narrates for the conception of Washington:

"Captain," said Carson, who for some time had been looking suspiciously at some whitening appearance outside the nearest islands, "what are those yonder?—won't you just take a look with the glass?" We ceased paddling for a moment, and found them to be the caps of the waves that were beginning to break under the force of a strong breeze that was coming up the lake.

No other portents were encountered. The set of the strong lake current bore to no whirlpool, after all. Whitely encrusted with salt from the spray, they made landing upon the broad beach of the rugged silent island. After a survey from the highest peak, and a night's stay upon the island, whose haunted solitude undoubtedly was, on this September day, 1843, for the first time broken by "the cheerful sound of human voices," the adventurers returned to the mainland. Carson dramatically relates in his *Own Story:*

We ascended the mountain and under [a] shelving rock cut a large cross which is there to this day.

Next morning started back. Had not left the island more than a league when the clouds commenced gathering for a storm. Our boat leaking wind kept one man continually employed at the bellows. Fremont directed us to pull for our lives, if we do not arrive on shore before the storm commenced we will surely all perish. We done our best and arrived in time to save ourselves. We had not more than landed when the storm commenced and in [an] hour the waters had risen eight or ten feet.

The "bad medicine" dreams almost came true.

Frémont named the island (which Kit Carson says was fifteen miles out, a distance reduced to ten from the nearest shore line) Disappointment Island, by reason of its barrenness. The early Mormons named it Castle Island. Captain Howard Stansbury, of the Government exploring party of 1849-50, named it Frémont's Island. He found the cross chiseled into a rock-face of the summit; but the brass cap of the telescope, accidentally left upon the summit by Frémont, had of course vanished — probably had been soon dislodged by one of the visiting magpies that Frémont noted.

Time pressed. The genii of the lake had been roused. The lake had been scientifically located, its aspects remarked, but the circuit of it by land or water had to be left to future explorers. Vastly taken with the fertile bottoms of the Bear, Frémont led the march northward to Fort Hall beside the Snake.

It was now late in September, and very stormy, with rain and snow. According to the Wiggins narration, when the whole company had made rendezvous at Fort Hall and the onward march clear to the coast was still the prospect the Carson contingent from Taos balked.

Several of them had been to the westward, and they knew what a tough trail that was, down the Snake; and that the desolation would be heightened by the bleak weather. California, it appears, was mentioned; and this made matters worse, for the California Sierra divide had been a spectre ever since the Jedediah Smith and Joe Walker experiences with it. Smith had recoiled from the snow, in spring; had lost a lot of horses. The Walker party, in the fall of 1833, had been twenty-three days fighting over from the desert.

Wiggins asserts that the Carson men told Frémont they would continue with him and Kit if he would winter at Walla Walla and postpone further exploration until spring. As for

California, at this juncture, "the nervy youngster was told by the mountaineers in the party that to be caught in the passes with sixty or seventy feet of snow to block the way would be certain death." Carson, it is stated, was somewhat dubious, himself; but he directed the men to do as they pleased — he was going on with the lieutenant.

However, Fremont placed us under arrest, as a matter of form, allowing us to retain our arms. The Irish sergeant with whom I had been unpleasantly mixed up early in the year was in charge of the party, and we were sent on ahead. A particularly rocky cut caused a hurried order from the explorer to the prisoners to return and assist in clearing a passageway for the wagons, and we sent back a very saucy answer. When the messenger returned, full of wrath, our men were far up the mountains in another trail, going faster all the time, and with the helpless Irishman, whom we all hated, trying to hustle along and keep track of his prisoners.

The "sergeant," Patrick White, abandoned the long-winded mountain-men as impossible charges and rejoined the main command. As for the Taosans, "it broke us all up to leave Kit to the whims of Frémont, but we knew our traveling with the Frémont party was all off, and we started back alone." Blankets and a few supplies were obtained at Fort Hall. Taos was not reached until January, and if Josefa heard at all from Kit, she heard then.

Adventure attended the home trail. On the Sweetwater, while the party were divided and were hunting in two squads, the Sioux took toll of them. DeBleury, in the advance squad of six, was killed; the Wiggins squad of five met his runaway horse, with bloody saddle, galloping up the defile, and lying in ambush killed the five on-coming Indians.[288]

The onward-bound expedition — the van commanded by Frémont and guided by Carson, the rear in the hands of Thomas Fitzpatrick — marched along the Oregon Trail down the Snake; passed more emigrants and noted where at Fall Creek — a short distance east of the Raft River of Idaho — there branched to the southwest a fresh wagon trail: the trail left by the main Chiles company for California, piloted now by the veteran Joe Walker.

Twenty miles west of Raft River, or seventy west of Fort Hall, the advance camped at Swamp Creek, central southern Idaho. "Returning with a small party in a starving condition from the westward 12 or 14 years since, Carson had met here three or four buffalo bulls, two of which were killed." Carson may have referred to his trip under Thomas McKay of the Hudson's Bay Company out of Fort Hall and into the Mary's River country with circuit back by way of the Snake. But if Frémont quoted him correctly Carson erred in point of time, for he was not in the mountains in 1829 and in 1831 had only just entered them, to spend the late fall and the winter on the Salmon, far to the north.

At the Dalles of the Columbia Fitzpatrick was still in the rear. Frémont here embarked in a canoe for Fort Vancouver down near the mouth of the river. "In charge of the party which was to remain at the Dalles I left Carson, with instructions to occupy the people in making pack saddles and refitting their equipment." On November 7 Frémont called upon Governor McLoughlin at Vancouver, "who received me with the courtesy and hospitality for which he had been eminently distinguished."

This completed the cross-country survey as ordered. Lieutenant Frémont was officially expected to seek his station. "He might then have returned upon his tracks, or been brought home by sea, or hunted the most pleasant path for getting back," Senator Benton proclaimed; "and if he had been routine officer, satisfied with fulfilling an order, he would have done so."

Life would possibly have flowed more smoothly for Frémont had he been more of a routine officer, and he would have been spared resentment and humiliation. But he would have been less of a man. For political ends he was styled the Pathfinder. The paths that he actually found were of scant public utility and were bettered by other paths. He was however a Pathseeker, and there can be no quibbles as to the inspirational values, to the common mind, of his gallant initiative. For Frémont testified to the fact that things could be done.

The matter of returning, in winter, by the trail of the Snake and the South Pass presented a problem, but nothing to daunt Frémont had he been minded to tackle it. On the other hand he now had been farther into the northwest than Kit Carson and even Thomas Fitzpatrick, who in 1841 had guided the Father DeSmet party down the lower Snake; had personally inspected the route from Fort Hall and tabulated it; and back-tracking through country already covered would be time and efforts wasted.

The Great Basin between the Salt Lake and the California Sierra haunted Frémont. In the words of Senator Benton: "All that vast region, more than seven hundred miles square — equal to a great kingdom in Europe — was an unknown land — a sealed book, which he longed to open and read." Senator Benton and his expansionist colleagues had some curiosity as to that region, themselves.

Frémont fostered the idea, fathered by the Benton circle, of a march southeast through southeastern Oregon and central Nevada, from the lower Columbia to the Rio Colorado of the present Nevada-Arizona line. By that to cleave the heart of this mystic mid-region of the desert West. Governor McLough-lin of the Hudson's Bay Company headquarters at Fort Van-couver encouraged him in the project, even drew him a rough map of the interior, locating for him the Buenaventura River.

The Great Basin had been traversed, in latitude, by Jedediah Smith, Joe Walker, the Bartleson-Bidwell party, and more than half way by Carson. Peter Skene Ogden had been well into it. A division of the Chiles party, led by Walker, at this very time were taking wagons through to the west slope of the Sierra divide. But the basin plateau, with its arid desolation and many broken ranges, had not been and yet has not con-tinuously been traversed between north and south. The trails still are desultory, and no crimson woof of the railroad from border to border shows upon the map.

Although the Bonneville map and report, and the Albert Gallatin map, half a dozen years in circulation, and the later

Wilkes map, argued to the contrary, it suited a credulous world, including Senator Benton, to conceive that rivers or a river flowed from the interior of the Great Basin to the western sea. The interior spurs and the barrier ranges were ignored, the distance was ignored, the thirsty atmosphere and the thirsty sands were ignored, the lack of material evidences of such a stream was ignored, and only the fairy tales nurturing superstition which feeds romance were believed.

The principal stream, dating back to Father Escalante, should be the Buenaventura; and the Buenaventura, with its head in the Salt Lake or a Lake Salado; or the river Los Mingos or Timpanogos; or other river, draining that Arabian Nights country into the Pacific Ocean at San Francisco Bay, extended a water-way (with only the Rockies interrupting) from the Missouri to the coast. It was another elusive Northwest Passage. Might Lieutenant Frémont announce this river the horizons of the march of empire would be vastly expanded.[289]

To produce this river thoroughfare "with rich bottoms covered with wood and grass, where the wild animals would collect and shelter"; to locate, on the way, a rumored Tlamath (Klamath) Lake; to locate a life-giving oasis lake termed "Mary's," in the midst of the desert: these were the three chief objects of the desert venture by Lieutenant Frémont in the winter of 1843-44. He also hoped to cross, in the farther southeast, the divide between the heads of the California Gulf waters and of the Arkansas, and follow the Arkansas down to Bent's Fort "and home."

He did not quite do this, in direct line; and none of the three chief objectives was attained. Two were unattainable. Carson is of record as having been to the sink of the Mary's (the Sink of the Humboldt) on his trip under McKay; but for most of the year this is an alkali mud-flat rather than a sweet-water lake.

In number twenty-five, "of many nations, American, French, German, Canadian, Indian, and colored [for Frémont had

brought out with him a colored boy retainer, Jacob Dodson]
— and most of them young, several being under twenty-one
years of age"; with 104 mules and horses, many of "thin, inferior quality," and the howitzer as the only thing on wheels,
at noon of November 25, "weather disagreeably cold, with
flurries of snow," they started from the Protestant mission at
the Dalles.

The excitement of "turning towards home" and of facing
adventures in a storied *terra incognita* had routed them out
of their robes and blankets while the stars were still shining.
Frémont sets down his appreciation of the "fine spirit of this
brave and generous commencement."

California west of the mountains seems not to have been in
the budget; but on March 6 asylum was made at Sutter's Fort,
inside of California, within the present limits of the city of
Sacramento.

Of all the party only Carson, as of record, had ever been in
that desert basin or in California. On the way over, Klamath
Marsh in southern Oregon, instead of Klamath Lake thirty
miles to the southward, was reconnoitered (according to Frederick Dellenbaugh's *Frémont and '49*), and here, or at the lake
either, Frémont would look in vain for three rivers, of three
directions — "one west, to the ocean; another north, to the
Columbia; the third [the Sacramento] south, to California."
The only outlet is the Klamath River, flowing southwesterly
through the northwest corner of California.

Not Carson nor Fitzpatrick nor anyone else of the company
had before gazed upon this well-defended freehold: the lush
meadowlands, the rounded reed huts of its semi-aquatic people
— hardy, vigorous Indians of seeming frankness but with formidable bows and shafts. There was a talk. "We pronounced
them a mean, low-lived, treacherous race, which we found to
be a fact when we were in their country in 1846," Carson declares after the fact had been accomplished. For the next visit
to the Klamath country was of positive flavor; in night camp
a day's march in the south, Klamath arrow and Klamath ax
were the Klamath greeting.

Misled by the Klamaths' information as interpreted, and by even the McLoughlin map ("disastrously erroneous," Senator Benton condemns it), Frémont turned eastward into the high desert, on quest of not only Mary's Lake and the Buenaventura, but the main Sacramento on its way to the bay of San Francisco. The heads of the Sacramento, however, were embedded in the southwest, beyond a divide.

There was no Sacramento, save by guess. There was no Mary's Lake oasis, and no Buenaventura connecting with the California coast country, although Kit Carson hopefully searched for beaver cuttings in errant stream after errant stream. The course was east, it was south, paralleling the white Sierra; in desperation it was westerly, for the heights themselves. The land had proved to be one of plateau ridges and of basins independent one of another. Upon the timbered or brushy highlands the party were frozen and were impeded by snow; in the lowlands they were constantly baffled by blind leads, by salty waters and impoverishing herbage, by camps of thirst and starvation for men and animals, succeeding to camps of comparative plenty.

The general route is fairly plain upon the map: Klamath Marsh, Summer Lake, Lake Abert, Warner Lake, Pyramid Lake, the lower Truckee River, Carson River with the future Virginia City of the Comstock Lode yonder on the right, Walker River, Markleeville south of Lake Tahoe, thence westerly again to the basin source, in the high mountains, of the West Carson River, and on to Carson Pass, of the summit of the Sierra Nevada divide — a pass, of name long absent from the atlas, but there, shortly west of the present town of Woodfords, Alpine County, Northern California, and announced by a granite boulder for the eyes of touring motorists.

The march for the snow divide and for California upon the Western slope had been commenced January 19; the summit pass was reached by the whole party a month later, or February 20; the howitzer had been abandoned three weeks back. As they had been warned by the Indians, the party had encountered snow "as deep as a man" and precipices from which man and animal would fall for half a mile. Of the sixty-seven horses and mules still animate at the eastern base only thirty-three won over to the western base. Among the lost was the buffalo-horse Proveau. The march from the summit followed a watershed ridge between two canyoned creeks (Silver and Strawberry) until that dropped off to the intercepting course of a thin, icy river rushing westward from the lake (Lake Tahoe) above. Encouraged by fires seemingly near but far distant below, and following the little river (the South Fork of the American, as happened) which, fed by trickling side streams, became a torrent, in the last of February the party had descended from winter into greening spring. By this route of the South Fork they brushed the treasure site of the Sutter historic mill race that flooded the world with golden dreams.

The romance-invested valley of the Sacramento (Carson's promise) beckoned them forward. Vastly stimulated by the sight of domesticated Indians and by the civilly spoken Spanish of a vaquero from Sutter's Fort itself, Frémont with Kit Carson and a squad continued to push on ahead while Thomas Fitzpatrick brought on the cripples and the baggage.

Fitzpatrick and band had to be met out from the haven of the fort; and were met and succored — "a woeful procession" of men and beasts, "each man, weak and emaciated, leading a horse or mule as weak and emaciated as themselves."

Wonder may again be expressed as to why Frémont insisted upon making this mid-winter passage of the Sierra when the physical strength of his company had touched bottom. He knew, for he had seen it, that on the desert side there were sheltered coves with fuel, fodder, water, and game of fish, antelope and rabbits, where he and his men might winter in and reconnoitre at their leisure. The snowfall on the desert side is moderate. The Indians were of low morale. Carson, Fitzpatrick, Godey, had wintered in, elsewhere, among other Indians and under less weatherable conditions. But this wintering in spelled inaction for possibly long periods, it portended a stop of operations and a lapse of the discipline always hard to enforce among idling men. Furthermore, his animals ˋwere disappearing, day by day — cleverly stolen by the skulking desert folk. In time his command might be stranded, immobile. For one reason or another, then, without passport he crossed into that thither California of Mexico where foreigners were subject to decree and an armed company of North American explorers were the least welcome of all strangers. He kept to the known latitude of Sutter's Fort, the lower Sacramento and San Francisco Bay.

But here was the compelling bourne of Alta California, and here was the Sacramento River flowing on to the world-trade bay of San Francisco. It was not the Buenaventura water-way, however, from the desert to the sea. As Frémont ascertained, the only Buenaventura existent was a pleasant little stream of the coast mission country to the south. And he had to report, to his chiefs, Senator Benton and Colonel Abert, that the only waterway from the Rockies to the Pacific was the Columbia system in the Oregon Northwest. The Sacramento had source far short of the desert.

And here was the rumored Sutter's Fort — that northern outpost built since Kit Carson's visit to the southern end of the valley. And here was Captain John Augustus Sutter, German Swiss-American who, from Santa Fé and from the fur rendezvous of the summer of 1838 having arrived in California via Oregon and the Sandwich Islands, in 1839 had founded, with his "eight Kanakas, three white men, an Indian and a bulldog," this fortified colony of New Switzerland. Now having out of his awarded inch taken an ell, as self-styled *Gobernador de Forteleza de Nueva Helvetia* he seemed to be as secure as any Crusoe or any baron of a rock-eyried castle on the Rhine. Governor John McLoughlin of Fort Vancouver was a seigneur scarcely more powerful than he was for his appointed time ere the human deluge of Forty-nine.

The pack animals, says Carson, "had through hunger eaten one another's tails and the leather of the pack saddles, in fact everything they could lay hold of"; and "when we arrived at the Fort we were nearly naked and in as poor condition as men possibly could be. We were well received by Mr. Sutter and furnished in a princely manner everything we required by him."

As return in part for his hospitality Captain Sutter accepted drafts upon the Topographical Bureau — which he complains he had to discount twenty per cent. for cash. He gained a blacksmith, Samuel Neal, and four other men of abilities less valued; all of them, reports Frémont, being discharged by their own wishes — two of them, including Blacksmith Neal, records Sutter, being charged with, if not discharged for, stealing sugar.

And at the last he speeds the welcomed guests, March 24, in advance of a visit by a Mexican officer and twenty-five soldiers from the coast sent to inquire, in the name of His Excellency Governor Micheltorena, what was the purpose of this armed invasion.[290]

Baptiste Derosier, Mrs. Frémont's asserted courier in hour of need, also had been left behind; not discharged, but deranged and wandering loose somewhere in the hills as though his sin of commission had found him out. Frémont says that he was never heard of again. But Carson says in his dictated biography:

Remained a few days waiting his return, but as he did not come in, we departed. Left word with Sutter to make search and, if possible, find him. He done so, and, sometime after our departure, he was found, was kept at the Fort and properly cared for till he got well, and then Mr. Sutter sent him to the States.

Derosier reappeared in Missouri some two years after the return of the expedition.

From the vicinity of Sutter's Fort, where Frémont had talked with several American settlers, Chiles already one of them, the march southward traversed the lower end of the valley of the Sacramento River and headed up the broad valley of the San Joaquin. The next objective was a pass "at the head of the San Joaquin," which opened upon the southern extension of the great desert, crossed by the Spanish Trail from Los Angeles to Santa Fé — the trail revived, in part, by William Wolfskill.

Frémont still had in mind that yet unknown interior river of drainage functions equalling those of the Colorado. By swinging in a far-flung half circle around the southern rim of the basin interior and connecting with his out trail at the Salt Lake he would cut the course of that river or else lay its ghost forever. The solid barrier of the Sierra divide and the fact that the established traders' trail between California and New Mexico did not cut such a river were matters for his personal report. There is this to be said about John Charles Frémont: as a true explorer he depended as little as possible upon the statements of others. Carson of course had been across the southern arm of the desert, had wide acquaintance among trappers and traders of that southwest; but he was a cautious man, not given to argument.

The march was up the valley of the San Joaquin, between the river and the foothills of the Sierra. Carson had been in this region before, in the spring and summer of 1830, when as a youth he had trapped and hunted through with Ewing Young. Ewing Young had been dead three years, and the California as he knew it was soon to be dead, also.

The route was ever southeast through a country such as Kit Carson had pictured in his stories in the camps back amid the desert and the snow. A sweet, fair, bountiful country, well watered, at this season, by rains and streams; blanketed with orange poppies and purple lupins, and livened by elk, antelope, wild horses and fowl. There were groves of spreading oaks, for camping spots, and tracts of grass and pea-vines for beast forage.

At the southern end of California's long central valley the desert divide and the coast range meet, forming a pocket. A Christian Indian, mounted and attired á caballero, joined the evening camp. He was upon a visit to relatives in the mountains; was from San Fernando, "one of several missions in this part of California, where the country is so beautiful that it is considered a paradise, and the name of its principal town (*Pueblo de los Angeles*) would make it angelic." Carson could have informed Frémont that the Los Angeles of his own experience was anything but angelic. As to San Gabriel and San Fernando — they were good places.

The Indian, Spanish in trappings and tongue, volunteered to guide the strangers through the pass to the desert. And there they went, emerging, for the zest of Frémont:

> guided by a civilized Indian, attended by two wild ones from the Sierra; a Chinook from the Columbia; and our own mixture of American, French, German — all armed; four or five languages heard at once, above a hundred horses and mules, half wild; American, Spanish, and Indian dresses and equipments intermingled . . . Scouts ahead, and on our flanks; a front and rear division; the pack animals, baggage, and horned cattle, in the center; and the whole stretching a quarter of a mile . . . looking more like we belonged to Asia than to the United States of America.

Thus, by way of Tah-ee-chay-pah (Tehachapi) Pass, of the railroad route between Bakersfield and the desert, they made exit into the desert again whence they had mysteriously come. The California authorities might be hugely relieved by this riddance of such barbarians, whose purposes were questionable. But the leader had seen the land, and he came again with another wild troop.

It was the Mohave Desert. When, squinting into it from above, Kit Carson translated for Frémont the guide's Spanish, "*No hay agua, no hay zapate — nada!* (There is no water, there is no forage — nothing!)", he only voiced his own thought. He had toiled westward across this desert on his first trapping trip, that with Ewing Young in 1829; and back across it he and Captain Young had retreated from the pressing demands of civil and military Southern California. This third trip, of 1844, however, faced more favorable circumstances; for the month was April, when the desert softens and blooms.

The erratic Mohave River was rediscovered; the Spanish Trail — a sure desert guide at last — was struck. It led north by east, as if skirting the Great Basin, but it crossed no dis-

gorging river. On May 3 (1844) the company camped upon
the site of Las Vegas, Nevada. The redoubtable Joseph Walker
himself, of desert experience exceeded by that of no other
white man, overhauled the company just beyond the next
springs camp-place of Las Vegas de Santa Clara (the Santa
Clara Meadows, there in southwestern Utah, and of Mountain
Meadows Massacre rechristening), and engaged to guide them
on. He with eight other good American rifles had spurred
ahead of a "great caravan" of horses and mules — the first of
the spring caravans from California for New Mexico, over the
Spanish Trail.

Lieutenant Frémont took occasion to learn much from Captain Walker, but he did not learn that lovely Utah Lake, thirty
miles south of the Salt Lake, is not and was not "the southern
limb of the great Salt Lake" connected by a narrow passage;
and Captain Walker did not explain "a problem which
requires to be solved" — that of a lake with one part living
fresh water and the other a dead sea of saturated salt water.

Utah Lake is not a member of the Salt Lake, but discharges
into the Salt Lake by the river Jordan. In after years the Mormon leader, Brigham Young, held Frémont to account for his
fresh-and-salt water story as published — although the error
really was of no lasting injury to the Mormon settlers. The
fresh water was there, and elsewhere, and plenty of it.

Now the company crossed the Wasatch watershed of northeastern Utah to the Uintah where Antoine Robidoux was
maintaining his post in its last year. They hastened, well-fed
and happy, through Brown's Hole of the upper Green (where
Fort Davy Crockett was an unnamed ruin) and eastward up
the Yampa, thence along the Colorado-Wyoming line where
the veteran Fraeb had forted and died and where Carson
pointed out the site of his buffalo-hunters' camp of 1835, scene
of the night attack of the wolf-imitating Sioux and the death
of "poor Davis" with five bullets in his body; and turning
southward they descended through the three famed mountain
parks: North or New Park (the Bull Pen, the Cow Lodge),

Middle or Old Park, South Park or the Bayou Salade, familiar and reminiscent ground to all fur and meat and robe hunters, but yet, as Frémont explains, "unknown to science and history."

Crossing from the Bayou Salade to the upper Arkansas (but by no means to the head-waters of the Arkansas, as Frémont had planned to do), with Pike's Peak as their landmark on the left, they headed for the pueblo at the mouth of Fountain Creek, "where we had the pleasure to find a number of our old acquaintances." And now

our cavalcade moved rapidly down the Arkansas, along the broad road which follows the river, and on the 1st of July we arrived at Bent's Fort, about 70 miles below the mouth of the Fontaine-qui-bouit. As we emerged into view from the groves on the river, we were saluted with a display of the national flag and repeated discharges from the guns of the fort, where we were received by Mr. George Bent with a cordial welcome and a friendly hospitality.

Carson relates:

On the 4th of July, Mr. Bent gave Fremont and party a splendid dinner. The day was celebrated as well, if not better, than in many of the towns of the States.

From Bent's Fort Kit Carson, likely enough with Joe Walker on his way to Santa Fé, rode to Taos, home and Josefa; reported there after a year's absence and the completion of his longest continuous trail, roughly 5,500 miles, wherein the trail of the explorer outdid the trail of the trapper.

Chapter XXIX

Kit Carson's Star in the Ascendant

WITH his spoils of the country — his Indians, his Mexicans, his saddle-horse Sacramento, iron-gray "of the best California stock," a gift from Captain Sutter — Lieutenant Frémont arrived in St. Louis to the great relief of his wife and family circle. His "eight months" of absence had been extended to fourteen. He arrived "inspired with California," full of facts and theories, convinced that the Buenaventura and other alleged rivers draining the Great Basin into the Pacific were myths, but after all to write upon his map the confession, in a long arc covering that still white area from the Salt Lake to the Sierras, from the Columbia River in the north to the Mohave River in the south:

THE GREAT BASIN: diameter 11° of latitude, 10° of longitude; elevation above the sea between 4 and 5,000 feet; surrounded by lofty mountains: contents almost unknown, but believed to be filled with rivers and lakes which have no communication with the sea, deserts and oases which have never been explored, and savage tribes, which no traveler has seen or described.

He returned to fame, and to the double brevet (well earned) of First Lieutenant and Captain; and, if conquered by the desert, nevertheless to spread word, by authority, of

The Great Salt Lake, the Utah Lake, the Little Salt Lake; at all which places, then desert, the Mormons now are; the Sierra Nevada, then solitary in the snow, now crowded with Americans digging gold from its flanks; the beautiful valleys of the Sacramento and San Joachim, then alive with wild horses, elk, deer, and wild fowls, now smiling with American cultivation; the Great Basin itself, and its contents; the Three Parks; the approximation of the great rivers which, rising together in the central region of the Rocky Mountains, go off east and west, toward the rising and the setting sun:—all these, and other strange features of a new region, more Asiatic than American.[291]

He returned, into the midst of a national campaign waged over the acquisition of Texas and Oregon — with California as the inevitable by-product. The cause demonstrated for victory. In Washington, in the spring, Frémont met the new President, James K. Polk, Democrat and pro-Texas Whig champion from Tennessee. President Polk politely doubted the accuracy of Frémont's analysis of the Great Basin, inasmuch as a map in the Congressional Library files really showed three rivers connecting the Salt Lake with the Columbia, the Gulf of California, and San Francisco Bay; but he believed in California as desirable territory.

President Brigham Young of the Church of Latter Day Saints and the Mormon State of Deseret was another dignitary who questioned the reports of Lieutenant Frémont; and that, as late as 1877. "Good soil and good grass adapted to civilized settlements," Frémont had said, speaking of the territory along the east approach to the Salt Lake. And there was the "fresh water limb" of the lake. "From Frémont's reports," President Young said in an interview in the *New York Times* of June 2, 1877,

we determined to get our wagons together, form a grand caravan and travel through the country to the Salt Lake, 1000 miles from any civilized settlement. We started out with 147 people and 73 wagons. This was in 1847 . . . Salt Lake plain is a natural desert. When he struck this plain there was nothing on it but sage-bushes.

Frémont answered this by quoting from his published report; but by a curious mental lapse he denied that he had stated that the south end of the lake was fresh water.

Daniel Webster, ex-Secretary of State, also doubted Lieutenant Frémont's reports: accepted the values of Oregon but was suspicious of the asserted values of California save as a maritime base for trade with the Orient. To him California was a sandy strip along the ocean, with an occasional fertile spot, but with the harbor of San Francisco which was worth twenty Texases. England might have Oregon, Texas was no prize to be bought by bloodshed and a Union disrupted, but the harbor-indented coast of California should not pass to any European power.

While the Frémont second expedition did indeed materially

exploit the practicability of the Oregon Trail from the South Pass on, the Columbia River water-way and the honest worth of the Pacific Northwest, it advertised the foreign land of California with a greater appeal — the appeal to the fancy of adventurer and settler. The very change from cold to warmth, from want to plenty, in a measure from poverty to riches, was a picture as telling as that of any advertising lay-out of today. In this expedition Kit Carson might have just pride. It was a distinct achievement, and he had borne a good part.

The first expedition, that to the South Pass, had put his name into the public prints, had established him as a romantic figure ahorse, a skillful hunter and a safe guide. In this second expedition his character was developed less conservatively, contrasting with that side of his character which had induced him to make his will (an untimely act, Frémont had complained) when Indian trouble threatened. In this second expedition he was off to a brave start when, so unexpected by the reader, in true story fashion he met Frémont, and faithfully kept rendezvous on schedule with the mules replacement.

Thereafter, inasmuch as Fitzpatrick was assigned to duty with the baggage train, and Godey with him, Kit Carson, in the fore with Frémont, got the breaks, so to say. Through Frémont he had a speaking rôle and a rôle of action. He enjoyed special privilege. And although the hard-working Fitzpatrick, fighting to get the animals through, and carefully husbanding the supplies, in the approach to the Sierra is mentioned as appointed to scouting squads, Carson was Frémont's chosen companion.

He did not discover the pass which was later named for him. The location of the pass, by general direction, had been indicated by the Indian guide before he deserted. The pass was first viewed from a flanking peak by an advance squad composed of Frémont, Fitzpatrick, and several others unnamed in the report. Frémont says only: "February 6.—Accompanied by Mr. Fitzpatrick, I set out today with a reconnoitering party, on snowshoes. . . . Crossing the open basin, in a march of about ten miles we reached the top of one of the peaks, to the left of the pass indicated by our guide." Carson, however, proves to have been with the party.[292]

It had fallen to Carson to encourage the company in their attack upon the Sierra barrier and in their final live-or-die effort to surmount the pass itself. As he says: "We were nearly out of provisions and cross the mountain we must let the consequences be what they may." He, of all the company, was the only one who had been in that California and out of personal knowledge could guarantee its existence as a substantial sanctuary. Frémont accordingly narrates:

I reminded them [the company] of the beautiful valley of the Sacramento, with which they were familiar from the descriptions of Carson, who had been there some fifteen years ago, and who, in our late privations, had delighted us in speaking of its rich pastures and abounding game, and drew a vivid contrast between its summer climate, less than a hundred miles distant, and the falling snow around us.

And it was for Carson, out of accurate memory, to hail the promised land from that overlooking peak, and to give assurance that the summit of the Sierra divide had been reached, that the valley of the Sacramento was actually in sight below. Thus he ended doubts. To quote Frémont:

Far below us, dimmed by the distance, was a large snowless valley, bounded on the western side, at the distance of about a hundred miles, by a low range of mountains which Carson recognized with delight as the mountains bordering the coast. "There," said he, "is the little mountain — it is fifteen years ago since I saw it; but I am just as sure as if I had seen it yesterday." Between us, then, and this low coast range, was the valley of the Sacramento. . . .

Carson again stabilized the hopes of the company, during the first descent, by routing the fears that yonder distant broad sheet of water might be only another "vast interior lake" of bitter waters rather than San Francisco Bay. A river joined it in the south as well as in the north; but he "had entered the valley along the southern side of the bay, and remembered perfectly to have crossed the mouth of a very large stream."

It was Carson's ready fortune to plunge into an icy stream

for the rescue of Frémont, whose moccasins had slipped; and Carson should have been the interpreter to translate the Spanish of the voluble Indian vaquero announcing that Sutter's Fort was at hand "just over the hill" and had a welcome for its countrymen. It was Kit Carson the American (as Frémont emphasizes) who, moreover, starred with Alexander Godey the Frenchman in the most actively dramatic episode of the entire march.

On the homeward way across the California desert two Mexicans of California, Andrés Fuentes and an eleven-year-old boy, Pablo Hernández, came as refugees into the Frémont camp, to report that the remainder of their party (the wife of Fuentes, the father and mother of Pablo, and one Santiago Giacome) traveling in advance of a spring caravan out of Los Angeles had been left eighty miles to the eastward surrounded by Indians. They two, on herd, had managed to burst free with the thirty loose horses, which were now at the Aqua de Tomaso spring-hole about twenty-five miles out. Frederick Dellenbaugh (*Frémont and '49*) suggests that this was properly Agua de Tío Meso, or Uncle Meso's Spring.

The next morning the Frémont company took the back trail of the two Mexicans; and regaining the Spanish Trail which ran a little to the north of their camp on the last reaches of the Mohave River, in the afternoon arrived at the watering place where the horses had been left. The horses of course had been herded away by the Indians in pursuit of them. Fuentes implored Frémont to help him recover the animals. Carson says, in his *Own Story:*

He [Fremont] stated to the party that if they wished to volunteer for such a purpose they might do so, that he would furnish animals for them to ride. Godey and myself volunteered with the expectation that some men of our party would join us. They did not. We two and the Mexican took the trail of [the] animals and commenced the pursuit.

"Well mounted," Frémont relates, "the three set off on the trail." Near dusk Fuentes was back again, his horse, if not his heart, having failed him; but Carson and Godey had gone on, following the hoof tracks leading into the rougher country of the eastern border of the San Bernardino Desert, southeastern California. Frémont waited in camp throughout the next morning. And then in the afternoon,

a war-whoop was heard, such as Indians make when returning from a victorious enterprise; and soon Carson and Godey appeared, driving before them a band of horses, recognized by Fuentes to be a part of those they had lost. Two bloody scalps, dangling from the end of Godey's gun, announced that they had overtaken the Indians as well as the horses.

Frémont says that the pair had followed the trail by moonshine until, afraid of losing it in a dark defile of the mountains, they had been obliged to bivouac, without a fire, and there wait for daylight. Carson says they rode during the night, "it was very dark," they had to dismount and "feel for the trail," and finally, requiring rest, they lay down in their wet saddle-blankets and "passed a miserably cold night." Made a little fire, at daybreak, in a deep ravine, in order to warm themselves before starting on.

By the signs the Indians had gone through the place after sunset; they therefore could not be far ahead. At sunrise they were discovered in camp about two miles before, and engaged in feasting upon horse meat. Had killed five horses. By Carson's story:

We were compelled to leave our horses, they could not travel. We hid them among the rocks, continued on the trail, crawled in among the horses [i. e.: the remainder of the stolen herd]. A young one got frightened, that frightened the rest. The Indians noticed the commotion among the animals, sprung to their arms. We now considered it time to charge on the Indians. They were about thirty in number. We charged. I fired, killed one. Godey fired, missed, but reloaded and fired, killing another. There were only three shots fired and two were killed. The remainder run. I then took the two rifles and ascended a hill to keep guard while Godey scalped the dead Indians. He scalped the one he shot and was proceeding towards the one I shot. He was not yet dead and was behind some rocks. As Godey approached, he raised, let fly an arrow. It passed through Godey's shirt collar. He again fell and Godey finished him.

A fugitive account, possibly based upon Godey's story of the scrimmage, states that Godey did not miss his mark with his first fire but that he and Carson aimed at the same man — no doubt a captain or chief — and felled him. Godey then quickly reloaded and fired again, while Carson reserved his own loaded piece, as was the mountain-man custom on defense. Frémont cites the fact that the body of one of the two Indians killed had two bullets in it.

Carson, dictating his story a dozen years later, when the incidents had cooled, did not tell all. It should be borne in mind that he narrated of Frémont's expeditions at the time, 1856-1857, when Frémont was in the public eye as Presidential timber. That some things were not to be told is evidenced by the striking fact that in none of the three campaign biographies of Frémont, issued in 1856, is this matter of the attack and of the return with bloody scalps dangling referred to.

But in his enthusiasm Frémont had made report with all the gruesome details. In the first flight of arrows a shaft grazed Godey's neck. When the enemy had vacated the camp Godey proceeded to scalp the victims while Carson stood guard. The Indian shot by Godey was dead; the other Indian, with two balls in him, revived under the sting of the knife and

sprang to his feet, the blood streaming from his skinned head, and uttered a hideous howl. An old squaw, possibly his mother, stopped and looked back from the mountain side she was climbing, threatening and lamenting. The frightful spectacle appalled the stout hearts of our men; but they did what humanity required, and quickly terminated the agonies of the gory savage.

An abandoned boy, the bulk of the stolen horses, a quantity of horse beef boiling in large clay pots, and several baskets containing fifty or sixty pairs of moccasins, were the other fruits of the victory.

This performance, climaxed in the return to camp with war-whoop and scalp trophies, and probably further colored by the narration of the exuberant Godey, moved Frémont, sensitive to the dramatic, to the grand gesture:

They had rode about one hundred miles in the pursuit and return, and all in thirty hours. The time, place, object, and numbers, considered, this expedition of Carson and Godey may be considered among the boldest and most disinterested which the annals of western adventure, so full of daring deeds, can present. Two men, in a savage desert, pursue day and night an unknown body of Indians into the defiles of an unknown mountain — attack them on sight, without counting numbers — and defeat them in an instant — and for what? To punish the robbers of the desert, and to avenge the wrongs of Mexicans whom they did not know. I repeat: it was Carson and Godey who did this — the former an *American,* born in the Boonslick country of Missouri; the latter a Frenchman, born in St. Louis — and both trained to western enterprise from early life.

There is something defensive in this; but as a recital of thrilling Western knight-errantry it scored a deep notch for Carson in the fancy of the public — Kit Carson again, an American in rivalry with a Frenchman. Carson and Godey, however, had not expected to go alone; but once committed to the trail, go they had to. The chances are that they thought less of avenging the wretched Mexicans (of a class whom Carson was wont to hold in small esteem) than of clearing the trail ahead and throwing fear into those desert Indians who as yet knew little of the white man's prowess and weapons. One theft, if unpunished, would lead to another.

Whatever qualms Frémont may have had over the thorough scalping were doused when the original camping spot of the Mexican party was reached. Silence reigned here except as broken by the whines of a frightened little dog. The bodies of the two men, Hernández and Giacome, were found riddled and stripped and mutilated. The two women had been carried away. The oncoming caravan from Los Angeles discovered them naked and lifeless, staked out upon the adjacent desert.[293]

The camp spot had been called the Archilette; Frémont renamed it Agua de Hernández; on the old trail maps it is Resting Springs, about seventy-five miles southwest of present Las Vegas, southwestern Nevada.

This tragedy, of deed more serious, as a crime, than that of robbery (albeit horse theft, in the West, tops the list), was not avenged. Apparently no volunteers had been called for to ride, cavalier, in behalf of Pablo's father and mother. Carson and Godey had done all when they had regained the horses and had exacted penalty for the theft. The end was not yet, but no further vengeance was attempted as a measure of gallantry.

Return of Carson and Godey

During the onward march a company of bold insulting Indians were met. They were assumed to be the "same people who had murdered the Mexicans," Frémont reports. He had the chief in his power, but he acted wisely, "peace being our object," in avoiding a general fracas. There was too much at stake, with home and success now in view, to risk inviting a mêlée, a course of bush-whacking attacks, if not a desert siege, and loss of men and animals. With difficulty, however, he restrained his command, particularly Carson, enraged by the chief's contemptuous count of the small number in the camp, including a mule that was being shod. "Why, there are none of you. We are many. If you have your arms, we have these," and the chief twanged his bow. Carson blurted: "Don't say that, old man! Don't you say that — your life's in danger." To Frémont these Diggers were as irresponsible as wild animals; to Carson and the other mountain-men they were a vicious species of Indians.

Next, Baptiste Tabeau disappeared. He had gone back to the camp of the night before to look up a lamed mule and had not returned. Carson vented his anxiety over the absence. Even while he and Frémont were discussing the situation a "kill" smoke signaled from the back trail. Carson and squad were sent to investigate. They returned in the night with the report that they had found the mule, dying from an arrow, and a separate little puddle that looked, in the darkness, like blood.

Investigation by daylight brought proof that Tabeau had been shot from his horse, had vainly struggled, had been dragged to the river there and thrown in. Thus the Indians had made an end of vengeance, for they were not sighted again. So went the game of tit for tat. In his next expedition Frémont handled the Indians more roughly.

As to Baptiste Tabeau, Carson says in his dictated memoirs:

I was grieved on account of the death of the Canadian. He was a brave, noble-souled fellow. I had been in many an Indian fight with him and I am confident, if he was not taken unawares, that he surely killed one or two before he fell.

Chapter XXX

Out Again with Frémont — 1845

GRANTED that his wages had been those of the first expedition, $100 a month, when Kit Carson now arrived home from some twelve months of steady work he was in good funds. There was money in beaver when beaver were plentiful, and he had profited in fur before he married Josefa. The government vouchers in hand were something more substantial, however: cash, with no trade discount nor expenses to be figured off.

They were a stake outside whatever reserve he may have had. He was past thirty-four, was responsible for the welfare of a young wife who was no lodge-keeping Indian but required white man's care approved by her relatives and gossipy Taos; the size of his future household he could not foresee; it was time that he dropped that anchor to windward and hauled taut.

"I arrived in Taos and remained till March, 1845," he dictates. But he was not so constant as that. James Josiah Webb relates, in his *"Journal of a Santa Fé Trader,"* that while he was upon his way, in September, 1844, to Taos and Santa Fé by route of Bent's Fort and the Mountain Branch of the caravan trail:

One day we camped on the Rio Culebra (a small stream running from the mountains into the Rio Grande), and in the early afternoon saw three men approaching camp at a brisk gallop, each with a led horse. They dismounted, unsaddled, and in a few minutes had a fire kindled, and the coffeepot over the fire. They were soon recognized as old mountain-men and acquaintances of several of the party — Kit Carson, Lucien Maxwell, and Timothy Goodale. As soon as they got dinner cooking (coffee boiling, a prairie dog dressed and opened out on a stick before the fire), Carson and Maxwell came to our camp. . . . I can remember nothing of the interview except that they had left Pueblo that morning and expected to reach Taos that night. They soon left, ate their dinner, saddled their horses, and were off, Kit galloping up to the trail rope, or lariat, of his horse and stooping in his saddle, picked it up and was off without breaking a gallop, giving us this word of caution:

"Look out for your ha'r, boys! The Utes are plenty about here."[294]

Whereupon, with his portion of the prairie dog under his belt, Kit Carson took to the home trail and Josefa again.

It was the next March, after another birthday (by which he turned thirty-five), when, as a husband of two years, with his fellow mountain-man and Taosan, Dick Owens (the Owens of the Joseph Gale company in that fire-fighting scrimmage with the Blackfeet back in the fall of 1835), who was still a free lance, he at last dropped anchor on the Cimarroncito or Little Cimarron, fifty-five miles east of Taos. He and Owens had "concluded that, as we had rambled enough that it would be advisable for us to go and settle on some good stream and make us a farm." There "we built ourselves little huts, put in considerable grain, and commenced getting out timber to enlarge our improvements."[295]

This was a futile gesture. In less than six months Carson and Owens both were out once more on the long trail. Even had Frémont not sounded the rally to his standard the ranch on the Little Cimarron was likely to prove poor holding ground. Before an inch of the ranch land had been cleared Texas with her train of war had been annexed, and before Frémont set face to the farthest west again the thunder heads were growling in the horizons. Ere the second ranch crop could have been reaped, Kearny's Army of the West would raise the signal dust, betokening a different crop, across the plains from Leavenworth to Bent's Fort, and there, under the streaming flag, and at Santa Fé, enlist the services of men such as William Bent, Thomas Fitzpatrick, Antoine Leroux. It is scarcely conceivable that Kit Carson and Dick Owens would have bent their backs over hoe and sickle when they saw a ready adventure for rifle and saddle, steady eye and hand.

Carson's isolation must have been quite complete if he really thought that he had settled down to ranching. He played the ostrich with its head in the sand. In Washington Frémont had finished his stirring report of that second expedition, on March 1 it was submitted to the War Department, for the action of Congress; on this day the joint resolution of Congress, consummated February 28, for the admission of the state of Texas into the Union, by the approval of President Tyler became a law, and the Mexican minister, pronouncing the measure to be an act of war, demanded his passports.

The citizenship of the United States had waxed militant. The expansionist notion of a peaceful conquest of the Southwest and Northwest by barter and infiltration was overborne by the swelling blather "Texas and Fight," "Fifty-four Forty or Fight."

Texas was a child of trouble. By adopting her the United States adopted also her boundaries dispute with Mexico, for Mexico never had conceded her claim to the Rio Grande border upon either west or south. The condition of the war with Mexico was the annexation of Texas, a "rebellious province." The occasion was made when General Taylor's Army of Occupation crossed the Nueces and became, in the eyes of Mexico, an army of invasion.

The ways of Texas were the ways of the hot-blood South. The ways of Oregon were the ways of the cool North. Oregon was temperately breaking one set of ties ere contracting another set. July 5, 1843, almost coincidental with the arrival of Lieutenant Frémont at Fort St. Vrain on his second expedition, this time clear to the coast, the self-styled "we, the people of Oregon Territory," having in regulation town meeting fitted Oregon with an American jacket shaped upon a provisional territorial government, announced home rule "until such time as the United States of America extend their jurisdiction over us." The prospective *casus belli* up there was not the theory of foreign soil acquired against the law of nations, for Oregon was in substance as in theory American territory; it was that of boundary again — the satisfaction of the American jingo and Anglophobiac, and the British bulldog, as to whether the northern boundary should be the established 49°, the more southern valley of the Columbia, or the far northern latitude 54° 40' which, if applied today, would cut off a third of British Columbia.[296]

Those United States, then, of which Bent's Fort and, in measure, Taos, were outposts, and to which Kit Carson and

Dick Owens, on their ranch, as Americans paid fealty, were in way of ordering two wars at once, in fields widely separated. But not for only two prizes; for three. There was California.

That fetish the Monroe Doctrine, and the covetous designs of State and people governed the destiny of California. To State there were 800 miles of fair coastline with harbors opening upon the prolific Orient. It was a coastline worthy of other cargoes than those of hides and tallow. The bogy of France or England controlling those harbors and the trade of the Pacific was conceivable as a violation of North American supremacy but was unthinkable. One time, the waterway of the Columbia to the Orient had been the expansion code of Western empire; it still was a *sine qua non,* but opportunity had burgeoned afresh. That opportunity was Texas and those negotiations of war and peace which should run the southern boundary of the Republic clear through to the Pacific in the south as the northern boundary was in process of being run clear through to the Pacific in the north. "Manifest destiny" declared that the eastern and western boundaries of the United States should be only the two oceans.

Senator Benton, pointing generally west, might declaim: "There is the East. There lies the road to India," but to the people of lesser vision yet equal imagination California allured as "the richest, the most beautiful, and the healthiest country in the world." It was the desirable end of trail; so Frémont and sundry others had found it.

There California dangled like a red and savory apple; temptingly near the Sierra fence, far from the Mexican house, and bound to be the spoil of the first bold hand. The northern side was ripe to American eyes. Sutter's Fort was promise of this, for having raised, from his initial small sowing, a dragons-teeth crop of retainers, in November, 1841, Captain Sutter the independent had defied the California authorities to interfere with his stronghold. That same fall Captain Charles Wilkes of the Navy had surveyed San Francisco Bay and the rivers emptying into it. The next fall Commodore Thomas ap Catesby

Jones, by sudden mysterious notion, had landed a force of marines and had seized Monterey — an act portentous but reversed by apology profuse. Lieutenant Frémont of the Army had successfully marched in and out again. Americans had taken up land and settled upon it. Where went the known ripened half of California, there went the other half, equally as ripe, and, with its tropical latitude, perhaps more tasty. And who was Mexico, with pretense to such possessions?

With the common people it was a case of the superiority complex. It was an outcrop of the racial antipathy between the Saxon and the Latin. All the Southwest was lost to Mexico in the Texan war for independence, and the aftermath of feud. The Alamo, the massacre at Goliad, the prison cells of Chihuahua, the exhibit of the bleeding ears of Texan-Americans in the Santa Fé Expedition — these and such as these, to the American not only of the West and the South but even of the far Northeast, made up Mexican history. Besides, there was a heavy list of damage claims by American merchants against Mexico, unpaid. Thus both valor and purse were touched. And whereas to Mexico the North Americans were barbarians, Mexico, to the American, was an outlaw nation, with property title subject to the right of might. When Americans, in this wise minded with despite for the very Spanish language, dropped from the heights into California, the rule of Mexico there, already questioned by the natives, became the mere shadow of a form.[297]

How much of the unrest and the thunderings of 1845 in the States seeped over the Santa Fé Trail and spread to Kit Carson and Dick Owens baching upon their ranch east across the mountains from Taos, *quién sabe?* They contacted Taos and Bent's. There were talk and papers to tell of an Oregon and California migration renewed and of a Texas migration in the throes — to the result that ere the year had waned the beaten road from St. Louis to Texas by way of Fort Gibson on the lower Arkansas in present Oklahoma was "literally lined (as Lieutenant J. W. Abert reported in October) with the wagons

of emigrants." At Fort Jesup, western Louisiana along the
Texas border, on June 30 Colonel Zachary Taylor had received
orders to land troops upon Texas soil and be in readiness to
evict Mexico from the State of Texas as far as the Rio Grande.
At Nauvoo, Illinois, the Mormon dictator Brigham Young was
considering the hejira of 1846-47; yet unannounced but pre-
saged by those other evictions which forced it. And Brevet
Captain John C. Frémont's report of his discoveries of 1844-45
had been printed in 10,000 copies, and Kit Carson himself, the
epitome of derring-do, was of greater popular repute than Colonel Taylor or Brigham Young either.

It is not reasonable to assume that Kit Carson was unconscious of the surge of events. Furthermore he had made poor
provision for dodging issues. His ranch venture was contingent
upon a promise to Frémont that he would join him any time
upon call. By this he had tossed a sop to fortune, for he knew
Frémont. And here, to the ranch, there came, the first week in
August, an express messenger from Bent's Fort with the word
that Frémont was at the post and expecting him.

With remarkable promptness the two ranchers sold out, lock,
stock and barrel, for about half the worth of the holdings and
improvements; Carson consigned Josefa to the care of her sister
Ignacia and Don Carlos Bent, Ignacia's husband and his friend,
and with Owens took off to join Frémont again. For Dick
went, too. During the months he had been regaled with stories
of the desert and of California, and of Frémont.[298]

"This was like Carson, prompt, self-sacrificing, and true,"
Frémont records. Just so, considering that Frémont apparently
asked a great deal of him. But Carson did well to stick to the
main chance; Frémont and government pay were sure things,
the ranch proposition was an experiment. Oliver Wiggins states
that Carson, returned from the previous expedition, had grown
wary of Frémont and hoped to break from him. There is no
indication of this. As to slim Josefa — she had to rest content
in the knowledge that her Cristobal was highly valued. She
had seen little of him since they were married but he was do-

ing man's work in accordance with the ways of the Southwest.

The Frémont third expedition, starting from St. Louis but organizing at Bent's Fort, contained many familiar faces. Carson was there; Lucien Maxwell was there; Basil Lajeunesse was there — not to return again; Godey was there, and Talbot of Washington, Jacob Dodson, the negro, and Thomas Fitzpatrick, and Joe Walker, and the iron-gray horse El Toro del Sacramento — the Bull of the Sacramento.

Among the new faces were twelve Delawares and an Ioway half-breed, under the Delaware chiefs Swanok and Sagundai; Lieutenant J. W. Abert and Lieutenant G. W. Peck; Edward M. Kern of Philadelphia, topographer, succeeding the German Preuss; Archambeau, the Canadian hunter, "general favorite . . . tall, fine-looking, very cheerful, with all the gaiety of the voyageur"; Stepp, the gunsmith, who was to spike the cannon at the Golden Gate; and Richard Owens, "Dick" Owens, within a year to be Captain of Company A, First California Battalion of Mounted Riflemen, Colonel John C. Frémont commanding, but at present characterized only as a friend of Kit Carson — "cool, brave, and of good judgment; a good hunter and a good shot; experienced in mountain life . . . "; forming with Carson and Godey the perfect triangle. According to the story by Thomas S. Martin as contained in H. H. Bancroft's *History of Nevada, Colorado and Wyoming,* Bill Williams accompanied the march as far as the Salt Lake.[299]

Lieutenants Abert and Peck, with Thomas Fitzpatrick as guide and the trader Hatcher (whom Lewis Garrard in his *Wah-to-yah* makes famous) as hunter, and with some thirty other men, were detached for reconnaisance from Bent's Fort down the Canadian River country through northern Texas to the lower Arkansas, thence north to St. Louis. The War Department would stress the theory that these explorations of the Forties were in line of routine, with no direct military bearing. They were, however, most timely — and in nick of time. As far back as November, 1835, the old war-horse Major General Edmund P. Gaines, reporting from St. Louis headquarters to the Adjutant General, had advised: "The approaching disturbances in Texas would seem strongly to admonish us of the immense importance of our officers and men being thoroughly familiar with the whole line of our southwestern frontier, from the Sabine bay to the Rocky Mountains."

As affairs shaped, all the frontier, facing south and facing west, required attention. To Mexico in the south there was added Mexico in the far west also, and England in the northwest and possibly in the far west as well. To the unknown quantity of Texas the unknown quantity of California and of Oregon were added. To the one hand goes Lieutenant Abert and his inoffensive civilian command; to the other hand, Captain Frémont once more.

Captain Frémont had arrived at Bent's Fort on August 3. He left there August 26, with a brave cavalcade of 200 horse animals, and a "well-appointed compact party of sixty; mostly experienced and self-reliant men, equal to any emergency likely to occur and willing to meet it." This last clause is significant, although framed forty years after the facts, when things that might have been could appear as things that were.[300]

There should, however, have been men in the party who realized that this expedition of the noted Frémont might be a venture into something more serious than mere hardships. War was in the air — war with Mexico and war with Great Britain. And Frémont, apparently out of ample funds (which he had), while bidding for a larger party than ever before expertly culled the proffered rank and file.

A reporter for the *Weekly Reveille* of June 9 (quoted in Nevins' *Frémont*) shows the captain surrounded by an importunate crowd of wage and glory seekers, in St. Louis, and stipulating "fifty men — good riflemen and packers — been to the mountains before —" by which and by other stipulations he "took the *starch* out of many a good fellow." Having his men, he hung up a dozen of the best rifles obtainable as prizes for excellence in target shooting. The Pacific Railroad Survey parties through Indian country in the early Fifties and even the advance survey parties for the Union Pacific, and for the Kansas Pacific during the Cheyenne war in the buffalo country, were less exacting in their make-up.

The expedition set out ostensibly to explore "that section of the Rocky Mountains which gives rise to the Arkansas River, the Rio Grande del Norte of the Gulf of Mexico, and the Rio Colorado of the Gulf of California; to complete the examination of the Great Salt Lake and its interesting region; and to extend the survey west and southwest to the examination of the Cascade Mountains and the Sierra Nevada."

The expedition was designed, moreover, to open a shorter, southern route for travel to California, and a travel trail between interior northern California and Oregon. There lay the import of the reference to the "examination" of the Sierra Nevada and the Cascade ranges, in addition to that of the "interesting region" of the Salt Lake. Roads of occupation are as useful in war as in peace.

To quote Frémont, looking backward and incited to tell all:

As affairs resolved themselves, California stood out as the chief subject in the impending war; and with Mr. Benton and other governing men at Washington it became a firm resolve to hold it for the United States. . . . This was talked over fully during the time of preparation for the third expedition, and the contingencies anticipated and weighed.

William L. Marcy, Secretary of War, in his annual report, December 5, 1846 — a time also when all could be told — asserted:

The objects of this service [Frémont's] were, as those of his previous explorations had been, of a scientific character, without any view whatever to military operations . . . and his whole force consisted of sixty-two men, employed by himself for security against Indians, and for procuring subsistence in the wilderness and desert country through which he was to pass.[301]

Frémont presumably served two masters. It should not be said that there was a deep dark plot by which his movements were directed from the outset, but he was prepared by his advisers to deal with circumstances other than those pertaining to the physical aspects of the country. His troop was mobile. This time he did not cumber himself with carts.

Having marched from Bent's Fort up along the Arkansas to the mouth of the Grand Canyon of the Arkansas (the neighborhood of present Cañon City, Colorado), thence northward through the region of Cripple Creek and westerly to strike the head of the Arkansas, again, near Buena Vista, the company thence ascended the dwindling stream about by route of the later Denver & Rio Grande Railroad, to make a camp on the west short of the upper of the beautiful Twin Lakes; from the Leadville district (where they noted the lakes of that high country) they headed on northward, by Frémont Pass (with the Mount of the Holy Cross unnoted) crossed the divide there between the sources of the Eagle and the Blue, followed down the Piney River to the Grand, and crossing over to the White River (this country well known to Carson at least) descended it by Indian and trapper trail to the Green of present Utah. The White River trail to the Green had been taken by Carson and Captain Lee in their trading trip of the fall of 1833.

The company pressed westward through the Uintah country beyond the Green, and to present Provo near the shore of Utah Lake. The southern part of the Great Salt Lake was within easy march. The further trail had yet to be proved out.

With Carson and several others Captain Frémont visited, ahorse, Antelope Island, well stocked with wild meat, and put it on the map. From his camp at the south end of the Salt Lake he gazed across the washboard ranges of the desert, toward California. "The country looked dry and of my own men none knew anything of it; neither Walker nor Carson. The Indians declared to us that no one had ever beeen known to cross the plain, which was desert."

Jedediah Smith, returning from California, had crossed this Salt Lake Desert here in the summer of 1827, but there was no one in this company to bear witness to his feat nor speak of the Albert Gallatin and Captain Wilkes maps limning his route.

On October 28, Kit Carson, Lucien Maxwell, and Auguste

Archambeau the hunter, and, according to Carson, Basil Lajeunesse, but according to Frémont, an attendant for a water-
carrying mule, were sent ahead to cross the salty, bare plain
and scout for water at the base of a landmark peak on the
western edge; were to raise a smoke signal if they found good
country.

Carson says in his *Own Story:*

It [this desert] had never before been crossed by white man. I was often
here. Old trappers would speak of the impossibility of crossing, that water
could not be found, grass for the animals, there was none.

Fremont was bound to cross. Nothing was impossible for him to perform if required in his explorations.

Before we started it was arranged that at a certain time of next day
we [he] should ascend the mountain near his camp, have with him his
telescope, so that we could be seen by him, and if we found grass or water,
we should make a smoke, which would be the signal to him to advance.

Frémont says, writing some seventeen years after Carson's
dictation, that he was to start the next day and make one
march into the desert, there to wait for news.

The Carson squad made a forced march, by night and early
morning, of sixty miles and discovered grass and water at the
foot of the lone peak. They signaled by smoke, and Archambeau rode back, on into another night, to meet Frémont; announced, as Frémont says, by welcomed jingle of spurs, came
upon him and his camp fires, in the midst of the desert, before
dawn; found the company abandoned by their Indian guide,
whose terror of the unknown had been such that "his knees
really gave way under him."

"And next evening at dark he [Frémont] got across having
lost only a few animals." (Carson).

Frémont bestowed the name Pilot Peak upon the friendly
mountain. It served as a guide for emigrant parties who, beginning with the summer of the next year, 1846, ventured upon
this new trail from the southern end of the Salt Lake to the
first water, and thence to the Mary's River in the northwest.
The first of the parties, in which was Edwin Bryant who wrote

the chronicle *What I Saw in California,* followed in the very traces of Frémont; but the new desert trail was dubbed the Hastings Cut-Off, for the California enthusiast Lansford W. Hastings, who had been a member of the Chiles company of 1843, and his co-operate James M. Hudspeth, in company with James Clyman and others, on return from California that spring had taken to that new route of which they had heard from the Frémont men.

On the regular emigrant trail along the Mary's River (the Humboldt)—

at 14 miles we encamped this being the point whare Mr. Freemant intersected the wagon Trail last fall on his way to california and Mr. Hastings our pilot was anxious to try this rout but my beleef is that it [is] verry little nearer and not so good a road as by fort Hall ... after long consultation and many arguments for and against the different routs one leading Northward by fort Hall and the other by the Salt Lake we all finally tooke Fremonts Trail by way of the Salt Lake Late in thee day.[802]

Forthwith Hastings and Hudspeth stationed themselves at Bridger's Fort on the emigrant road to Fort Hall and other junctions of the Snake River trail to Oregon and the Humboldt River trail for California, and shunted travel to California by promise of a new, shorter route around the southern end of the Salt Lake. Captain Joe Walker, however, there at Bridger's Fort advised the Bryant company against the new trail; succeeding parties of emigrants met disaster on the wide, pitiless salty plain whose reflected sunshine and acrid dust distressed man and beast, and more disaster amid the rough country beyond; so that one road or another passing north of the Salt Lake, for the Humboldt River trail to California, was favored over Hastings Cut-Off.

Now by circumvention of short low range after short low range the Frémont company proceeded westward until, November 5, at the eastern base of the East Humboldt Mountains system in northeastern present Nevada, they divided. The larger detachment, under Topographer Edward Kern and guided by Joe Walker the desert veteran, was directed to strike the Mary's

or Ogden's River in the northwest, and follow it down to its
head by the emigrant road; thence continue to rendezvous
at Walker Lake in the southwest[303]

To the mountains and to the river Frémont gave the name
Humboldt — not in arrogance, nor in ignorance of the long-
standing name for the river, but as a bow to the celebrated
physical scientist and naturalist Alexander von Humboldt, of
Germany. Humboldt's study of mountains did not take him
into North America — they were of general value, nevertheless, and a tribute of one explorer to another was fitting; but
Peter Skene Ogden and his Indian wife had prior claim to the
river at least, and the name Humboldt was misplaced.

Frémont, with ten selected men, "some of whom were Delawares," the rest including Carson, Dick Owens, Lucien Maxwell, Basil Lajeunesse, rode on by course southwest through
central Nevada for that lake which then bore and ever since
has borne the name of Joe Walker.

At the reunion near reedy Walker Lake the call of California and Sutter's Fort and of intrigue yet to be determined
was insistent. The well-timed approach of winter was excuse
enough for making port, although this desert frontier of the
Sierra Nevada had turned out to be not inhospitable. As Frémont recorded:

Instead of a barren country, the mountains were covered with grasses of
the best quality, wooded with several varieties of trees, and containing
more deer and mountain sheep than we had seen in any previous part
of our voyage.

But it was the close of November. Light falls of snow here
in the lower country and the cold breath from the Sierra ramparts beyond those foothills counseled haste if the experiences
of 1844 were not to be repeated. The Kern-Walker party, with
the main baggage, set on southward to cross the mountains by
southern pass known to Walker, and to come in to the upper
San Joaquin; the Frémont party of fifteen picked men struck
northwest up Walker River, to Carson River, thence on to the
Truckee and up the Truckee into the mountains — the

Truckee trail of the Fortyniners, of the Overland Stage and the Pony Express, and of the first transcontinental railroad.

By pass that may have been Truckee or Donner's Pass, of present Summit, Frémont crossed the divide. Emigrants had been ahead of him, and he saw the year-old ruts left by the wheels of the first wagons to climb over the mountains. Lake Tahoe was far on his left, the pass of 1844, to be called Carson Pass, was still further. Descending, in due time he paralleled the North Fork of the American River and continuing at ease, with men and animals in great contrast with his sorry squad of his previous invasion, on December 9, 1845, he made camp beside the American just above the fort.

He, Kit Carson, Alex Godey, Basil Lajeunesese, possibly others present, were in the beautiful "California Valley" once again. The Delawares, Dick Owens, Lucien Maxwell, and others, for the first time. Outside there lay the desert Great Basin branded with the Frémont irons: Pilot Peak, Humboldt Mountains and River, Basil Creek, Crane Creek, Sagundai Spring, Walker Lake and Walker River as may be, Carson Lake and Carson River, added to Pyramid Lake, Lake Abert, Christmas Lake, Summer Lake and Winter Ridge, of the first entry from the north. Some of the brands have stuck, others have been changed and may scarcely be recognized upon the desert's hide.[304]

By this traverse of the Nevada desert interior from east to west another joint (the first being the Mary's River) had been found in the armor of the Great Basin. The map submitted by Frémont in 1848, based upon his explorations of 1845, was vastly different from his map of the Great Basin of 1844. Where much had been white, save for the arching legend "Unknown," now much was etched with physical symbols and place names. And although the Frémont southern route was improved upon and shortened by later explorations; although, in consequence of the California troubles, his feat of 1845 received less notice by the world and was less exploited by himself than his previous feats, he really pioneered a permanent feasible trail between the Salt Lake and Northern California. Moreover he and his stalwarts were the first white men, as he rightfully asserts, to make survey of this, the prospector's end of Nevada, long thereafter to be *terra incognita* save to the emigrant, the stage, the pack animal, the Mormon station-keepers, the treasure delver, and the wandering Indian.

In 1859 Captain J. H. Simpson of the Topographical Corps, which no longer knew Captain Frémont except as a name, surveyed for a central route across the Great Basin. He approximated the Frémont trail in places. By reason of Indian attacks throughout the emigrant trail of the Humboldt route and in order to shorten the running time the Pioneer Stage Line of the Overland Mail was moved south, to the northern one of the two routes reported upon by Captain Simpson — the latitude of the Frémont crossing. Beginning in the winter of 1859-60 the dusty Concords plied between Salt Lake and Placerville by the Simpson Central Route; the Overland Stage Line and the Pony Express took the same central route; in this case at least Frémont was the Pathfinder, and it had been his to sow where others should reap.[305]

Chapter XXXI

In Again with Frémont — 1846

TAKING Kit Carson, on the second day, Frémont rode down from the camp to report at Sutter's Fort, about three miles. He found, he naïvely says, "that our previous visit had created some excitement among the Mexican authorities"; and that Captain Sutter had explained away the intrusion with the statement that a party "engaged in a geographical survey of the interior" had been obliged to seek food and shelter at his place.

It is hard to credit that Frémont was only now getting this news. Closely following upon his previous visit, Captain Sutter had reported it and the circumstances attendant upon it, to United States Consul Thomas O. Larkin at Monterey, by a letter of March 28 — the day after Colonel Tellez and soldiers had appeared, investigating; and Consul Larkin had reported the whole matter, by dispatch of April 12, to the Secretary of State. Frémont was in Washington during the next fall and winter and spring.

He had camped, this time, opposite the *rancho* of the sea-captain Eliab Grimes, and from the Americans who undoubtedly came into his lines he should have learned that by orders from Mexico, date of June 10 and published in California September 12, the influx of foreign immigrants without passports into California was to be stopped, and that General José Castro had warned American settlers that unless they obtained regulation licenses to occupy lands as Mexican citizens, they could not remain. Rumors of war with the United States, emanating from Mexico and based upon the annexation of Texas, had been eight months in circulation throughout Northern California.

He should have heard, also, of the revolt of the Californians against Governor Manuel Micheltorena, who represented Mexico, and his imported *cholos* or convict soldiery; and how Captain Sutter, with an enlisted force of settlers recruited at his fort, had aided Micheltorena in the brief campaign, last January, against ex-Governor Juan Bautista Alvarado and General José Castro. Micheltorena was ousted, Don Pío Pico, native son, was installed in his place; and it might seem that Captain Sutter had been on the wrong side.

In a frame of mind only to be conjectured, then, Frémont, taking Carson, rode down the river to call upon Captain Sutter. He says, and Carson also says, that the captain received them with delight and supplied them with everything desired. But John Bidwell, of the Bartelson-Bidwell emigrant party of 1841, relates that on this day he himself was in charge of the fort during Captain Sutter's absence on a trip out to the Bay of San Francisco.

Frémont camped on the American River about three miles above the fort. The first notice of his return to California was his sudden appearance, with Kit Carson, at the fort. He at once made known to me his wants.

Bidwell replied that he was unable to furnish the sixteen mules but could furnish horses; could make the required pack-saddles and could turn over the blacksmith shop but that there was no coal for the forge. Whereupon Frémont "became reticent, and saying something in a low tone to Kit Carson, rose and left without saying good-day." Having heard that as he rode away he complained of his treatment, Bidwell went up to his camp in order to set matters right. There Frémont

stated in a very formal manner, that he was the officer of one government and Sutter the officer of another; that difficulties existed between those governments; and, hence, his inference that I, representing Sutter, was not willing to accommodate him.[306]

Frémont accordingly had not been unaware that his presence in California might be unwelcome. Captain Sutter returned the next day and made amends the best he could; rounded up fourteen mules and meanwhile reported the arrival of the party of Americans to General Mariano Guadalupe Vallejo, commanding the northern frontier, with headquarters at Sonoma presidio north of the Bay of San Francisco; explained that the party wished to recruit themselves in a mild climate. Captain Sutter played the game two ways. As the landed proprietor of a trading post he would not rebuff this gift-horse in shape of Anglo-Saxons descending to him from the mountains — a horse that might prove to be as dynamic as the wooden horse of the Greeks in Troy; and as a Mexican citizen and official besides he should not yet risk the displeasure of the powers that were. Duties were expected of him as Representative of the Government on the Northern Frontiers and Commissioner of Justice.

Having been placated by Captain Sutter (whom he later deposed as a "Mexican"), on January 14 Captain Frémont marched south with cattle and horse stock, to find his main party under Edward Kern, Theodore Talbot and Joseph Walker. He marched in confidence; that his presence again in the country, this time with some sixty mounted men armed each with "three to six guns, rifles and pistols," might rouse fresh alarm in the nervous authorities, did not trouble his mental horizon.[307]

He did not temporize with the Indians, as he had done the year before when the Paiutes had infested his march. He set out to be the master at once. Striking the trail of horse-eating Indians, on his way up the San Joaquin Valley, he sent Dick Owens, Lucien Maxwell and two Delawares forward to locate the thieves; followed, and in the act of making night camp heard the sounds of a fracas on ahead. Charging to the rescue, he came upon Owens, Maxwell and the Delawares driven to cover upon a little hill by an angered Indian village and about to lose their own horses. Owens deftly shot an Indian, a safe retreat was accomplished, and although this night the Indians roundly cursed the invaders and threatened death to all in the morning, the party succeeded in side-stepping the enemy and making on.

It was a bootless affair — and worse than that. It encouraged further hostilities, even to the end that the California officials, were they so minded, might incite the California tribes to scourging the American trespassers from the land. Indeed, this accusation against the authorities was soon made. By thus early shedding blood Frémont was shifted from the defensive to the offensive; he had adopted the feud of the settlers with the horse stealers — for that matter, the feud of the Mexican military and *rancheros* also, but received no thanks for that.

Carson had engaged these horse eaters of California in this very valley in 1830 and likely enough had warned Frémont of their tricks. Captain Sutter had conducted a successful expedition against the marauders last year. Frémont did not act without reasonable caution, and, of course, he had not forgotten the Hernández tragedy and the fate of Baptiste Tabeau laid at the door of those other horse eaters, on the desert. He sent a squad forward to scout and to insure against surprise. Nevertheless, it may be accepted that Owens, Maxwell and the two Delawares did not make the peace sign from their post upon the hill. The way in from the Salt Lake had been void of excitement; the Delawares particularly, warriors in leash, lusted for new varieties of scalps.

The next day Maxwell sighted an Indian, gave chase to him, overhauled him and in a duel of a brace of pistols against bow and arrows killed him. Whether the Indian had been up to mischief was not learned; Frémont, galloping to the scene with Alex Godey and two Delawares, was too late to stop Maxwell, already flushed with victory.

A circuit of the valley of the San Joaquin was made, but the main party were not found. The beef cattle and the horse stock were diminishing. To quote Carson's *Own Story:*

From the head of King's River we started back for the prairie [the valley bottoms of the lower country on this western side of the Sierra] and when we arrived we had no cattle, they all having given out. Had to leave behind all except those we killed for meat. As we were getting from the mountains, during the night, some Indians crawled into our camp and killed two of our mules. Next morning we started back for the Fort. Through some mistake we had not found our camp [the Talbot-Kern-Walker camp at appointed rendezvous] and, as we had lost nearly all our animals, it became necessary to return. The same evening we came on a party of Indians, killed five of them, and continued on to the Fort. Arrived at the fort safely.

Frémont does not mention this affray save by inference in a letter to his wife — "[we] fought our way down into the plain again and back to Sutter's. Tell your father that I have something handsome to tell him of some exploits of Carson and Dick Owens, and others."

They were still the sixteen in number when they returned to Sutter's Fort. All were afoot, Carson says. The tour had been disastrous. The day was January 15 — the year '46 had dawned and the pen of History was poised over the opening chapter in another annual of National events.

In August, while Captain Frémont was organizing at Bent's Fort, General Taylor had moved forward to the Gulf coast of Texas. Now, by orders of January 13 from the Secretary of War, he would move, in due course, forward again and this time to the Rio Grande border, on the farther edge of 119 miles of territory never relinquished by the Mexican government to Texas, nor as yet occupied by Texas. The diplomatic advances to Mexico by President Polk had failed; the military advance of General Taylor was to be a success. Of these developments Captain Frémont, in California, knew nothing.

On this date, the middle of January, one Lieutenant Archibald H. Gillespie of the Marine Corps, having left Washington early in November last with confidential instructions for Consul Larkin and Captain Frémont in California, and having traveled privately through Mexico from Vera Cruz of the east coast to Mexico City, there to be stayed by anti-peace demonstrations which placed a militant dictator in power, is pressing on again, for Mazatlan of the west coast. Of this slow Mercury from the Washington Olympus which debated peace and war, Captain Frémont in California can have no knowledge. And Lieutenant Gillespie himself, secret agent and dispatch bearer, can only repeat, parrot like, the instructions confided to him. Of the actual events that pursue him but do not overtake him he knows no more than Frémont, excepting that in the Mexican capital he has had opportunity to contact the temper of the Mexican people. He speaks the Spanish very well.

Kit Carson says that the Frémont party now had to refit from the settlements on the coast.

At Sutter's Frémont found United States Vice-Consul William A. Leidesdorff, pro-American Dane of West Indian blood, and Captain William S. Hinckley, Mexicanized Yankee skipper, ex-alcalde of Yerba Buena and captain of the port of San Francisco — arrived, the two visitors, by skiff up the river from the bay, to follow rumors to their source. Captain Sutter gave a dinner to his assembled guests of state. And having rested four days and exhausted the spare supplies on hand, Captain Frémont, taking eight of his men, and having been furnished with a passport at last by Captain Sutter, set out in Sutter's schooner launch for San Francisco Bay.

He does not mention the names of the eight — who, however, by the manuscript of William Swasey, Sutter's bookkeeper, as written for historian Bancroft, included Alex Godey. Nor is it stated who the men remaining were, or what they did; but they probably were left in charge of Carson, for Carson says: "We now started for San José. . . . Got a few animals and crossed the coast range to see if we could hear anything of our party under Talbot."

As to the Talbot-Kern-Walker detachment, whereabouts unknown, Frémont had no worries. They were surely on the right side of the Sierra, in a good game country, and were strong enough to look out for themselves. It was high time that he himself proclaimed for himself to official California.

At Yerba Buena village of San Francisco pueblo he took stock, as a sight-seer, of the noble bay, and was entertained by Vice-Consul Leidesdorff and Captain Hinckley; here wrote a letter, January 24, to Jessie, his wife, recounting his successful trip, to date, into California — "I am now going on business to see some gentlemen on the coast, and will then join my people, and complete our survey in this part of the world as rapidly as possible." And, that having been accomplished, in good season "we turn our faces homeward . . . *et le bon temps viendra.*" That promised future was rainbow's end; the fairy gold never quite materialized, but for John Charles Frémont it always turned to the false, fool's gold.[308]

From Yerba Buena he set on, with Vice-Consul Leidesdorff, inland by way of San José, to present himself to Consul Thomas O. Larkin at Monterey, the military and commercial capital of Alta California. It was necessary for him to learn the news, to establish his credit with the authorities, and to open the avenues for refitting his company. His men followed.

In Monterey, January 27, the captain called upon Consul Larkin. He found in the person of this Thomas Oliver Larkin of Massachusetts a close, practical Yankee who with his short side-whiskers and firmly compressed lips was the very type of a New England merchant or Methodist deacon. The captain's coming was not unexpected, for the date of his departure from Yerba Buena had been immediately communicated to headquarters by vigilant Sub-Prefect Francisco Guerrero y Palomaris. And on January 29 Consul Larkin received from Don Manuel Castro, prefect of the district, a formal note of query as to the business, in these parts, of an officer of the United States Army with a body of troops.

The answer, made immediately by Frémont through Consul Larkin's office, was ready and simple. This was an expedition under Government orders to find a more direct route to the Pacific; his command were not soldiers but civilians; he had left them, about fifty, on the frontier, and had himself come to Monterey for the purpose of getting supplies; after having rested his company he would march northward into Oregon.

There was no written reply to this explanation, and silence was taken for assent. Don Manuel, however, had at once sent a dispatch to Governor Don Pío Pico and the provincial government at Los Angeles, for instructions. Then in an interview with Don José Castro, commanding general of California, and other officials, Captain Frémont was granted permission, so he testifies, "to winter in the valley of the San Joaquin" and there recruit his men "where there were no inhabitants to be molested by our presence." He said, in later day, that he proposed, to General Castro, to march out southward to the Gila River and home by that route.[309]

But the exact words of the interview are not of record, and Frémont, pleading his latitude of action before the Congressional committee sitting upon the claims to indemnity for services rendered him during the conquest, seems to have had a number of after thoughts.

The California authorities had little knowledge of those unmilitary employes — American, French, avid Delawares; bearded, hairy, swart, with "from three to six guns, rifles and pistols, each"; and for that matter Frémont himself did not then know where his said fifty men were nor what they were up to. Anyway, he did not retire to the San Joaquin, in the interior upon the eastern side of the coast range; he remained on the settlements side of the mountains.

The Talbot-Kern-Walker party were over in the east, at the end of a hard trip in which the lean had equalled the fat. Had not been obliged to kill any Indians, although Captain Walker, while ascending to his pass on a previous trip, had killed twenty-five. Having failed to meet Captain Frémont at the assumed rendezvous, they were heading down the San Joaquin for Sutter's Fort when, February 6, Captain Walker and Fabbol, scouting in advance for news, encountered one William O. Fallon — "Mountaineer" Fallon, "Big" or "Gros" Fallon, he was called — an Irishman of the country, who said that Frémont was over at San José puebelo, with the rest of the company. Walker started back with him, from the camp on the Calaveras of the lower San Joaquin, to open communications; and then, on the 11th, Kit Carson and Dick Owens appeared; and on the 15th the march from the San Joaquin and across the coast mountains was met, just outside of San José, by fresh horses sent from the Frémont camp; and that noon the whole company were together again, in camp some thirteen miles southeast of San José — upon the Laguna Seca *rancho* of the American William Fisher and near to the public road through this Santa Clara Valley.[310]

The spectacle of the hardy cavalcade of half a hundred more *extranjeros* North Americans shuffling by the traveled road through little San José, for the camp beyond, should have set the 500 inhabitants agog; but for the department officials at Monterey the period was one of watchful waiting. Thus Governor Don Pío Pico, making no objections as yet, enjoined upon Prefect Don Manuel Castro, by letter of February 18.[311]

Getting the report of Topographer Kern, Frémont gave the name Owens, for Dick Owens, to a lake passed by the detachment high up amid the eastern slopes of the Sierra. The river along which descent from the Sierra had been made took the name Kern River.

The valley camp was visited by Californian *caballeros*. There were rivalries of horsemanship and marksmanship. With his rifle an American brought down a vulture on the wing. Kit Carson, like Joe Walker, had been hereabouts before. In the summer of 1830 he, with Captain Ewing Young, from their trappers' camp over on the San Joaquin had come to the Mission San José twelve miles north of the town, and probably had gone down into Monterey, to help apprehend the mutinous Frenchmen. His elder half-brother, big Mose, now was about to come up from the south to take resident charge of the Fitch *rancho* up above Sonoma. That Kit saw him this spring, however, is doubtful. He was to see him a little later.

Americans from the outlying districts also visited the camp. Among them was Dr. John Marsh, Harvard medico and active proprietor of the extensive Los Médanos *rancho* lying between the delta of the San Joaquin and the northern base of Mount Diablo. He was one of the settlers who had enlisted with Captain Sutter's force on the side of Governor Micheltorena last fall. But he really had nothing against the Castros and could assure Captain Frémont that Americans were promised good treatment by the present power in California. Captain John Gantt, Carson's old trapper captain, should have been among the visitors. He had quarters at the Marsh *rancho;* had raised a company of riflemen in the Sutter command for Micheltorena's cause; and after the governor's downfall he, with Dr. Marsh, had contracted with Governor Pío Pico to hunt horse-thief Indians — but the job fizzled out. Neal the blacksmith, who had been discharged at Sutter's in 1844, turned up — if not here, then below, far from his ranch in the upper Sacramento Valley. At any rate, Captain Frémont and his camp drew many visitors, of many kinds.

The camp was only about thirty miles from the ocean, which a wooded range in the west shut from the view. San José lay in a coast valley. From a little hill up at the mission (a short ride) an arm of the bay of San Francisco itself could be seen. Monterey was about seventy miles by road, in the southwest at the other side of the lower end of that Cuesta de los Gatos (Wild-Cats Ridge) which is the Santa Cruz Mountains.

This was by no means the San Joaquin Valley, removed from the settlements. Prefect Don Manuel Castro and General Don José Castro, and perhaps Consul Thomas O. Larkin as well, may have wondered how long Captain Frémont and his sixty armed men were to remain here ere proceeding to winter upon the San Joaquin frontier. The winter was passing; it had practically passed before Captain Frémont had asked permission to spend it.

There was a disturbing incident. Don Sebastian Peralta, of a very respectable family, a brave Indian fighter, one time *regidor* (magistrate) at San José, and *mayordomo* or superintendent of secular affairs at Santa Clara Mission there a little way northwest of San José, and now owner of the large *rancho* Rinconada de los Gatos adjoining Santa Clara, complained to the alcalde of San José that when he had approached the American commander with claim to horses of his that were in the American *caballada* he had been treated insultingly and ordered out of the camp.

Alcalde Dolores Pacheco, who was, himself, a man of high standing, thereupon addressed a note, February 20, to Captain Frémont, summoning him to satisfy the claims of Don Sebastian. But the American commander only replied with a tart letter. He said that all his animals had been bought and paid for, except four taken from the Tulares Indians; and the one horse in especial claimed by Sebastian Peralta had been brought out from the United States. He said that Don Sebastian "should have been well satisfied to escape without a severe horse-whipping" for having tried to "obtain animals under false pretences."

Any further communications on this subject will not, therefore, receive attention. You will readily understand that my duties will not permit me to appear before the magistrates of your towns on the complaint of every straggling vagabond who may chance to visit my camp. You inform me that unless satisfaction be immediately made by the delivery of the animals in question, the complaint will be forwarded to the governor. I would beg you at the same time to enclose to his Excellency a copy of this note.[312]

There was nothing more to be done, for on the day after, February 22, the Americans broke camp and moved on southward, by the road to Santa Cruz of the coast. Alcalde Pacheco transmitted the correspondence to Prefect Castro at Monterey, and endorsed Don Sebastian as being *hombre de bien* — an honest man.

Frémont's attitude in this matter is somewhat puzzling. His best course, it seems, if he were so certain of his rights, would have been to challenge full investigation, and thus make good his previous avowment that his mission in the country was entirely peaceful. There is the chance that Carson had told him of the toils cast about Ewing Young and company in Los Angeles, and that with a sense of guilt at having already overstayed his welcome in these parts he proposed not to be trapped by any trumped-up charges. One thing would lead to another, and he had men who were getting out of hand — as is seen later.

As for Don Sebastian — in the fall of 1833 he, with a party from San José, had taken twenty-seven stolen horses from an American party of traders captained by one Joaquin Jóven or Ewing Young, in the San Joaquin Valley, and he knew how

these *caballadas* in the interior were made up. The majority of
the horses acquired from the Indians had been stolen first.[313]

When, this spring, Frémont marched up the Sacramento for
the north he was followed by a letter from Captain Sutter
asking him to send back twenty-one stolen horses out of a
gather from the Indians; this letter Frémont resented by not
replying to it at all.

Breaking camp on February 22 (while, as happened, the
messenger Gillespie was leaving port at Mazatlan) Frémont
marched, not northeast for the San Joaquin, with Oregon of
the north in prospect, or, by other choice, with the goal of the
Rio Colorado and Rio Gila of the southeast in view. He took
to the traveled road to the settlements on the coast in the west
and southwest. He showed no inclination of retiring to the
unsettled frontier.

This was the road to Santa Cruz and Monterey of the Bay
of Monterey. Frémont states in his *Memoirs* that he wished to
examine the coast slopes, with the idea of sometime making a
home there. Consequently the vagrant trip was not one of exploration for the Government. The reports of Consul Larkin
would supply sufficient information upon that region. The
company did not require further recuperation by this kind of
a jaunt, and he himself had engaged to keep away from the
settlements.

He states that his route was designed to take him to a pass
in the coast range south of Monterey, by which he would cross
into the interior. But the Cascade Mountains and the way to
Oregon did not lie in that direction, and the Government instructions apparently did not contemplate a swing back home
through the extreme southwest.

Now this erratic move by Captain Frémont — who was in
California at all merely by suffrance of the supreme authorities, his passport from Captain Sutter, an under official, being
a temporary affair — was rightly viewed with suspicion. Something may have been said, by Consul Larkin, of his visiting
Monterey again after he had collected his men but it had not

been expected that he should bring all his men with him. Having leisurely crossed the water-shed of the Santa Cruz Mountains, he descended to the coast at Santa Cruz of the northern end of Monterey Bay; thence, by no one's leave, he marched southward through the cattle pastures fronting the bay, into the Salinas plains east of Monterey at the south end of the bay; and on March 3 was camped, with all his armed men, on the *rancho* Alisal of the Englishman William E. P. Hartnell, near present Salinas, and about twenty miles from the presidio and customs port of Monterey.

This Don Guillermo Hartnell was customs house inspector and interpreter, and was known to favor foreign rule in California — but that of England rather than of the United States. The camp of the Americans on his lands was nothing reprehensible in that, perhaps. The men, however, still here in the settlements and so near to Monterey itself, were making a nuisance of themselves.

Three of them intruded upon the *rancho* Los Paicines of Don Angel María Castro of the Castro family — an uncle of General Don José Castro, and justice of the peace at San Juan Bautista Mission; frightened the women, and one man, who was drunk, forced one of Don Angel's daughters to drink wine with him. Further and more serious offense was alleged. Don Angel, not a young man, ordered the fellow out; he drew a pistol but his two companions finally got him away. For this low business he paid a fine of ten dollars at San Juan, but the native people did not know what might happen next.[314]

There appears to be no record of Frémont's having communicated with Prefect Castro or General Castro at Monterey, with explanation of his approach to the coast. He received a letter from Consul Larkin, inviting him to come in to Monterey and, by report — for this letter seems not to be on file — suggesting that he fullfil expectations. Frémont responded, March 5:

It would have afforded me pleasure to thank you personally for the kindness of your late letters, but I am unwilling to leave my party, and the presence of my little force might be disagreeable to the authorities in Monterey. . . . I shall soon be laboriously employed; the spring promises to be a glorious one, and a month or two will pass quickly and usefully among the flowers while we are waiting on the season for our operations in the north.[315]

A "little force" of over fifty armed foreigners might indeed be unwelcome in Monterey. Whether or not the allusion to a "glorious" spring had double meaning must be left to that veil of mystery in which Frémont moved about. But if he thought that he was free to proceed down to Santa Barbara of the coast (as had been planned), why lay a smoke screen over his intentions? And if he apprehended that he would be exceeding his rights, why go there?

His period of special grace was sharply challenged. This very afternoon a young provincial officer with two soldiers as his escort rode into the camp. He introduced himself as Lieutenant José Antonio Chavez, sent by General Don José Castro. He was an imperious caballero, with bearing of contempt for the men and their commander. His manner therefore was offensive, but it was not necessarily official; the notes that he delivered were official.

Comandante General Don José Castro wrote:

This morning at seven, information reached this office that you and your party have entered the settlements of this department; and this being prohibited by our laws, I find myself obliged to notify you that on the receipt of this you must immediately retire beyond the limits of the department, such being the orders of the supreme government, which the undersigned is under the obligation of enforcing.

Prefect Don Manuel Castro wrote that he had "learned with much displeasure"

that in disregard of the laws and authorities of the Mexican republic you have entered the pueblos of this district under my charge, with an armed force, on a commission which the government of your nation must have given you to survey solely its own territory. Therefore, this prefecture orders you as soon as you receive this communication, without any excuse, to retire with your men beyond the limits of this department; it being understood that if you do not do it, this prefecture will adopt the necessary measures to make you respect this determination.[316]

Frémont's reaction was instant. He took no time for a formal response by the written word, as military custom demanded. To him the spirit of the orders was reflected in the brusque delivery of them. He informed Lieutenant Chavez that he was astonished "at General Castro's breach of good faith, and the rudeness with which he committed it," and bade him say to General Castro that "I peremptorily refused compliance to an order insulting to my government and myself."

Lieutenant Chavez, stiff of neck, rode away. He should have been pleased with the effect of his insolence, and the mischief which he had contributed to the situation. In the camp there were fingers that itched to loose a bullet after him. But he was not all popinjay; he was possessed of valor and resources. Might Frémont and the men have read his future they would have smiled. The next January Lieutenant Chavez, as a wounded fugitive from the battle of near-by Natividad, finally escaped capture at Monterey by lying *perdu* in a four-poster bed and there bulwarked on either side by a fair and loyal companion— "their dark locks floating over the pillows, and their large eyes closed in seeming slumber," as remarks the Navy chaplain Walter Colton. A Don Juan, but booted and spurred! The American searching squad withdrew with apologies. The episode was long a picaresque tale for the California countryside, and burdened Lieutenant Chavez with a train of embarrassing congratulations.[317]

Chapter XXXII

American Rifles in California

KIT CARSON says:

After we had all got together again [outside of San José] we set out for Monterey to get an outfit. When we arrived within about 30 miles of Monterey, Fremont received a very impertinent order from General Castro, ordering him to immediately leave the country and if he did not, that he would drive him out.

Senator Benton says, in a letter of November 9, 1846, to *Niles Register* (Vol. LXXI), that when Frémont had retired, by permission, "to that beautiful valley" of the San Joaquin, General Castro would have attacked him on the pretense that he was inciting the American settlers to rise against the government.

Secretary of War, General Marcy, says in his annual report, date of December 5, 1846:

The leave [to recruit in the valley of the San Joaquin] was granted; but scarcely had he [Frémont] reached the desired spot for refreshment and repose, before he received information from the American settlements, and by expresses from our Consul at Monterey, that General Castro was preparing to attack him with a comparatively large force of artillery, cavalry and infantry, upon the pretext that, under the cover of a scientific mission, he was exciting the American settlers to revolt.

Whereupon Frémont "took a position on a mountain overlooking Monterey, at a distance of about thirty miles." The geographical horizons of Senator Benton and Secretary Marcy were rather vague.

General Castro says, reporting, March 6, to the Minister of War:

This man [Captain Frémont] presented himself at my headquarters some days ago, with the object of asking permission to procure provisions for his men, whom he had left in the mountains — which was given him. But two days ago I was much surprised at being informed that he was only two days' journey from this place. Consequently I at once sent him a communication, ordering him, on the instant of its receipt, to put himself on the march and leave the department. But I have received no answer, and in order to make him obey in case of resistance, I sent a force to observe his operations, and today I march in person to join it and to see that the object is attained.[318]

Frémont says, writing to his wife April 1 (*Memoirs*): "The Spaniards . . . ordered us out of the country, after having given me permission to winter there."

Without a shadow of a cause, the governor suddenly raised the whole country against us, issuing a false and scandalous proclamation.

Early in the morning of March 6 Captain Frémont moved back a few miles, to the ridge divide between the Salinas and the San Benito rivers. Here, about thirty miles from Monterey, he established himself on "a small wooded flat" at the summit of the rugged Gavilán or Hawk Peak dominating the northern slopes of the Gavilán Range and the road, through the pass there, between Monterey and the inside country whence he had come; hastily erected "a rough but strong fort of solid logs" and "amidst the cheers of the men" broke out, from a tall sapling, the Stars and Stripes.

Thus the United States flag by land floated belligerently for the first time in Alta California of Mexico, and to all effect was not sheathed again as the emblem of conquest. At this time, or on March 8, General Taylor's first division crossed the Rubicon of the Nueces in Texas, on the way to the Rio Grande and war. At this time, or on March 1, John Slidell, special envoy to Mexico, in limbo in Jalapa short of the capital, was again demanding an audience to purchase a peace — only, on March 6, to be denied once more and on March 21 to be issued his passport papers for his return to his own country. At this time, or on March 13, special messenger Lieutenant Gillespie was in the port of Honolulu, for the last leg of his journey from Washington to California, there to seek out Captain Frémont and discharge himself of his secret mission. From this the second week of March, 1846, there dates 5,000 miles of new American seacoast and 1,000 miles square of new American interior, for at the same time President James K. Polk's absolute declaration, in his first message to Congress, December,

1845, that he stood upon the principle "Fifty-four Forty or Fight" had reached the British ministry. The compromise of the forty-ninth parallel was in the offing.

From the hilltop the Frémont sixty, of one mind to bait the Mexican, now watched the forces of General Castro mobilizing at the San Juan mission below. It is doubtful if any of the rank and file made appeal to reason among themselves, paused to question the right and the wrong, even knew what the arrangements had been and, for that matter, cared what this all was about. Frémont was not a commander who discussed the aye's and no's of action with his men. He went ahead and required their support, and got it.

In this instance the men knew — they could see — that the captain had been bullied by the sprig emissary and the bidding he delivered from Monterey quarters. They all had been told to get out. Somebody had interpreted Frémont's reply for the Mexican lieutenant to deliver, and the tenor of that soon spread through the camp. There were men like Carson, of experience in New Mexico with Mexican bad faith, and schooled by the practices of Ewing Young and a long line of trappers and traders to trust in no bargain with the Spaniard. Considerable had been heard of this General Castro and his plan — as so reported — to drive the Americans out of the country and keep them out. But he had tackled the wrong crowd, here.[319]

Whatever Frémont's rights in the present business were, he acted only as a man of spirit could act. He acted in character; if he had docilely turned tail, so to say, and obeyed the letter of the uncompromising instructions, instead of demonstrating his resentment of the accredited spirit of them, he would have lost face with his command and with the California settlers generally.

He recalled General Castro much less pleasantly than when posed as a gracious host at military headquarters in Monterey. A suave, swarthy man, resplendent in full Mexican uniform, collared to the ears and booted to the knees. A man of forehead "high but not broad, indicating a fair average of brains"; of

hair "black as a raven's wing" and "arranged in thick clustering curls"; of "black bushy whiskers and moustaches" forming
"an unbroken cordon of hair from ear to ear via the upper lip";
complexion, "a dark olive"; eye, "a brilliant black, indicating
intelligence"; lips, thick; nose, aquiline; "figure stalwart, inclining to stoutness." These attributes now bespoke the worst,
and Frémont never saw General Castro again, to change this
opinion of him.[320]

The raising of the flag of the United States above the soil of
Mexican California was a spectacular gesture. It gave the men
something tangible as well as theoretical to fight for, and moreover it further enraged and mystified Castro. Whether these
men were pirates, revolutionists, or military invaders commissioned to seize the country in event of the threatened war between the two republics, he did not know. And what the
real but confidential status of Captain Frémont was, Consul
Thomas O. Larkin now wondered also. In his letter to his wife
Jessie, Frémont says: "Of course I did not dare to compromise
the United States, against which appearances would have been
strong." He scraped the ragged edge, however.

At any rate, this was not to be another Alamo. Frémont,
suddenly in command in a moment of civilized war — but an
officer appointed from civilian life to a corps which required
no tactical training — made the most of the experience and
acted alertly. When a body of cavalry were sighted filing up
the wood road as if for the summit, he took forty men and
hastened down to ambush the foe. Fortunately, the column
halted, in time, and turned back. They were Captain Joaquin
de la Torre and company, on a reconnoissance — and not unwilling to test the temper of the bear.

General Castro reported that in this sally Captain Frémont
sent warning to neighborhood rancheros not to join either side.

The Upham *Life of Frémont* (1856) pictures the Delawares
on "unfailing watch from every peak, or lofty crag"; Frémont,
in one portentous sunrise, addressing his men, and assured by
them "with one voice" that they would die "on the spot rather

than surrender"; the Delawares riding the camp in their red
war-paint, with their "war and death songs"; Frémont making
a moonlight sortie with twenty-five men and putting the on-
stealing foe to flight; Frémont boldly reconnoitering the lower
country by daylight; Frémont opposing the plea of his men
for a night attack upon the Californian camp — which may be
true. Rifles had been a long time loaded and the hilltop was
getting irksome.

Meanwhile, down below things were at sixes and sevens.
General Castro was making a great show of gathering troops
and cannon; and not the least of his preparations were the
reports, the proclamations, and the summons to the field, in
process of issue. Consul Larkin was in a flurry. He feared a
conflict, with bloodshed, that would embroil the whole countryside and endanger the lives and property of all Americans
— and he owned considerable property, himself. How far
Captain Frémont was empowered to go Consul Larkin could
not determine. He hazarded the guess that the captain had
confidential instructions not yet evolved.

He feared that the captain had misunderstood the wording
of the notes. Inasmuch as Prefect Castro had transmitted copies
of the notes to the consular office, Consul Larkin dispatched a
correct English translation of them up to the captain, for his
rereading. He warned the captain that the natives were firmly
resolved to "break you up," that a force of 200 soldiers were
being organized as if to attack him, and suggested that he consider an agreement that would enable him to remove his camp
to a greater distance from the settlements. At the same time the
consul ventured to suggest to the prefect and the general that
the officer in command of the Gavilán expedition should be
selected with caution, in order to guard against a needless
conflict. There were explanatory dispatches to the Secretary
of State in Washington, and a fervent appeal to Mazatlan for
a warship.

Frémont replied to the consul's letter of advices, saying that
he would not take time to read it, since the messenger was wait-

ing, but that he had done no wrong, if unjustly attacked would fight without accepting quarter, and "we will die, every man of us, under the flag of our country." Having supplied the Californian messenger with a passport to insure him in his trip out and back, Alcalde Diaz of Monterey now requested a copy of the American captain's note. Consul Larkin furnished it. Fortunately it put him above any suspicion of connivance with the affair and by its apparently honest spirit should have a salutary effect; unfortunately, however, Frémont's "will not accept quarter" was turned, by William Hartnell the Englishman, official interpreter at Monterey, into the Spanish "will not give quarter."

The successful messenger, Prudencio Espinosa (an American messenger, with duplicate dispatches, had been captured by Castro videttes and his budget confiscated) tried to hearten the consul by informing him that 2,000 men could not drive those Americans from their hill. But during this night, of March 9, Frémont vacated his position.

He says that the flag pole fell down — an indication, his men agreed with him, that the time had come for moving on. General Castro had been given opportunity enough to execute his threats. And the captain felt bound, as he ingenuously puts it, to obey the obligations imposed upon a scientific expedition in foreign territory.

It is alleged that the warning implorations from Consul Larkin, voicing at the same time every support within his power as a fellow American, had something to do with the night evacuation. Kit Carson says, reflecting the attitude of the men:

General Castro came with several hundred men and established his headquarters near us. He would frequently fire his big guns to frighten us, thinking by such demonstrations he could make us leave.

We had in the party about forty men armed with rifles, Castro had several hundred soldiers of Artillery, Cavalry and Infantry. Fremont received expresses from Monterey from Americans advising him to leave, that the Mexicans were strong and would surely attack us. He sent them word that he had done nothing to raise the wrath of the Mexican commander, that he was in performance of a duty, that he would let the consequences be what they may, execute a retreat he would not.

We remained in our position on the mountain for three days, had become tired of waiting for the attack of the valiant Mexican General. We then started for the Sacramento River. . . .[321]

There then was no retreat; there was only the retirement at last, after a delay of three days. The Frémont rights in the country, however, were the same on the third day as they had been on the first day. His move was timely, none the less. Castro claimed that on March 9 he received additional, more positive orders, from Mexico City itself, relative to unauthorized foreigners in California and directed particularly against the man Frémont. They might have discouraged his hesitancy to assault a hill garrisoned by half a hundred dead-shot riflemen, posted behind log parapets.

At noon of the 10th he discovered, through scouts, that the Americans were no longer upon the hill. Investigation revealed odds and ends of camp refuse, of little value; and a number of horses — which were announced as the spoils of war but which really were strays cut out from the Frémont *caballada* and left behind. Whether any of the horses bore the Don Sebastian Peralta brand is not stated. Nor is there reliable mention of the amount of that specie — expedition funds as obtained through Consul Larkin — which, as "abandoned," salted the rumors for both Californians and Americans.

Consul Larkin, like General Castro, was relieved in mind. He had already sent up another dispatch for the captain, this time by the hands of "the Blacksmith Joseph who formerly belonged to that company under your command," a reference which seems to point to Samuel Neal. But Frémont and his men had gone. The consul did not know where they had gone. Whereas, in the first week of March, he reported to the Secretary of State that Captain Frémont would proceed from the Monterey latitude to "the Oregon," in a report of April 2 he conjectured that the captain was on his way to Santa Barbara, on the coast in the south, there to pick up supplies and funds which the "undersigned" had mysteriously provided for him ahead of time.

General Castro did not know where the captain and men had gone, save that they had retired a short distance into the interior. He did not pursue, to find out. He followed a posted proclamation that called upon his fellow citizens to rally to "lance this ulcer" which, in the shape of a band of robbers, threatened their independence, with another, that announced that the insulting highwaymen had fled the sight of 200 patriots assembled and had retreated toward the Tulares.[322]

Frémont, however, was upon his way back to the north. He was possibly mindful of those instructions from the War Department which, according to Secretary of War Marcy (annual report of 1846) named as an objective the discovery "of a new and shorter route from the western base of the Rocky Mountains to the mouth of the Columbia River." He retired, as he wrote to his wife April 1, "slowly and growlingly before a force of three or four hundred men, and three pieces of artillery." His trail had become one of unwholesome excitement. His men had been bilked of a lusty fight. The foreigners of Anglo-Saxon blood had been roused, near and far, by his reported straits. He could have doubled his force, but "refrained (he says) from committing a solitary act of hostility or impropriety."

Captain William D. Phelps of the American merchant ship *Moscow* sent him word from Monterey to come aboard at any point on the coast if he were hard pressed. March 14, Dr. John Marsh dispatched a courier ahead of Frémont to Sutter's Fort, with details of the events. On March 17, up near the head of the Napa Valley north of San Francisco Bay James Clyman heard the news:

A report is now rife that Capt. Frémont has raised the American flag in Monteray and all good citizens are called on to appear forthwith to appear at Sonoma armed and Equiped for service under General Byaho [Vallejo] to defend the rights and privileges of Mexican citizens.

By March 21 he had heard more details, but

no report However can be relied on as but few men in this Country can write you may form some idea of what reports are carried verbally from one to two hundred Miles by an ignorant supersticious people.[323]

Whereupon Clyman addressed a note to Captain Frémont, offering him the reinforcement of a company of frontiersman immigrants.

Meanwhile, as before indicated, Castro had sounded the call to arms in San Francisco itself, and from Los Angeles to the Bay region the countryside was in a moil of fear and fervor.

What flag did these men serve who served this Captain Frémont? The flag of lawless filibustering, the flag of California independence, or in truth the flag of a conquering republic? Unmolested and unpursued, in the sweet aftermath of the California rainy season the Frémont company marched, at first by short, defiant stages, down the lush, green valley of the San Joaquin and up the sister valley, poppy strewn, of the Sacramento; on March 21 were again in camp near Sutter's Fort of New Helvetia — there to be congratulated by their fellow Americans for their spunk in bearding the obnoxious Castro, to be hailed as authoritative spokesmen of a new era, and without doubt to find Captain Sutter among the few who were perturbed by the threatened decisive break in profitable relations with the California powers and populace.

The Frémont company as counted upon Hawk's Peak by the messenger Prudencio Espinosa numbered sixty-two. Consul Larkin says that the captain discharged four or five men. He somewhere lost Captain Joe Walker, for Walker was at Bridger's Fort in July with a gather of California horse stock, which he delivered at Bent's Fort in August, for sale to the army in the Southwest. The facts "of considerable interest," in "reference to recent occurrences in California," communicated by him to Edwin Bryant at Bridger's appear not to have excited that gentleman and did not deter him from continuing his journey. During the trip northward, at least, Frémont granted quittance (it would seem) to Steppenfeldt, otherwise

Stepp, the gunsmith, and to William Sigler — if Sigler is to be accepted as having been one of the command. The men were ready to fight or to farm. For many years Kit Carson looked to a return to California, there to stay.

Or Frémont may have dropped off his men to form a line of communication with the rear. To Captain Sutter his actions were "mysterious and suspicious."

Upon the day of Frémont's return, triumphant but resentful, to the bank of the American River above Sutter's Fort, the Mexican Government was closing the door to all overtures from the United States by handing his hat to Mr. Slidell, special envoy of peace proposals backed, apparently, by an American naval squadron off Vera Cruz. General Zachary Taylor was dictating a dispatch announcing that in battle order he had crossed the deadline of the Arroyo Colorado, thirty miles from the Rio Grande, in the face of a Mexican armed force and the written warning that this further advance would be deemed a declaration of war. In Washington, President Polk was looking to war, if there were any, with England rather than with Mexico, and was cherishing the idea of a boundary treaty with Mexico, founded upon advance payment of half a million or a million dollars, calculated to obtain cession of all the remaining west and southwest north of the line of El Paso del Norte run through to the Pacific Coast.

Secret messenger Lieutenant Gillespie was two days out of Honolulu with his cautionary instructions for Consul Larkin and Captain Frémont. Monterey was now four weeks distant; the whereabouts of Captain Frémont were an unknown quantity. The lieutenant's instructions, dated last October, projected California independence as that of another Texas bonded to the American Republic by popular friendship pre-arranged.

All in all, the processes of peace and war had formed bewildering cross currents.

Leaving Theodore Talbot at Sutter's to go by the Sutter launch down to Yerba Buena of San Francisco for supplies, and eventually sending Alex Godey and Thomas Martin south to the Tulares country of the San Joaquin after horses from the Indian herds, Frémont continued north up the Sacramento Valley. In Monterey, General Castro was fuming over a letter from Governor Pico jealously reprimanding him for having usurped Government by issuing proclamations to the citizens; and Consul Larkin was holding again to the fond belief that, regardless of the Frémont excitement, "the flag, if respectfully planted, will receive the good will of much of the wealth and respectability of the country."

Frémont marched steadily northward, as though he were bound far, even to the Cascades and a new route over to the Columbia. Since he had cut loose, he could not strip his *caballada* by returning, at the instance of the fussy Captain Sutter, animals purchased from the Indians for government service and the good of all. Striking the Feather River in the Valley of the Sacramento he followed that up, past the mouth of the Yuba and the site of present Marysville, and dropping over into the main valley again he visited briefly at the ranch of the blacksmith Samuel Neal, turned farmer, on Butte Creek south of present Chico. Still northward, on Deer Creek about a mile from the Sacramento, approximately halfway between present Chico and Redbluff, there was the inviting ranch of Peter Lassen. The distance from Sutter's Fort was almost 200 miles. The outposts of the immigrant settler were ever advancing.

The date of the camp upon Samuel Neal's *rancho* was March 28. On this day, to the discordantly mingling notes of Yankee Doodle and Star-Spangled Banner and the lusty crowing of the First Dragoons' headquarters game-cock, the American Army of Occupation raised the flag on the left bank of the Rio Grande opposite Matamoras. On this day President Polk entered in his *Diary* the receipt of favorable dispatches from Envoy Slidell, peace negotiator in Mexico. But Mr. Slidell had now been a week dismissed by the Mexican Government.

After six days of rest and outfitting at Peter Lassen's — preparation, says Kit Carson, for "the homeward trip" — Frémont marched on into the north, with face to Oregon. In the words of Carson, "[we] started for the Columbia River by going up the Sacramento and passing Shasta butte." The company, however, were not yet fairly off. Blustery spring weather whitened the ground of the upper valley with hail, and much as though genial California had weakened their stamina they were back, within a week, or on April 11, at Peter Lassen's.

Possibly the horse gather by Alex Godey and Thomas Martin, in the south, was yet incomplete. Possibly news as well as horses from the south was looked for. Theodore Talbot should be bringing a packet from Yerba Buena. What of the political weather? The storm season had only just begun.

Frémont stayed at Lassen's *rancho,* this time, almost two weeks. It apparently was during this period, and somewhere between Lassen's and Sutter's Fort, that his men entertained a company of Oregon-bound immigrants at a barbeque and dance — to a result that a San José Indian, one Antolino, posted to the coast with word for Monterey that 200 armed foreigners were making ready, in the mountains, to attack it. It seems to have been during this period that Captain Frémont replied, by letter of unestablished date, to the offer of assistance from James Clyman. "On the eve of my departure for home" — "perplexing circumstances" — " a declaration of war between our government and Mexico is probable" but the news is unconfirmed — "the California authorities . . . threaten to overwhelm me" — in case of peace "I have no right or business here," in case of war "I shall be outnumbered ten to one" and compelled "to retreat, pressed by a pursuing enemy." Additional men, living off the country on the way east, would therefore be only an incumbrance.[324]

It may have been during this period that, as by the assertions of Kit Carson and Thomas Martin, the Frémont company responded to the pleas of the alarmed settlers by shattering villages of the valley Indians — hostiles in mind if not yet in deed. According to Martin "the men were told to do as they pleased about the Indians," and, thereafter, "we followed up the Sacramento, killing plenty of game and an occasional

Indian. Of the latter we made it a rule to spare none of the bucks."

It certainly was during this period that Lieutenant Gillespie, the messenger from Washington, arrived, a month late, at his first goal. On April 17 the *Cyane* sloop-of-war, last from Honolulu, hove to in the Bay of Monterey and dropped a boat which bore Lieutenant Gillespie's credentials to Consul Larkin and the request that he come aboard "as early as possible." The lieutenant's Washington budget was almost six months old, his own cross-country advices were more than two months old, for he had left Mazatlan of Mexico on February 22 and Mazatlan was two weeks removed from the City of Mexico, news center.

On this day there was issued, at Monterey, for Yerba Buena, the *bando* or proclamation that unnaturalized foreigners in California could not hold land and were subject to being expelled.

As though he had been waiting for something — even as though he had been waiting for tardy information but hardly with knowledge of any Lieutenant Gillespie tacking in upon his trail — Frémont did not break camp at Lassen's until April 24. He then headed north once more. His purpose, he says, was definite: to connect this line of survey up the Sacramento Valley and on, with his line of survey south from the Columbia in the late fall and early winter of 1843. Next, a passage through the Cascade coast range of Oregon, on the west, was to be investigated.

In all seeming he was done with California — and the dilatory Castro. Whether he fooled himself, and his men — therein sorely disappointing them; or whether he engaged himself for a return from Oregon through California, is a matter of this and that conceit. At any rate he was playing against loaded dice.

On this day, April 24, when he apparently cast loose again, United States dragoons had also ridden out — to be attacked and roundly whipped, the next morning, by a Mexican detachment, on the north side of the Rio Grande. "Hostilities may now be considered as commenced," General Taylor grimly reported. The news was received in Washington May 9; by Commodore Sloat at Mazatlan, May 17; by Consul Larkin at Monterey, June 19.

On April 24 Lieutenant Gillespie was safe and sound, with all his secrets (except his identity) intact, at San Francisco; for he had left Monterey, with horses and guides, at midnight of April 19, following a ball during which General Castro, suspecting his official character, had vainly plied him with wine. The smiling American officer, the very model of correct deportment, kept his own tongue.

May 8 Captain Frémont, with his company, was camped beside the north end of the main Klamath Lake, across the boundary of Oregon. He was only some twenty miles, air flight, short of his southernmost camp in the Klamath country on that line down from the Columbia in the close of 1843.

At that time, up there, winter had set in. The only pleasing prospect was the oasis valley of the legended Buenaventura waiting in the mute Great Basin. At this time, down here, spring had burgeoned, the men had dispensed with tents, the trail from Lassen's had been one of hunter's delight, only near the end of the survey had the country become bleak and sterile, with winter still lingering; but yonder in the west there were the romantic Cascades, whitely cloaked as yet, to be sure, nevertheless heavily timbered and well watered, promising game and forage, and with pleasant valleys at their eastern base wherein a party of explorers might range at will while waiting upon the season for new and profitable adventure in those higher precincts so rosily alluring with each dawn light. Briefly, according to Frémont in his *Memoirs,* the prospects, at this juncture, all were pleasing. His narrative, to date, has no reference to any complaints by his men. May 6, at the foot of the lake, "Animals and men all fared well here." May 7, he was certain that he could obtain plenty of lake fish when game lacked, while he was completing his survey of the Klamath region ere proceeding to the Cascades. The night of May 8 he was ruminating, with keen anticipation of the work and scenery in store for him, beside his headquarters fire, when he heard the trampling and clinking of hoofs in the black recesses of that wilderness which, he had fancied, was within the human knowledge of only him and his, and the Indians.

The sounds strengthened. In a few minutes two men rode wearily into the firelight. They were the rancher blacksmith Samuel Neal and William Sigler. Neal said that he had important news. The hour was late but the camp had roused. The two horses were turned into the camp herd; the two men were seated by the fire and handed cups of hot coffee from the ever ready pot. Then Neal opened his pack.

He said that a United States lieutenant by the name of Gillespie had been left, two days back, coming on with dispatches from Washington for the captain; he now had only three men — Peter Lassen, Stepp, and a black-boy servant; the trail was hard to follow, the horses were petering out again, the Indian signs were bad, he (Neal) and Sigler had ridden ahead to catch the captain, with heads down and pistols leveled right and left had charged through one party of reds cutting their trail, had covered 100 miles in the two days, and were of the opinion that Gillespie and his little squad were stalled.

All the camp heard. Frémont acted promptly, as always. Nothing was to be gained, he decided, by risking the accidents of a rough trail in the night. He tolled off Carson, Dick Owens, Alex Godey, Lucien Maxwell, Basil Lajeunesse, Denny the half-breed and four Delawares — Crane, Swonok, Sagundai and Charley; ordered them to be ready to take the back trail with him at daybreak; and after the camp had quieted he lay awake wondering what urgency of events had brought a Government messenger from Washington in search of him in these far, wild mountains.

At dawn they all started. In the afternoon they were at their camp of May 6 near the foot of the lake, thirty miles, having made the two marches in one spurt. The spot was in the clear, the lieutenant, if coming, would naturally come this way and could not be missed. At sunset he and his three toiled in.

The meeting of Dr. David Livingston, the Scot explorer, and Henry M. Stanley, American journalist, in the depths of darkest Africa, was scarcely more dramatic than this meeting of John C. Frémont, Army officer, and Archibald H. Gillespie, Marine officer, in the glades of the virgin Northwest.

Chapter XXXIII

Frémont Marches and Counter-Marches

WHEN, at sunset of May 9, in this piece of meadowland on the border of Klamath Lake of southwestern Oregon, Brevet Captain Frémont and First Lieutenant Gillespie shook hands, night had fallen upon the smoking battlefield of Resaca de la Palma of the Rio Grande border of southeastern Texas; the dismayed Mexican soldiery fleeing the Taylor "devils" had lashed the dark surface of the river with fugitives in the last throes, and had filled Matamoras, upon the other side, with cries of lamentation.

In Washington, President Polk had, this evening, received the General Taylor dispatch of April 26 announcing the attack upon the dragoons, and was preparing his war message to Congress declaring that Mexico "has invaded our territory and shed American blood upon the American soil."

While Frémont was camped at the upper end of the lake, May 8, the battle of Palo Alto had been fought; and while he was on his way to the lake from Peter Lassen's, Fort Taylor, opposite Mamatoras, had been enduring a bombardment that would last for practically a week.

Now here was Lieutenant Gillespie. As though to add to the importance of his presence as a messenger from that outer world of national intrigues and sudden actions, some stress has been laid upon the long train of events which pursued him. But those details have resulted for only an anti-climax; the news of the events of the past four months overtook him only as mutterings, and the events themselves can serve as only a historical background.

The lieutenant had left Washington about November 3, for Vera Cruz across the Gulf; had arrived in the City of Mexico late in December and there been detained by the revolution of the Mexican war party; had sailed from Mazatlan February 22; had sailed from Honolulu March 19; had headed north by land out of Monterey April 19; had continued on, up the Sacramento, from San Francisco, April 25; had left Sutter's Fort April 29, and Lassen's ranch, May 2. Three hundred miles by trail north of Lassen's he had found Frémont.

A naval officer who had put in six months and several thousand miles of travel by sea and land for the purpose, apparently, of finding Captain Frémont and delivering dispatches to him from Washington itself should well have excited the curiosity of not only Frémont but all the Frémont company and all the persons, with knowledge of his character, contacted along the way.

As William L. Todd narrates, afterward:

> A great curiosity was awakened by the sudden arrival of a young man in Monterey from Mazatlan, in a United States sloop of war, having left Washington in November, 1845. The young man was Lieutenant Gillespie, of the United States Navy, and his immediate inquiry was for Captain Fremont. Learning his route he sets out to overtake him with all haste. This he succeeds in doing on the southern border of Oregon.[325]

Lieutenant Gillespie's dispatches consisted of a note of introduction, without reference to his rank or real functions, from Secretary of State Buchanan, dated November 1; a packet of newspaper prints and of "home" letters under the seal of Senator Benton, Frémont's father-in-law; and confidential instructions from Secretary Buchanan to Consul Larkin and likewise Frémont — these of date October 17.

The lieutenant had committed the instructions to memory and destroyed the written copy before he landed at Vera Cruz. A duplicate copy was upon its way to Monterey by the *Congress* frigate around the Horn. It would reach Consul Larkin in June and form a pleasing addition to his private official files; for during all the year 1845 he had received but one letter from the Department of State! Comparing this signed document with the transcription written from memory by Lieutenant Gillespie he will find no variation of any consequence. The lieutenant's mind had been extraordinarily retentive.

The instructions appointed Consul Larkin confidential agent for the United States in California; conferred the same duties upon the lieutenant and Captain Frémont; these were, to keep closely in touch with local affairs in California, to cultivate the goodwill of the Californians toward the United States, to counteract any opposing influence of England or France, and by friendly offices to incline the authorities and people to independence of Mexico with the view of voluntary union with the American Republic. The instructions provided for the methods of Statecraft and peace, not for those of force and war.[326]

Frémont attached more importance to the contents of the Senator Benton packet. The family letters he accepted as communicating to him, by cryptic allusions to be understood only by him through discussions in Washington last year, the conditions that actually should govern him. Emphasis was laid upon the threat of England, upon the probability of war with Mexico, upon the necessity of his being ready to take advantage of his opportune presence in California. The letters, he claimed, he was justified in accepting as his warrant, from the Administration, for taking decisive steps, if deemed by him imperative, to secure California.

The letters may have informed him of the warning, transmitted last summer by Baron Gerolt, former Prussian minister to Mexico, to Secretary of the Navy Bancroft and Senator Benton, that the Mexican Government was determined to drive the Frémont company out of California. This, Frémont would not like. Or he may have been so informed by Lieutenant Gillespie, for the lieutenant had things to say which, aside from the confidential State instructions, he could not trust to paper.

These things were of even more importance than the letters. In after years George Bancroft, Secretary of the Navy in 1846, stated that Lieutenant Gillespie was authorized by him to "absolve" Captain Frémont from the duties of an explorer and bid him assume the duties of an Army officer commissioned to the acquisition of California. "It was officially made known to you that your country was at war."[327]

Lieutenant Gillespie had other matters to retail, for the ears of Captain Frémont, here where the wilderness campfires flickered upon earnest, weathered countenances and the back drop of low-branched evergreens. He is assumed to have repeated verbal monitions from Senator Benton, adviser to the President and chairman of the Senate Military Committee. He might have been delegated to speak for the President himself. The Polk *Diary* of October 30, 1845, reads:

I held a confidential conversation with Lieut. Gillespie of the Marine Corps, about 8 o'clock P. M., on the subject of the secret mission on which he was about to go to California. His secret instructions and the letter to Mr. Larkin, United States consul at Monterey, in the Department of State, will explain the object of his mission.[328]

And then, again something very important, he had observations of his own to make, colored by his experiences in Mexico, by what he had further learned at Mazatlan and possibly Honolulu, and by what he had ingested at Monterey and San Francisco.

Kit Carson says, in his *Own Story* dictated ten years after this event of which he chronicled:

A few days after we left [that is, left Lassen's rancho, April 24] information was received in California that war was declared between the United States and Mexico. Lieutenant Gillespie, U. S. Marines, and six men were sent after us to have us come back.

Frémont says, writing forty years after these events of which he chronicled in his *Memoirs:* "Now it was officially made known to me that my country was at war, and it was so made known expressly to guide my conduct." By this he repeats exactly the assertion of ex-Secretary Bancroft in the letter of review written for him, of current date, or in 1886.

The Carson statement may be taken as the guess of the men generally. The Navy lieutenant could not have come this far at risk of his life with any news less than that of war — and of a California to be seized as a prize of war. But Lieutenant Gillespie could not officially, nor personally, have announced a final declaration of war nor even the active existence of war.

The declaration of war by Washington was issued May 13 and reached Mazatlan and the Naval force there near the last of June, and Monterey not until the middle of August. The news of the first bloodshed by an act of war did not reach Mazatlan until May 17, a month after Lieutenant Gillespie had arrived at Monterey. When he was last in Washington, early in November, no one there could assure him, more than by venturing an opinion, that war with Mexico was a certainty. Indeed, there was strong belief, in official circles, in a resumption of friendly relations with Mexico and a peaceful settlement of the territorial dispute between the two republics; and efforts were being directed to a peaceful acquisition of California. The very dispatch which, date of October 14, Lieutenant Gillespie bore to Commodore Sloat at Mazatlan, in addition to those instructions for Consul Larkin and Captain Frémont, enjoined the commodore also to "conciliate toward our country the most friendly regard of the people of California."[329]

A great deal had happened, however (including Frémont on Gavilán Peak), to the relations between the United States and Mexico, since Lieutenant Gillespie had had his confidential interview with President Polk and his talks with Secretary Buchanan and possibly Secretary Bancroft and beyond doubt with Senator Benton, and had set out with his dispatches. What did he now know that he had not known then?

He had been in the City of Mexico in January when the National war party, the military faction, had ousted President Herrera, inclined to negotiations of peace, and elevated Paredes, of the Army. But this was known in California several weeks before the lieutenant's arrival there. On April 2 a military *junta* or council, convened at Monterey, proclaimed for Paredes and although the act was not made public for a time Consul Larkin should have been aware of it. In fact, he should have known of the triumph of the war spirit in the Mexican capital, through advices from Mazatlan, when Frémont had been in contact with him in March. And there were the later contacts established by Frémont with San Francisco through Peter Lassen's, Neal's rancho, and Fort Sutter. Whether Gillespie's news of the revolution was news to Frémont, then, is doubtful.

The lieutenant would know that the peace ambassador, Slidell, had not been received by Mexico, but he could not know that Slidell had been handed his hat — the act which declared for war.

He would know that General Taylor had assembled an army upon the coast of Texas, and Frémont's letters and papers from home would convey the same news (if news it was, to Frémont at this late date); but neither the lieutenant, of his own knowledge, nor the letters and papers, could inform Frémont that by orders of January 13 General Taylor had, on March 8, begun that forward movement to the Rio Grande, which, as accomplished, Mexico viewed as a declaration of war.

Traveling in advance of the decisive war news, the lieutenant had carried to Commodore Sloat the latest advices from the Navy Department, and to Consul Parrott perhaps the latest report of conditions in interior Mexico. From the day he sailed, February 22, from Mazatlan, until the day, April 17, of his arrival at Monterey, he was on the sea, save for five days, March 13 to March 19, in the harbor of Honolulu. The *Cyane,* direct from Mazatlan to Honolulu by a voyage of twenty days, brought news there rather than found it there. Only when, at the finish of the second or last leg of his Pacific voyage, the lieutenant met Consul Larkin at Monterey, after the middle of April, could he have been in touch with comparatively late news of real war import. And that amounted to little beyond the consul's own surmises.

Upon his way again, the lieutenant carried letters of introduction from the consul to Vice-Consul Leidesdorff, Jacob Leese and others of the San Francisco district; to Captain Sutter and Peter Lassen; to Charles Weber of San José and others whom he might encounter in passage. It seems that the consul, although he apparently had not heard from Frémont himself since the Gavilán affair, suspected that the captain might be in the north beyond Peter Lassen's.

The letter of transmission to Mr. Leidesdorff:

I have given to Archibald H. Gillespie, Esq. (of N. Y.) a letter of introduction to you. . . . He has not good health, and wishes to travel through your part of California to enjoy the climate, etc. I believe he has some personal acquaintance with Capt. Fremont, and may wish to see him if the trouble and expence is not too much. . . . You will find Mr. Gillespie a gentleman of much information and well acquainted with the countries he has passed through, as he is well acquainted with the Spanish language. Perhaps he has done business in some Spanish port. You will oblige me by paying to him every attention in your power. . . .[330]

Mr. Gillespie, the gentleman of mystery who may have "done business in some Spanish port" but whose official status was recognized, was followed to Yerba Buena by a letter, April 23, from the consul — who now announces the *Portsmouth* with the latest news:

Capt. Montgomery of the Portsmouth being under sailing orders (the 1st or 2nd instant) at Mazatlan, was waiting for the Mexican Mail, when Commodore Sloat heard per Brig Hannah of the situation of Capt Fremont near San Juan and immediately dispatched the Ship. She was 21 days from Mazatlan to Monterey. I send you 4 or 5 New York and 1 Mexican newspapers the former to the 5th of Feb. the latter of March. New York papers of Feb. 25 were in the hands of the Com. Capt. Montgomery has not yet any certain information of Mr. Slidel's situation in Jalapa, in March, he says that the Cammandant General of Mazatlan had later news by six days than Com. Sloat, that all Custom House and other Government Officers had left Mazatlan taking away the archives, and government property, publishing in the street, that Com. Sloat would in all probability declare a state of Blockade the next day (thereby giving reasons to suppose they were aware of the cause). Mr. Parrott [in] private letter to Don Pablo LaGuire [LaGuerra] has an oppinion that Com. Sloat may by the next mail (6 or 8 days) have a declaration on the part of the U. S. against Mexico in which case we shall see him in a few days take the country.[331]

The consul was preparing General Castro and other influential citizens for a change of flag "in thirty days."

But there is doubt as to whether Lieutenant Gillespie conveyed this news by the *Portsmouth,* and Consul Larkin's dicta, to Captain Frémont, for: "He did not receive this letter till his return from the upper Sacramento to Sutter's Fort, May 30, 1846."[332]

Vice-Consul William Leidesdorff, however, should have received the same information — possibly in time to impart it to the lieutenant. Now he writes, April 25, to Consul Larkin at Monterey:

> According to your request I have done everything in my power for Mr. Archibald Gillespie. he leaves this place in a few hours for the Sacramento. . . . Glorious news for Capt. Fremont. I think I see him smile, by your letters it appears that this news was not generally known. however here they must have some news as the Sub Prefect is busy dispatching couriers in different parts of the country and Capt. Hinckley has been heard to say that Guerrera [the said sub-prefect] had received a courier yesterday advising him of the expected war with Mexico. . . .[333]

Consequently, in view of the foregoing, whatever verbal news of war Lieutenant Gillespie could have delivered to Captain Frémont was reported news subject to ratification. No formal declaration of war had yet been made. Active hostilities had in truth begun, but they were still below the southeastern horizon. Frémont says (*Century Magazine,* 1891), that the idea of conciliation "was no longer practicable, as actual war was inevitable and immediate; moreover, it was in conflict with our own [his and Gillespie's] instructions." One may wonder, then, why if they had special instructions, Consul Larkin, who had just been made trusted confidential agent with Government instructions, was not apprized of those conflicting instructions.

Secretary Buchanan's instructions to Consul Larkin, and repeated to Frémont (and Secretary Bancroft's instructions of the same time, delivered to Commodore Sloat by Gillespie) stipulated that there should be no open interference with California affairs, "unless [Mexico] should commence hostilities against the United States." As Richman puts it in his *Cali-*

fornia Under Spain and Mexico: Is it likely that what was forbidden to the agent [Larkin] was permitted to the officer [Frémont]? And since Frémont assumed, with reason based upon the latest news, that "actual war was inevitable and immediate," he could have awaited his near release. That the Bancroft instructions to him, and those to Commodore Sloat, were opposed in their advices, is hard to accept, although credible.[334]

The designs of Frémont breathed love of Country. As the rule, historians writing near to the California scene have questioned his methods of approach. The influence of his course of conduct upon his men, Kit Carson and others, who without clear understanding of the angles of the situation looked up to him as their mentor and guide, is important in that it promoted arrogance and despite among men who already were adventurers. His influence upon the settlers who were led, directly or indirectly, to count upon his support, moral or material, of their seizure of California property, is likewise important in characterizing the conquest events. The spirit of despite and filibuster was reflected in the acts of the later immigrants. The side-lights of history emphasize the local color with which Frémont invested his trail wherever he went.

He was in his thirty-fourth year. It is true that, as is pointed out, he was alone here in California (at least, he deemed himself to be sole arbiter, irrespective of Consul Larkin) and delegated to his initiative. The Gillespie monitions may have been a word to the wise, emboldening Frémont to decide, as he says, "to move forward on the opportunity." But only his modified statement, in the *Century* article by Mrs. Frémont in 1891, that (as he conceived it) "actual war was inevitable and immediate," is a sortable premise to his argument that he felt authorized to take military measures in advance.

These measures were framed to counter the plans of England as well as the equally conjectural plans of his arch foeman, General Castro. It was not for him to admit that the threat of British sovereignty over California raised only the specter of a theory. The specter was made animate, like a puppet, by foreign agencies such as that of James A. Forbes, British vice-consul in California where the small British commerce should not have required a consular office. Great Britain therefore was maturing a protectorate. Consul Larkin himself was suspicious of rival intrigue. And the maintenance of a major British squadron in the California Pacific provided sources for portentous rumors.[335]

If the tales are believable, a singular situation had developed down there at Mazatlan, with the British and American squadrons playing cat and mouse — with every move of an American ship attended by a like move of a British ship. Just why, with California in view, a British squadron should have been stationed at Mazatlan apparently with the sole purpose of waiting upon the American squadron; and just why, as H. H. Bancroft questions, the British admiral should have felt bound to wait upon the American admiral's advices rather than upon his own advices, which were as timely, and on occasions were even first at hand, is not clear. A sailor's yarn (Purser Rodman M. Price in Frémont's *Memoirs*) has it that when Lieutenant Gillespie turned up with his belated dispatches for California he was shunted on the *Cyane* to Honolulu in order to deceive the British admiral. But we see that when the sloop *Portsmouth* set sail, with all speed, in answer to Consul Larkin's truly alarming summons, she went direct and no British ship tagged her.

It has been suggested that the British ships in Pacific waters waited upon the matter of Oregon rather than upon that of California; and something is said about the American squadron's being so far out-weighed, out-gunned, out-numbered and out-classed by the British warships upon the California station of Mazatlan, that "an understanding concerning Mexican affairs between the Cabinets of St. James and Washington" would seem to exist.[336]

When in 1842 Secretary of State Daniel Webster had contemplated negotiating with Mexico for the harbor of San

Francisco — or, as diplomatically put, "a good harbor on the Pacific" — the British ministry announced, in due time, that "the Queen's government . . . had not the slightest objection to an acquisition of territory [i.e.: by the United States] in that direction." The last of December, 1844, Vice-Consul Forbes at Monterey had been informed by the Home Office that his government "would view with much dissatisfaction the establishment of a protectoral power over California by any other foreign state"; but when in January of this year, 1846, Consul Forbes had protested, to the California government, the presence of Frémont in the department, and had repeated the very warning issued to him only two years back, the British Foreign Office, with the Oregon question in process of peaceful settlement, and with no desire to take on a California dispute, rebuked him with curt mandate: "Her Majesty's Government do not approve of his late proceeding." Consul Forbes acknowledged the corn to Consul Larkin.[337]

So much for the attitude, static rather than dynamic, of the British ministry toward a United States in California. As with Oregon, California was lost to any power save the United States when the American immigrants descended from her helpless borders with the first skirmish columns of that army of the West. The Monroe Doctrine did not need to be enforced, although it made a pleasing sentiment. While it assumed to be a law of Nations it had to be recognized as a law of national nature. Captain Frémont was not deputed to know, and Lieutenant Gillespie, Kit Carson, and the others could not know, those State and Foreign Department exchanges that presumptively revealed the official mind of the British Government. Senator Benton, whose prejudices equaled the volume of his vanities but were offset by his patriotism above party — Senator Benton, the Old Gladiator, did not choose to know. The dogma of British dominance of the Pacific coast was ever-ready fuel for the fire of Western expansion. Secretary Buchanan, in his cautionary confidential instructions, was fending a voluntary drift by California to European supervision. Secretary

Bancroft, of the Navy, bore into the wake, in this instance at least, of Secretary Buchanan. A British protectorate over California could have been only temporary, as a measure to secure claims against Mexico; but Washington was not yet so secure of its tenets as to risk even this precedent.

As has been related, the messages finally delivered to Captain Frémont by Lieutenant Gillespie were a traveler's note of introduction from the Secretary of State, letters and papers from the Benton family, those confidential instructions (as repeated from memory) by Secretary Buchanan and applying here the same as down at Monterey, the oral pronouncements of Senator Benton (speaking of course for Government), the oral advices of the Secretary of the Navy to an officer of the Army transmitting, as an order (according to ex-Secretary Bancroft's recollections in 1886), the determination of the President to possess California; possibly the context of the confidential instructions by the Navy Department to Commodore Sloat at Mazatlan (which paralleled the State Department instructions), and assuredly the live and latest facts and fancies as gathered by Lieutenant Gillespie himself, arrived with his other budget six months old. There was nothing from the Secretary of War.

Now, this interruption of story action has been necessary to the purpose of finding out what motivated Frémont to decide to disregard the politic instructions of State and turn conquistador — aside from the excuse that those instructions counseling the conciliatory methods of diplomacy and intrigue were made obsolete by *post factum* events.

The instructions, it seems, were the only tangible exhibit for evidence when he argued the legality of his campaign expense claims before the Congressional committees in 1847-1848. His plea that he had acted upon Government authority was based upon nothing of record and had to be supported by circumstantial and opinion evidence in the way of testimony — with Lieutenant Gillespie (who himself appeared to know little) as chief witness. Senator Benton, driven to laudation of the Frémont energies, boldly cited his son-in-law as having acted "without any authority from his government, except the equivocal and enigmatical visit of Mr. Gillespie." And "equivocal and enigmatical" that visit must always remain, for the parties to it take refuge in vague mystery.[338]

In August, 1848, the House committee reported adversely upon the expense and damage claims for the period prior to the official raising of the flag in California, on the ground of lack of proof that Frémont had acted by Government authority. A portion of the claims were eventually allowed as a matter of justice.[339]

That President Polk, in this same period in California affairs, projected aggressive military service for Frémont might be indicated by his jumping him, May 27 (1846), from a lieutenancy in the Engineers to the lieutenant colonelcy of the newly organized Regiment of Mounted Riflemen. It was understood, however, that he was to be retained upon exploration duty.

It may be said that Frémont's compelling impulses now were: Senator Thomas Hart Benton, statesman militant, presumptive mouthpiece for the secrets of the Administration's inner circle, with a son-in-law commanding opportunities yet unattained by the West Point "clique"; Jesse Benton Frémont, with a husband whose advancement was her glory, in whose welfare she was a very Amazon — a loving, loyal wife whose miniature was carried by Kit Carson clear across the continent, from heart to heart; Lieutenant Gillespie himself, arrived victor over difficulties, arrived brimming with speculative information, a quick, narrow and confident man, disdainful of those clumsy attempts to sink him at Monterey and now further incited by the romance of empire likely to materialize from this union with a well-led, well-armed, truly American party sequestered amid these wild environments; Frémont's ambitions, personal, professional, and patriotic — a Urim and Thummim by which he read between the lines of Duty while still not unmindful of duty as he saw it; the urge from his interpretation of the interpretation by Lieutenant Gillespie of the oral message from Secretary Bancroft; and the urge of General José Castro. There was always General Castro, responsible for a score that should be erased.

And the men themselves. They were Richard Kern and Theodore Talbot, educated in the East, bred to controlled thought but now wonted to adventure and long chances. They were Kit Carson, Dick Owens, Lucien Maxwell, Alex Godey, Basil Lajeunesse, the fierce Delawares, and all, recruited from the professional hunting-shirt ranks — men of the rifle, pistol and butcher-knife, free lances to whom liberty was license, whose gospel was blow for blow, who were accustomed to obey only those laws agreeable to them, who were at large in a land much to their taste and who had light regard for the Don and possible consequences of action. They were men who, all of them, looking to their captain and like their captain did not relish being rated as an "ulcer."

Frémont significantly wrote to Senator Benton, in retrospect:

You will remember how grossly outraged and insulted we had already been by this officer [Castro]; many in my own camp, and throughout the country, thought that I should not have retreated in March last. I felt humiliated and humbled; one of the main objects proposed by this expedition had been entirely defeated, and it was the opinion of the officers of the squadron (so I was informed by Mr. Gillespie) that I could not again retreat consistently with any military reputation.

Senator Benton indeed remembered. And enclosing Frémont's letters to the President he made comment, for publication: "To my mind . . . the noble resolution which they took to die, if attacked, under the flag of their country, four thousand miles distant from their homes, was an act of the highest heroism, worthy to be recorded by Xenophon."[340]

Quite of a sudden the prospect of the Cascades north no longer pleased. The complexion of country and company had changed. Writing thus in retrospect; summarizing the events, as he says, of the ten weeks which included the formal con-

C.N. Rankin

Stand Saw Blas 1 Pack
60496   60503
60497   60504
60498   60505
2 Blades each Total 12Pack

ITEM
#4 81117.WP
Spinel Blds

Balsa. 1/4 in Plywood
OR LESS

Phone No
1-800-235-1066

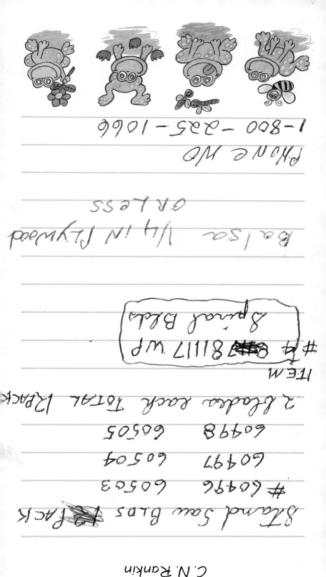

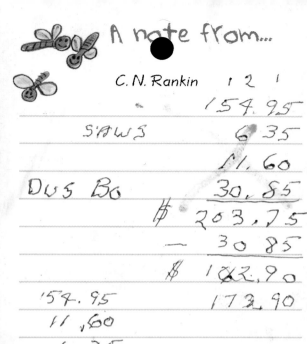

A note from...

C. N. Rankin   1 2 1

154.95

SAWS   6 35

11.60

DUS BG   30.85

$ 203.75

— 30 85

$ 182.90

154.95   172.90

11.60

6 35

172.90

154.95
6.35
11.60
172.90

PREMIUM SAM BLDS.

5 # 80858

5 # 80857

10 PACK

12 PACK

#

81117 TYPE
      SP

4

2 each OF #

60496
60497
60498
60503

on Too

2 of each

quest; writing, moreover, in a strangely defensive vein for an officer who had acted by delegated authority, Frémont prefaced his letter to Senator Benton:

When Mr. Gillespie overtook me in the middle of May, we were encamped on the northern shore of the greater Tlamath Lake. Snow was falling steadily and heavily in the mountains, which entirely surround and dominate the elevated valley region into which we had penetrated; in the east, and north, and west, barriers absolutely impassable barred our road; we had no provisions; our animals were already feeble, and while any other way was open, I could not bring myself to attempt such a doubtful enterprise as a passage of those unknown mountains in the dead of winter. Every day the snow was falling; and in the face of the depressing influence exercised on the people by the loss of our men, and the unpromising appearance of things, I judged it inexpedient to pursue our journey further in this direction. . . .[341]

But Senator Benton saw things from a wider angle. Busy with celestial telescope, barometer, thermometer, sketch pencil, and pen, it was

in the midst of such dangers, and such occupations as these, and in the wildest regions of the Farthest West, that Mr. Frémont was pursuing science and shunning war, when the arrival of Lieutenant Gillespie, and his communications from Washington, suddenly changed all his plans, turned him back from Oregon, and opened a new and splendid field of operations in California itself.[342]

Kit Carson may take over the narrative of this night of May 9, a night momentous here upon the Oregon southwestern border as upon the lower Rio Grande of the Gulf coast. No fresh Indian signs had been found on the back trail from the main camp. The lieutenant said that he had not been followed.

Mr. Gillespie had brought the Colonel letters from home — the first he had had since leaving the States the year before — and he was up, and kept a large fire burning until after midnight; the rest of us were tired out, and all went to sleep. This was the only night in all our travels, except the one night on the island in the Salt Lake, that we failed to keep guard; and as the men were so tired, and we expected no attack now that we had fourteen in the party, the Colonel did not like to ask it of them, but sat up late himself. Owens and I were sleeping together, and we were waked at the same time by the licks of the axe that killed our men. At first, I did not know it was that; but I called to Basil, who was that side: "What's the matter there? What's the fuss about?" He never answered, for he was dead then, poor fellow — and he never knew what killed him. His head had been cut in, in his sleep; the other groaned a little as he died. The Delawares (we had four with us) were sleeping at that fire, and they sprang up as the Tlamaths charged them. One of them (named Crane) caught up a gun, which was unloaded; but, although he could do no execution, he kept them at bay, fighting like a soldier, and did not give up until he was shot full of arrows, three entering his heart; he died bravely. As soon as I had called out, I saw it was Indians in the camp, and I and Owens together cried out "Indians." There were no orders given; things went on too fast, and the Colonel had men with him that did not need to be told their duty. The Colonel and I, Maxwell, Owens, Godey and Stepp jumped together, we six, and ran to the assistance of our Delawares. I don't know who fired and who didn't; but I think it was Stepp's shot that killed the Tlamath chief; for it was at the crack of Stepp's gun that he fell. He had an English half-axe slung to his wrist by a cord, and there were forty arrows left in the quiver, the most beautiful and warlike arrows I ever saw. He must have been the bravest man among them, from the way he was armed, and judging by his cap. When the Tlamaths saw him fall, they ran; but we lay, every man with his rifle cocked, until daylight, expecting another attack.[348]

Basil Lajeunesse and the Iowa breed Denny had been killed where they were lying. Carson's rifle had been useless by reason of a broken cap-tube; he dropped it and shot with his pistol at the chief who was pouring arrows into the defenseless Crane. The pistol ball only cut the half-axe from the red wrist. Maxwell fired, as the chief now dodged, and wounded him in the leg. The fellow was about to plunge into the cover of the low-boughed evergreens and twinkling shafts when the rifle bullet of Stepp the gunsmith stopped him short.

The night passed with the camp on the alert. In the next afternoon, reunion with the main party was effected. The three bodies had been buried along the way. An ambush was arranged; the Delawares appeased the spirits of their slain' brothers with two fresh scalps. The march was north again. Carson says that "Frémont concluded to return to California but take a different route from that which we had last entered the country," and so he did.

Affairs of State could wait; the news center of Sutter's Fort, the coveted Bay of San Francisco, Monterey the hotbed of conspiracy, the nearing British flag, General Castro himself, Consul Larkin who should be anticipating a contact and an understanding with his co-workers in the cause, could wait until this spot job was finished. It might be considered as a part of the whole. The Indians evidently had been outfitted by the British Hudson's Bay Company for the offensive against Americans; to Senator Benton, who conveyed the idea to the Secretary of War, they had been "excited" against Frémont himself by that General Castro 400 miles air-line to the south. But whatever the theories, blow demanded double blow, and vengeance in the north could not wait upon vengeance, or anything else, in the south.

In weather and through country that did not oppose ready travel, under skies that did not prevent night observations, with men not so depressed in spirit that they could not shoot straight, Frémont, pack train and all, made complete circuit of Klamath Lake — up the west side and down the east side. There were battle, skirmish, and duel.

Detached with ten men to find a village ripe for attack, Carson found it, near the head of the lake; was seen by the Indians, did not pause to send back report, but charged in. Frémont heard the rumpus and came at the gallop with reinforcement. Arrived in time to lend a hand, he says; arrived too late for service, Carson says. The enemy were routed, leaving their fourteen dead; the woven huts were fired. "The flag being dry," says Carson, "it was a beautiful sight." With thought of Basil, Denny, and Crane, why not? The chief of this or other village had given Lieutenant Gillespie a salmon at one time and used a hatchet at another; and the captain had shared his store of tobacco with these or similar murdering Indians.[344]

On the trail again Carson's gun snapped; his Indian foeman was quick to level an arrow upon arched bow, he threw himself aside in the saddle but the poisoned point would surely have lodged in his vitals had not Frémont, charging past upon his war-steed El Toro del Sacramento ridden the Indian down, for Sagundai the Delaware, following close, to finish off with the war-club. "I owe my life to them two — the Colonel and Sacramento saved me," Carson said in the Washington *Union,* the next June.

Lucien Maxwell, Archambeau, Dick Owens, Godey, Stepp, Jacob the black boy — they too had their trail encounters with, and lifted the hair of, these tigerish Modocs who reckoned no odds. A warrior, standing fast, with his rapid arrows closed the trail to a whole party until Carson, stealing around upon his flank, deftly shot him.

"By Heaven, this is rough work!" Gillespie declared. "I'll take care to let them know in Washington about it."

"Heaven don't come in for much, about here, just now," Frémont answered; "and as for Washington, it will be long enough before we see it again; time enough to forget about this."

Gillespie occupied the same lodge with him. They two "remained long awake," discussing the day's incidents "and speculating over what was to come in the events that seemed near at hand." So says Frémont.

On May 24, two weeks after the messenger lieutenant had delivered his commissions, the Frémont command were back at Peter Lassen's on the way to the lower Sacramento again.[345]

Chapter XXXIV

California for Free Americans

CAPTAIN FRÉMONT of the United States Army, who had taken the trail north for Oregon only a month past, was back at Peter Lassen's with the Government man who had gone in search of him! The word traveled on south and so did the captain. On May 27 he was at Neal's *rancho*, on May 30 he was at the Buttes, in the lower Sacramento Valley about sixty miles north of Sutter's Fort and admirably designed to command the approaches from the south and the Sonoma northern frontier in the southwest.

On the day of his arrival at Lassen's, Frémont had written to Senator Benton, reciting his experiences with the Indians in the north, his suspicions of British influence up there, and announcing that he would be home in September — might be in Washington upon the very heels of the letter. "I shall now proceed directly homewards, by the Colorado." By the same mail courier, the rancher Samuel Neal, Lieutenant Gillespie sent off a letter to Consul Larkin, relating of his own experiences and also stating that Captain Frémont was now proceeding home. "There was too much snow upon the mountains to cross. He now goes home from here."[346]

With the sealed letter to Senator Benton, Frémont enclosed a note for Consul Larkin:

Dear Sir:
  Not being able to detain a present opportunity to write to you, I will beg you only to forward the enclosed through some of your friends in Mazatlan, so that it may *not be interrupted*. Please see to this for me. I will write you soon more at length and acknowledge all favors.
                    Yours truly,
                                    J. C. FRÉMONT.[347]

The letters brought by Rancher Neal, May 31, were the first definite word of Frémont in over a month, at the least. And the Frémont note was evidently the first communication from Frémont direct since he had left Hawk's Peak, the night of March 9. For Consul Larkin replied immediately, to acknowledge the note; to say that he had "expected a long letter" a month back, but that it may have miscarried; and to wonder whether Frémont had ever received newspapers and a packet of letters sent to him while he was at San Juan, before driven to the Peak. The consul then took pains to explain certain of his official acts while the captain was on the Peak. And the next day he wrote to Secretary Buchanan that Captain Frémont was starting home.[348]

The records apparently do not show that Frémont ever discussed matters with or co-operated with Consul Larkin, or in fact communicated with him at all, save by the brief note of transmission, from the time of the Hawk's Peak episode until he appeared in person again at Monterey with his conquering crusaders. The consul might reasonably be mystified. The instructions to Frémont from the Secretary of State were those to himself also; and as confidential agents of the Government he and Lieutenant Gillespie and Captain Frémont were to work together.

Frémont wished to go on record, at present, as being done with California and as heading home. His functions in California were those of a non-combatant, save on defense. He did not contemplate offense. Even after the capture of Californian horses by "a party of twelve from my camp," and the capture, by his asserted direction, of Sonoma, prisoners from which "were placed at New Helvetia, a fortified post under my command," both events occurring after he had "decided [June 6] on the course which I would pursue" (an aggressive and not a defensive course), and all as detailed in his letter of June 25 to Senator Benton, he wrote, June 16, to Commander Montgomery of the sloop-of-war *Portsmouth* in San Francisco Bay:

It is therefore my present intention to abandon the farther prosecution of our exploration and proceed immediately across the mountainous country to the eastward ... and thence to the frontier of Missouri. ... The nature of my instructions and the peaceful nature of our operations do not contemplate any active hostility on my part, even in the event of war between the two countries. ...[349]

Kit Carson, who was probably no more hazed in his mental horizons than the rest of the men were in theirs, says (*Own Story*): "Here [the Buttes] camp was made to await positive orders in regard to the war, to hunt."

Frémont discovered that he was short in necessary supplies. It therefore would have been folly for him to have pushed on, in good weather as in bad, to the Cascades and the Columbia. The last four weeks of backing and filling had stripped him, so that, at Lassen's once more, he had found himself "destitute." His change of plans, encouraged by Lieutenant Gillespie, had indeed been a fortunate move, inasmuch as, again fortunately, he had learned that the sloop-of-war *Portsmouth* had anchored in the Bay of Monterey.

Through the lieutenant he made requisition upon the Navy stores carried by the *Portsmouth* for the supplies necessary to his march out of the country. There were 8,000 percussion caps, 300 pounds of rifle lead, a keg of powder, flour, sugar, coffee, tea, tobacco, pork, and so forth — material only proper for men, as Lieutenant Gillespie stated in his own appeal to the *Portsmouth*, "engaged upon a laborious and dangerous expedition." Moreover, "Captain Frémont is also in want of funds for the purchase of animals, as, upon leaving for the United States, it will be necessary for him to purchase more horses." The stock on hand was unfit for further service.[350]

Evidently the "official" news of war between the United States and Mexico had been premature, else Frémont would not have risked obtaining such valuable supplies by such a long line of communication. But the need was the more compelling since a courier had arrived, May 28, at the Neal *rancho* camp, from Captain Sutter with word that "two Spaniards" sent by General Castro had been among the Indians inciting them against the foreigners; the Indians therefore were "flying to the mountains" in preparation for the attack.[351]

This day Gillespie posted off with the requisition; was greeted at Sutter's with the reproaches of the nervous Captain Sutter for having returned a $300 riding mule ruined by hard usage, and with the assurance that the Indians and General Castro were leagued to destroy not only the settlers and their crops but the Frémont company also. The lieutenant now borrowed the captain's launch; was followed down river, the next day, May 31, by a letter from the captain to General Castro warning him that this Gillespie was a United States officer on secret dispatch duty — "I recommend you to station a respectable garrison at this point before the arrival of immigrants from the United States . . . may number some thousands. . . ." And, believing that the government (Californian) will buy his establishment, he was "putting a new story on the large new building ·.. . quarters for two or three hundred soldiers, with sufficient parade grounds. . . ."[352]

Thus the thrifty Captain Sutter held to the principle of self-preservation. As an accredited Mexican official in time of peace he had much to keep; as the lord of a buffer state in time of strife he had much to lose but he purposed to lose it with profit. A plague on this mysterious, trouble-making Frémont who disturbed the surface current of settler and Mexican affairs!

Lieutenant Gillespie, down at Yerba Buena of San Francisco on June 7 (apparently having been in no great haste), by the best of good fortune found that the *Portsmouth* was right there in San Francisco Bay, having come up from Monterey following the receipt, May 31, through Consul Larkin, of the news of Captain Frémont's whereabouts.

The stars of Commander John B. Montgomery and Captain John C. Frémont rode the same orbit. Lieutenant Gillespie was spared the trip to Monterey. Commander Montgomery (for whom and for whose timely ship a street and a square in San Francisco are named) was very glad to honor the requisition of Captain Frémont of the Topographical Service of the Army, and was pleased to learn, from the lieutenant, that the captain "may find it convenient to visit the *Portsmouth* at Santa Barbara should we have occasion to go there."[353]

At the same time, however, Lieutenant Gillespie, writing,

date of June 7, from Yerba Buena to Consul Larkin, made profession:

Capt. Frémont's party being very much in need of supplies before starting for home, and he being desirous not to give the authorities of the country any cause to complain of his traveling by the Sea Coast, induced me to come [to arrange for supplies, etc.].[354]

It is difficult to see how the captain could visit the *Portsmouth* at Santa Barbara without diverging to the sea coast on the west in his travel route to the south or east. But any course that suited the plans of Captain Frémont (the nature of whose enterprise, the commander said, he did not seek to know) suited the plans of Commander Montgomery. The "occasion" therefore became "the prospect in view," to employ the commander's words of response. And now that Frémont was projecting a march south to the coast below Monterey, into the midst of the forbidden settlements, even perilously near General Castro on the one hand and Governor Pico on the other, the request for the 8,000 percussion caps, the lead and the powder, was all the more impelling. Especially since, in a military *junta* convened at Monterey on April 11, an appeal to Governor Pico at Los Angeles had been drawn up, for defensive measures against "the imminent risk of an invasion founded on the extravagant design of an American Captain in the United States Army, Mr. N. Frémont [Frémont did not like the ignorance displayed in that 'N' Frémont]" who had retired to the interior only, according to report, to gather force for further aggression.[355]

The Frémont camps, from Lassen's *rancho* on down to the Buttes, were centers of alarms daily renewed by the settlers who made the most of the presence, again, of this Army officer and his proved fighting men. If he had not back-tracked by Government orders to make California American territory, then why had he come? That was it. He was the one who had stirred up Castro to fresh enmity and he ought to see the business through. That also was it.

Indeed, this settler north was in a pretty mess! There was

the *bando* issued from Monterey April 17 and made public April 30 — a copy had been brought up to Sutter's, was official, signed by Sub-Prefect Guerrero down at San Francisco:

Being informed that a multitude of foreigners abusing our invested regulations without having come with the requisites provided for by law are residing in the district, and that many of them who should not be admitted into this country have made themselves owners of land, this being a right belonging only to citizens,

the sub-prefect felt obliged to declare that unnaturalized foreigners without legal papers could not possess land and unless they voluntarily retired from the country were "subject to being expelled from it whenever the Government may find it convenient."[356]

This spread uneasiness among the squatters who had not taken the trouble to apply for citizenship papers — or even passports. And other proclamations were reported, as emanating from General Castro himself, threatening to evict all Americans. And there were the warnings, from first-hand sources — from Captain Sutter and from Indians themselves — that the California Indians had been engaged, by Castro, to burn the settlers' wheat fields and carry war to the ranches. The Indians were painting and dancing, and organizing in the mountains. General Castro was preparing to follow up by bringing soldiers to the Sacramento; he was already recruiting an army.

Of the evils actual and imaginary, the Indians were the nearest. War, there, was independent of any commission from Washington. Frémont says that he led his expedition out of the Buttes — which are commonly known as the Marysville Buttes, in the plain between the Sacramento and the locality of present Marysville of the Feather, and give the name to Butte Creek. Carson and others say that they all started from Peter Lassen's, farther north. Frémont says that "several Indians" were killed in their war paint, in the surprise first attack upon the first village, up the west bank of the Sacramento. The other villages took warning and fled the approach of the mounted rifle-bearers. The Indians' fancied security had been broken; the Indians had learned "that Castro was far and that I was near." Kit Carson says: "The number killed I cannot say. It was a perfect butchery. Those not killed fled in all directions and we returned to Lawson's [Lassen's]."

Captain Frémont had demonstrated. He not only had protected his rear but he had saved the settlers from the torch and the war-whoop and had opened the trail for the incoming immigrant trains. More power to his arm, for what, now, of Castro and those Californians conspiring below! Frémont's attitude may be dismissed in a sentence. With him it was aye, yes and no, while he blew warm and chill, never very hot, never very cold.

For an officer directly instructed by Washington to take California he had developed a singular bump of caution; seemed to prefer being an observer of events rather than participator in them. All the mass of testimony, narrating appeals to him, interviews with him, discussions with him, reduces apparently to the fact that he said one thing to one man and another thing to another man, and withal, as the discourager of hesitancy, bade the settlers to go ahead and his own command to keep back.

He was having some difficulty in holding his men in hand. And there were settlers, like to them, in the camp: ex-trappers, backwoodsmen, some respecting God, few respecting the Devil, and none respecting the Don.

There was "Dr." Robert Semple, Kentuckian printer and dentist, built to fit a post-hole, six feet eight inches tall "and about fifteen inches in diameter, dressed in greasy buckskin from head to foot, and with a fox-skin cap" which he delighted to wear with tail to the fore.[357]

There was Ezekiel Merritt, of similar physical dimensions, said to have been one of Captain Joe Walker's free-booter trappers of 1833 in California — to Captain Frémont "a rugged man, fearless and simple; taking delight in incurring risks, but tractible and not given to asking questions when there was something he was required to do"; and, as suited to Frémont's notion of such, selected to be the Frémont "field-lieutenant" among the settlers, but of chief repute as a "phenomenal tobacco-chewer" by token of his reeking long beard dyed with the constant leakage.[358]

There was William Brown Ide, New England carpenter, Ohio and Illinois school-teacher — envisioned head of the California Republic only to be embittered by unappreciative Fate in same measure that James Marshall, discoverer of California gold, and Captain John August Sutter, California's pioneer host to all comers, were embittered.

There was William O. Fallon — "Big" Fallon — wanderfoot trapper, Irishman from New Mexico, California adventurer, ready to seek the desert and mountains again but finding a billet in the Frémont camps and a patron in their captain, companions among their men and new hazards in the prospect.

There was John Bidwell, thrifty, conservative, of New York birth, of school-teacher service in Ohio and Iowa Territory, a man of solid parts, of wide views and large vested interests.

There was John Neal, Irish sailor, two-fisted and quick-tempered, much at Sutter's Fort but not of the Sutter staff, as John Bidwell was. When last of record, a fugitive from justice, having killed a man in a quarrel.

There was Samuel J. Hensley, Kentuckian, trapper from New Mexico, Mexican citizen of California, respected *ranchero*, a Sutter valued retainer and agent, "of strong will and well-balanced mind, generous, temperate, and brave."

There was Samuel Neal, no relation of John; blacksmith, ex-Frémont man, prosperous rancher and stock raiser, of energy and loyalty in the cause of his old commander.

There was Peter Lassen, the Dane; sturdy and courageous, blacksmith, hunter, outpost rancher, ever a pioneer until murdered, in 1859, north of Pyramid Lake.[359]

And there were other settlers actual or so-called, of degree high and degree low, with much to lose and with little to lose, and the majority of them seeing, in the *bandos,* the rumors, and a present Frémont who did not promise to stay but who yet did not go, the opportunity to make of California another Texas.

Of the men mentioned by name, Semple and Ide, Ezekiel Merritt, "Big" Fallon, John Neal, were not land owners. Merritt had citizenship papers, but no property; Semple and Ide lived upon other persons' lands. Bidwell, Hensley, Samuel Neal, Peter Lassen, were land owners by legal grant and would appear to have been secure against ejection by any published *bando.* But these men and their kind had their ideas upon Mexican methods with foreigners, and save for a few *Anglos* who through family connections or timidity stayed neutral, they stuck together for the common good. Once they set hands to the plow, they turned the whole furrow.

Nevertheless, the California authorities had been fair, on the whole, with the foreign element. California was different from New Mexico, which was a border province subject to the sharp practices of transients who found all defensive laws unjust. New Mexico, with its seat of power at watchful Santa Fé, was in close contact with dominant Old Mexico, and was in the focus of jealously restrictive regulations directed against North Americans especially. California, remote from the central power and neglected by it in time of need, was much to itself and thereby was strongly infused with a native independence. California was even more Spanish than New Mexico, and for that matter Mexico. Its landed class of undiluted descent from pure-blood origins, its climate, and pastoral easy life adhering to traditions of hospitality that made every stranger a guest — these built for a Spanish, not a Mexican California, and for a community moreover free and unique. It was a generous country, of estates feudal in their liberties, democratic in their customs, simple in their needs, and carelessly tolerant of all comers. Settled California fronted upon the sea, a broad highway; and men of other flags arrived, for intercourse business and social — some to stay in port, else to ride the roads from mission to mission, pueblo to pueblo, *rancho* to *rancho,* to take out citizenship papers, and to marry among the native people. Thus California was early wonted to the foreigner, whereas in New Mexico, of a rural populace extending through the interior and insulated from the world, the white skin of the foreigner was long a curiosity. There was only the one entrance road, the caravan road to Santa Fé; and the leaven of foreign blood was confined mainly to Taos of the northern frontier, its influence in Santa Fé was slight.

Strangely enough New Mexico, thoroughly of Mexico, readily yielded to foreign conquest — yielded spiritually as well as physically. But it was of course in the line of march by horse and foot and was virtually delivered to the invader by a governing general who had no patriotic love of the land. California, which had nurtured independence of Mexico and was not unmindful of a future under another flag, earnestly tried to resist the change thrust upon it.

The causes of the revolt by the militant foreigners are less obscure than they are defensible. They seem to have been due to a state of mind rather than to material conditions. As the rule the foreigner who conformed himself to the laws was welcome in California. The regulations pertaining to foreigners were not irksome; they bore most heavily upon the transient, the free-booter, the paperless sojourner who claimed special privilege by plea of accidental entry. Laws that might prove irksome were indulgently applied, and the edicts of exclusion, issued from Mexico as late as 1842 and thereabouts, were quashed before they had gone into effect.

In California, as nowhere else in the Mexican states or provinces, the foreigner merged with the native life, social and business. Eleven square leagues of land were his privilege, and by his own location. Upon his grant he was unmolested, practically unsupervised. In the settlements he pursued his business and moved about at will, so long as he was deemed to be an honest man.

Taxes were not onerous nor prejudicial, and there was little religious intolerance. California was not priest-ridden. And when the foreigner married into a Spanish family he became one of the family. Indeed, a large number of the adopted *rancheros* speedily grew to be as much of the soil, in their garb and habits, as the native Californians. The marriages were almost uniformly happy ones; and the loyalty of the Spanish women to their American husbands during the conquest itself is noteworthy.

In 1846 the foreign population of California was between 700 and 800, including the Frémont company, as differentiated from a Spanish population of not more than 7,000. The Americans were much in the majority, owing to the immigration from the east and from Oregon. These immigrants came seeking land, and free land. The most of them entering California in the north stopped short of the coast settlements and for their knowledge of the California proprietary practices and regulations depended upon go-betweens and hearsay. They had traveled a long, hard trail, and believed that they had earned whatever they might take; and when hunters, trappers, adventurers, without home ties, they confused their alleged rights of free men with those of freebooters. And they all, like all Americans of that day, believed in the destiny of Americans to rule wherever they set stakes. Only Americans knew *how* to possess the earth.[360]

The causes of the revolt of a foreign element in California founded in racial antipathies as well as in that heritage of conceit. It should be remarked that the movement originated in Northern California — not in Southern and Central California where, as in the San Diego, Los Angeles, Santa Barbara districts, and extended even to Monterey, mutual interests governed the various peoples living without distinct cleavage. The San Francisco Bay district, however, was a border line. The Sacramento Valley, of that temperate northern interior congenial to the hardy Saxon, with its lands, otherwise wasted, consigned chiefly to the Anglo-Saxon, its wild upper reaches beyond which lay free Oregon, its defiant post of Sutter's Fort, its gateway immigrant trail from the east, its coveted gateway of the tossing San Francisco Bay in the southwest, and its flanking, American-settled valleys on the west, north of the Bay, by the very spirit of its attributes bred independence.

The occasions of the revolt were the distrust of Mexico who would be encouraged to reprisals by hostilities with the United States; the alarms of edicts in fact and fancy, and of Indians subsidized for war, both threatening the security of Americans whether with papers or without; and the disturbing but inciting presence of Frémont. And there was England to be forestalled now if ever.

Had Frémont not served as a joker running wild, so to say, and had there been no gesture of an inimical Mexico and a covetous England, a Bear Flag would have been eventually raised, none the less — granted that diplomacy failed. It was written of California, as it had been written, in prophecy fulfilled, of Texas and Oregon, and as it was being written, prior to conquest by arms, of New Mexico and all the Southwest.

To the degree that it fended off a European power, the movement was patriotic. But it had its selfish side: that of feud, special privilege, private venture, personal ambitions and aims. William Ide, for one, was sorely disappointed in that Government, through Frémont, the Navy and the Flag, demonstrated so soon, ere he had completed organization of his California Republic as a unit to be submitted, by treaty, to the United States. There were others who opined that the front-rank victors missed the spoils.[361]

A Boston tea party and a Lexington, in Texas a little affair at Gonzales and a Bejar, now in California a horse raid at the Cosumnes and a follow-up at Sonoma. General José Castro's native intelligence would seem to have been of poor quality or small quantity. Else he may have trusted in Consul Larkin's profession that the United States were waiting for California to declare for the flag. He dared to appear at Sonoma presidio north of San Francisco Bay. He was getting more munitions of war there, almost under the eyes of settlers of the Sacramento — and of Captain Frémont. He well knew of that rendezvous of the malcontents, and of the growing threat of Sutter's Fort — another ulcerous condition. And back again at Santa Clara of the San José and Monterey district he sent Lieutenant Francisco Arce, his private secretary, and Lieutenant José María Alviso and eight men up to Sonoma for the 170 horses engaged from General Vallejo, *comandante* of the northern frontier.

The horses were to be used in a campaign against Governor Pico. Governor Pío Pico would so say, and Governor Pico should know. But as quite another matter the horses, by the alleged word of the boastful Lieutenant Arce, were to be used against the *gringo* trespassers of the Sacramento Valley. Riding hard, rancher William Knight of the crossing of the Sacramento — the lowest ford, today Knight's Landing, shortly above Sutter's Fort and Sacramento City — brought the news to Frémont's camp at the Buttes in the northward; and so did a traditionary Indian, who announced the spectacle of 200 mounted soldiers advancing up the valley, destroying settlers' crops and taking settlers captive.

The Frémont camp was ready to believe the worst, and thereby was hoping for the best. As a coincidence in line with the coincidence of his prolonged stop-over in California, Captain Frémont, on June 6, as he afterward said in writing to Senator Benton, which was during the time of General Castro's defiant visit to Yerba Buena and Sonoma, "decided on the course which I would pursue, and immediately concerted my operations with the foreigners inhabiting the Sacramento Valley." But by that date Lieutenant Arce had not made his brag, and the horses or the horsemen had not been reported. On June 16 Frémont assured Commander Montgomery of the "peaceful nature" of his operations "even in the event of war between the two countries," but Sonoma had already been taken and that by his direction, if he is to be believed, and *Comandante General* Vallejo seized. Nothing of this letter appears in his *Memoirs,* nor in his testimony at Washington to establish his rights as conquistador; and now that he was enabled with horses, and with supplies from the *Portsmouth,* there was naught, except disinclination, to prevent his abiding by the "nature of my instructions," assertedly peaceful like that of his operations, and proceeding "immediately across the mountainous country to the eastward," for the Missouri frontier.

It is necessary to study Frémont, in order to get at the mental squint of Carson and others in the camp. There should have been considerable uncertainty and speculation. To Carson, Frémont was waiting for news of war. The conjectural "declaration" brought by Lieutenant Gillespie had been a flash. And meanwhile the Frémont command, like Frémont himself, served events rather than mastered them. It may have been a deep and double-dealing plot, but it more resembles indecision dandled for the arms of accident.

The Californian *caballada* had passed through Sutter's Fort and were heading down the Sacramento by the road, the only road, to the south and the lower country. The outward swing from Sonoma had been required for a crossing of the river clear of the marshes of the bay district. Ezekiel Merritt the gaunt tobacco eater led a dozen men to the pursuit. The object of the party was known. The first blow for American freedom in California was to be struck. It would be followed by other blows. The settlers had risen, and the Spaniards were to be given a lesson. It was their turn, now that the Indians had been properly handled. The Frémont company strained on the leash. Up and at 'em — particularly Castro — in the cause of vengeance, brotherhood, scalps and booty!

What do some of them say, who for one reason or another were interested in the enterprise? Captain Sutter says:

Merrit [Merritt], a mountaineer, formerly a long time with me, but now with Fremont, came to me . . . and told me he was going to seize those horses for Fremont, which he did.[362]

Thomas Martin, Frémont man whose recollections were of the dramatic vein, says:

Fremont called us together and told us that we were going to take the country and called for volunteers to go and capture this band of horses. . . . That evening 15 of us under Capt. Swift went and caught them at daylight the next morning. We arrested 17 men, 14 officers and 2 privates and 1 citizen. . . . We took back with us about 400 head of horses. . . .[363]

Martin never reversed the telescope. William Ide says, however:

Several persons, among whom was Kit Carson, begged of Fremont their discharge from the service of the exploring expedition that they might be at liberty to join us. Fremont, in my hearing, expressly declared that he was not at liberty to afford us the least aid or assistance; nor would he suffer any of his men to do so; that he had not asked the assistance of the emigrants for his protection; that he was able, of his own party, to fight and whip Castro if he chose, but that he should not do so unless first assaulted by him; and that positively he should wait only for a supply of provisions, two weeks at furthest, when he would, without further reference to what might take place here, be on his march for the States.[364]

Frémont says only "A party of twelve from my camp," and Kit Carson says nothing at all, this being one of the occasions when inactivity staled him.

Early in the morning of June 10 the Ezekiel Merritt party, swelled to fourteen, surprised the Alviso-Arce party of ten camped, with their *caballada,* on the Don Martin Murphy *rancho* of the Cosumnes tributary of the Sacramento; bade them rise and deliver, or fight if they preferred; deftly stripped the corral and with best wishes to General Castro scoured away on the back trail with the loose horses.

The night of June 7, the day before the sally, Frémont had made the last astronomical observation of his record as an explorer. That he did not know. To him it was only the finish of his present scientific tour. "Latitude 39° 14′ 41″, longitude 121° 33′ 36″, Buttes of the Sacramento (on a small run or spring at northeastern base)." This was the legend in his field-book.

On June 8 he moved, with all his retainers, down across the valley, to the Feather River; thence, June 9, down to its juncture with the Bear, whence the immigrant trail from the high Sierra wended on to Sutter's Fort. Field-Lieutenant Merritt and party had cantered out, athwart the low sun, upon errand purposeful. And in the morning of June 11 a charging cloud of dust, the thud of rapid hoofs, the flicker of whirling riatas and the glint of rifle barrels, and wild cheers crescendo heralded the triumphant return.

"I sent Merritt into Sonoma instructed to surprise the garrison at that place," Frémont narrates. Merritt, not at all wearied of well doing, a rough-and-ready kind to whom a nod was word enough, went that very afternoon with some twenty minute-men.

At Sutter's Fort the dismayed Captain Sutter was privately denouncing Merritt and co-operates for a "band of thieves," and much distrusting the values of Captain Frémont in the country. John Bidwell, quite innocent of the importance of the alarms, was up the American prospecting for a sawmill site. Down at Santa Clara pueblo General José Castro, apprized, by *violento extraordinario* — hard-riding special courier — of the disaster to his horse herd, returning in haste to Monterey there dictated indignant letters calling for aid against those "irresponsible highwaymen" of the north committing outrages at the instigation of Frémont. Consul Larkin, on June 14, tried still to play the mediator by offering to help regain the animals and punish the robbers, if United States citizens had taken part in the foray. And on this day, June 14, by another dawn-light surprise a *banda* of lawless Americans, in number increased to some thirty, seized Sonoma and everybody in it.

The house of General Mariano Guadalupe Vallejo, fronting the plaza of the ruined mission of San Francisco Solano, was surrounded and invaded, much to the fright of the women in bed; the general had been summoned in his negligé — would have formally surrendered his sword but could find no one who ranked to take it. Therefore he did the hospitality of refreshments, wine and brandy, which eased the situation. He was known to favor the North Americans — although this unshaven, greasy-buckskin crowd, ferociously armed and apparently on the loose, showed to better advantage outside his threshold than inside.

In the course of the refreshments, the to-be-expected bluster and merriment, and the palaver over the correct form of capitulation, it was discovered, through the medium of Don Jacob Leese who acted as official interpreter (being that none of the visitors spoke dependable Spanish), that these men came from Captain Frémont and claimed to represent the "republican party" of California. Consequently General Don Mariano, and Captain Don Salvador Vallejo his brother, and Lieutenant Colonel Don Victor Pruden his French secretary, gave their written parole as prisoners of war and received their guarantees of safety — and amid something of a wrangle among their captors were started off, to their further astonishment not unmixed with relief, with an escort squad, for delivery to Captain Frémont. Don Jacob Leese, Mexicanized Ohioan, Don Mariano's brother-in-law, went along as interpreter.

Captain Frémont had moved his camp again, this time to the American River once more, three miles above Sutter's. When he had been found he sent down an order for the arrest of Don Jacob also. He wrote, in his dispatch before mentioned, to Commander Montgomery:

New Helvetia, June 16, 1846.

... This evening I was interrupted in a note to yourself by the arrival of General Vallejo and other officers who had been taken prisoners and insisted upon surrendering to me. The people and authorities of the country persist in connecting me with every movement of the foreigners and I am hourly in expectation of the approach of General Castro.[365]

If he was threatened by "a repetition of the recent insults" and "any hostile moves are made in our direction" he felt bound by the national character of his duty to meet or anticipate them.

As for the four prisoners, the captain would not recognize their paroles; said that he was not responsible for the Sonoma seizure, that the people had risen in self protection, that he had no means of caring for prisoners, and thereupon he sent the squad back down to be stowed under lock in Sutter's Fort.[366]

The short Kit Carson, fixed lieutenant, and the long Ezekiel Merritt, roving lieutenant, rode ahead with orders to Captain

Sutter. Whether any men of the Frémont expeditionary command had been in the party to Sonoma is debatable. Lucien Maxwell's name appears in one list.[367]

At Sutter's the four prisoners-of-war put in a time, as Jacob Leese (who had been acting as Consul Larkin's sub-agent in the north) records, "in the most aughful manner a reflecting on the cituation of our familys and property in the hands of such a desperate set of men"; General Vallejo, mazed by the shuffle of events, resigned himself to the will of God "Who doubtless had decreed that June 1846 was to be the black month of my life"; flustered Captain Sutter, unwilling jailer, despaired now of selling his *forteleza* to the old government but had hopes of floating upon the new tide, and meantime treated his charges "with kindness and so good as I could."[368]

Meantime, or on June 15, the amateur revolutionists in garrison at Sonoma had recovered from the spasms of their temerity, had codified their ideas, and having at last organized by electing William B. Ide captain, this day (if not the day before or the day after) proclaimed by running up an unbleached cotton flag "sufficiently significant of their intentions — a white field, red border, with a grizzly bear eyeing a single star, which threw its light on the motto, 'The Republic of California.' "[369]

On this day a proclamation (written full speed by William Ide "between the hours of one and four that morning") of principles, and of amnesty to all noncombatants, was issued subject to the criticisms of the literate; a special messenger from Sub-Prefect Guerrero of Yerba Buena informed Prefect Castro at Monterey that Sonoma had been taken by "70 men under the 'Doctor of the Sacramento' " and a quarrelsome character, name unknown [Merritt]; a messenger from General Vallejo boarded the *Portsmouth* with the news of the ravishment and with the petition that Commander Montgomery intercede to prevent acts of violence by this band who seemed to have no organization.

Whereupon the commander, as much surprised as General Vallejo had been, sympathetically disavowed any connection of the United States, or himself, or Captain Frémont, with the affair — and then, at first opportunity, the next week, by hearty letter congratulated Captain Frémont: "The capture of the horses and the surprise of Sonoma were masterstrokes, but should have been followed up by a rush upon Santa Clara" where Castro "might have been taken by thirty men."[370]

On this same day a messenger from the insurgents themselves boarded the *Portsmouth,* to announce for them, as the commander's fellow countrymen, the grievances which had called for the new bill of rights, the founding of the Republic of California, the honorable intentions of the defenders thereof, and the lack of powder. Whereupon the commander replied he was happy to learn of the high sentiments governing, as they should, this protest against oppression; but inasmuch as he was here "as a representative of a government at peace (as far as I know) with Mexico and her province of California" he could not "furnish munitions of war," nor in any manner take sides with any popular movement.

At the mouth of the American just below Sutter's Fort, Captain Frémont had finished transferring the supplies sent up the Sacramento by Commander Montgomery; and from camp, the next day, June 16, following the delivery of the hostages from Sonoma, will write the commander a letter of thanks — with the assurance of his own peaceful functions and of his purpose to march across the Sierra for home.

Neither Commander Montgomery nor Consul Larkin had received any news confirming the war alarms of two months back. Returned to Captain Frémont from his trip to the Bay, Lieutenant Gillespie would have picked up (if it had not been delivered to him at the earlier date) his letter of April 23 from the consul, announcing the information, to date of April 1, brought from Mazatlan by the *Portsmouth.* He might have been apprized, at Yerba Buena, of the contents of another letter, written, April 27, after Consul Larkin had waited five days for further word of war, to the consul's sub-agents, Abel Stearns at Los Angeles, Jonathan Warner at San Diego, and

Jacob Leese at Sonoma. In part, but as to war developments:

Mr. Polk in Dec. 1845 objected to do anything with Mexico, relative to our demands against the Nation, until one more Minister should have been sent to Mexico. Mr. Slidell has now been there, and from my Mexican papers to March 12th or 14th and New York to February 25th I find that Mr. Slidell Ministry has been refused. General Paredes has put out Herrera, the people are now putting him out. The northern Departments of Mexico wish to seperate and become two Nations. The Portsmouth was on the 1st waiting for the last Mexican mail (the Commandant General of Mazatlan, had a very late one, as express) when Com. Sloat heard of the situation of Captain Fremont, and at once dispatched her for this Consulate jurisdiction, when the Portsmouth sailed the Commandant General of Mazatlan had published a Bando informing the inhabitants that the Commodore would on the morrow declare the Port in a state of Blockade, thereby giving the Americans reason to suppose that there was war. And the Commodore had the news, which he had not, but was expecting it. The Government Officers had left Mazatlan for Rosario taking the archives.[371]

This was merely a rehash of the letter of April 23. The consul now said that he expected, in the event of war, to see the flag flying over California by the 4th of July. By Carson's statement, made with his usual latitude, "after the Fort [Sonoma] had been taken, Frémont had heard positively of the war being declared," it would seem that Lieutenant Gillespie only now, June 12 or 13, brought the consul's information to Frémont and his waiting camp.

At Yerba Buena the lieutenant would have received a letter, of June 1, from the consul, saying that he had reason to believe that intervention by England was not likely. But this would not alter the general opinion.

On this day, June 15, 1846, at Washington there was signed, by the Secretary of State and the British Minister, the Oregon treaty which recognized the parallel of Forty-nine as the international boundary from the Rockies to the Pacific. Three stars at once — Oregon, Washington, Idaho — were added to the flag. Another — California — had risen with the Bear Flag. At the same time 16,000 Mormons, trudging westward, had crossed the Mississippi River, their van had reached the Missouri at Council Bluffs, Iowa, and in the farther west their State of Deseret, future Utah and Nevada, only waited.

Two thousand emigrants for the Pacific coast had left the Missouri River border, but the host of invasion which should over-run California materialized, out there, as some 400 persons. Among them, however, were the Donner party, of tragic experience in the snow-bound Sierra, and the party of Edwin Bryant whose resultant narrative of the trail, the conquest, and California by and large of those days, is a standard document. Among the immigrants due this summer were members of the Boggs family, of Missouri and the Santa Fé Trail — a family which included Thomas O. Boggs who became Carson's close associate on the Arkansas and executor of his will; they would gravitate to the popular Napa Valley north of San Francisco Bay and neighbor with Moses Carson who was over at present Healdsburg of the Russian River Valley. There was also William H. Russell of Kentucky, self-acclaimed "bosom friend of Henry Clay," who as Frémont's ordnance officer, secretary of state, profound and expatiatory admirer, would defend his chief's privacy from intrusion by petty orders and visitors.[372]

In the States of South and West 50,000 volunteers from a populace contending for service against Mexico had rallied to the colors, "to see the elephant" and "revel in the Halls of Montezuma." On the Rio Grande the badgered "Old Zach" Taylor, now brevet major general, was soon to receive quickstep orders, date of June 12, from the general-in-chief, Winfield Scott, at Washington, urging him to "conquer a peace" by "pressing" his operations "toward the heart of the enemy's country," even clear to Mexico City the capital; and he will be privately admonished to "take foot in hand" and be off upon the war path.

At Fort Leavenworth beside the Missouri River, Colonel Stephen Watts Kearny, mustering the Army of the West for the occupation of New Mexico, has received instructions, date of June 3, that the President had assigned him to the important objective of "taking the earliest possession of Upper Cali-

fornia." The naval forces in the Pacific should be "in possession of all the towns on the sea coast" and will co-operate with
him. It might be that "a considerable number of American
citizens" understood to have "settled on the Sacramento River,
near Sutter's establishment, called 'Nuevo Helvetia,' " and to be
"well disposed toward the United States," would prove helpful
to him in holding the country. But there is nothing of Frémont in this.[373]

On June 15, Commodore Sloat, commanding the naval
forces in the Pacific, having been convinced, June 7, that active
hostilities had opened on the Rio Grande border and that
Commodore Conner was blockading the eastern ports, was a
week out of Mazatlan upon his way to plant the United States
flag ashore at Monterey.

But these ordered impulses of a Nation at stride were yet as
something remote from the local scene and events in the "California Republic." Now the simple minded Kit Carson, under
thirty-eight, rode forth for Empire, couching his lance against
tyranny and entering the lists of War and State to an extent
that he had little dreamed when he left his ranch on the
Cimarroncito, and Josefa.

Kit Carson Days

Chapter XXXV

Carson on the Glory Trail

REGARDING the properties of the local scene Kit Carson says (*Own Story*):

A party was sent from here [the Buttes] to surprise Sonoma, a military post. They captured it, took one General and two Captains prisoners, several cannon and a number of small arms. After the Fort had been taken, Fremont had heard positively of the war being declared. Then marched forward to Sonoma, and found it in the possession of the men he had sent in advance.

Frémont says (*Memoirs*): "I sent Merritt into Sonoma instructed to surprise the garrison at that place." And, in his letter of June 25 to Senator Benton (*Memoirs*):

I had scarcely reached the Lower Sacramento, when General Castro, then in the north (at Sonoma, in the Department of Sonoma, north of the bay of San Francisco, commanded by General Vallejo) declared his determination immediately to proceed against the foreigners settled in the country, for whose expulsion an order had just been issued by the governor of the Californias. For these purposes Castro immediately assembled a force at the Mission of Santa Clara, a strong place, on the northern shore of the Francisco Bay.

And having been once "humiliated," as he has stated in a preceding chapter, and being posted with his back to the wall of snows and famine, he "determined to take such active and anticipatory measures as should seem to me most expedient to protect my party and justify my own character."

Senator Benton says (Washington *Union* letter, fall of 1846):

. . . he found his further progress [in the Klamath Lake region] completely barred by the double obstacle of hostile Indians, which Castro had excited against him, and the lofty mountains, covered with deep and falling snow. These were the difficulties and dangers in front. Behind, and on the north bank of the San Francisco Bay, at the military post of Sonoma, was General Castro assembling troops, with the avowed object of attacking both Frémont's party and all the American settlers. Thus, his passage barred in front by impassable snows and mountains . . . menaced by a general at the head of tenfold forces of all arms; the American settlers in California marked out for destruction on a false accusation of meditating a revolt under his instigation; his men and horses suffering from fatigue, cold, and famine;

"after the most anxious deliberation"

Captain Frémont determined to turn upon his pursuers and fight them instantly, without regard to numbers, and seek safety for his party and the American settlers by overturning the Mexican government in California.

And Senator Benton, transmitting his private information, assured the President (*Niles Register,* LXXI, 1846):

I make this communication to you, sir . . . with the sole view of vindicating the American government and its officer from the foul imputation of exciting insurrection in the provinces of a neighboring power with whom we were then at peace. I could add much more to prove that Captain Frémont's private views and feelings were in unison with his ostensible mission — that the passion of his soul was the pursuit of science and that he looked with dread and aversion upon every possible collision either with the Indians, Mexicans, or British, that could turn him aside from that cherished pursuit.

Moreover, as Senator Benton saw the matter in his *Thirty Years' View* (1856), in addition to the already operating campaign of Castro, 400 miles distant across a wilderness, and his Indian allies:

Juntas were in session to transfer the country to Great Britain; the public domain was passing away in large grants to British subjects; a British fleet was expected on the coast; the British vice-consul, Forbes, and the emissary priest, Macnamara [the Reverend Eugene McNamara, Irish Catholic priest, had applied to Mexico for a California grant upon which to settle 2,000 Irish colonists], ruling and conducting everything, and all their plans so far advanced as to render the least delay fatal.[374]

Secretary of War William Marcy, inspired by word at second hand, says (annual report, December, 1846):

. . . he found his further progress in that direction [Oregon] obstructed by impassable snowy mountains and hostile Indians, who, having been excited against him by General Castro, had killed and wounded four of his men, and left him no repose either in camp or on the march. At the same time information reached him that General Castro, in addition to his Indian allies, was advancing in person against him with artillery and cavalry, at the head of four or five hundred men; that they were passing around the head of the Bay of San Francisco to a rendezvous on the north side of it, and that the American settlers in the valley of the Sacramento were comprehended in the scheme of destruction meditated against his own party.

And so the story grew. Frémont accordingly turned upon his "Mexican pursuers." As Secretary Marcy further confirms:

It was on the 6th of June, and before the commencement of the war between the United States and Mexico could there have been known, that this resolution was taken; and, by the 5th of July

not only General Castro but the other Mexican authority in California had been totally overthrown.

Down at Santa Clara field headquarters, south of the Bay, the harried General Castro, exercised over the jealous Governor Pico on the one side of him and the mysterious Captain Frémont on the other, issued proclamation June 17:

The contemptible policy of the agents of the government of the U. S. of the north has induced a number of adventurers, regardless of the rights of men, to boldly undertake an invasion, by possessing themselves of the town of Sonoma, and taking by surprise the military commander of that frontier, Col. Don M. G. Vallejo, Lieut.-col. Victor Prudon, Capt. Don Salvador Vallejo, and Mr. Jacob P. Leese.[375]

Fellow-countrymen are besought to rise and unite for the defense of liberty and the succor of the loudly-calling prisoners.

Down at Santa Barbara, Governor Pico, about to discipline the obnoxious General Castro with an armed levy, by another *violento extraordinario,* from Prefect Castro at Monterey, learned, June 23, of the Sonoma thunder-clap; and he, too, issued a proclamation to his fellow-citizens:

At this moment your department government has received the unfortunate news, officially communicated by the political authorities of Monterey, and dated four days ago, that a gang of North American adventurers, with the blackest treason that the spirit of evil could invent, have invaded the town of Sonoma, raising their flag, and carrying off as prisoners four Mexican citizens.[376]

Mexican compatriots are urged to "quit the domestic hearth, and fly, gun in hand . . . to avenge the country's honor." The North American nation "has stolen the department of Texas, and wished to do the same with that of California."

At Monterey, Consul Thomas Larkin, having heard the news by dispatch, June 16, from Commander Montgomery, doubting the very words wrote, June 18, to the Secretary of State. Frémont and Gillespie were said to be the true culprits, and he, the consul, was himself being accused of connivance. Consul Larkin now saw those confidential instructions from Washington, counseling the professions of brotherly friend-ship and an attentive ear, badly scrambled by this muddle of the traffic signals. And he had reason to fear that Governor Pico might now indeed bring England upon the scene, to in-quire into this threatened rape of Sabine — otherwise Mexican — California. The consul could at least write to Governor Pico, as he did, protesting that neither he himself nor his govern-ment was in any way concerned in the seizure of Sonoma.

Frémont, in the north, had not yet sighted General Castro who, 100 miles away, with those forces "tenfold" in number, "artillery and cavalry," seemed to be making a prodigiously slow advance around San Francisco Bay. Lieutenant Gillespie had been enabled to go down to the Bay and return with a boat load of supplies; and thirty civilian riflemen had captured and were holding that very Sonoma, reputed fortress and war magazine of the northern frontier.

While dispatching and receiving couriers for a roundup of the latest news from the south Frémont, on June 19, with twenty men visited Sutter's Fort, took it over, in fact as in theory, to a result that Topographer Edward Kern remained there as commanding officer and that ex-commander Sutter tearfully bewailed the Frémont dictum which consigned him (if he did not like the way in which things were being run), as a Mexican (and a Mexican citizen and official he was), to his fellow Mexicans beyond the San Joaquin River.[377]

By resolution ante-dated June 6 in order, apparently, to

cover, by post-dated announcement, all the operations, Frémont was now ready to proclaim. He perceived that the "individual action" of the settlers, in a movement, he asserts, "due to my presence in the valley," would result in only disaster as soon as the forces of the Mexican Government were brought to bear. Since California had no regular military establishment, lacked leaders, guns, and powder — the fearsome fortress of Sonoma was a relic citadel without a garrison, naked San Francisco could have been taken by a launch, the proud presidio Monterey pleaded that it could not even answer the proposed salute by Commodore Sloat — there was no great likelihood that a Californian offensive from the south would have advanced very far into the American north. And Mexico herself was a laggard in this kind of a war; she had learned the worst in Texas.

The outcome, left independent of Frémont, as promoted by the reinforcements of immigrants from Oregon and the East might have been a State of Northern California with a State of Southern California set off later — a final arrangement not without favor today.

All this, of course, had there been no international war and had the United States not seized the California coast. The war news, however, was still unaccountably delayed. Frémont says: "I knew the facts of the situation. These I could not make known. . . ." Whatever those facts were which he never did reveal, one should have been the fact that he not only "assumed the responsibility," as he says, but ordered the fitting of it in advance.

The responsibilities of the business did not bother Kit Carson and others, to whom war had been declared sufficiently for the exercise of local option. If the captain proposed to fight for the stake of California they needed no further urging. Nevertheless, there was one man, Risdon Moore of Illinois, a "Cromwellian" type, as Frémont saw him, and, as a seeming anomaly in the ranks, a "reasoning man." Or, singularly again, although he was a reasoning man he failed to find the reason why he, hired as a civilian for exploration duties, should now march as a soldier for attack upon the authorized government of California. He may have asked for the captain's orders. He foresaw "bad consequences probable," argued the matter, and balked.

Risdon, with that calm, strong Cromwellian face which belied him, might have been discharged and abandoned to his blindness; but, since he was a reasoning man, he was deemed by Frémont to be "open to conviction," and during his night of "solitary reflection" in a close, dungeon-like room of the fort, the fleas there stimulated him with that appeal to reason in which Frémont, Carson, the Delawares and all, had failed. The next morning, thoroughly converted to the war proposition, he resumed his rifle and horse, and his place in the ranks.

Frémont states that, as the representative of the Army and the Flag in California, by his alliance with the revolution he gave to his (and thereby its) movements "the national character which must of necessity be respected by Mexico" and foreign governments. But, his instructions fom Government being secret and tentative, and he himself being a reasoning man, he hedged on the "national character" of his enterprise as endowed with the Army and the Flag, by writing out his resignation from the United States service, to be transmitted to Senator Benton, for the hands of the War Department in case that politics demanded a sacrifice.

Had Risdon Moore known of that scrap of paper he might not have yielded to even the contentions of the dungeon fleas. To Carson and the Delawares, of doglike devotion, the gesture would have mattered little. But this prospective release of the United States Government from complicity in the seizure of California not only indicated how uncertain Frémont was of his authority to act, as yet; it portended a situation of unpleasant possibilities.

Granted that the war with Mexico had not occurred to make, as Frémont would accept it, "an open situation" for him; rather the situation had proved to be a closed situation.

Granted that his filibustering campaign (for such it now was) short-circuited. Projects with like ambitions have been shorted in these Latin countries. Granted that the Republic, in line with potentates and princes, was ungrateful and chose the path of least resistance; or, at the worst, was helpless by the judgment of international law. Then there was, for adventurers, the firing squad and the "I told you so" of Risdon Moore. But Frémont's star ruled in conjunction with the star of Carson. He got away with this bold design, as he did with the howitzer. De Raousset-Boulbon and Captain Crabb in Sonora, Walker in Nicaragua, yes, and Maximilian in Mexico, were less fortunate in their horoscope.

About this time, June 18-19, the revolutionists Fowler (possibly George) and Thomas Cowie were sent from the Sonora garrison to bring back a keg of powder from Moses Carson, overseer of Captain Henry Fitch's American *rancho*, Sotoyomi, in the Russian River Valley to the north. They did not return — through their carelessness in keeping to the main road they never got there; for their stripped and (as claimed) mutilated bodies were found, by report of four weeks later, or July 16, buried upon the Santa Rosa *rancho,* half way. The word of the capture and the killing, however, appears to have reached Sonoma within a couple of days after the occurrence.[378]

A party of Californian irregulars who had been chased and fired upon by the *Osos* or Bears were accused of the murders — with special emphasis laid upon the bloodthirsty knife of one Jack Four-fingers, a Mexican import, politely Manuel García, politely again, Bernardino García, and destined to parade through California outlaw history as Jack Three-fingers or Three-Fingered Jack, throat-cutter of squealing Chinese and a lieutenant of the renowned bandit chief, Joaquin Murieta. Four-fingers apparently was confined at Sonoma for trial; but he lived to die by the bullets of a Ranger posse in June, 1853.[379]

Rumors rode the sunny air like the flying feathered cork in battledore and shuttlecock. General Castro heard that Captain Frémont was advancing upon him with 400 men. Through messengers from Sonoma, Captain Frémont heard that General Castro was advancing in force with three divisions, to assault Sonoma first. The gods of war so willed it that never the twain, of south and north, did meet, but Frémont, watchfully waiting in his camp above Sutter's Fort for some overt act to be directed against him that he might strike in defense of honor, life and liberty, gave ear to the appeal.

As the thing was put to him, only he could save Sonoma and its garrison. Forthwith he unleashed his hardy little legion, sounded the trump, and at the head of ninety horsemen including a muster of settlers thundered into Sonoma at two o'clock in the morning of June 25, after a forced march of eighty miles.

He had left behind him a Sutter's Fort all on the alert for enemy attack. Thus Lieutenant Joseph Revere of the *Portsmouth,* arrived June 26 in the ship's launch on a tour of inspection for the curious Commander Montgomery, found it —

... with its crenulated walls, fortified gateway, and bastioned angles; the heavily bearded, fierce-looking hunters and trappers, armed with rifles, bowie knives and pistols; their ornamented hunting shirts, and gartered leggings; their long hair turbaned with colored handkerchiefs; their wild and almost savage looks, and dauntless independent bearing; the wagons filled with golden grain; the arid yet fertile plains; the "caballados" [caballadas] driven across it by wild, shouting Indians, enveloped in clouds of dust, and the dashing horsemen, scouring the fields in every direction. .... Everything bore the impress of vigilance and preparation for defence — and not without reason; for Castro, then at the Pueblo de San José, with a force of several hundred men, well provided with horses and artillery, had threatened to march upon the valley of the Sacramento.[380]

Only Captain Sutter and the hostage prisoners were unhappy.

Frémont was in time, and moreover was timely, at Sonoma. The enemy was near — had crossed the Bay and had already been encountered. Lieutenant Henry Ford of the garrison had taken seventeen or eighteen men and scouted to the south in search for the irregulars who were accused of having done Fowler and Cowie to death and who had captured John Todd and another Bear, besides. After one successful little surprise of a guerilla squad at the *Rancho* San Antonio half-way between Sonoma and the old mission San Rafael the Ford Bears had continued on for San Rafael itself, there to complete the job. But in another charge, the same morning, upon the suspicious horse-filled corral and occupied premises of the *Rancho* Olompali short of San Rafael they were surprised in turn. This was a Castro detachment of some fifty irregulars and militia under no less a leader than Captain Joaquin de la Torre. The hasty Bears took to cover in a strip of brush and trees, with their rifles out-ranged the muskets and lances of the Californians, killed at least one man and wounded others, and sent the foe scouring away to the south. They probably had united with the main column at San Rafael.

The opportunity to drive the invaders back upon their haunches was not to be lost. The very day following that of his arrival at Sonoma, Frémont as captain of 130 riders — his own retainers, Lieutenant Ford's victorious warriors, loose-foot settlers, but all Bears together — marched again for San Rafael, eager to close accounts with that Captain de la Torre, "one of his [Castro's] best officers," as he says. The case now appeared not to be the United States vs. Mexico in California but Frémont vs. Castro. As Frémont pronounced within a few days to Captain Phelps of the *Moscow,* "his government had been outrageously insulted in his person" and "he would compel from Castro a public apology, or hunt him from the country."

To the disappointment of the Ford Bears and their swart and hairy allies among whom the scalp-trophied Delawares were high of hope — to the greatest disappointment of Frémont himself, San Rafael proved to be only a deserted, peaceful old mission. Captain de la Torre had declined combat; his present whereabouts seemed to be unknown. He should be still in this vicinity north of the Bay, however, and General Castro was reliably reported as in readiness, with his two other divisions, to cross from Point San Pablo on the mainland in the east to Point San Pedro of the coast upper peninsula on the west — those opposing landings of the narrows between San Francisco and San Pablo bays.

Therefore, Frémont held to his advance post of breezy San Rafael on its rolling plain at the head of a small estuary — a scant Spanish league inland from the San Pedro shore of the narrows and commanding a view of narrows and opposite shore.

It was on the second day, Sunday, June 28, when three men in a boat rowed by a fourth man were seen setting out from Point San Pablo as though to cross to Point San Pedro. Where he was pacing in the mission outer corridor fronting the narrows Frémont ordered Kit Carson to take two men and cut off the landing party. Carson turned back for further instructions; he galloped on, down the cover of the little estuary; he was in time — he and his two dismounted, and halted and shot the three on-trudging strangers. One of them was an old man; the others were young fellows. They had left saddles on the tidelands beach near the mouth of the estuary and seemed to be coming to the mission. The fourth fellow had pulled away in the boat.

Of this killing, by Carson and companions, of old José de los Reyes Barreyesa of Santa Clara and his nephews the twin brothers Francisco and Ramon de Haro of Yerba Buena, Frémont says (*Memoirs*):

... letters were intercepted which required De la Torre to send horses to the Point [San Pedro] the next morning to meet troops from the other side; but the enemy did not cross the straits. ...

Both the settlers and the men of my command were excited against the Californians by the recent murder of the two Americans [Cowie and Fowler], and not by the murder only, but by the brutal circumstances attending it. My scouts, mainly Delawares, influenced by these feelings, made sharp retaliation and killed Barreyesa and de Haro, who were the bearers of the intercepted letters.

And again, in his long report of July 25 to Senator Benton: "Three of Castro's party having landed on the Sonoma side in advance, were killed on the beach; and beyond this there was no loss on either side."

Taking the cue, Senator Benton says, reviewing this report in *Niles Register* of the same year (Vol. LXXI): "... in return for which [the murder of Cowie and Fowler] three of De la Torre's men being taken were instantly shot."

José S. Berreyesa, son of old José, says (Los Angeles *Star*, September 27, 1856):

Occupying the office of first alcalde of Sonoma in the year 1846, [I] having been taken by surprise and put in prison in said town in company with several of my countrymen, Col. Fremont arrived at Sonoma with his forces from [the] Sacramento. He came, in company with Capt. Gillespie and several soldiers, to the room in which I was confined, and [he] having required from me the tranquility of my jurisdiction, I answered him that I did not wish to take part in any matters in the neighborhood, as I was a prisoner. After some further remarks he retired, not well satisfied with the tenor of my replies. On the following day accompanied by soldiers he went to San Rafael. At the time that the news of my arrest had reached my parents, at the instance of my mother, that my father should go to Sonoma to see the condition in which myself and brothers were placed, this pacific old man left Santa Clara for San Pablo. After many difficulties he succeeded in passing (across the strait), accompanied by two young cousins, Francisco and Ramon Haro, and having disembarked near San Rafael they proceeded towards the mission of that name with the intention of getting horses and return to get their saddles, which remained on the beach. Unfortunately Col. Fremont was walking in the corridor of the mission with some of his soldiers and they perceived the three Californians. They took their arms and mounted — approached toward them, and fired. It is perhaps true that they were scarcely dead when they were stripped of their clothing, which was all they had on their persons; others say that Col. Fremont was asked whether they should be taken prisoners or killed and that he replied that he had no room for prisoners and in consequence of this they were slain.

On the day following this event Fremont returned to Sonoma and I learned from one of the Americans who accompanied him, and who spoke Spanish, that one of the persons killed at San Rafael was my father. I sought the first opportunity to question him (Fremont) about the matter, and whilst he was standing in front of the room in which I was a prisoner, I and my two brothers spoke to him and questioned him who it was that killed my father, and he answered that it was not certain he was killed, but that it was a Mr. Castro. [A Castro of San Pablo had rowed the boat.] Shortly afterwards a soldier passed by with a serape belonging to my father and one of my brothers pointed him out. After being satisfied of this fact I requested Col. Fremont to be called and told him that I believed my father had been killed by his orders and begged that he would do me the favor to have the article restored to me that I might give it to my mother. To this Col. Fremont replied that he could not order its restoration as the serape belonged to the soldier who had it, and then he retired without giving me any further reply. I then endeavored to obtain it from the soldier, who asked me $25 for it, which I paid, and in this manner I obtained it.

Jasper O'Farrell, an Irishman resident of San Rafael, says in the same issue of the *Star:*

I was at San Rafael in June 1846 when the then Captain Fremont arrived at that mission with his troops. The second day after his arrival there was a boat landed three men at the mouth of the *estero* [tide-water creek or estuary] on Point San Pablo [San Pedro]. As soon as they were descried by Fremont there were three men (of whom Kit Carson was one) detailed to meet them. They mounted their horses and after advancing about one hundred yards halted and Carson returned to where Fremont was standing on the corridor of the mission, in company with Gillespie, myself, and others, and said: "Captain shall I take those men prisoners?" In response Fremont waved his hand and said: "I have got no room for prisoners." They then advanced to within fifty yards of the three unfortunate and unarmed Californians, alighted from their horses, and deliberately shot them. One of them was an old and respected Californian, Don José R. Barreyesa, whose son was the alcalde of Sonoma. The other two were twin brothers and sons of Don Francisco de Haro, a citizen of the Pueblo of Yerba Buena. I saw Carson some two years ago [1853] and spoke to him of this act and he assured me that then and since he regretted to be compelled to shoot those men, but Fremont was bloodthirsty enough to order otherwise, and he further remarked that it was not the only brutal act he was compelled to commit while under his command.[381]

Alexander Godey says (New York *Evening Post,* October 30, 1856):

I now come to the "killing" of the "Berregeses" by the "accomplices of Fremont," and to convey an adequate idea of all the circumstances attending this matter, I will advert to an affair which transpired a few days previous. While we were on the march for San Rafael, the bodies of Tom Cowie and two companions of his were encountered in the road, having been murdered by a party of the enemy under Juan Padilla, the individual about whose cattle such ado is being made; their bodies presented a most shocking spectacle, bearing the marks of horrible mutilation, their throats cut, and their bowels ripped open; other indignities were perpetrated of a nature too disgusting and obscene to relate.

Tom was well known to many of our men, with whom he was a favorite, and the sight that his lifeless remains presented, created in the breasts of many of his old friends a feeling of stern and bitter revenge, and if many a deep and solemn oath was taken to meet our stern vengeance upon the perpetrators of the foul deed, those conversant with men will not be surprised. (It has always been understood that Padilla with his own hands tore out the bowels of Tom Cowie and placed them to his lips, thanking God that he at last had tasted the blood of an American.) San Rafael was surprised soon after, and occupied by our troops. Subsequently, being myself officer of the day, it was reported to me that a boat was crossing the straits containing two persons. Kit Carson, who was on patrol duty with his party, intercepted the men when they landed, and upon their resistance shot them both; upon their persons were found letters to the commander of the enemy's force, who was still supposed to be at San Rafael. Had they submitted, and not attempted to escape, they would have received no harm, but they furnished a pretext which, to the friends of Tom Cowie, was, perhaps, not unwelcome.

These are the facts, as they occurred. These men possessed no "goods"; they had nothing but their saddles, and the letters above mentioned, and the entire story of their peaceful business, property, the mode of their death, and the killing of their father, is sheer fabrication. There were but the two men; they had no goods, and were upon a hostile business; and according to all rules of warfare, they were subject to imprisonment, if taken, or death, if resisting.[382]

Kit Carson, in his *Own Story*, says nothing at all. But he makes a statement through William M. Boggs of Napa Valley and Sonoma. Boggs, arrived that year, 1846, in California, relates:

A boat containing three Californians landed at the Embarcadero [the San Rafael landing], when Carson and his two comrades captured them. Kit left the prisoners in charge of the two men with him and rode back to where Col. Fremont and his party were resting and reported the capture of three Californians, who had brought their saddles with them, and Kit asked Col. Fremont what he should do with the three prisoners. His reply to Carson was, "Mr. Carson, I have no use for prisoners — do your duty"— and that was all that passed. Kit returned to where his comrades, Capt. Swift and Jack Neil [Neal], were standing guard over the three men. They held a short consultation and decided to kill the prisoners, and shot them dead. This I had from both Swift and Carson himself . . .

After I had served in the service of the U. S. in the closing of the war in the conquest of California, I settled down in old Sonoma, and became intimately acquainted with nearly all the leading men of the Bear Flag Party, and all agreed on the same story, and one of the men who was with Kit at that time, Capt. Granville P. Swift, who became one of Fremont's most famous captains, told me of the part that he took in the killing of these three prisoners.

In about the year 1852 [it was 1853] my brother Tom and Kit came to California and were at my house together, and it occurred to me to ask Kit, in brother Tom's presence, if he was not at San Raphael [Rafael] with Fremont in 1846. He said he was. I then said, "You took some prisoners there, you and Swift." "Yes," he replied. "And you killed them?" I said. "Yes." "Well," I said to him, "what did you kill them for after you had them in your power?" He then related how he had reported them to Fremont and he told him to do his duty, and it was soon after the Californians at Santa Rosa Ranche had captured two young men of the Bear Flag Party on their way to Fort Ross [Bodega] on the coast to get ammunition for the party at Sonoma. . . .

An Indian who had witnessed this terrible affair reported it to old Moses Carson, the elder brother of Kit, who was living on a ranch in the Russian River Valley, about 16 miles above Santa Rosa. He came and took the remains of these young men and buried them. And Kit said his reason for the killing of these three Californians was to retaliate for the horrible manner in which the Californians had treated these two Americans, which so enraged the few American settlers that the act of the Americans retaliating was approved by nearly everyone.[383]

In the beginning, Tom Boggs had not believed this reputed action by his Santa Fé Trail and Bent's Fort friend, Kit Carson, and Carson evidently had never referred to it, while he was back in New Mexico. Captain Ford does not mention the matter in his Bear Flag manuscript. The chronicler, William Swasey (Bancroft *Collection* manuscripts) says: "The firing was perfectly justifiable under the circumstances." Captain William B. Ide (*Biographical Sketch*) says, in his customary florid style, that the three men, carrying deceptive letters "in their boots . . . fell on their knees begging for quarter," but were shot by orders "to take no prisoners from this band of murderers." John Fowler of the Bears says (*Ms.*, Bancroft *Col-*

lection) that Carson and a Frenchman his companion (in that case possibly old Beaulieu, a Sonoma recruit) were drunk; and he adds: "The killing of old Barreyesa and two youths in the most wanton manner somewhat opened the eyes of the officers in command to the fact that they must assume a stricter control over the doings of their subordinates." Charles Brown, an American who later, however, married a sister of the de Haros, says (*Ms. Early Events,* Bancroft *Collection*): "The murder of José Reyes Barreyesa and the de Haros was a most infamous act."

Bancroft (*History of California,* Vol. V) says that one of the de Haro boys volunteered to bear a message from General Castro to Captain de la Torre; his brother engaged to accompany him, and old Barreyesa took the opportunity to cross in the same boat for the purpose of getting to his son at Sonoma.

So to Kit Carson fell the doubtful honor of firing one of these, the only hostile shots fired by men under Frémont's direct command during all the conquest of California. There is no defense for the act, save the excuse of obeying orders; and there is no defense for the orders. In the matter of prisoners, there already were prisoners at Fort Sutter and Sonoma, with secure quarters for more. It was not known that those three men were possessed of dispatches, until after they had been killed and searched — and dispatches were no violation of the laws of war, anyway. It never was known that the three could have been connected with the murder of Cowie and Fowler. Those two Americans had not been of Frémont's company, nor had they been trail associates of Carson. If retribution were to be exacted for the murder, it was not for Frémont and his company, who were still in the service of the United States, to lend themselves to the job. There were prisoners, suspected of being from the very band, in the custody of the Bears at Sonoma, where a drum-head trial could have been held by the revolutionists with their own row to hoe.

No allowance is due Frémont. The killing was not done by his Delawares who, as he intimates, got out of hand; nor were the killed men belligerents in the Castro advance. Some slight allowance may be made for the settler Swift, known as a "crack shot" and rated as "a bitter hater of Mexicans"; and for that other named partner of Carson's, John Neal, whose character has been remarked. That Carson chose to read his orders as he did only shows how little, in these heady times, he thought for himself. The wine, in any shape, of the filibuster was too much for him; his confidence in Frémont and his ignorance of the true situation were the false bead on the cup, inducing him to believe that he was quaffing of a holy war, in which crusaders can do no wrong against the infidel.

The next prisoner taken was not killed. He was an Indian, he also carried a dispatch, this time one from Captain de la Torre himself, announcing to General Castro a projected attack upon Sonoma. Frémont, Carson and all rode hard, by night march, to the succor of Sonoma; arrived just before dawn and with the trampling of their horses roused the garrison to a sense of peril.

It seems to have turned into a Frémont harebrained joke, such as he had risked when on the Kansas plains he, with a squad, stripped and yelling like Indians, had charged the main camp and had almost been shot. Now in the words of sarcastic William Ide of the garrison:

The blankets of the advancing host flowed in the breeze. They had advanced to within 200 yards of the place where I stood. The impatience of the men at the gun became intense, lest the enemy came too near, so as to lose the effect of the spreading of the shot. I made a motion to lay down my rifle [in signal]. The matches were swinging. "My God! They swing the matches!" cried the well-known voice of Kit Carson. "Hold on, hold on!" we shouted, " 'tis Fremont, 'tis Fremont!" in a voice heard by every man of both parties, we cried, while Captain Fremont dashed away to his left to take cover behind an adobe house; and in a moment after he made one of his most gallant charges on our fort; it was a noble exploit; he came in a full gallop, right in the face and teeth of our two long 18's.[384]

The joke, however, was on Frémont as well as on the garrison. Having put the chase upon a paper scent, de la Torre and his force were recrossing the Bay for the safer south. Made suspicious, Frémont, Carson and all dashed back, this same day, to San Rafael, but the trail of retreat was cold.

Carson, still confused by events still looming large to him, says (*Own Story,* 1856):

> During our stay here [Sonoma], General Castro ordered one of his captains and large force from San Francisco to attack us and drive us from the country. He came over, found two of our men that were carrying news to the settlers that Sonoma was taken and war declared, whom he brutally murdered. He found that we were anxious to meet him and commenced his retreat. We followed him some six days and nights. He could not be found. He made his escape leaving his animals and he reached San Francisco and from there went to Pueblo of Los Angeles, General Castro joining him — their object being to reorganize their forces.

Carson's memory, at this time ten years after events, may have been faulty in details; but his loose statements tend to show, rather, the faulty perspective and the catch-as-catch-can notions with which he and his fellow valiants performed. His intelligence of the angles governing the activities seems to have been on a par with that of the Delawares.

During this Sonoma period he should have met his big half-brother Mose, whom he probably had last seen in New Mexico, fifteen years back. He does not refer to the reunion; it was a small incident of great and busy days. But Moses was in evidence here and hereafter — by the evidence of his bill as purveyor, at least, to the cause.

Well, the clever Captain de la Torre, of ferocity suddenly punctured, had cleared out — had "fled with his command in a most cowardly manner to Sausalito," as Gillespie testified before the Claims Committee in Washington; and with his fifty men, countered by 150, had escaped across the Bay. Frémont and company were brought up short at Sausalito, there upon the tip of the northern peninsula facing the Golden Gate. Here, June 30, Captain William D. Phelps, of the American trading bark *Moscow* lying off Sausalito, curiously inclined visited the camp.

Upon the *Portsmouth,* lying at Yerba Buena of San Francisco, Commander Montgomery, having learned of Captain Frémont's militant operations as the now committed head of the revolution, ruefully entered in his diary, date of June 28:

The course of Captain Fremont renders my position as a neutral particularly delicate and difficult. Having avowed not only my own but Captain Fremont's entire neutrality and non-interference in the existing difficulties in the country, it can scarcely be supposed, under the circumstances, that I shall be regarded as having spoken in good faith and sincerity.[385]

Inasmuch as Commander Montgomery, "in demeanor polite to all," consistently informed Frémont upon the movements of the enemy and was prepared to meet him at Santa Barbara, his neutrality might indeed be questioned. He may have feared more for his future usefulness than for his reputation.[386]

Through the medium of "Doctor" Semple — discovered as a "tall, lank, Kentucky-looking chap, dressed in a greasy deerskin hunting-shirt, with trousers to match, and which terminated just before his knees, his head surmounted with a coonskin cap, tail in front"— the skipper of the *Moscow* found Frémont sitting at the entrance to his tent while his men diligently overhauled their equipment, preparing for further action. Captain Phelps was somewhat surprised by, but was well satisfied with, the slender person and neat but "excellent rig" of this the "King of the Rocky Mountains," and was impressively informed that General Castro should either publicly apologize or be hunted out of the country.[387]

The next day Captain Frémont and Lieutenant Gillespie paid a return call upon Captain Phelps aboard the *Moscow,* and, as Frémont says, arranged with him "for the use of one of his boats, with which he met me at the landing before daylight in the morning," the captain and his boat's crew being "excited and pleased to aid me in the work on hand"; this the more so, perhaps, in that, according to the testimony of Captain Phelps, he had been assured by the two officers that war had been declared and that they were "acting in obedience to orders of the United States government"; and the more so, again, in that Captain Phelps conceived that the arduous transportation, and the risk and hazard attached to "capturing and dismantling" the fort across the Bay, and "spiking the guns thereof" (ten heavy brass and iron pieces), entitled him to $10,000 from said government.

The fort was El Castillo de San Joaquin, built in 1794 and humbled by its half-century of conflict with Time. There was no garrison, and, in truth, none was apprehended. Supplied by Captain Phelps with rat-tail files from the *Moscow's* cargo of Yankee notions, and taking "twelve of my men singled out as the best shots" (Carson thereby included in the muster), Frémont — but he tells (*Memoirs*) the better story, as always:

Pulling across the strait or avenue of water which leads in from the Gate [en route he named this salty Delaware, Chrysopylae or Golden Gate] we reached the Fort Point in the gray dawn of the morning and scrambled up the steep bank just in time to see several horsemen escaping at full speed towards Yerba Buena. We promptly spiked the guns — fourteen — nearly all long brass Spanish pieces. The work of spiking was effectually done by Stepp, who was a gunsmith, and knew as well how to make a rifle as to use one.

Carson should have thrilled to that crossing of the silent, gray-misted strait and the charge upon the high batteries. This was war. The spiking was so effectually done that the pieces were rendered unserviceable not only to the Californians but also to Commander Montgomery — although it was thought that new vents might be drilled in the brasses. His officer placed in command found there not fourteen but ten pieces of armament — three brass 12's and 18's (dated 1623, 1628, and 1693), "three long iron 42's, and four smaller iron guns," with the carriages of the few mounted pieces rotted and the round-shot rusty.[388]

It was really left to Senator Benton and Secretary of War Marcy, incited by Frémont's home letter (July 25) pronouncing of de la Torre's narrow squeak, the spiking of (now) "six large and handsome pieces" and the capture or destruction of all "boats and launches," to wave the flag — "the Mexican commander, de la Torre, barely escaping with the loss of his transport boats and nine pieces of brass artillery, spiked," as Secretary Marcy affirmed in his annual report before mentioned. There may be little wonder that Carson saw largely. But Lieutenant (then Major) Gillespie, summoned by the board of California Claims commissioners in Washington, September 19, 1853, rehearsed the matter without actual disparagement of Captain Frémont:

> I hereby certify that in July, 1846, Captain W. D. Phelps did transport a party of men under the command of John C. Frémont from Sausalito across the bay of San Francisco (seven miles) to the fort at Yerba Buena, commanding the entrance to the harbor, for the purpose of spiking the guns of the fort, which was in a very dismantled condition and could not have been reoccupied without having been almost entirely rebuilt. There was no enemy present, and the sole object Captain Frémont had in view was to prevent the Californians from using the guns at any future time. There was no risk or personal danger incurred, and the service would be well paid for at fifty dollars.[389]

Whereupon Captain Phelps was required to lower his own belated flag. Those his services, as related in his deposition approved of by Frémont and as considered by Frémont "to have been very valuable to the United States," passed in measure with *sic transit gloria mundi.*